1990

Lordship and Military Obligation in Anglo-Saxon England

Lordship and Military Obligation in Anglo-Saxon England

Richard P. Abels

UNIVERSITY OF CALIFORNIA PRESS
Berkeley · Los Angeles · London

University of California Press
Berkeley and Los Angeles, California

University of California Press, Ltd.
London, England

Copyright © 1988 by the Regents of the University of California

Library of Congress Cataloging-in-Publication Data

Abels, Richard Philip, 1951–
  Lordship and military obligation in Anglo Saxon
England.

  Revision of thesis (Ph. D.)—Columbia University.
  Bibliography: p.
  Includes index.
  1. Great Britain—History, Military—Anglo-Saxon
period, 449–1066. 2. Anglo-Saxons—England—History.
3. Feudalism—England—History. 4. Land tenure—England—
History. I. Title.
DA59.A24   1988   942.01   87-10787
ISBN 0-520-05794-5 (alk. paper)

Printed in the United States of America

1 2 3 4 5 6 7 8 9

To Ellen

Contents

Abbreviations

Anglo-Norman Studies	*Proceedings of the Battle Conference on Anglo-Norman Studies,* ed. R. Allen Brown. Cited by volume number and year of publication.
ASC	Anglo-Saxon Chronicle. Cited by year (from the manuscript with the corrected date in square brackets) and recension.
BCS	Walter de Gray Birch, ed., *Cartularium Saxonicum,* 3 vols. and index (1885–1899, reprint New York, 1964). Cited by number.
DB	Domesday Book. Cited by volume and folio (b stands for verso).
EHD	*English Historical Documents.* David C. Douglas, General Editor.
EHR	*English Historical Review*
H.E.	Bede, *Historia Ecclesiastica.* Cited by book and chapter.
ICC	*Inquisitio Comitatus Cantabrigiensis*
IE	*Inquisitio Eliensis*
KCD	J. M. Kemble, ed., *Codex Diplomaticus Aevi Saxonici.* 6 vols. London, 1839–1848.
MGH	*Monumenta Germaniae Historica* (*Ep.* stands for *Epistolae* and *SS* for *Scriptores*).
S	P. H. Sawyer, *Anglo-Saxon Charters: An Annotated List and Bibliography.* London, 1968.
Stenton, *ASE*	F. M. Stenton, *Anglo-Saxon England.* 3d ed. Oxford, 1971.

T.R.E.   "Tempore Regis Edwardi" ("in the time
                                of King Edward"). The Domesday Book
                                formula for 1066.

TRHS   *Transactions of the Royal Historical So-
                                ciety*

T.R.W.   "Tempore Regis Willelmi" ("in the time
                                of King William"). The Domesday Book
                                formula for 1086.

VCH   *The Victoria County Histories*

Acknowledgments

While I cannot hope to repay the scholarly debts I incurred in the preparation of this book, I can at the very least acknowledge them. Malcolm Bean, who guided my graduate education at Columbia University, was the model sponsor. He and I discussed and argued our way through every line of the dissertation that was to become this book; his intellectual imprint lies not only upon the present work but upon me as a medievalist. For the demands that he made and for the constant encouragement he gave me I offer my sincerest thanks.

I am also very much indebted to Warren Hollister for his kindness and generosity. My many stimulating conversations with him, Robin Fleming, and Katharin Mack, and the constructive comments that they have offered on drafts of this manuscript have saved me from many errors. I have benefited personally and professionally from their friendship.

I feel fortunate to have been associated with Columbia University and with the U.S. Naval Academy. Columbia University offered me the opportunity to teach in its Contemporary Civilization program, an experience which changed my life and determined my career, and to work with Malcolm Bean and John H. Mundy. The Naval Academy Research Council has provided generous financial support for this work. My colleagues in the Works in Progress Seminar of the History Department, U.S. Naval Academy, read several chapters of this work in manuscript and offered helpful editorial and substantive suggestions. I am especially indebted to Thomas Brennan, Phyllis Culham, Nancy and Matthew Ellenberger, Frederick Harrod, Michael Isenberg, Anne Quartararo, Craig Symonds, and Larry Thompson.

My former colleague at the Naval Academy, Dr. Don Alexander (Major, U.S.A.), helped me think through problems of military tactics and strategy. I am grateful to Emily Tabuteau and Carroll Gillmor, both of whom generously shared unpublished research with me. G. D. Snooks offered a frank and useful critique of my statistical method; Rae Jean Goodman, my colleague in Economics at the U.S. Naval Academy, gave me invaluable assistance in avoiding the pitfalls Dr. Snooks had pointed out.

Portions of this manuscript were presented at meetings of the Haskins Society, the AHA, the International Congress on Medieval Studies at Western Michigan University, and the Battle Conference. I profited immensely from the critical comments I received and from discussions with conference participants, particularly Bernard Bachrach and Nicholas Hooper. Parts of chapters five and six were published in an earlier form in *Anglo-Norman Studies VIII* and appear here with the kind permission of Boydell Press.

The maps and graphs were redrawn by William Clipson. The plates from the Bayeux Tapestry are reproduced with the special authorization of the Town of Bayeux. The illustration from the Canterbury Heptateuch appears with the kind permission of the British Library, and the photograph of the Franks Casket, with that of the Trustees of the British Museum.

My greatest debt belongs to my wife, Ellen, to whom I dedicate this book. To thank one's wife in extravagant terms has become an academic cliche. Nevertheless, Ellen deserves this and more. She was quite simply my best critic as well as my best friend. Her patience with my obsessive revisions bordered on the saintly, and her interest in Anglo-Saxon military obligation, on the miraculous. If it had not been for her I could never have written this book.

Introduction

The Anglo-Saxon period was a violent one. Warfare dominated its history and shaped the nature of its governance. Indeed, war was the natural state for the patchwork of tribal kingdoms that composed pre-viking England. Chieftains engaged in a seemingly endless struggle against foreign enemies and rival kinsmen for authority, power, and tribute, even after Christianity had supplied them with an ideology of kingship that did not depend on success in battle. These petty wars were ended by the viking invasions. From the sacking of Lindisfarne in 793 until the last years of William the Conqueror's reign, England was to lie under the shadow of the Northmen. Initially, these pirates sought plunder, but in the 860s their goal changed, as the various Danish war bands united for conquest and settlement. Within a decade the Danes had extinguished and replaced all the native royal lines but one. King Alfred's Wessex survived.

Alfred's success was due in large measure to his willingness to innovate. He reorganized the West Saxon military forces and began to build a system of fortified towns throughout southern England, thereby promoting royal power and authority. Alfred's sons and grandsons consolidated his gains. Carrying the war across the Thames, they redeemed the territories that had fallen under Danish rule, creating through their conquests a unified kingdom of England. The measure of their success was that Alfred's great-grandson, Edgar "the Peaceable," could enjoy a sixteen-year reign (959–975) conspicuous for its lack of political events. As one version of the Anglo-Saxon Chronicle put it, "Nor was there fleet so proud nor host so strong that it got itself prey in England as long as the noble king held the throne."[1]

The peace and prosperity that Alfred's successors had purchased with the sword lasted but a few decades. England faced an even graver crisis toward the end of the tenth century from a Denmark that had itself recently become a unified state. Thirty years of fighting culminated in Cnut's accession to the English throne, and a quarter century of Danish rule followed. This conquest proved far milder than the one that was to follow a half century later. Although England had changed dynasties, its system of government, laws, and customs survived the conquest virtually unchanged, as Cnut assumed the trappings and responsibilities of his English predecessors. Cnut's victory strengthened the monarchy, continuing the process begun by Alfred, and gave England a peace guaranteed by its conqueror's overwhelming military power.

Unlike Francia, the English state had weathered the ravages of the Northmen, emerging in the eleventh century with an apparatus for royal governance as sophisticated as any in early medieval Europe. War had tempered and strengthened the Anglo-Saxon monarchy. It was also to destroy it. The last king of Saxon England, Harold Godwineson, spent his ten-month reign preparing for and fighting two costly engagements against foreign claimants to his throne. Harold's victory at Stamford Bridge over Harald Hardrada, a viking warrior of almost legendary proportions, and the English king's subsequent death at Hastings are both the stuff of sagas and the grist of Anglo-Saxon history.

Who fought in the armies of Anglo-Saxon England, and why? Our very conception of early English society and the Anglo-Saxon polity depends upon how we answer these questions. Military obligation and indeed military institutions in general are crucial to the understanding of the culture of this people. Anglo-Saxon England has not been served well by its historians in this regard. Frederic Maitland's complaint that "no matter with which we have to deal is darker than the constitution of the English army on the eve of its defeat"[2] remains as true today as it was when he penned it almost ninety years ago. One might add only that far more is known about Harold's forces at Hastings than about King Oswiu's at the Winwaed or Alfred's at Edington.

Most of the work that has been done on the armies of the Anglo-Saxon kings has focused on the eleventh century. It is not difficult to account for this; the character of Harold's forces is relevant to the long and often bitter debate over the impact of the Norman Conquest. Those who have wished to portray the Norman conquerors as the architects of the feudal system have minimized the resemblance of the royal army of pre-Conquest England to the Anglo-Norman feudal host.[3] Others have argued with equal vehemence that the Anglo-Saxons developed dependent military tenures at least a full century before Hastings.[4] The question haunting all these works is whether the origins of English feudalism are to be found in the Confessor's England. This is, of course, an important question. It is also one that, I believe, has obscured our understanding of the concept of military obligation among the Anglo-Saxons. One cannot truly understand why Harold's forces served him in 1066 without first identifying the historical forces that shaped these warriors' conception of their duty to him. Anglo-Saxon military institutions evolved over the centuries in response to foreign threats and changing social needs.

Although it has generally been conceded that the fyrd was an actual institution, the royal army of Anglo-Saxon England, the consensus ends there.[5] Even before Maitland's time historians argued about the composition of the fyrd and the nature of its warriors' obligation to serve the king in arms.[6] But the modern phase of this controversy began with Maitland and his contemporaries. The Victorian scholarly tradition represented by Bishop William Stubbs confidently reconstructed Anglo-Saxon society as *ceorl*-centered and defended by an army of free husbandmen. As Sir Frank Stenton, the most prominent modern defender of this view, put it, "fyrd service . . . is plainly the duty of peasants, not of nobles. . . . [T]heir obligation to service was of more ancient origin than manorial lordship itself."[7] In other words, the military organization of Anglo-Saxon England was pre-feudal; it arose from the ancient Teutonic duty of all free men to defend their country in battle.[8] The fyrd was quite simply "the nation in arms."

Stenton, it should be emphasized, merely restated what had been a historical truism throughout the nineteenth century. In a sense, it was the military corollary of an assumption shared by most Victorian scholars about the nature of early Germanic society. If Anglo-Saxon England had been a peasant "commonwealth" with a constitutional kingship, as most then believed, it must have been defended by a free peasant militia. Not every scholar, however, was comfortable with this reconstruction of early English society and its military. Three prominent historians writing around the turn of the century, H. Munro Chadwick, Frederic Maitland, and Paul Vinogradoff, seemed especially dissatisfied. The latter two had discovered from their close studies of Domesday

Book that the notion of a peasant army did not sit well with the reality of Anglo-Saxon military service in the eleventh century.[9] Unwilling to abandon completely the received theory, they argued that the fyrd had evolved over time into a proto-feudal host. Thus, even if J. H. Round were correct and the Conqueror had defined the amount of military service due him from each of his tenants-in-chief, it was doubtful that the Normans introduced "any very new principle," since the fyrd itself already contained tenurial and contractual elements.[10]

H. Munro Chadwick, whose specialty was early Anglo-Saxon institutions, was even more radical in his speculations. Rather than seeking the meaning of fyrd service in Tacitus, which had been done with monotonous regularity, he turned directly to the early English sources. And in these he found royal armies made up of noble warriors who were personally commended to the ealdormen under whom they fought. Only the local forces, ill-armed rabble barely deserving to be called "armies," were peasant levies. Chadwick concluded that lordship lay at the heart of Anglo-Saxon military obligation—even in Bede's day— and that warfare was ordinarily an aristocratic pursuit.[11] Chadwick's analysis of the sources, however, seems to have been largely ignored or dismissed as an interesting, if eccentric, theory, at least until the appearance of Eric John's *Land Tenure in Early England* in 1960. In the course of John's vociferous attack upon his predecessors in the field of Anglo-Saxon studies, he argued briefly for Chadwick's conception of the fyrd, a line of argument that he developed more fully in his second book, *Orbis Britanniae*.[12] Reviewing the evidence, most notably the writings of Bede and the poem, *The Battle of Maldon,* he concluded that the fyrd had always been composed of aristocratic warriors serving under an earl, reeve, or magnate to whom they were bound by the tie of vassalage. In essence, John turned Stenton's thesis on its head. For him, fyrd service was plainly the duty of nobles, whose obligation to fight derived from the lordship bond. John dispensed entirely with the notion of a warrior ceorl. In his view, peasants farmed and aristocrats fought.

Any dialectical debate demands not only a thesis and its antithesis but a synthesis, and this was provided by C. Warren Hollister. In *Anglo-Saxon Military Institutions on the Eve of the Norman Conquest* (1962) he attempted to reconcile the apparently contradictory evidence for the composition of the fyrd and, following a course first suggested by Vinogradoff,[13] proposed an ingenious solution: Stenton and Chadwick were both right, for there had been not one but two types of fyrd. There had been a "select fyrd," a force of professional, noble warriors, each of whom answered for a five-hide holding. But in addition to this host there was a second levy, the "great fyrd," which was much as Stenton had thought it to be—the nation in arms.[14] Hollister's solution, elegant in conception and persuasive in presentation, soon achieved the status of orthodoxy. It has not, however, gone unchallenged. Critics have pointed out that the division of the late Anglo-Saxon military forces into two distinct bodies lacks specific confirmation in the sources. Hollister coined the terms "great fyrd" and "select fyrd" precisely because the contemporary Old English and Latin sources did not distinguish in their language between forces raised for local defense and those raised for offensive expeditions. Nicholas Hooper has also questioned Hollister's heavy reliance upon post-Conquest and continental materials for his portrayal of the "great fyrd," claiming that such sources cannot be used to establish the existence of an Anglo-Saxon *levée en masse*.[15] Hooper's criticism is well taken; it is also ironic in light of the historiography of the fyrd. When Hollister wrote his book, few seriously doubted that the Anglo-Saxons, like other early Germanic peoples, obliged all free men to defend their localities. Since the existence of such a levy was beyond dispute and its actual military value questionable,[16] Hollister concentrated his discussion upon the point that he found most interesting: its survival after the Conquest. Hence his use of post-Conquest materials. If Hollister was controversial, it was in his insistence that the late Saxon kings had relied mainly on a "select fyrd," for here he was straying from the teachings of Stenton. It is little wonder, then, that the bulk of his book was an argument for and an analysis of the select system of military recruitment. Ironically, after dismissing almost all of Hollister's evidence for universal military service as irrelevant and declaring the little that remained "insufficient to prove the existence of a 'great fyrd' obligation," Hooper concluded that "Stenton was correct when he said 'the king's right to call on all men for the defence of the land was never abandoned. But insofar as can be seen, it was rarely exercised in the last centuries of the Old English state.' "[17] The logic of Hooper's argument ought to have carried him elsewhere. That it did not is eloquent testimony to the power retained by the traditional conception of the fyrd.

Michael Powicke's *Military Obligation in Medieval England*, published in the same year as *Anglo-Saxon Military Institutions*, advanced an argument similar in a number of respects to Hollister's. According to Powicke's reading of the evidence, the Anglo-Saxon army was divided into royal, provincial, and county forces. The first two were closely related—the royal army was in fact composed of provincial divisions—and consisted primarily of mounted, thegnly warriors, whose obligation for service was assessed on the land they held according to a five-hide rule. County forces, essentially peasant militias under the command of the shire's thegns, supplemented the provincial and royal armies by defending the localities. For both thegn and ceorl the obligation to serve was personal rather than tenurial. The *assessment* of service, however, was territorial.[18]

The difficulties encountered by such eminent historians are quite understandable in light of the paucity of the extant sources. Historians of the Anglo-Saxon period, especially those concerned with military matters, are not blessed with an abundance of primary source material, and what has survived is often obscure to the modern reader. The most valuable source for conditions in late Anglo-Saxon England, Domesday Book, is a case in point. One who approaches this land register for the first time in hope of learning something about the nature of society under the last Anglo-Saxon rulers will probably depart more confused than enlightened. The reader is given an overwhelming amount of data concerning individual estates during the reign of Edward the Confessor, but upon examination these figures prove a most precarious foundation for a historical reconstruction. Scholars are not even certain what the units of measure used in the survey, the hide and the ploughland, actually measured. Domesday Book's scattered references to pre-Conquest military service are even less satisfying, since the compilers of the register were only interested in the financial renders associated with such service. And these problems are not unique to the great survey. Practically every piece of evidence that we possess seems tolerant of two or more plausible interpretations, and very little of that evidence is directly concerned with the composition of the fyrd or the nature of Anglo-Saxon military obligation.

The other major sources for Anglo-Saxon institutional history include diplomatic materials, legal compilations, narratives, and the archaeological record. Each presents difficulties. If the term "charter" is used in a general sense to embrace not only formal diplomas but writs, wills, leases, records of lawsuits, and miscellaneous memoranda as well, there are approximately fifteen hundred extant charters.[19] This figure is misleading. Only two hundred or so of these documents have survived in contemporary manuscripts. The vast majority are preserved in the medieval cartularies of various religious establishments, intended as evidence of title to property, and many of these are either outright forgeries or pious "improvements" of lost originals. Historians are divided on how much credence should be placed in spurious or "improved" charters. Some argue that a genuine substratum underlies even the most obvious medieval forgeries and that such documents can be quite valuable if used carefully; others reject this approach entirely and are willing to credit only those charters that are unquestionably genuine. Moreover, the technical criteria used for assessing authenticity are so vague that a diploma judged to be trustworthy by one expert may be deemed an outright fabrication by another. Even those charters that are undoubtedly authentic present problems to the historian. The accounts of lawsuits, perhaps the most informative class of documents, assume that the reader will be familiar with the circumstances surrounding the suit and the proper legal procedure required in the case. These, moreover, are not in any sense unbiased transcripts, but give one party's view of the facts, and hence may be tendentious. The formal diplomas and writs, on the other hand, are couched in such stereotyped formulas that many are of little apparent interest to the historian.[20]

The Old English lawbooks are also not without their difficulties. The early codes and, to some extent, the lawbooks of Alfred and his successors were ideological and political documents intended to present an image of kingship rather than comprehensive codifications of existing law. They ignore such basic matters as the rules of inheritance, the differences between types of land tenure, and the structure of Anglo-Saxon kindreds. We see in them a mixture of selected customs and fresh legislation, an indistinguishable heap of old and new law.[21] One cannot even assume that the codes, or at least the pre-Alfredian codes, were meant as practical legal manuals. Justice in that society was rendered by noblemen, and we can only wonder what use could have been made of written law by seventh- and eighth-century judges who were undoubtedly illiterate.[22]

One thing, however, is certain: the Anglo-Saxon lawbooks represent royal law, decrees established by authority of the king for the benefit of the king.[23] Like the royal genealogies with which they are associated, they were intended as demonstrations of a king's regality.[24] The Church had taught the early Anglo-Saxon rulers that lawgiving was a function proper to kingship and that the legislation so promulgated ought to be in written form upon the model of the Romans.[25] By issuing a code of law a king was asserting his right to rule.

One may argue, in fact, that the law codes are more valuable for the

light they shed upon "abuses" than as evidence of legal practice. If king
after king promulgated decrees against an abuse, or if the same ruler
issued a series of laws aimed at curbing a particular practice, it is safe
to assume that the "crime" was not uncommon at the time. We cannot,
however, assume that the legislation eradicated the abuse; we may be
certain only that the king viewed the practice as criminal.

The narrative sources, notably the Anglo-Saxon Chronicle, Bede's
History and saints' lives, the early hagiographies, and the medieval
historiae of the monastic houses, are hardly objective presentations of
fact. Each has a viewpoint and a patron's interest at heart, and this
must be taken into account when using these documents as historical
evidence. The literary sources are also an important and somewhat
underutilized source of information for Old English society. Many of
the poems, including *Beowulf,* are, however, undated,[26] and even those
that can be placed within a temporal framework, such as *The Battle of
Maldon,* may well be misleading, since as literary creations they are
governed by their genre's conventions, many of which appear to have
been deliberately archaic.

We should also mention the archaeological evidence, including in
this category numismatics and settlement studies. While archaeology is
the one area in which discoveries are constantly occurring, one need
only read the report of the findings of a dig to see how dependent
archaeologists are on historians' interpretations of Anglo-Saxon society.
Like other sources, artifacts must be interpreted and are, in fact, sus-
ceptible to a number of different constructions.

Historians concerned with the fyrd and Anglo-Saxon military obligation must face still a further problem with the sources. Bede, *Beowulf,*
and the Anglo-Saxon Chronicle are one in describing a society constantly engaged in warfare, and yet, apart from a few Domesday custumals, we possess few texts that deal explicitly with the nature of
Anglo-Saxon military obligation. Such evidence precludes dogmatic
conclusions; the source material simply does not permit a reconstruction
of the fyrd in any age that can be accepted with complete confidence.
Nevertheless, a careful study of the available sources, unclouded by
preconceived notions of the nature of primitive Germanic society and
as free as possible from the obsession with the origins of English "feudalism," can yield insight into the changing character of Anglo-Saxon
military arrangements.

This work is not intended as a comprehensive study of warfare in
Anglo-Saxon England. Its aim instead is to answer a specific though

wide-ranging question: What was the relationship between Anglo-Saxon lordship and military obligation? It thus will concentrate upon topics such as military tactics and the development of the English navy only insofar as they are relevant to the question at hand. Nor does this work pretend to answer all the questions related to Anglo-Saxon lordship. The relationship between lords and their peasant cultivators has been largely ignored, as have technical disputes over the nature of Anglo-Saxon commendation.

Before we begin, a note of caution should be sounded. Friedrich Nietzsche's observation that only that which has no history can be defined ought to be taken to heart by all who study institutions. Societies continually reinterpret their institutions to meet ever-changing needs. Anglo-Saxon history is, of course, both long and eventful. Much of the confusion surrounding the study of Old English institutions has arisen from the mistaken assumption that one can and ought to define a static "institution." The only way in which we can hope to understand what lordship and military obligation meant in pre-Conquest England is to trace their evolution through the available sources.

Because of the paucity of source material for this period, historians have often based their arguments upon a mass of evidence that is, to say the least, heterogeneous. Nothing is thought of presenting an "Oswaldslow" charter of the late tenth century to bolster a thesis derived from a seventh-century West Saxon lawbook, or of using the early eleventh-century poem, *The Battle of Maldon,* to illuminate the wars described by Bede. To be sure, if we attempt to do away entirely with the conflation of disparate sources, we will be left with too little material upon which to draw for any conclusions at all. Yet we must also be aware that arguments based upon this practice have a source of possible error built into them from the start. We can neither simply presume that Anglo-Saxon England retained the same character throughout its turbulent six-hundred-year history nor ignore the possibility that institutions developed differently in different localities. Whenever it is feasible, the historian ought to examine Anglo-Saxon institutions within a regional and temporal framework.

Map 1
Southern Britain in the early eighth century

Lordship, Land Tenure, and the Early Anglo-Saxon Fyrd

FYRD SERVICE IN EARLY WESSEX

War was endemic to the kingdoms of seventh- and eighth-century Britain. An Anglo-Saxon ruler of this period was above all else a warlord, a *dryhten*, as the Old English sources put it. His primary duty was to protect his people against the depredations of their neighbors and to lead them on expeditions of plunder and conquest. As the *Beowulf*-poet sang about the mythical founder of the Danish royal line,

> Often Scyld Scefing took mead-benches away from enemy bands, from many tribes, terrified their nobles . . . [He] became great under the skies, prospered in honors until every one of those who lived about him . . . had to pay him tribute. That was a good king.[1]

Scyld was a good king because he was the lord of a mighty war band that profited from his leadership. As long as he lived, his people were safe and enjoyed tribute from the surrounding tribes.

This portrait of a king was not merely a convention of a heroic genre. Even the saintliest of Bede's kings, the Northumbrian Oswald, was a warrior who earned glory and met death in battle. His head and hands were displayed on stakes for a full year before they were removed by the saint's brother, King Oswiu, and venerated as Christian relics. Acceptance of the new saint came slowly to those who remembered him as a rapacious conqueror. Oswald's reputed sanctity mattered less to the monks of Bardney than his subjugation of their homeland, and when Queen Osthryth of Mercia, the martyr's niece, decided to enrich that religious house with the bones of her uncle, the monks refused to receive in death one who had been their enemy in life. It took a miracle to make them forget their feud and view the queen's gift as a blessing.[2] King Sigeberht of East Anglia, another of Bede's royal saints, also died in battle, despite having exchanged his crown for a monk's habit some years before in order to escape the affairs of this world. The East Anglian nobility could not forget what he had once been, and when the kingdom was threatened by Penda of Mercia, the same heathen king who slew Oswald, they turned to Sigeberht, begging him to lead them to victory as he had done so often in the past. The unwilling monk was dragged protesting to the battlefield, where, armed only with a staff, he earned his martyr's crown.[3]

Oswald and Sigeberht were unique only in their sanctity. The latter's violent death was characteristic of the kings of his dynasty: his immediate predecessor on the East Anglian throne had been murdered and each of the three kings who reigned after him met his end in battle. Oswald was no less typical of his line. Of the eight kings who ruled Northumbria in the seventh century, six perished in war. This record is hardly surprising in view of the constant warfare that marked the age. A seventh- or eighth-century king most often came to his throne through violence or through the threat of violence, and kept his crown by warding off domestic and foreign rivals. Peace was simply the aftermath of one war and the prelude to another. In this world of ubiquitous violence, it was necessary that a chieftain secure (in the words of the *Beowulf*-poet) "beloved companions to stand by him, people to serve him when war comes."[4] But how could he obtain these warriors? What obliged men in seventh-century England to attend a king's army? One cannot claim to understand early Anglo-Saxon society without first answering these basic questions.

Our earliest source for the organization of an Anglo-Saxon royal army is a provision in a late seventh-century West Saxon law code attributed to King Ine which defines the penalties to be exacted from those who failed to attend that king's "fyrds." The linguistic evidence suggests that the term "fyrd" had originally meant "a journey."[5] By Ine's day, however, "fyrd" had acquired a distinctly martial connotation. The term was used in the Old English biblical translations and literary sources to mean an "armed expedition or force." In royal or "official" documents, such as charters, writs, and legal compilations, the word assumed a more technical meaning, denoting a specific type of military expedition, one conducted by or in the name of a king.[6] This is its meaning in Ine's code. Since the relevant provision, *Ine*, c. 51, is critical evidence for the nature of military obligation in pre-viking Wessex and is frequently cited as evidence for "the nation in arms," it merits close examination. The clause reads in full:

> If a nobleman who holds land [*gesithcund mon landagenda*] neglects military service [*forsitte fierd*], he shall pay 120 shillings and forfeit his land; [a nobleman] who holds no land [*unlandagende*] shall pay 60 shillings; a *cierlisc* man shall pay 30 shillings as penalty for neglecting the fyrd [*to fierdwite*].[7]

On the surface, this law appears straightforward. It stipulates the penalties to be exacted from individuals of various ranks if they fail to attend the king's host. But when one attempts to analyze the provision further, the difficulties of interpretation become readily apparent. Consider, for example, what this text reveals about the military obligation of the free man of common birth, the ceorl.

Much has been written about the ceorl, especially by those historians who would place him at the center of early Anglo-Saxon society. Frederic Maitland's vision of seventh-century England as a land of free peasant proprietors has persisted into the most recent surveys of Anglo-Saxon history. Modern historians are far too aware of the prevalence of slavery and the early importance of lordship and hierarchy to speak of this society, as their predecessors did, as a "primitive Germanic democracy" or a "peasant commonwealth." But this has not affected the basic conception of the seventh-century English countryside as dotted with communities of free peasants, and of early Anglo-Saxon society as ceorl-centered. The most recent historian to write about Anglo-Saxon legal and administrative institutions, Henry Loyn, has echoed Sir Frank Stenton's dictum that English social history begins with the community of free peasants.[8] The actual evidence for the activities and character of the seventh-century ceorl, however, is anything but conclusive. The word "ceorl" itself simply means a "man" or a "husband"; in itself it denotes nothing about an individual's economic or social status. And while the early Kentish and West Saxon laws do present the ceorl as one who was "folk-free," the nature and extent of his "freedom" are debatable.[9] One cannot even say with confidence that *cierlisc* men formed the largest class in early English society, since there is some evidence to suggest that slaves may have outnumbered the free in the seventh and eighth centuries.[10] The evidence urges caution in our claims about the early English ceorl. We would not be straying too far from the truth if we were to say that the term "cierlisc man" in Ine's laws described free commoners, who enjoyed the protection of a wergild and a free kindred, but who were unequal in their possession of status and wealth. Nor would we be going beyond the evidence to note that the ceorl's freedom did not mean that he regarded only the king as his superior.

Most surveys of early English history state flatly that ceorls were obliged by their free status to defend the homeland, and, by extension, that the armies of seventh-century England were "nations in arms." Despite this near consensus, there is remarkably little evidence for the existence of mass levies of freemen in early Anglo-Saxon England. Upon careful examination one discovers that only a single early English text speaks explicitly about the military service of ceorls, the aforementioned *Ine*, c. 51. The historian who wishes to discuss "the nation in arms" and expound upon the nature of the ceorl's military obligation is forced by necessity to appeal to continental (or even post-Conquest) evidence and analogy, with the tacit assumption that all early Germanic kingdoms were essentially alike.[11] But even the continental evidence is far from certain. It is well known that the Carolingian capitularies required military service from the Frankish "liberi homines." The meaning of this phrase and the precise identity of these warriors, however, have been matters of great dispute. These "freemen" may have been warrior peasants endowed with allodial property and hereditary freedom or they may have been semi-servile military settlers. Suspicion is also raised by the absence of any reference to a general military obligation in the earliest barbarian law codes.[12] It is possible that, like other archaic forms of service, the obligation to serve in arms was so familiar that it was unnecessary to define it in the Salic law (an argument which has also been used to explain the puzzling paucity of information on the military service of ceorls). It is equally possible that traditional Frankish custom did not enforce universal military service. The military organization of the Frankish kingdom under Clovis and his descendants was greatly influenced by late imperial institutions and practices, and we cannot be certain that the local levies of Merovingian Gaul were not recruited upon the basis of decayed Roman custom. It seems significant in this context that the local levies described by Gregory of Tours were raised from the heavily Romanized cities of southern Gaul rather than from the Frankish homeland of Austrasia or the Burgundian countryside. The Anglo-Saxons, of course, were not exposed to Roman law and custom to the same degree that the other successor kingdoms were. The argument from analogy is thus fraught with uncertainties.

We return then to the one explicit statement in the sources that free men of all ranks served in the royal hosts of pre-viking England, *Ine*, c. 51. Traditionally, the clause has been interpreted to mean that all free men were obliged to fight in the fyrds of seventh-century Wessex and, hence, that these fyrds were "national" levies.[13] This reading, of course, is colored by the notion that early English society was ceorl-centered. Sir Frank Stenton, for instance, had no doubt that seventh-century West Saxon society was based on the free peasant, an individual who was oath-worthy and weapon-worthy. To defend the nation, according to him, was not only the obligation but the privilege of a free man. Only the free man was fyrd-worthy; he alone had the right to bear arms, a right symbolized in the bestowal of weapons during the manumission ceremony. Hence the ceorl who shirked his duty to king and country was liable to pay *fyrdwite* to the king. Some recent scholars have rejected the logic of this argument, largely because of their conceptions of the structure of early English society. Eric John, who has stressed the aristocratic complexion of Anglo-Saxon society, can find nothing in *Ine*, c. 51 to prove that ceorls actually bore arms in battle, although he is willing to concede, based on the archaeological evidence, that some ceorls possessed weapons. Arguing by analogy from a tale in Bede's *Historia Ecclesiastica*, John suggests instead that the cierlisc man's fyrd service amounted to no more than the provisioning of the king's aristocratic troops when they were called on expedition.[14]

Although Stenton's and John's interpretations of *Ine*, c. 51 are fundamentally opposed, both assume that the law was intended to apply to all free West Saxons. They differ on what sort of fyrd service ceorls were neglecting, not that the king expected all ceorls to attend his fyrds. One need not, however, read the text to imply universal military service of one sort or another. The clause is simply a tariff of penalties. It never explicitly demands fyrd service from everyone, but merely stipulates the penalties to be assessed against those who ought to have gone on campaign with the king but did not. Can we be sure that every cierlisc man was required by his free status to attend the king in battle? Are we justified, in other words, in assuming that the seventh-century West Saxon ruler would have expected every free man to fight at his side, and would have had the right to punish those who did not? I think not.

Even if *Ine,* c. 51 was meant to apply to all free men in his realm—
and this in itself is far from certain—it need not follow that the law
reflects actual practice.

Admittedly, the tenor of Ine's code supports the view that all free
West Saxons were duty-bound to serve him militarily. In fact, when
one considers the laws as a whole, the impression received is of a strong
monarchy exercising authority over all its subjects, noble and commoner
alike. This is not in the least surprising; it is also hardly the soundest
foundation upon which to erect a thesis. The early Anglo-Saxon law
codes did not simply reflect tribal custom or practice of the period; they
were ideological and political documents intended to demonstrate a
king's regality. Lawgiving had a symbolic meaning for these barbarian
rulers that transcended the practical use to which these codes could be
put. Ine's decrees no more reveal the true state of late seventh-century
West Saxon society than King Alfred's pedigree preserves his actual
descent from Woden.[15] Rather, both were meant to project a royal ideal
of kingship. By issuing a code of laws, Ine was asserting his right to
rule both the West Saxons and their confederates. While Ine's code
undoubtedly preserves much in the way of genuine customs, it recasts
customary law as the king's law and places Ine's own decrees upon the
same footing as the "old right" (*eald riht*). The preamble to Ine's code
thus states:

> I, Ine, by grace of God king of Wessex . . . have been taking counsel . . .
> in order that just law and just royal decrees [*cynedomas*] may be estab-
> lished throughout our people, so that no ealdorman nor subject of ours
> may from henceforth pervert these our decrees [*thas ure domas*].[16]

Ine's laws thus emphasize, and perhaps even exaggerate, the power and
status of the West Saxon monarchy.

In at least one respect the image of kingship projected by Ine's legislation must be questioned. From other early sources, it is clear that
the claims of lordship outweighed the loyalty owed to a king when king
and lord came into conflict. The retainers of a nobleman were duty-
bound to follow him into exile if he fell from the king's favor. If they
failed to do so, if they chose to serve their king rather than their rebellious lord, they could expect only ridicule and scorn. This sentiment
was deeply ingrained in the aristocratic ethos of early Wessex, so much
so that Ine's own bishop and kinsman, St. Aldhelm of Sherborne, demanded similar fidelity from the clergy. When Aldhelm learned that
Bishop Wilfrid had been driven from Northumbria after quarreling with

King Aldfrith, he addressed a letter to the exile's monastic followers, admonishing them

> that no one of you in sluggish inaction may grow dull in faith, even if necessity require you to be driven from your native land with the prelate who is deprived of his episcopal dignity, and you have to go to any parts of the broad realms across the sea. . . . Behold, if laymen, ignorant of the divine knowledge, abandon the faithful lord whom they have loved during his prosperity, when his good fortune has come to an end and adversity befallen him, and prefer the ease of their native land to the afflictions of their exiled lord, are they not regarded as deserving of ridicule and hateful jeering, and of the clamor of execration? What then will be said of you if you should let the pontiff who has fostered you and raised you go into exile alone?[17]

One was morally obliged to follow one's lord into exile, enduring all the hardships that he was forced to bear. If, moreover, a nobleman did not accept his exile meekly but waged war against the king, as happened so often during the turbulent seventh and eighth centuries, his men were expected to fight at his side. The well-known Anglo-Saxon Chronicle entry for 757 provides a striking illustration of this.[18] King Cynewulf of Wessex and his retinue were ambushed by the *ætheling* Cyneheard, a disaffected member of the royal house whom the king had attempted to exile. After killing the king and all those with him, Cyneheard's men found themselves surrounded by Cynewulf's main body of followers. Rather than abandon their lord, Cyneheard's men refused all offers of clemency, preferring to stay and die with the rebel prince. The Chronicler's attitude is unambiguous: he approved of the behavior of Cyneheard's men, even though he found their lord's actions reprehensible.

It is noteworthy that the early sources use the language of lordship to express the obligations owed a king.[19] When Wiglaf followed Beowulf into combat against the dragon, he did not speak of his duty to "king and country," but of the responsibility of a thegn, that is, a retainer, to protect his lord.[20] One might, in fact, be justified in regarding kingship among the early Anglo-Saxons as but an exalted form of lordship, the king being simply the lord of nobles.[21] H. M. Chadwick's study of the early Anglo-Saxon sources led him to conclude that the term *cyning* (literally, "of the kin") originally designated a member of the royal lineage without reference to royal authority, while the office of king was expressed by the titles *hlaford* and *dryhten,* both of which meant "lord."[22] Certainly, the literary and hagiographical sources give no

warrant for distinguishing between the king-subject and lord-client relationships.[23] An *ætheling*'s noble descent gave him the right to gather
about him a war band, which in some cases grew to royal proportions.
Indeed, within this band his position, based as it was upon a mixture
of blood-right and commendation, may well have resembled that of a
king.[24] Even the early Anglo-Saxon Church, which exalted the role of
the king, recognized that the obligations of lordship and kingship were
not dissimilar. Thus the *Penitential of Archbishop Theodore,* a compilation of the late seventh or early eighth century, stipulated the same
penance for one who killed upon the order of his lord and one who
killed in a "public war."[25] This tendency to associate kingship with
personal lordship culminated in the tenth-century Colyton oath, in
which King Edmund, desirous of strengthening the monarchy, commanded his subjects to swear fealty to him, not as it behooves a man
to be loyal to his king, but "just as a man ought to be faithful to his
lord."[26]

As a number of commentators have noted, Ine's code does portray
him as having the right and power to regulate relations between his
nobles and their dependents. Chapters 63 through 68, a series of laws
concerned with the conditions under which one might leave a holding,
thus decree that a nobleman who wishes to give up his estate and depart
from the land may only take with him his reeve, his smith, and his
children's nurse; his other dependents and tenants must remain behind.[27] Moreover, if a nobleman were to become involved in a feud,
those who held *gesett land* from him, that is, his tenants,[28] were to be
safe from his enemies, an eloquent reminder that peasants as well as
nobles in pre-viking England were constrained by the demands of lordship to pursue vendettas.[29] The image of a powerful monarch exercising
control over his nobility and their followers is unmistakable; it may
also be specious. Royal grants to noblemen at this time did not alienate
the land from the royal fisc. If, as seems likely, the abandoned estates
of clauses 63–68 were such donatives, then this series of laws should
be read as defining the rights retained by the king over the peasants
dwelling upon royal loanland. In other words, *Ine,* caps. 63–68 may
be concerned with a question of disputed lordship rather than an assertion of royal sovereignty.

If Ine's code is read carefully, it is clear that the king's jurisdiction
over the households of his *gesiths* was in fact limited. *Ine,* c. 50, for
example, reads:

> If a nobleman comes to terms with the king or with the king's ealdorman, or with his lord, on behalf of his dependents [*inwihan*], free or unfree, he, the nobleman, shall have no right to any fines, because he has not previously taken care at home [*æt ham*] to restrain them [his men] from evildoing.[30]

Undoubtedly, this provision was intended to emphasize the king's authority over his noblemen's dependents. Every individual, whether the man of the king or of some noble, had to obey the king's law.[31] Yet chapter 50 concedes that the wrongdoer's lord, rather than a royal officer, had the primary responsibility and privilege of meting out punishment and collecting the fines of justice. Moreover, a gesith who wished to protect his men could come to terms with his own lord instead of with the king or his ealdorman. It would seem that in certain circumstances the king exercised authority over his nobles' households through the nobles themselves.[32]

The powers of seventh-century West Saxon kings were thus circumscribed by the demands of the lordship bond. Ine's code should be interpreted with that in mind. A dependent would have been expected to follow his lord into battle or exile, and the king's jurisdiction over the retainers of a nobleman, including his ability to fine them, was limited and indirect. If we are to take Aldhelm and the Chronicler seriously, Ine could not have expected fyrdwite from a dependent of another lord, since a commended man was obligated to defend his own lord against all enemies, including the king.

This line of argument leads one to question the traditional interpretation of *Ine*, c. 51. It is more reasonable to read this provision as imposing penalties upon royal retainers who failed to attend their lord's host than upon all free men. On this view, the cierlisc men of the clause were commoners who stood in an immediate relationship to the king. Among these king's ceorls may be numbered the "Welsh horsemen" (*horswealas*) who rode upon the king's errands and the humbler members of the royal household.[33] Ine may have also regarded those ceorls who held fiscal land and rendered rent and services for their tenures, the *gafolgeldan* and *geburas*, as his men, since they fell under his personal protection (*mund*).[34] This would, at any rate, explain why the ideas of *gafol* ("tribute" or "tax"), fisc, and royal lordship are so closely linked in the early glosses.[35] If the foregoing analysis is correct, then the ceorls of *Ine*, c. 51 followed the king into battle not because they were free men defending their homeland but because he was their lord.

In this they rendered him a service that every lord expected from his commended men and dependents.

That there was a separate class of "king's cierlisc men" in seventh-century Wessex may be inferred not only from the dooms of Ine but from place-name studies and from analogy with contemporary practice in neighboring kingdoms. The numerous West Saxon Charltons (*ceorla tuns*) adjoining royal estates seem to point to the existence of "king's ceorls" in early Wessex.[36] There can be no doubt, moreover, that such a class existed in seventh-century Sussex and Kent. When Æthelwalh, the first Christian king of the South Saxons, bestowed Selsey upon St. Wilfrid, he gave him free men as well as lands and slaves for the support of the monastic community.[37] This was not merely a conveyance but also a transfer of lordship; the free men of Selsey, who had formerly looked upon Æthelwalh as their lord, were now Wilfrid's men. Similarly, the *frigmen* ("free men") of Æthelberht's code regarded the king of Kent as their personal lord and protector (*hlaford and mundbora*)[38] and consequently enjoyed his protection. If, for example, someone were to kill the dependent of a Kentish nobleman, he would have to pay that nobleman twelve shillings for the violation of his protection,[39] but if the victim were a frigman, the slayer would owe fifty shillings to the king.[40] On the evidence of the early Kentish law-books, frigmen were dependents of the king who dwelled upon their own holdings.[41] Considering that the gafolgeldan were also householders protected by the king's mund, one might reasonably regard them as the West Saxon equivalent of these Kentish frigmen.

The term *frigman* in Æthelberht's laws is reminiscent of the *liberi* ("free men") of the Frankish capitularies. The resemblance is more than linguistic. Nineteenth-century German historians generally conceived the liberi to have been free farmer-warriors possessed of allodial holdings and obliged by their freedom to defend the folk. Although the classical doctrine still has its ardent supporters, it is no longer accepted by the majority of German historians. Over the last forty years scholars such as Theodor Mayer, Heinrich Dannenbauer, and Karl Bosl have undertaken a major reevaluation of the nature of "freedom" in early Germanic society, a reevaluation that has been largely ignored by American and British historians of Anglo-Saxon England. For the historians of the *Königsfreiheit* school, "freedom" in the early Middle Ages was not the birthright of ordinary peasants. Only the tribal aristocracy was fully free. The lesser freedom enjoyed by commoners had been acquired for the most part through service. The liberi of the Merovingian and Carolingian law books were thus actually *Königsfreien*, "king's free" soldier-colonists settled upon public land and rendering service and taxes (*servicia* and *tributa*) to the king for their tenancies and free status.[42] Among these services were watch and ward, riding and carrying service, repair of bridges and fortifications, and, above all else, attendance in the king's host.[43] Such duties ring familiar to the student of Anglo-Saxon England; they read like a catalog of the services rendered by the sokemen and "free men" (*liberi homines*) of early East Anglia and Kent.[44] In addition, the Frankish "king's free," like the Kentish "gavelkinders" and the West Saxon gafolgeldan, were distinguished from other commoners by their payment of a land-tax arising from their use of fiscal land.[45]

The Königsfreien were settled in royal administrative districts termed *centenas,* which, like the lathes of Kent and the "shires" of early Northumbria and Wessex, were organized around the king's estates and strongholds.[46] The similarities between the Frankish centenas and these early Anglo-Saxon "hundredal manors"[47] are striking. Before the creation of the Domesday hundreds in the tenth and the early eleventh century, centena-like districts prevailed throughout most of England. These consisted of discrete villages and hamlets attached to a fortified royal residence (*cynges tun*), in which dwelled a king's reeve who did justice and to whom the peasants paid the king's *feorm,* or food rent. One might cite the example of Selsey here; the eighty-seven hides that King Æthelwalh granted to Wilfrid consisted of a royal villa and the scattered villages that owed tribute and services to it.[48]

The evidence is, of course, too fragile to support a conclusive argument. Still, there are provocative parallels between the early West Saxon gafolgeldan and the continental Königsfreien,[49] parallels that should be viewed in light of the modern reassessment of primitive Germanic society. Scholars now tend to dismiss the traditional notions of peasant commonwealths and proto-democracy in the Teutonic forests as romantic fictions. The strongly aristocratic complexion of early Germanic society has been so fully revealed by archaeological,[50] linguistic,[51] and historical investigations[52] that even the critics of the Königsfreiheit school have been forced to admit that the "common freedom of the peasant" (*Gemeinfreiheit der Bauern*) was limited by the demands of lordship and the claims of the aristocracy. This complex of evidence leaves little doubt that Germanic society in the age of the migrations was characterized by a landholding upper class and its dependent peasantry. Lordship and hierarchy were present in Germanic society from the very beginning of the Middle Ages.

The thesis that fyrd service in seventh-century Wessex was an obligation of king's men is thus consistent with recent continental scholarship. More importantly, it harmonizes better with the early Anglo-Saxon sources than do the received interpretations. On the present reconstruction, neither Bishop Aldhelm's insistence that a man ought to follow his lord into exile nor the Chronicle's approval of the bravery of Cyneheard's men was a challenge to the king's law and authority. The suggested reading of *Ine,* c. 51 also resolves a puzzle of early West Saxon history: how a young exile, Cædwalla, managed to wrest the crown from a reigning king.[53]

When Centwine came to the West Saxon throne in 676,[54] he drove his kinsman and rival, Cædwalla, into exile. The young nobleman sought refuge in "the desert places of Chiltern and the Weald" and there gathered about him a following, which in time grew so large that he was able to plunder the land of the South Saxons, killing their king in the process.[55] After nine years of brigandage, Cædwalla turned his eyes toward Wessex and, to use the words of the Chronicle, "began to contend for the kingdom." The military resources available to the reigning king proved no match for those of the savage young exile; Cædwalla met his kinsman in battle and decisively defeated the West Saxon fyrd.[56] Would it not be more reasonable to view Cædwalla's victory as the triumph of one war band over another than as the conquest of a "nation"?

As with the ceorls, only those nobles who were bound to the king by the tie of lordship were obliged to serve him with arms. Theoretically, this would have included all the higher nobility,[57] but theory and practice do not always coincide. To be sure, a king owed his rank precisely to the submission of the *principes* of the people.[58] Not all magnates, however, participated in the election of a new king, and not all men of noble birth entered the royal retinue.[59] Without an established rule of royal succession, the early Anglo-Saxons were plagued with chaotic interregna and chronic civil strife. Although only those of royal blood could legitimately claim the throne, the *stirps regia* included all men within the sixth or seventh "knee" of the founder, and the descent of the crown within this group depended more upon ad hoc considerations, such as the relative strengths of the claimants' retinues, than upon any settled constitutional principles. Thus the phrase "chosen to be king" (*geceosan to cyninge*) encountered in both *Beowulf* and the Chronicle did not imply a constitutional election by the representatives of the "folk," but rather the submission of the dead ruler's household and nobility to the lordship of a prince (ætheling), who through their submission became king.[60] This process was often drawn out and bloody. As the *Beowulf*-poet admonished the sons of kings, "a young man ought by his good deeds, by giving splendid gifts while still in his father's house, to make sure that in later life beloved companions will stand by him, that people will serve him when war comes."[61]

The Chronicle annal for 757 vividly illuminates just such an election. King Sigeberht alienated his nobles through "unjust acts" and consequently lost the kingdom to his kinsman Cynewulf. One of the West Saxon ealdormen, however, refused to abandon Sigeberht, and because of this Sigeberht managed temporarily to retain Hampshire. Three decades later, King Cynewulf attempted to exile Sigeberht's brother, Cyneheard, who responded, as we have seen, by killing the king in an ambush. The ætheling was then himself trapped by the late king's thegns. He attempted to strike a bargain with them; if they would grant him the kingdom, they could have whatever lands and treasures they desired. But Cynewulf's men refused the offer, since it would have been dishonorable to serve the man who had murdered their lord. It is clear that if Cynewulf's men had accepted Cyneheard's lordship, the ætheling would then have been king.

Cædwalla's success and Cynewulf's murder cast a shadow over Ine's code and its portrait of royal power. Cædwalla was not the only West Saxon ætheling "to contend for the kingdom." From the last years of Ine's reign to the murder of King Cynewulf in 786, there was internecine conflict between the collateral lines of the house of Cerdic. In 721 Ine killed his kinsman, also named Cynewulf. A year later, Ealdbeorht rebelled and managed to seize a royal vill before being driven from the kingdom. Ealdbeorht seems to have pursued his claim with the aid of the South Saxons, since in 725 we find Ine invading Sussex and slaying his rival. When Æthelheard came to the throne in 726, after Ine abdicated to go on pilgrimage, he was immediately challenged by Oswald, who also traced his descent from Cerdic. King Cuthred faced in quick succession rebellions by Cynric (748) and Æthelhun, "the presumptuous ealdorman" (*ASC*, s.a. 750). And Cuthred's successor was the Sigeberht who lost the throne to Cynewulf. Even Ecgberht, the most powerful English king of his day, was an exile during the reign of his predecessor. Endemic dynastic struggles thus form the backdrop to Ine's laws.

Such historical considerations would lead one to conclude that *Ine,*
c. 51 could not have applied to every aristocrat, but only to those
noblemen who had chosen the king as their personal lord; in other
words, to the royal retinue. The distinction drawn between the "land-
owning gesith" and the "gesith without land" in this law would then
have reflected a division in the upper echelons of the king's following.
The former was an aristocrat to whom the king had granted land as a
reward for service; the latter was a noble retainer who received maintenance in the king's household.[62]

Ine's legislation about the lands of his nobility supports this interpretation of the landed nobleman in clause 51. Under the traditional
notion of family land, it would be difficult to explain Ine's apparent
interest in and authority over the estates of the aristocracy. *Burghbryce,*
the act of breaking into a fortified dwelling, is not simply the concern
of a nobleman and his family, but is treated as a crime against the
king.[63] Similarly, a breach of peace in the house of an ealdorman, a
distinguished advisor (*gethungenes witan*),[64] or even of a gafolgelda is
to be compounded through a payment to the king.[65] Ine even claimed
the right to regulate the relationship between his nobles and their tenants, declaring that a nobleman had to settle a certain percentage of his
land with tenants before the king would permit him to leave his
holding.[66] The very fact that a gesith would voluntarily leave an estate
to pursue his fortune elsewhere suggests that the estate was not part of
his familial inheritance.[67] It is far more plausible to interpret these
tenures as royal donatives over which the king retained a proprietary
interest.

Early Anglo-Saxon diplomas confirm the existence of such precarious
tenures.[68] A late seventh-century Kentish charter from the reign of King
Oswine speaks of land that "princes had possessed in olden time by the
gift of kings," and a number of other early Kentish landbooks mention
that the land being granted by the king had formerly been held by other
tenants.[69] Similar evidence can be obtained from eighth-century charters
of the West Midlands. One, BCS 245 (S 125), records the transformation
of a loan into bookland; the grantees, a thegn and his sister, were now
to hold "in perpetuity" and with the right of bequest the same property
that their late father had held at the pleasure of the king. In BCS 183
(S 55), the Hwiccean *subreguli* Eanberht, Uhtred, and Ealdred gave an
estate to St. Peter's, Worcester, which had previously been held by a
comes, Tyrdda. There is even some suggestion that by the middle of

the eighth century Hwiccean and Mercian kings were recording their gifts of loanland, just as though they were booking these estates.[70]

If the gesith's land was held precariously of the king, one would expect it to revert to the king if the donee failed in his duty to his royal lord. And this is exactly what we find in the first clause of chapter 51. Just as an ealdorman who neglected his responsibilities lost his *scir*, his sphere of authority,[71] so a *gesithcund mon landagende* who ignored the king's summons to the fyrd forfeited his land. The parallel is instructive. In both cases that which was forfeited had not been held by hereditary right—although a man's descent may have made him worthy of the grant—but as a reward for past service with the implied condition of continued service.

FYRD SERVICE IN EARLY NORTHUMBRIA AND MERCIA

A similar picture of the fyrd emerges from the early sources for Northumbria and Mercia. Any examination of Northumbrian society in the seventh and eighth centuries must begin with the works of Bede. Among the salutary tales that Bede relates in his *Historia Ecclesiastica Gentis Anglorum* is one set in the aftermath of the Battle of the Trent, A.D. 679. A young follower of the Northumbrian king Ecgfrith, Imma, was struck unconscious during the fight and revived somewhat later to find himself lying among the corpses of the slain. Binding his wounds as best he could, he went in search of his comrades, only to encounter instead a band of Mercian soldiers (*uiri hostilis exercitus*), who took him captive and presented him to their lord (*ad dominum ipsorum*), one of King Æthelred's gesiths.[72] Imma feared to admit that he was a warrior (*miles*), lest he fall victim to a blood-feud, the inevitable consequence of war at this time.[73] Instead, he passed himself off as a "rustic" who was both married and poor, adding that he had come on campaign with others of his ilk to bring provisions to the warriors.[74]

What are we to make of this? Eric John, following the lead of H. Munro Chadwick, concluded that "Bede takes it for granted that gentlemen fight and yokels supply; a captured gesith is in quite different case from a captured ceorl."[75] Consequently, Stenton's vision of the fyrd dissolves, and we are left from the start with a limited and select force of aristocratic warriors. But does Bede's text bear the weight of this interpretation? Chadwick and John both ignored another passage in the *Historia Ecclesiastica* that is damaging to the thesis of bellicose nobles and passive peasants:

> In these favourable times of peace and prosperity, many of the Northumbrian race, both noble and simple [*tam nobiles quam priuati*], have laid aside their weapons and taken the tonsure, preferring that they and their children should take monastic vows rather than train themselves in the art of war [*bellicis exercere studiis*].[76]

The term *priuati* is unusual. It occurs only one other time in the *Historia*, in a passage borrowed from Gildas.[77] But in both cases the meaning is unmistakable: the priuati were the baseborn, the non-noble element within the *gens*.[78] Apparently, Bede believed that some "yokels" did fight.

The *Vita Wilfridi* confirms this view and supplies a clue to the military organization of Northumbria in the seventh and the early eighth century.[79] When Wilfrid reached the age of fourteen, he decided to leave his father's "fields" (*rura*) and seek "the kingdom of Heaven." Apparently, the road to the Kingdom passed through King Oswiu's court,[80] since we find Wilfrid's father, himself no doubt a king's thegn, bestowing upon his son and his son's "boys" (*pueri*) suitable weapons, horses, and garments, so that Wilfrid "could stand fitly before the royal presence."[81] (One is reminded of the Danish coastguard's comment on first sighting Beowulf: "I have never seen a man more noble [*maran eorla*] on earth than is one of you, a man in battle-dress. That is no retainer [*seldguma*] made to seem good by his weapons."[82])

Who were Wilfrid's "boys"? The text suggests that the young saint's following was made up of commoners drawn from his father's household. Their weapons, their horses, and even their clothes were given to them so that they might better serve their master, Wilfrid. Although it is possible that the saint's companions were young noblemen given in fosterage to Wilfrid's father,[83] the passage militates against such an interpretation. If they had been foster-sons, Wilfrid's father would have been obliged to commend them at court, as Wilfrid himself was later to do for his own foster-sons,[84] and there is no suggestion in the text that he did so. On the contrary, Eddius leaves little doubt of the entourage's purpose; they, like the horses they rode and the raiment they wore, were given to Wilfrid so that he might make the desired impression upon the king and his nobles.[85]

Even the word that Eddius chose to describe the saint's following, *pueri*, implies their humble origin. At least this is the sense that *puer* had in Francia at this time. In Merovingian Latin the term denoted a servant or retainer, a usage that found its precedent in both classical and patristic writings.[86] Moreover, the Frankish pueri who swelled the retinues of the kings and their magnates were usually *pauperes;* some in fact were mere freedmen.[87] Although the Northumbrian evidence is not as clear as one might wish, Bede does use puer for "household servant" on at least one occasion, and he seems to have been aware that the term could connote a military retainer.[88] Eddius, it should be added, referred to Wilfrid's later "regal" following as his *sodales,* "companions," rather than as his pueri.[89]

But we need not rest our argument for cierlisc warriors on mere inference. We have the testimony of no less a personage than Alcuin for this. In a letter to his pupils "Calvinus" and "Cuculus," Alcuin candidly assessed the tribulations of Eanbald II, Archbishop of York.[90] His sympathy was limited, to say the least. The archbishop, it seems, had been playing a dangerous game, harboring the king's enemies in return for their landed possessions.[91] As a result, his following had swollen to an unseemly degree:

> And what does he want with such a number of thegns in his retinue [*in comitatu suo tantus numerus militum*]? He seems to maintain them out of pity. He is harming the monastic folk who receive him with his following. He has, as I hear, far more than his predecessors had.[92] Moreover, they too have more of the common sort, that is, low-born soldiers, than is fitting under them [*illi gregarios, id est ignobiles milites, plures habent, quam deceat, sub se*]. Our master [Æthelberht, Archbishop of York] allowed no one of his followers [*ex suis satellitibus*] to have more than one such, except for the heads of his household, who had two only. The pity is imprudent that benefits a few—and those perhaps criminals—and harms many—and those good men.

The prelate's household was clearly divided into two distinct grades: Eanbald's personal retainers and, under them, their retainers. The former were men of distinguished ancestry. A number of them had been wealthy landowners who, having fallen from favor with the king, had sought refuge in the archbishop's following. The latter were men of a far different sort. Unlike their masters, they were low-born warriors (*ignobiles milites*), men whom Bede would no doubt have termed priuati and whom Ine would have recognized as cierlisc. If Alcuin's use of *gregarii* is not merely a literary conceit, these commoners may well have formed the rank and file of the war bands at this time.

What then is to be made of Imma's tale? Chadwick and John, as we have seen, concluded from Imma's pretense that a ceorl's fyrd service ordinarily consisted of supplying the troops; the rustic did not himself fight, and hence was not subject to the vendetta. But we have also seen contrary evidence that asserts the existence of low-born warriors. The contradiction, however, is only apparent. Imma claimed not only to be a "rustic" but also a "pauper bound by the chains of marriage." Chadwick and John, taking note only of *rusticus,* ignored Imma's professed economic and marital status. Yet is it not truer to the text to see Imma's safety hinging upon being accepted as a particular sort of *cierlisc mon,* one who was both poor and married? If so, then it is quite possible that Ecgfrith's followers and those of his nobles included young, unmarried peasants, who, like their "betters," hoped to advance themselves through military service. The more prosperous husbandman, the ceorl who rendered gafol from a hide or more of fiscal land, may also have been called upon to serve his royal lord in arms. Only the poorer heads of households discharged their duty in the commissariat.

In Northumbria, as in Wessex, at least some ceorls owed fyrd service. The parallel between the two kingdoms, however, does not end here, but extends to the military obligation of the landholding aristocracy, the *gesithcund men landagende,* to use Ine's terminology. For what Ine's laws imply about the land tenure of the nobility and its relationship to fyrd service, the Northumbrian evidence confirms. The Northumbrian gesiths, like their southern counterparts, appear to have held land at the king's pleasure as a reward for faithful service with the understood condition of future service.

Once again we must turn to Bede for our evidence. In 734 Bede composed a long epistle to Ecgberht, Bishop of York, concerning the state of the Church in Northumbria.[93] He drew his superior's attention to a number of ecclesiastical abuses, both of omission and commission. Among the more serious of the latter was the scandalous proliferation of spurious monasteries. Since the death of King Aldfrith some thirty years before, laymen, especially the king's officers and servants, had been acquiring estates and villages, which they secured by royal charters, under the pretense of establishing monastic foundations.[94] But instead of devoting themselves to the religious life, these so-called abbots were marrying and raising families upon the lands they had purchased ostensibly for the use of God. Bede knew full well the reason for this charade; by calling their lands "monastic houses," laymen were able both to secure hereditary estates and to free themselves from all service, divine as well as secular. The consequences of this practice were equally obvious; not only would the quality of religious worship decline and immorality spread throughout Northumbria, but "by a dwindling of the supply of secular troops" there would be an insufficient number of men to defend the kingdom from "barbarian" incursions.[95]

Donations of this type had become so prevalent that the sons of noblemen and of veteran warrior-retainers (*filii nobilium aut emeritorum militum*) found themselves without hope of marriage and family in their native land. They faced an unpalatable choice: either they could seek their fortunes in foreign adventures, "abandoning the fatherland for which they ought to fight," or, if they wished to serve their own king, they could remain in Northumbria "and with greater guilt and shamelessness devote themselves to loose living and fornication."[96] Why, one might reasonably ask, were these youths not content to dwell upon their fathers' lands until they could obtain their patrimonies? Why, unless this was not an option? Charles-Edwards has sought to reconcile Bede's epistle to Ecgberht with the assumption that nobles possessed hereditary familial estates. He reasons that young warriors may have been serving the king in order to augment the estates which they would receive upon the deaths of their fathers. He assumes that the familial lands were too small to support the households of both father and son, and that the father's life expectancy was such that the son could not anticipate his father's death. Neither assumption is compelling.[97] Moreover, there is little positive evidence for aristocratic allodial estates before the introduction of bookland. Ine's laws demonstrate that ceorls ordinarily expected to inherit property from their parents, but there is no analogous evidence for the gesithcund men.[98] On the contrary, as we shall see, the literary sources suggest that noblemen received their patrimonies as gifts from the king. It is not paradoxical to think that peasants might have had a hereditary right to cultivate and dwell upon a plot of land, while their betters had to "earn" their inheritances. The estates of these noblemen were not "farms" which they worked, but rather political units over which they enjoyed rights. The conclusion to be drawn from Bede's letter seems inescapable: if a young Northumbrian nobleman wished to marry, he first had to secure a suitable endowment, and such land could only be earned through service to the king or his magnates.

Great nobles as well as kings rewarded their followers with loanland, and this system was crucial to the defense of the kingdom. Bede thus describes the Northumbrian warriors who defended the frontiers as "the warriors or companions of secular powers."[99] Who were these "secular powers"? In another passage of the same letter, Bede tells us that laymen were securing charters for their spurious monasteries, and that bishops, abbots, and "secular powers" (*potestates seculi*) were witnessing these documents. One can therefore identify Bede's "secular powers" with the royal *comites* and *principes* whose names appear in the witness lists of the early charters.[100]

The rapid multiplication of spurious monasteries held by book-right was threatening the traditional career pattern of the Northumbrian nobility. Previously, the "sons of noblemen and tried warriors" had been raised on their fathers' estates or on those of foster-parents until they reached the age of maturity and entered a noble or royal retinue. Here they began as junior members of the household (*geoguth* or *juventus*) and, if they pleased their lord, could expect as their reward "a landed possession suitable to their grade."[101] As veteran warriors, the *duguth* of poetry and the *nobiles aut emeriti milites* of Bede's epistle, they lived upon royal lands, married, and raised a new generation of warriors.

If we read the literary sources without romantic preconceptions, this quid pro quo of land for military service stands out in bold relief. Beowulf, a grandson of the Geatish king Hrethrel, was seven years old when his father gave him to the king to be raised in the royal household. When the poem opens, Beowulf's father is dead and yet the young warrior is landless. It is not until he has proved his worth in foreign adventures that his royal kinsman Hygelac endows him with an estate suitable to one of his birth. Like Widsith,[102] Beowulf wins treasure abroad, returns to his native land, and, as is only proper, hands over his booty to his royal lord. Hygelac concludes the transaction by giving his kinsman and retainer a valuable sword, a hall, "a princely seat," and seven thousand hides of land. As the poet explains: "To both alike there was land by birth in that country—an estate, ancestral right; but a great kingdom belonged rather to the one who was higher in rank."[103]

This exchange of gifts reflects the principle of reciprocity.[104] Beowulf's land was in a very real sense his not only by birth (*gecynde*) but by royal gift. The ætheling's descent made him worthy to be Hygelac's "companion"—this is, after all, the literal meaning of gesithcund[105]— and his deeds proved him deserving of an estate suitable to one of his birth, which he could receive only through the favor of the king. In the world of the *Beowulf*-poet, a nobleman earned his land from his royal lord.

The gift-giving lord is a familiar figure in Old English poetry, and it is not surprising that the Anglo-Saxons should have regarded munificence as a great virtue in their rulers.[106] In that society, as in so many other primitive communities,[107] gift-giving was a tool of governance. The flow of goods between lords and retainers sustained the social hierarchy. When Beowulf, Weohstan, and Widsith offered their lords the wealth they had won, they did their duty as retainers, and when their lords answered with as much or even greater treasure, they too acted as they should have. A gift in that society bore a value beyond its simple market price, for it created, symbolized, and confirmed the relationship between a man and his lord. The offer of a gift and its acceptance established a social relationship; the recipient of the largess placed himself in the debt of the donor and morally obliged himself to requite the favor. The ring, the mead, and, above all, the land given a man by his lord constrained that man to respond appropriately, to "love all that his lord loved, and to hate all that he hated."[108]

In this scheme a grant of land answered a retainer's loyal service and called forth from him a further gift of service. Both land and service were "free" gifts required by the lord-man relationship.[109] As Beowulf boasted to his hearth-companions before his fatal engagement with the dragon:

> I repaid in war the treasures that he [Hygelac] gave me—with my bright sword, as was granted me by fate: he had given me land, a pleasant dwelling. There was no need for him, any reason, that he should have to seek among the Gifthas or the Spear-Danes or in Sweden in order to buy with treasure a worse warrior.[110]

Neither gift was "complete." Gift and counter-gift sustained one another. Although it was customary that a thegn should receive an estate for life (either his or his lord's), this should not blind us to the donation's precarious character. If one failed in one's duty to the king or, like Benedict Biscop,[111] chose to abandon the *militia regis* for the *militia Dei,* the royal grant could be forfeited. Even if a thegn served his lord faithfully, this in itself did not guarantee his tenure, as the minstrel Deor discovered to his dismay.[112] Thus the king's gift was as open-ended as his retainer's counter-gift of service; the former was continually renewed and confirmed by the performance of the latter. In this way land cemented a man to his lord, compelling him to render whatever aid the lord might require.

To receive land from one's lord was a sign of special favor. A landed estate was a symbolic as well as an economic gift. It differed from other gifts in that its possession signified a new, higher status for the thegn within his lord's retinue. King Hygelac's decision to endow his heroic kinsman with seven thousand hides of land meant that Beowulf was no longer to be regarded as a "youth" (*geoguth*).[113] He had proved himself a warrior through his Danish adventures; he had shown himself worthy of his own land and household.[114]

The distinction between "tried men" (*duguth*) and "youths" is crucial to a proper understanding of early Anglo-Saxon lordship. In Bede's day, the following of a king or of a great noble was divided into his *geoguth* and his *duguth*. The former were young, unmarried warriors who, having as yet no land of their own, resided with their lord, accompanying him as he progressed through his estates. When a retainer of this sort had proved himself to his lord's satisfaction, he received from him a suitable endowment, perhaps even the land that his father had held from the lord.[115] This made him into a duguth, or, as Bede put it, a "companion [*comes*] or tried warrior [*emeritus miles*]."[116] He ceased to dwell in his lord's household, although he still attended his councils; rather, he lived upon the donative, married, raised a family, and maintained a household of his own.[117] The Mercian nobleman who held Imma captive may be considered representative of this class; Imma himself was undoubtedly one of King Ecgfrith's geoguth.[118]

The duguth received their landed estates from the king. By accepting these gifts, they bound themselves even more closely to their royal lord, since their obligation to him was now greater. When a king assembled his army, the duguth were expected to answer his summons at the head of their retinues, much as they would attend his court in time of peace.[119] The fyrd thus would have been the king's household warriors augmented by the followings of his landed retainers. Although the sources provide little detail on the organization of early Anglo-Saxon armies, we find support for this view of the fyrd in two narratives: Bede's brief account of the Battle at *Degsastan* and the related notice of this battle in the northern recension of the Chronicle.[120] According to Bede, Aedan, ruler of the Scottish kingdom of Dal Riada, invaded Bernicia in A.D. 603 to put an end to the encroachments of King Æthelfrith of Northumbria. The Northumbrians, led by the ætheling Hering, son of Hussa, intercepted the Dal Riadans near Dawston in Liddesdale and decisively defeated them. Only Aedan and a few of his bodyguards managed to escape the slaughter. The Northumbrians did not, however, emerge unscathed. Among the fallen were Æthelfrith's own brother, Theodbald, and his entire following. In other words, despite the overwhelming nature of the victory, an entire war band from the victorious side was annihilated. The evidence is hardly conclusive, but it would appear that this particular Northumbrian fyrd consisted of individual retinues, such as Theodbald's, each of which fought separately under the leadership of its lord.

Landed retainers not only continued to serve the royal lord with arms but were, in fact, of great military value, for they and their own retainers constituted the bulk of a king's forces. This is amply borne out by the circumstances surrounding the battle by the River Idle (A.D. 616/617).[121] Rædwald, king of the East Anglians, gathered a large force of men and attacked his powerful rival, Æthelfrith of Northumbria. Rædwald had moved so swiftly that he caught Æthelfrith totally unaware, leaving the Northumbrian without sufficient time to summon and assemble his landed warriors. Æthelfrith was thus forced to rely upon those troops who were at hand, presumably his personal retinue. The result was disastrous for the Northumbrians; greatly outnumbered, they were routed by the East Anglians. Æthelfrith had been a great and feared warrior king who had previously enjoyed much success against the Britons.[122] Even a renowned king with a distinguished household could come to disaster if he lacked a sufficient force of landed retainers.

The career of Oswine of Deira, one of Bede's model rulers, points up this same lesson. Because of his generosity and personal qualities, Oswine had attracted a large household retinue from the nobility of "almost every province." The resources of his kingdom, however, were no match for those of its hostile northern neighbor, Bernicia. When he faced Oswiu of Bernicia in battle, Oswine found that his troops were greatly outnumbered. Rather than risk a disastrous engagement, "he disbanded the army that he had assembled at *Wilfaresdun,* and ordered all his men to return home." He himself went into hiding in the house of a noble supporter, who promptly betrayed him to Oswiu.[123] While geoguth may have provided the royal household guard, the duguth were necessary if a king was to wage war successfully against a powerful enemy.

If we accept the argument that the royal armies of this period were made up of a king's personal followers serving in hope of reward, the careers of early Anglo-Saxon rulers such as Oswald, Oswiu, and Ecgfrith become far more intelligible. Time and time again we are told in the sources that newly elevated kings had to defend their kingdoms with tiny armies. Later in their reigns these same kings, having weathered the attacks made upon them "while their kingdoms were still weak," are found leading great armies.[124] Victory, after all, meant tribute and land, and these meant in turn that a king could attract more warriors into his service.

It is tempting to read the distinction between "proven men" and "youths" into *Ine, c. 51*. If, as seems likely, the *gesithcund men landagende* of that clause were akin to Bede's *comites uel emeriti milites,* then one would indeed expect them to lose their landed estates if they refused to follow the king into battle. For, like their northern counterparts, they would have held their lands by a precarious tenure that depended upon their continued faithful service to their royal lord. Such land was held so that a king's gesith or thegn could better serve his lord. On this reconstruction, the noblemen of Wessex and Northumbria did not inherit their estates. Instead, they inherited status, which, when coupled with service, made them worthy to receive grants of land from the king. They could, however, forfeit or renounce this gift.[125] Thus aristocratic land tenure in both kingdoms during this period may be thought of as a benefit of lordship. It was the gesith's personal relationship and service to the king that both brought him land and obligated him to attend the king's host.

What was true of Wessex and Northumbria also seems to have been true of Mercia. Here too the seventh-century fyrd is best described as a royal war band made up of the king's personal retainers and their followers. Let us turn once more to Bede's narrative of the Battle of the Trent. Bede relates that Imma was captured by a band of soldiers whom he describes simply as "men from the enemy army" (*uiri hostilis exercitus*).[126] Who were these Mercian warriors? Although they served in King Æthelred's host, it is extremely unlikely that they were the king's gesiths or thegns. Rather than bringing their prisoner to the king, as one might expect from king's men, they took him to the residence of an unnamed *comes regis,* whom Bede terms their "lord" (*dominum ipsorum*). Obviously, these men were the armed retainers of a Mercian nobleman, who fought for him, just as he fought for his own lord, the king.

This interpretation of the fyrd harks back to the word's linguistic roots.[127] As has been noted, the custom of attending the king's host arose not from some ancient Germanic conscription of the folk, but rather from the obligation of a retainer to accompany and defend his lord upon journeys.[128] By the time that we first encounter it in the written sources, fyrd had come to mean a specific type of journey, a military expedition. It was, in fact, a particular application of this duty to follow and protect one's lord. When an Anglo-Saxon king of the seventh or eighth century chose to war, his retainers would follow him into battle, not out of a duty to defend the "nation" or the "folk," but because he was their lord. Similarly, their own men, also obliged by the bond of lordship, fought under them. Such a gathering might best be conceived as a king's retinue arrayed for war, which itself was but an assemblage of his followers' individual retinues.

This conception of the early fyrd also accords well with the evidence for small armies during this period. An oft-cited clause in Ine's laws (c. 13, § 1) defines an army (*here*) as a band totaling more than thirty-five men.[129] Despite its inflated numbers for later fleets, the Chronicle represents the early Anglo-Saxon invaders as arriving in a handful of ships: Hengist and Horsa, Ælle, and Stuf and Wihtgar, each with three; Port with two; and Cerdic and Cynric with five.[130] Although Bede goes on to say that the example of Hengist and Horsa inspired other Germanic war bands to follow them to Britain, he also stresses that the crews of the brothers' three ships were sufficient to defeat a Pictish army threatening Kent.[131] This is not to suggest that Gildas, Bede, Nennius, and the Chronicle preserve an accurate record of the forces involved in the original invasion; these accounts, each drawing upon both tradition and earlier narratives, are probably closer to myth than history. Yet it is worth noting that the Chronicler saw nothing incongruous about adventurers such as Cerdic or Ælle winning kingdoms with armies numbering no more than a few hundred warriors.

Although the sources are silent on the numbers attending the early fyrds, we can gauge the size of a private army in the late eighth century from the eighty-four men who fell by the side of the ætheling Cyneheard in his unsuccessful attempt to seize the throne of Wessex.[132] Nor should we assume too readily that the retinue of a great prince and the army of a king were of different orders of magnitude in the seventh and eighth centuries. Although Cyneheard's force proved in the end no match for the resources of King Cynewulf, an earlier West Saxon nobleman, Cædwalla, was able to defeat the fyrds of two kingdoms with his war band, a war band large enough to be called an "army" (*exercitus*) by Bede.[133] A seventh-century Mercian ætheling, the future saint Guthlac, also gathered about him a band of followers and for nine years "laid waste the towns and residences, villages and fortresses, of his opponents with fire and sword"—all this without the aid, or interference, of Æthelred, King of the Mercians.[134]

Even the military establishments of the powerful Northumbrian kings of the seventh and eighth centuries appear to have been quite modest in size. According to Eddius, the army that supported Osred's claim to the Northumbrian throne was so small that, when pressed by its enemies, it sought refuge in "a rocky, narrow cleft" in the fortress of Bamburgh.[135] The archaeological evidence also points to Northumbrian fyrds with hundreds rather than thousands of warriors. Among the more interesting structures uncovered by Dr. Brian Hope-Taylor in his excavations of the seventh-century royal vill at Yeavering was a grandstand that seated three hundred and twenty individuals. From all indications, this "amphitheatre" was intended as a meeting place at which the king could address and consult his retainers. It may also have served as a point of assembly for the king's fyrd.[136]

An Anglo-Saxon army of a few hundred men would have measured up well against the enemy forces that it would have faced in this period. If we can trust the evidence of the *Goddodin* poem, the core of which seems to have been composed by the poet Aneirin around A.D. 600, the army that Mynyddog Mwynfawr of Edinburgh led against the Anglo-Saxons of Deira consisted of either three hundred or three hundred and sixty-three mounted warriors.[137] If we grant each warrior a few servants, the entire army must have numbered only one thousand to fifteen hundred. This, moreover, seems to have been an exceptionally large force for a British king to take on campaign, since Mynyddog Mwynfawr had augmented his own troops with mercenaries drawn from neighboring kingdoms. Even the viking armies that ravaged Northumbria in the late eighth and the early ninth century numbered in the hundreds or low thousands.[138] The weight of the evidence thus suggests that the armies of early Northumbria were small, selective forces rather than levies of all free men.

CONCLUSION

The fyrds of early Wessex, Mercia, and Northumbria were neither select nor great levies. They were instead merely a king's retainers, his comites and milites, and their own armed followers, many of whom may well have been drawn from the cierlisc class. Lordship, not "kingship," cemented a seventh-century fyrd. One would probably have had difficulty distinguishing between the "royal armies" of this period and the war bands of æthelings such as the exiled Cædwalla or the young St. Guthlac.

The ceorl was not the key figure in an army of this sort, although the ranks may have included many commoners. The early fyrd, based as it was upon the lordship bond, was aristocratic in its basis and structure. While the Anglo-Saxon aristocracy, as we have seen, did not have a monopoly on warfare, nevertheless, warfare was deemed its proper profession. The reader of Bede can hardly help but notice the aristocratic flavor of the word *miles,* "warrior," in the *History.* To give but one example, Imma is introduced by Bede as a "youth from the army of the king" (*iuuenis de militia regis*) and is soon after termed a *miles.* Later, when his deceit is revealed, he admits to being "of the nobility" (*de nobilibus*). What is of special interest is that his captor had come to suspect Imma's noble birth "from his appearance, clothing, and speech."[139] The Anglo-Saxon nobleman, like his Frankish counterpart, belonged to a hereditary military caste[140] and, as the *Vita Wilfridi* makes clear, was born to be a warrior, whether in the *militia regis* or the *militia Christi.*[141]

The sources suggest that Dannenbauer's and Mayer's analyses of Frankish society might be applied profitably to Bede's England. Here too the nineteenth-century doctrines of "peasant freedom" and the proto-democracy of the Teutonic forests must give way. The fyrds summoned by King Oswiu and his contemporaries bore little resemblance to a "nation in arms." To be sure, cierlisc men did fight in them. However, they warred not as free men defending their homeland, but as the retainers of their "betters." In a word, the fyrd of the early Anglo-Saxon period, like English society itself, was hierarchical and dominated by the aristocracy.

AN EXCURSUS ON THE "FREEDOM" OF THE CEORL IN EARLY AND MIDDLE SAXON ENGLAND

Lexicographers and historians have so often translated the term "ceorl" as "free commoner"[1] that one might reasonably assume that there is some formal etymological connection between this word and the concept of freedom. Such an assumption, however, would be mistaken. Rather, ceorl derives from the primitive Germanic *karlaz,* which is thought to have meant "old man."[2] By the time we encounter ceorl in the written sources, it bears three distinct, though related, meanings: a "man" in the sense of gender, without regard to age or social standing;[3] a "husband," i.e., "man" as correlative to "wife";[4] and the head of a non-noble household.[5] It is this last sense that prevails in the legal compilations.

Although "free" may simply be a "modern gloss" upon ceorl, as Aston and others have argued,[6] it is nonetheless a reasonable gloss. For the legal writings do use *cierlisc mon* as a technical term for one who was less than noble (*gesithcund*), yet more than a slave (*theow*). The ceorl was "free" in that he had certain legal privileges and obligations, most notably the rights to take oaths and to defend himself and his own, his kin, his lord, and his dependents.[7] Unlike the slave, the ceorl of early and middle Saxon England enjoyed a blood-price. If a slave was killed, his owner could demand compensation for the loss of his property, but neither a master nor a slave's kinsman was obliged to ransom him from a vendetta or guarantee his safety.[8] By contrast, if a free man were injured or killed, his kinsmen and his lord had the legal right and moral obligation to take vengeance upon his enemy and his enemy's friends, or accept from them monetary compensation fixed by custom and law. It was more than coincidental that the medieval English manumission ceremony marked the transition from servitude to freedom through the ritual bestowal of arms.[9]

The ceorl, like the noble, was a free man, and this not inconsiderable link between them was underscored by the legal jingle *ge ceorle ge eorle* (*Alfred,* c. 4, § 2), used to encompass the entire free community. There were also profound differences between them. The ceorl's wergild in late seventh-century Wessex established his value as one-sixth that of a nobleman who held land, and one-third that of a landless noble or of a Welshman endowed with at least five hides of land.[10] The meaning of this difference in wergild is most clearly brought out by a Mercian text composed in the early eleventh century, *Ath:* "The oath of a man of a 1200 wergild [a thegn in Mercia[11]] is equivalent to the oath of six *ceorls;* for, if a man of a 1200 wergild is to be avenged, he is fully avenged on six *ceorls,* and his wergild is the wergild of six *ceorls.*"[12] The ceorl's more modest standing in society could also work to his benefit. The early law codes all agree that the monetary penalty for a crime or dereliction of duty should vary with the status of the male-factor. A man's wergild established not only his blood-price vis-à-vis his enemies but also the amount of compensation he had to pay for committing certain major crimes, such as participating in an armed foray or harboring a fugitive, and the value of the oath needed to clear him of an accusation of having committed these evil deeds.[13] But this did not mean that the king regarded the wrongdoings of a commoner more lightly. It seems significant that the laws of Ine stipulate that a ceorl of ill-repute caught in the act of theft was to have his hand or foot cut off, and that there is no similar penalty for one of nobler birth.[14]

The neat legal distinctions between noble, free man, and slave were probably oversimplifications of more complex economic and social realities. Ine's code itself suggests that the peasant class was anything but homogenous. The laws present a six-level tariff for Welshmen, establishing the value of a landless *wealh* (taken to be the equivalent of a slave) at a mere 50 or 60 shillings, a landed Welshman with half a hide at 80 shillings, a Welsh "tribute-payer" with a full hide at 120 shillings, his son at 100 shillings, a Welsh horseman in the king's service at 200 shillings, and, finally, a landed Welshman with five hides at 600 shillings.[15] The blood-price of a Welshman thus varied with his economic and social status, and it is possible that similar gradations may have obtained for his English neighbors. We will never know for certain, since Ine's laws do not supply us with a similar schedule for cierlisc men. In fact, they never even explicitly state that the wergild of the "ordinary" ceorl was 200 shillings; we may infer this, but we cannot prove it. As it is, we do know from the early sources that cierlisc men could and did hold unequal amounts of land and that the term "ceorl" embraced both "tribute-payers" (*gafolgeldan*) and lesser peasants known as *geburs*.[16] The boundary between free and unfree in early Wessex, moreover, seems to have been extremely fluid, as both manumissions and enslavements were common.[17] Finally, we cannot even begin to guess at the ratio between the free and the unfree in seventh-century Wessex, although the latter were probably numerous. In sum, some of the most basic questions about the early West Saxon ceorl and his place in society are unanswerable in our present state of knowledge.

We are on more secure ground in talking about the legal freedom of the ceorl than about his economic or social status. But we must take care to define what "freedom" meant in this society and to recognize that there were various degrees of freedom in early England. Even in ninth-century terms, the ceorl was not completely free. A fortuitous mistranslation in the *Old English Orosius*, a work apparently commissioned by King Alfred as part of his educational program,[18] allows us some insight into the contemporary understanding of the freedom of the ceorl. The translator relates that "[the Volscians] had freed some of their slaves and also became too mild and forgiving to them all. Then their ceorlas [Latin: *libertini*] resented the fact that they had freed the slaves and would not free them."[19] The translator evidently assumed that the cierlisc men of his time were in some way unfree. They resented the emancipation and merciful treatment of the slaves because their masters refused to do the same for them. The interpretation of the term ceorl in this text as a libertinus, a freedman, echoes its use in Alfred's treaty with Guthrum, for there the "ceorlas who occupy tributary land" (*ceorlas the on gafollande sit:* presumably *gafolgeldan*) are explicitly placed on the same footing with the Danish freedmen (*liesingas*); the murder of an individual from either class is to be compensated with a payment of two hundred shillings.[20]

What are we to make of Alfred's and the anonymous translator's understanding of the term *ceorl?* The key lies, perhaps, in the relationship between the ninth-century West Saxon cierlisc man and his lord, especially if that lord were also his "landlord" (*landhlaford*). From the seventh century on, the freedom of the West Saxon ceorl was circumscribed by the rights of his lord over him. The ceorl, in fact, was so tightly bound to his lord that if he attempted to seek another, the law prescribed that he be returned and fined sixty shillings—payable to the lord from whom he had fled.[21] Furthermore, a ceorl who held land from his lord could be obliged to labor upon the lord's command.[22] Indeed, if the peasant had accepted a dwelling-place when he covenanted for his yardland, he became tied to his tenancy. Because he had accepted the gift of a house (*botl*), he was no longer free to leave his holding, even if his lord were to demand increased services from it.[23]

It is likely that such tenancies were common in the tenth century. Certainly, the tenure of the ceorls of Hurstbourne was burdened in the time of Edward the Elder with labor services owed to the lord of the manor.[24] In this context one might also consider an interesting late tenth-century gloss: *peculium, ceorlic æhte* (the possessions of a ceorl).[25] If *peculium* retained the meaning it had had in the late Roman empire— and one cannot be certain of that—then the property of a ceorl was considered similar to the holding of a slave from his master.[26] This might illuminate the peculiar mixture of tenurial rights and servility that marked the "*geburs* who dwelled on tribute land" (*geburas the on tham gafollande sittath*) in the will of Wynflæd.[27] It is certain, at any rate, that in the ninth and tenth centuries freedmen and geburas could be bequeathed along with the estates in which they held land.[28]

In seventh- and eighth-century Kent, unlike Wessex, direct evidence survives of a more complex social structure than that of noble, ceorl, and slave. The Kentish laws speak of slaves, three classes of "læts," freedmen, ceorls, "freemen" (*frigmen*), and perhaps three classes of *eorls* (including the king).[29] It is uncertain which of these groups most closely corresponds to the ceorls of contemporary Wessex. The legal position of the West Saxon ceorl, at least in the late ninth century, was akin to that of the Kentish freedman of the Laws of Wihtræd.[30] Both were "folk-free" (*folcfry*), that is, free in the eyes of the community. Both enjoyed wergilds and had the right to seek compensation for other free kinsmen and kinswomen. Yet both were also only semi-free as regards their lords. In Kent the former master was to remain the guardian of his freedman's household, even if the man chose not to settle on the lord's estate. He was also to inherit his former slave's property and receive his wergild if he were slain.

The ceorl of early Kent, on the other hand, seems to have enjoyed a higher standing in society than did the West Saxon ceorl. When we first meet him in the Laws of Æthelberht, the Kentish ceorl is already a landholder and a lord in his own right with "loaf-eaters" (*hlafætas,* correlative to *hlaford* "lord"), who looked to him for maintenance and protection.[31] We also know from the will of a royal reeve that in the early ninth century Kentish men of cierlisc descent amassed considerable personal estates.[32] A direct comparison of the legal standing of Kentish and West Saxon ceorls also suggests the superiority of the former. The ceorls of early Kent enjoyed a blood-price of 100 Kentish shillings; their West Saxon counterparts were presumably protected by a 200 shilling wergild. The obvious conclusion, that the life of a West Saxon ceorl was worth twice that of a Kentish ceorl, is completely mistaken. If anything, the reverse was true. Kent boasted a gold shilling worth twenty *sceattas* and Wessex a less valuable silver one consisting of either four or five pence. Because the exchange rate between the two currencies is uncertain, it is difficult to compare the wergilds of Ine's laws with those of Æthelberht's and Wihtræd's. The question has become, in fact, a numismatic nightmare. Some historians have argued that the Kentish ceorl's life was set at more than twice the value of a West Saxon cierlisc man; others have found the ratio to be precisely two to one, and still others have contended that the wergilds were equal.[33] Until more evidence is uncovered, the question may be insoluble.

Whatever the precise relationship between their wergilds, we do know that the total value placed upon the life of a Kentish ceorl, the combined sum paid to his kinsmen and to his lord, was considerably higher than that of his West Saxon counterpart. Moreover, while the wergild of the West Saxon ceorl was assessed at one-sixth that of a nobleman, the blood-price of his Kentish counterpart was a full third.

The Kentish ceorl also enjoyed a far higher *mundbyrd:* if one violated the protection that he had extended to a dependent, he was to be compensated with six gold shillings as opposed to the West Saxon ceorl's *mund* of six silver shillings.[34] Regional diversity thus adds still another element of uncertainty in a discussion of the ceorls of early England.[35]

In short, both those who would entirely deny the ceorl his freedom[36] and those who would place him at the center of the Anglo-Saxon world go beyond the evidence. The most that can be concluded is that ceorls were "folk-free" in the sense that they had privileges and obligations to the community and were protected by customary law. Nevertheless, such freedom was limited by the demands of lordship, demands that may have grown increasingly harsh in the ninth and tenth centuries. The evidence, however, is hardly conclusive. Caution thus remains the safest course when dealing with the knotty problem of the ceorl and his liberty.

TWO

Bookland and the Origins of the "Common Burdens"

The military system sketched in the previous chapter did not long survive Bede. Even in his day it had been weakened in his native Northumbria by the rapid spread of bookland tenure. The *Epistola ad Ecgberctum* sounds the death-knell of the early fyrd arrangement. As Bede saw it, the proliferation of spurious monasteries had so depleted the stock of land used to reward the king's retainers that the young warriors could no longer look to the king for the land necessary for marriage and social advancement. They were forced instead to seek service in foreign courts, leaving their homeland vulnerable to the attacks of its enemies.[1]

To understand fully the impact of these spurious monasteries upon the ancient fyrd system, one must recall the relationship between land and military service in seventh- and eighth-century England. While the lordship bond, not the ownership of land, had been the source of military obligation,[2] the acceptance of an estate did oblige a man, according to the mores of the time, to serve his benefactor. The king's followers expected to receive estates appropriate to men of their birth, for such land both confirmed their inherited rank and conferred increased status. It is not coincidental that King Hygelac simultaneously bestowed land and status upon his victorious nephew Beowulf or that Wiglaf's possession of the "wealthy homestead of the Wægmundings" entitled him to "every folk-right enjoyed by his father."[3] Throughout the Anglo-Saxon period an individual's blood-price varied not only with his birth, but also with his landed wealth.[4] The king for his part expected that his generosity would be answered by his men's fidelity. By accepting the loan of land, a man acknowledged his dependency and implicitly promised his lord the counter-gift of faithful service.[5]

Since the early Anglo-Saxon kings granted merely the enjoyment of land rather than hereditary title to these possessions, each generation had to win its land (and hence rank) anew. Land tenure, then, was hereditable, but not hereditary. Only through service to his father's lord could a warrior hope to win his paternal estate. As the poet of *Widsith* sang, echoing the sentiments of Wiglaf in *Beowulf:*

> Then the king of the Goths treated me well; he, prince of the city-dwellers, gave me a ring in which there was reckoned to be six hundred pieces of pure gold counted by shillings; I gave it into the keeping of Eadgils, my protecting lord, when I came home, as reward to the dear one because he, the prince of the Myrgings, gave me land, my father's dwelling place.[6]

This was not merely a literary conceit. The evidence for pre-bookland tenures is, of course, slight, since by definition such tenures predated the introduction of charters. But the idea of earning one's father's estate persisted into the era of hereditary landed estates, and on occasion one can hear an echo of it in the early charters. A diploma from the earliest years of Edward the Elder's reign thus describes how a generation before a father disposed of his property: "During his lifetime the aforementioned Cenwald instructed that, if his son Census should serve the king or enter his following, he should be the lord of this land as long as he lived."[7]

The other side of the coin was that kings did not automatically inherit the loyalty of their followers' sons. Eddius assumed that a young warrior might serve a magnate instead of a king, but even this did not exhaust the possibilities for an ambitious youth of noble descent. Æthelings sometimes struck out on their own. As we have seen, the young Guthlac, not yet the athlete of God that he would become, led a war band "drawn from various peoples and from all directions," which pillaged, slaughtered, and ravaged the countryside for its own profit without any pretense of service to the Mercian king.[8] From the matter-of-fact way in which the saint's life as a chieftain is described, it would seem that such activities were not exceptional for a seventh- or eighth-century prince, a conclusion supported by the careers of Cædwalla of Wessex and Æthelbald of Mercia. In order to recruit warriors in the face of competition from nobles and rival monarchs, kings needed wealth, especially in the form of disposable land. The more land that a king had with which to reward followers, the more followers that king could attract, and consequently the stronger his kingdom would be.

Bede's *Epistola* contrasts these royal loans to warriors with the bookland usurped by the king's gesiths and thegns. Loanland, Bede asserted, was the endowment proper to laymen, while bookland was to be reserved for the use of God. In an age of endemic warfare and in a society that measured a king's greatness by his success in battle, a king's very survival depended upon his ability to gather around him a band of warriors. By rewarding his retainers with estates carved out of the royal fisc and held only at his pleasure, an Anglo-Saxon king was able to ensure that his resources would not be wasted upon those too young to fight, or pass into the hands of men of uncertain loyalty or ability. Rather, the king's lands would support those upon whom he most depended, his warriors and officials.

Bede understood the need for such tenures, for without them a king would have too few milites with whom to defend the "fatherland."[9] And since the king was the Church's lord, his fall could also prove calamitous to the men of God. Yet the very qualities that made loanland the ideal tenure for the *militia regis* rendered it unfit for the *militia Dei*. The Church needed a permanent endowment for its monasteries. It could not be subject to the whims of a king; it had to be preserved from the greed of rulers who, caring not for the souls of their predecessors, might be tempted to revoke what had been given a generation before.

Thus an eternally enduring body, the Church, sought an equally perpetual endowment that would be safe from "the uncertain vicissitudes of time" (a favorite sentiment of the early charters). Since native tenurial practice proved unhelpful, the churchmen naturally turned to Rome. The result was bookland, land held by a royal charter or "book" (*boc*).[10] The earliest surviving landbooks with any claim to authenticity date from the archiepiscopate of Theodore, and it is conceivable that Theodore and his contemporaries, particularly St. Wilfrid of Hexham and Hlothhere, the Frankish bishop of the West Saxons, had a hand in the charter's introduction into England.[11] In form, at least, these documents were transplanted Roman legal instruments.[12] They were modeled on the late Roman private deed and were written in the language of the West Roman vulgar law, the simplified law practiced in the late imperial countryside.[13] If the landbooks' formulae can be trusted, book-right resembled the vulgar law's *ius perpetuum,* and bookland was a type of *dominium* over fiscal land.

The concept of *ius perpetuum* in classical Roman law had involved a permanent lease of imperial possessions. By the sixth century this had evolved in the west into a vague type of *dominium* or ownership of the estate.[14] Early bookland seems to have created the same sort of complex of rights over property. The booking of an estate entailed both the conveyance of a demesne, *inland,* with all of its appurtenances, and a grant of superiority over the lands cultivated by the tenants, who owed rent and services to the named estate. The holder of a book would thus enjoy the king's food-rent (*feorm* or *tributum*) and all the services that had previously been rendered to the king and his reeve.[15] He would also possess some undefined jurisdictional rights. By Alfred's day, one who held bookland received fines of justice from those who dwelled in his territory. He was, in the terminology of the time, their "landlord" (*landhlaford*) or "landruler" (*landrica*). In earlier times the regalian perquisites of the book-holder may have been even greater. The earliest plausible reference to a grant of juridical superiority appears in a late seventh-century Kentish charter which records how King Wihtræd confirmed the ecclesiastical privileges of Abbess Mildred's minster on Thanet. According to the language of the charter, Wihtræd conceded that "the guardianship (*defensio*) over men and in all things" should belong to the abbess, "just as it had belonged to our royal predecessors."[16] Mildred's contemporary, the abbess Æbbe, also received from Wihtræd a grant of land along with the same rights "in men and in all things" that his royal predecessors had enjoyed.[17] In short, the abbesses rather than Wihtræd were to enjoy lordship over the tenants of their monastic lands. It would appear, then, that within their estates, the late seventh- and eighth-century book-holders enjoyed extensive, even regalian, rights over their tenants. Bookland was power as well as property.

The language of the early charters leaves little doubt that the framers of these documents had introduced into England a Roman vulgar law tenure borrowed from the countrysides of Italy and Francia. Not only did the early Anglo-Saxon charters follow *ius perpetuum* in emphasizing the eternality of the grant and the permanence of the donee's control over the gift,[18] but they also conferred the rights of alienation and bequest (i.e., free disposal *inter vivos* and *mortis causa*), which were long associated with ius perpetuum, and used vulgar law formulae to accomplish this.[19] It was the stability of the concession that made this form of tenure so suitable for the Church and so unsuitable for laymen. The earliest charters customarily described book-right as *ius ecclesiasticum* or *ius monasteriale,*[20] and indeed at first only the Church, the progenitor of bookland, was deemed worthy of a grant in *iure perpetuo.*

As Bede indicates in his *Epistola ad Ecgberctum,* a layman who desired
"land ascribed to him in hereditary right" could not simply request a
charter from a king or purchase one, but had to pose as a would-be
abbot.[21] The charter evidence fully supports Bede. All fifty-seven extant
authentic charters pre-dating Offa's accession to the Mercian throne in
757 are cast as donations to the Church, either directly or through the
mediation of a pious lay grantee who promised to found a monastery
with the land given to him.[22] In fact, the convention that book-right
was "ecclesiastical right" persisted long after bookland ceased to be a
preserve of the Church. By the last quarter of the eighth century, Anglo-
Saxon rulers were booking land to their gesiths and thegns without any
indication that these grants would be turned to pious uses. Offa, for
example, granted an estate near Salmonsbury, Gloucester, to his thegn,
Dudda, "with the liberty to bequeath the land to any of his kin," and
with the stipulation that any of Dudda's heirs who might be found
guilty of a major offense should pay the appropriate fine but not forfeit
the grant.[23] Yet even when the transaction was purely secular in purpose,
its landbook would often describe it in terms more appropriate for an
ecclesiastical endowment. Thus Offa conferred the property upon
Dudda and his kin "in church right."[24] One need only examine the
diplomas of King Edgar's reign to see how far the form of a charter
could diverge from its substance.[25] The formulae of such documents
tell the historian less about the donor's motivation than about the origins
of book-right in England.

The Church wanted bookland for obvious reasons. But why were
the early Anglo-Saxon kings receptive to the notion of ius ecclesiasticum? In other words, what did a royal donor hope to gain by giving
the Church a privileged tenure? The charters themselves supply the
answer to this question. Almost without exception, the seventh- and
eighth-century English charters portray the royal benefactors as moti-
vated by thoughts of heaven. Over and over one encounters formulae
such as "for remedy of my soul and for absolution from my sins"[26] as
well as pious proems that stress how transitory are the goods of this
world and how necessary it is to use them well so that one may procure
an everlasting reward.[27] Sentiments such as these again point to a continental origin of English book-right. Like the rights conferred by bookland tenure, the underlying idea of bookland—that, in the words of
BCS 187 (S 56), "the eternal rewards of the heavenly fatherland must
be purchased through terrestrial and transitory goods"—was not native
to the Anglo-Saxons but was brought to them by the early Christian

missionaries. A recent study has traced the development of the *pro anima* donation from the fifth through the seventh century in those territories that had once formed the Roman Empire and which now were in the hands of Germanic kings. One need only peruse the formulae used in the English landbooks to see how much they owed to the *pro anima* gifts made on the continent.[28]

We have already seen the Roman influences on book-right; the *donatio pro anima* allows us to glimpse a Germanic element in bookland, an aspect of this tenure that made it palatable to the early Anglo-Saxon kings. Bookland was, in effect, a type of *do-ut-des*. A Christian king gave a free gift to God in hope of receiving from Him the free gift of grace. If we view bookland in such a manner, it becomes clear that book-right had to be, at least initially, both *ius perpetuum* and *ius ecclesiasticum*. God had given man an eternal gift, salvation, and it was only fitting that man render something in return. While nothing that he could give to the Lord would be sufficient, for no man could hope to be God's equal, just as no vassal could aspire to be the equal of his lord, a king could at least respond with an eternal terrestrial gift, a perpetual concession of land and the rights over it. This exchange of gifts confirmed the relationship of lordship that existed between a king and his Lord God in much the same way that reciprocal prestation signified, and by signifying effected, a lordship relationship between a man and his secular lord.

This last point must be emphasized. The parallel between divine and earthly lordship permeates the sources. Just as a king's ealdorman owed his jurisdiction (*scir*) to the king (*Ine*, c. 36, § 1), and a king's gesith held his royal donative at the king's pleasure, the king himself is represented in the charters as owing his rank and lands to God, from whom all goods come. A number of charters, in fact, explicitly declare that what the king has granted to God and his servants is a return for the favors that God had previously shown him.[29] Even the fact that the king only gives to God that which is already His recalls the relationship between an Anglo-Saxon lord and his retainer.[30] All spoils of war by right belonged to the lord, who used them to reward his faithful men.[31] The death of a king meant the cessation of gift-giving and the loss of rights to property, a point emphasized by Wiglaf when he reproached his comrades for allowing Beowulf to fight the dragon alone: "Now shall treasure-receiving and sword-giving, all enjoyment of home [*ethelwynn*], all comfort, cease for your race."[32] The parallels between heavenly and earthly royal lordship and between the eternality of salvation and the perpetuality of book-right are explicitly drawn in a passage that King Alfred inserted into his translation of St. Augustine's *Soliloquies:*

> Every man, when he has built a hamlet on land leased to him by his lord and with his lord's help, likes to stay there some time, and to go hunting, fowling and fishing; and to employ himself in every way on that leased land, both on sea and land, until the time when he shall deserve bookland and a perpetual inheritance through his lord's kindness. May the bounteous benefactor, who rules both these temporary habitations as well as those eternal abodes, so grant![33]

Thus, while bookland tenure may have been foreign in origin, it flourished in England because the concept of *do-ut-des* informed Anglo-Saxon society; the notion that a man gave so that he might receive was anything but foreign to the pagan English. Bookland must have struck the early Christian kings as a reasonable demand on the part of the Church.

How did book-right impinge upon the early fyrd arrangement? What was it about this type of land tenure that brought it into conflict with the existing military system? On the simplest level, what was given to the Church could not be used to endow warriors. While in later times churchmen would bear arms at the command of the king,[34] both the genuine and spurious prelates who held the earliest books enjoyed their tenures without rendering military service for them. The evidence, scanty as it is, in fact suggests that until the second decade of the eighth century ius ecclesiasticum in both Northumbria and Mercia freed an estate from all secular service, so that the full resources of the land might be turned to God's use.[35] Thus, according to Bede, Oswiu celebrated his victory at the Winwæd by giving to the Church twelve small estates "on which, as they were freed from any concern about earthly military service, a site and means might be provided for the monks to wage heavenly warfare and pray with unceasing devotion that the race might win eternal peace."[36] Bede was less sanguine about the spurious monasteries of his day, as their "abbots" belonged to neither the *militia regis* nor the *militia Dei*.[37] Since warfare, as we have argued, was at this time largely the concern of the king's noble retainers and their often cierlisc clients, a policy of diverting land from its traditional use as a reward for service meant that the king could attract and maintain fewer warriors with whom to defend the kingdom or extend its borders.

Land granted in book-right, moreover, was characterized by the eternality of the concession. Unlike the endowments of royal warriors, once bookland was given to the Church, the king's "proprietary interest" (a term used here to approximate the king's rights over his fiscal lands) in the estate was severely curtailed. By giving the land in book-right, the king had removed it permanently from the fisc.

Kings faced a dilemma. They regarded the churchmen whom they had endowed with land as their commended men, but commendation, unlike bookland, was not hereditary.[38] What was to become a critical problem after the extension of bookland tenure to the laity was already a difficulty in the period when bookland was the preserve of churchmen. In theory, kings were booking land to God and his saints, but since human beings actually administered these estates, a donor could not be certain that the clerics who succeeded to a book would be as firm in their devotion to him as the recipients of the gift had been. This concern evidently underlies a curious passage in an early grant of privileges to the Church of Kent. In 699, King Wihtræd, echoing the first chapter of the law code he had issued some four years before,[39] confirmed those privileges enjoyed by the monasteries and ecclesiastical holdings in his realm, declaring that "from this day and moment they are to be free from all exaction of tribute as well as all expenses and attacks."[40] In return, Wihtræd demanded that the Kentish churchmen pray for him and show him "honor and obedience, just as they showed it to my royal predecessors under whom justice and liberty was served to them."[41] In other words, the king, who had succeeded to the Kentish throne after a period of anarchy during which "alien kings and usurpers plundered the kingdom,"[42] expected his churchmen to pray for the welfare of his soul and to refrain from aiding his enemies in any way, temporally or spiritually.

A bishop was the intermediary between a king and God, and a ruler needed clerics if he and his nation were to prosper militarily. In the mid-seventh century King Cenwealh of Wessex quarreled with both bishops whom he had set up in his kingdom and allowed the episcopacy to remain vacant until he was convinced by a series of military setbacks "that a kingdom which was without a bishop was, at the same time, justly deprived of divine protection."[43] Similarly, the exiled æthelings, Cædwalla of Wessex and Æthelbald of Mercia, each sought a holy man's support in their attempts to win their kingdoms.[44] We know of at least one case in which the clergy's spiritual aid was rendered on a battlefield, although the outcome in this particular instance suggests that God did not respond to every priest's prayers, especially when that priest was unsound on the Easter question. Bede tells how the pagan, Æthelfrith of Northumbria, the most powerful English king of the early

seventh century, served as God's instrument of vengeance on the ob-
stinate British clergy. The Northumbrian king had marched against the
Britons of Chester and was about to engage them in battle when he
noticed that a large group of unarmed men—1200 according to Bede
and a more reasonable 200 according to the Anglo-Saxon Chronicle—
was standing apart in a safe place with a small military escort. When
Æthelfrith learned that they were Christian priests who had assembled
to pray on behalf of the soldiers taking part in the fight, he declared,
"If they are praying to their God against us, then, even if they do not
bear arms, they are fighting against us, assailing us as they do with
prayers for our defeat." So he ordered that the priests be attacked and
massacred.[45] The biographer of St. Wilfrid tells a similar story, but one
with a happier ending. When the young Wilfrid was returning from
Gaul, where he had just been consecrated bishop, he and his companions
had the misfortune to be driven ashore on the coast of Sussex. Soon
their beached ship was surrounded by pagan warriors, who were more
interested in salvage and slaves than in salvation. Refusing Wilfrid's
attempt to purchase peace with a large cash payment, the South Saxons
massed for an attack. Their chief priest climbed on to a nearby mound
and began to curse the Christians, but before his magic could work he
was felled by a well-aimed stone. The Christian clergy proved more
effective in their appeals for supernatural aid, since Wilfrid's prayers
helped his companions to repulse three assaults, and, finally induced a
timely return of the tide.[46] Granted, our clerical sources must be sus-
pected of a natural tendency to exaggerate the importance of ecclesiastical support to secular success. Nevertheless, it would appear that
they were expressing a common attitude of the time that rulers needed
supernatural assistance mediated by churchmen. Early Anglo-Saxon
kings did, after all, endow monasteries in thanksgiving to God after
victories.[47]

Royal concern over the loyalty of prelates, moreover, was not un-
founded. While exiled from his bishopric in Northumbria, for example,
St. Wilfrid assisted the rebel Cædwalla against his kinsman Centwine.[48]
Fears of this sort were particularly acute when a powerful prelate managed to accumulate bookland in a number of kingdoms. Each of his
royal lords would naturally question his primary loyalty. St. Wilfrid's
difficulties in Northumbria again form a case in point. The saint held
vast holdings in Mercia and Wessex in addition to those in his native
country.[49] Since Ecgfrith of Northumbria and Wulfhere of Mercia were
fighting for supremacy over the English kingdoms,[50] the fact that the

bishop of York held land from the archenemy of Northumbria could only have aroused suspicion in Ecgfrith's court. For a gift of land, as we have seen, obliged the recipient to respond with "friendship." Land was wealth, and Wilfrid not only possessed spiritual powers but also maintained a large body of retainers. The bishop was an important man not only because of his office but also because of his episcopal and monastic holdings.

With the proliferation of bookland, the problem of royal control over such tenures became more acute. The evidence suggests that during the first half of the eighth century the rulers of Northumbria, Mercia,[51] and Kent[52] began to insist upon some service from the ecclesiastical estates in their kingdoms. This may well account for the sudden and otherwise puzzling introduction of immunity clauses in the charters of this period,[53] since such specific guarantees of exemption from *ius regium* would now have become necessary. Certainly, eighth-century kings, notably Offa of Mercia,[54] went even further, suppressing a number of monastic books and distributing the land thus recovered to their lay followers. The tendency, however, was toward the extension rather than the abatement of book-right. The desire of the laity for land held by ius ecclesiasticum, evidenced by Bede's complaint, eventually led to straightforward endowments of secular comites and ministri with bookland, with the result that by the end of the ninth century bookland was accepted as the proper reward for a king's thegn's faithful service to his royal lord.[55] The kings' willingness to impart land in book-right at a time when they were attempting to limit the rights associated with this type of tenure may be attributed to their need to attract and reward followers whose expectations were now higher and to their desire for ready cash, since many of these donations seem actually to have been sales.[56] It also points up the fact that in the second half of the eighth century a solution was found to the dilemma posed by *ius perpetuum*.

Military burdens upon the land, the so-called "common burdens,"[57] are first mentioned in a charter of 749, which records the privileges granted to the Church by King Æthelbald of Mercia at the Synod of Gumley.[58] In this charter, the Mercian king concedes a general immunity to all the churches and monasteries in his realm from all public renders, works, and charges, reserving only two things: the construction of bridges and the defense of fortifications against enemies. Æthelbald goes on to say that these burdens had been imposed upon the whole people by royal edict (*edicto regis*) and should not be remitted, since they are necessary for the welfare of the whole Church.[59] Although Æthelbald's diploma makes no mention of a precedent for this imposition, arguing from military necessity rather than tradition, it is tempting to think that the Mercian king found a model in contemporary Francia. The maintenance of roads and bridges was a service traditionally performed in Gaul by the residents of the immediate area, an obligation that probably found its legal roots in the Theodosian code and West Roman vulgar law.[60] Cultural contact between late Merovingian Gaul and Mercia may well have been a by-product of the vigorous cross-Channel trade of the second quarter of the eighth century.[61]

The notion that bridge-building and fortification defense, two of the ordinary three[62] "common burdens," arose during the eighth century fits well with the archaeological evidence; the earliest excavated English fortified boroughs are of Mercian provenance and can be dated to the middle of the eighth century.[63] It also makes sense historically when one considers the aggressive policies of Æthelbald against the other English rulers[64] and the Welsh. One should take special note of the failure of the charter to mention the third "common burden," service upon the king's expeditions. The comprehensive nature of the charter does not easily permit us to assume with Stevenson[65] that fyrd service was so taken for granted that there was no need to mention it, especially since Stevenson's argument linked military service with the construction and repair of fortresses, a burden which was considered worthy of mention.

The next earliest charters that speak of, and reserve, military burdens are BCS 202 and 203 (a contemporary text),[66] both of which refer to a grant of land by Uhtred, the underking of the Hwicce, with the consent of his overlord, Offa of Mercia, to his "faithful thegn" (fideli meo ministro), Æthelmund, the son of one of Æthelbald's ealdormen. The formula for the reservation comes from Æthelbald's privilege, and consequently refers only to bridge and fortress work. In fact, the requirement to send men on the king's expeditions does not appear in an unimpeachable charter until 793 X 796. BCS 274 (S 139) is a contemporary text describing a grant by King Offa of land in Gloucestershire to the same Æthelmund, now described as Offa's minister.[67] Offa gave this land free of all service to kings and principes "except for matters pertaining to expeditions, and the construction of bridges and fortifications, which is necessary for the whole people and from which none ought to be excused."[68] Apparently, by 796 fyrd service had joined bridge and fortress work as burdens upon bookland tenure in Mercia.

The evidence for the other kingdoms is less certain, though, if the charters in question are genuine, more revealing. As Brooks has pointed out,[69] the "common burdens" seem to have been imposed upon the Kentish churches by King Offa at a synod held at Clofesho in 792.[70] We need not search long for Offa's motivation in demanding such service; the acts of the synod explicitly state that the expeditions and fortifications were to be "against the pagan seamen" (*contra paganos marinos*), a phrase that recurs in authentic Kentish charters of the early ninth century.[71] It is possible that Offa was reorganizing his resources in the 790s to meet the threat of the viking invasions.[72] Certainly, Offa was unafraid of innovating.[73] Nor was he hesitant to demand money and labor from his subjects for the defense of his realm, a trait that was given concrete expression in the great dyke between England and Wales that bears his name.[74] Canterbury's Roman wall may have been refurbished in response to Offa's call for preparedness. We do know that the city was walled in the early ninth century, and its prominence made it a likely candidate for such "fortress work." In this context it is suggestive that a charter of 868 calls the inhabitants of Canterbury *burgware*.[75]

Nothing can be determined about the imposition of military burdens upon Northumbrian and East Anglian bookland tenure, since charters survive for neither kingdom. We can be fairly certain, however, that fortress work was unknown in seventh- and eighth-century Northumbria, since both the archaeological and written records indicate decay of the Roman defenses of York and Carlisle. Excavations undertaken in the early 1970s reveal that the walls of York had been repaired only once before the viking invasions, at some time during the seventh century.[76] Only the northern defenses of the city remained in use during the next two centuries, and when the Danes stormed York in 867 they discovered, in Asser's words, that the city "did not possess strong and well-built walls."[77] York, moreover, is exceptional in that there was any attempt to refurbish its fortifications in the seventh century. As Martin Biddle notes: "No other place in [England] has yet produced structural evidence for the reconstruction and strengthening of Roman defences in this period and it is a notable testimony to the importance of seventh- and eighth-century York."[78] Carlisle, for example, allowed its Roman walls to fall into such disrepair that by the late seventh century they were regarded as a mere curiosity.[79]

Wessex presents problems of a different sort. Fortress work is only first mentioned in the charters of the mid-ninth century, which again agrees well with archaeological findings, such as the results of recent excavations at Hamwih and Winchester.[80] Hamwih, a major trading center established in the beginning of the eighth century, was an undefended site, which was one of the reasons for its abandonment in the mid-to-late ninth century.[81] The decline of Hamwih coincided with the transformation of the nearby burh of Winchester from a royal residence and episcopal see into a thriving commercial city, the defenses of which were renovated in either the late ninth or early tenth century. Despite its function as an administrative and ecclesiastical center, Winchester's Roman walls had been allowed to decay during the seventh and eighth centuries.[82]

The other two "common burdens," host duty and bridge work, appear in a number of cartulary texts purporting to be copies of late eighth- and early ninth-century West Saxon charters.[83] Most of these documents, however, are outright forgeries. The first contemporary text mentioning host duty is BCS 426 (S 287), a grant by King Ecgberht of an estate near Canterbury dated 839. Since this is in form and substance a Kentish land grant, one might argue that the reservation of the "common burdens" reflects local rather than West Saxon usage. It is not until 848, in fact, that we find an unimpeachable landbook describing a grant within the borders of Wessex itself that reserves host service. This is BCS 451 (S 298), a well-known document that relates how King Æthelwulf booked himself twenty hides of land in Devon.

The only earlier charter that demands consideration in this connection is Æthelney 62, a grant by Beorhtric, king of the West Saxons, to one of his thegns in 794.[84] Unfortunately, this landbook survives only in an eighteenth-century copy, which is riddled with scribal errors. In its favor, the purported grant does employ genuinely early formulae, and its immunity clause has not been "borrowed" from some late charter. In fact, if it is a forgery, it is a remarkably inept one, for the immunity clause is inserted in Beorhtric's attestation, which is unusual, to say the least.[85]

Æthelney 62 represents King Beorhtric as granting ten hides to his ealdorman Wigferth, "free of all fiscal difficulties, royal works, and all things that pertain to the king's vill, except for expeditions, upon which all comites ought to go for the defence of the province and for the greater safety of the churches of God."[86] Since Beorhtric was Offa's ally and son-in-law,[87] it is not inconceivable that the reservation of fyrd service was due to Mercian influence. Certainly, Beorhtric would have had reason enough to impose military obligation upon bookland in his realm: it was during his reign that the vikings first began to ravage the coasts of Wessex.[88] More pertinent to our present inquiry, Æthelney 62 aids us in our understanding of the nature of the *expeditionales causae*. It would seem that, initially, at any rate, the reservation of this burden meant merely that the holder of the tenure was required to answer the king's summons to his host, just as if he were a gesith possessed of an ordinary royal læn. If this interpretation is correct, then the fyrd service spoken of in the charters was in fact a new royal burden upon the land, one which was only introduced toward the end of the eighth century by a powerful king, Offa, as a means of aggrandizing his military resources. One might best characterize it as the negation of one of the privileges associated with ius ecclesiasticum, namely, the freedom of the grantee and his estate from any military liability.[89] Certainly, the novelty of the "common burdens" is implied by the manner in which Offa demanded them from the Kentish clergy at Clofesho in 792: "It is my request and doctrine that you should consent to these three things [fyrd service and bridge and fortress work] so that by it this my grant of liberty should remain more stable."[90]

In short, the idea of military service as a stated condition of land tenure was a consequence of book-right. Under the traditional land-holding arrangement, a stipulation of this sort would have been unnecessary. A holder of loanland from the king was by definition a king's man, and his acceptance of the estate obligated him to respond with fidelity and service to his royal lord. Bookland tenure, a hereditary possession, was quite a different matter, for such a grant permanently alienated the land from the royal fisc without assuring that the future generations who enjoyed the property would recognize the king or his successors as their lord. The kings of the Mercian hegemony answered with the imposition of the "common burdens," which guaranteed the king military service from bookland and which tied the holders of the book securely to the ruler of the tribe. Their innovation worked. During Offa's reign military service was regularly exacted from bookland in Mercia and its subject kingdoms, and what had been a novel exaction a generation before was gradually transformed into custom. By 814 the process had advanced so far that a charter issued in that year by Offa's successor, King Coenwulf, described the "common burdens" as obligatory for all those who held their land by hereditary right: "Let this land be undisturbed and unshaken in all things, except these three claims alone, namely, going on expeditions, strengthening fortifications against the pagans, and repairing bridges, in the same way as all the people are accustomed to do concerning their own hereditary properties."[91]

The Mercian kings of the eighth century thus resolved the military dilemma presented by bookland. It remained for their successors in hegemony, the West Saxon kings of the ninth and tenth centuries, to exploit the possibilities presented by the "common burdens," and to use the Mercian solution to help create a state.

THREE

Royal Lordship and Military Innovation in Alfredian England

The kingdom of England was forged in the furnace of the viking invasions. The Tribal Hidage, a Mercian tribute list, reveals eighth-century England to have been dotted with petty kingdoms and *regiones*.[1] Before the advent of the *micel here*, the so-called "Great Danish Army," in the autumn of 865, there had been some movement toward a consolidation of power south of the Humber. But one cannot be certain that Ecgberht's "greater Wessex" would have been any more permanent a political association than Offa's Mercian hegemony had proved to be. Quite simply, the depredations of the Danes aided Wessex by extinguishing all other royal lineages. By A.D. 900 only the house of Cerdic remained, and the kings of this dynasty found that their survival depended upon a total reorganization of their realm, both administratively and militarily.

The Chronicle entry for 871 affords us a glimpse into the nature of the military system that Alfred inherited from his father and brothers. After describing six battles, the annal concludes with the observation that "during that year nine general engagements [*folc-gefeoht*] were fought against the Danish army in the kingdom south of the Thames, besides the expeditions which the king's brother Alfred and single ealdormen and king's thegns often rode on, which were not counted."[2] From this it would seem that the West Saxon military establishment consisted of three general types of army: the national host, shire forces led by individual ealdormen, and the war bands of individual thegns.

The first of these, occasionally described in the sources as the *folc*,[3] was characterized by the personal leadership of the king. Although this force drew its complement of warriors from various parts of the realm, it was nonetheless organized geographically by shire, each of which was under the command of an ealdorman or bishop.

Each of these territorial units was an army in itself. An eighth- or ninth-century ealdorman could wage war on his own initiative and was expected to do so in defense of his shire. Thus, in 802, on the very day that Ecgberht ascended the West Saxon throne, a West Saxon ealdorman, Weohstan, was engaged in battle with a Mercian army, also led by an ealdorman.[4] The Chronicler's account of the "great battle" fought near Kempsford makes mention of neither king. Similarly, in the winter of 878, at a time when King Alfred was huddled with a small band of followers in the woods and fens of Somerset, one of his ealdormen, Odda, won a great victory over a viking force of twenty-three ships that had descended upon the coast of Devon, killing the pirate chieftain and 840 of his men.[5] Such independence was militarily valuable—even essential—in an age of poor communications. But it also held its dangers. An ealdorman could raise his shire not only against the king's enemies and his own, but against the king himself, as the chaotic history of Northumbria in the late eighth century well attests.[6]

Just as the national host was made up of shire forces, so the shire forces were composed of the followings of individual local thegns. Asser's description of the Devonshire fyrd at Countisbury alludes to an organization of this sort: "For many of the king's thegns, with their followers [*multi ministri regis cum suis*], had shut themselves up for safety inside this stronghold."[7] These thegns, in turn, could mount raids of their own, much as St. Guthlac did a century and a half before. The sources unsurprisingly take little note of these small war bands; we only hear of them in passing, as in the annal for 871, or when a noble tried his hand at treason, as Cyneheard had done with his eighty-four retainers in 786 and the ætheling Æthelwold was to do with his commended men following the accession of his cousin Edward the Elder in 899.[8]

None of these forces, not even the folc, was "the nation in arms." All were war bands led by chieftains, whose troops were bound to them by personal ties. The royal armies that fought the Northmen in 871 thus had much in common with the fyrds of Bede's day. They remained the king's following arrayed for battle, and the language of lordship continued to characterize the relationship between the warrior-king and his subjects.[9] The military power of a ninth-century Anglo-Saxon ruler, like that of his seventh-century predecessors, remained dependent upon personal ties, that is, upon the willingness of the kingdom's nobles to recognize him as their "lord and protector."[10] Thus all that King Ceolwulf, the "foolish thegn" whom the Danes placed upon the Mercian throne, could promise his patrons was that he himself would choose their will and obey them in all things along with "all who would follow him."[11]

Mid–ninth-century fyrds differed most from the royal hosts of the seventh and eighth centuries not in their composition or leadership but in their relationship to bookland. As we have seen, book-right became increasingly common in the course of the ninth century. The devolution of book-right profoundly altered the relationship between king and landholder. In the days of Oswiu, one who held land drawn from the king's fisc was almost by definition a king's man. But now such land was inherited rather than earned and regranted. Granting land in book-right thus threatened a king's ability to exact service from his thegns, a problem that must have become obvious by the second generation of these lay books. BCS 303 (S 157), a charter dated 801, provides an example of one early attempt to rectify this problem. Coenwulf, king of the Mercians, and his brother Cuthred, king of Kent, granted some land in the latter's kingdom to "[their] shared thegn, Swithhun" to be held in book-right, both for his "pleasing money" and for his "pleasing service." This donation had an interesting—and revealing—condition. Swithhun was to possess the land with the right of free disposal and bequest as long as "he remain[ed] a faithful minister [*fidelis minister*] and an unshakeable friend to us and our magnates."[12] How the royal brothers were to guarantee the fidelity of Swithhun's heirs was another matter.

Viewed in this context, Æthelbald's and Offa's imposition of the "common burdens" upon bookland was more than an attempt to derive some profit from lands granted in "ecclesiastical right." It also represented their solution to the problem of non-hereditary commendation and hereditary tenures. For the military obligation incumbent upon bookland attached its holder securely to the king. One may see here stirrings toward a redefinition of kingship. Certainly, by the time of the Conquest all holders of books were considered to be in some sense king's men, and nobility itself had come to be defined by the possession of a book.[13]

The proliferation of book-right was particularly advanced in the West

Saxon kingdom of the mid-ninth century, due at least in part to the generosity of Alfred's father, King Æthelwulf. One need only consider Æthelwulf's famous "Decimation" of 855 to see the extent to which bookland had become the legitimate expectation of king's thegns. In preparation for his pilgrimage to Rome in 855, Æthelwulf "booked the tenth part of his land throughout all his kingdom to the praise of God and his own eternal salvation."[14] Although the language of this annal might lead one to believe that the Church alone benefited from the king's largess, the charter evidence proves such an inference mistaken. The purported texts of the "Decimation" all agree that king's thegns were to share in Æthelwulf's generosity, an arrangement confirmed by an authentic charter of 855.[15] BCS 486 (S 315) relates how Æthelwulf endowed his thegn (minister), Dunn, with a village and ten yokes of land near Rochester, Kent, "in consideration of the decimation of lands, which, God giving, I have ordered done for my other thegns" (*pro decimatione agrorum quam deo donante ceteris ministris meis facere decreui*).[16] Nor does this charter stand alone. We possess a contemporary charter dated the same year which describes how Æthelwulf booked land in Kent to another of his thegns, his "faithful minister Ealdhere, for his humble obedience and his fidelity to me in all things,"[17] to be free of all royal service with the exception of three charges, namely, host duty, fortification work, and bridge building. Apparently, Æthelwulf had divided a tenth of his private domain between his ecclesiastic and lay followers, hoping thereby to secure the favor of God for his journey and the loyalty of the West Saxon nobility during his absence, a wise precaution in light of subsequent events.[18] Because of these and previous grants of bookland to the laity,[19] Æthelwulf and his sons had to rely heavily upon the military dues attached to book-right and the willingness of the nobility to perform them.

Alfred's difficulties in 878 were due in no small measure to his dependence upon the "common burdens" for the defense of the kingdom. Once Guthrum's forces had established themselves in the royal vill of Chippenham in Wiltshire, they sent raiding parties, which "rode through the lands of many," compelling the owners either to submit to Danish lordship or to flee their estates.[20] Alfred, who was himself forced to take refuge on the isle of Athelney in the midst of the fens, discovered that his military resources had dwindled to the few men who followed Ealdorman Æthelnoth of Somerset into the forests and his own household retainers (*milites et faselli,*) reinforced by a small number of faithful noblemen. With these troops, he was able to harass the Danish military settlers, but he could not drive them out. It was not until Alfred managed to resecure the allegiance of the thegns of the western counties that he was able to engage the Danes in a pitched battle. While Alfred's "vassals" may have formed the core of his host, as the king's housecarls were to do in the Confessor's reign, the royal household alone could not wage a full-scale campaign.

The growing military importance of bookland aggravated certain problems previously encountered in connection with the seventh-century landholding gesiths.[21] Quite simply, it took time to summon and gather warriors from the various localities, and a highly mobile raiding band could devastate a region and move on before the king's host could engage it in battle.[22] To this one might add a second drawback. Those who held bookland were territorial lords with local interests, and were thus far more likely to seek terms with the Danish invaders, if by their timely submission they could save all or part of their inheritance. Asser leaves little doubt that many of the West Saxon nobles chose to accept Guthrum as their lord, just as King Ceolwulf and his followers had done in Mercia and King Ecgberht had done in Northumbria a few years before.[23] Nationalism, after all, was no impediment to dealing with the Northmen, and even their heathenism could be conveniently overlooked—or embraced—if the payoff was great enough. Twenty-two years after Alfred's flight into the marshes, his nephew Æthelwold was to flee to the vikings of Northumbria, asking their support against his cousin Edward the Elder. A great-grandson of Charlemagne, Pepin II of Aquitaine, was to do Æthelwold one better. He not only sought the vikings' aid in his quarrel with his uncle Charles the Bald but renounced Christianity in order to obtain it.[24] Pepin's apostasy found an echo in mid–ninth-century Ireland, where the Norse of Dublin took an active hand in tribal politics, and where wandering bands of native warriors adopted viking ways, ravaging their homeland with such ferocity that they earned the nickname *Gaill-Gaedhil,* "the Foreign Irish," from their compatriots. Everywhere the vikings went they found allies among the disaffected and ambitious, and Wessex was no exception.

Alfred had won a respite with his victory at Edington in the spring of 878, but this did not wipe out the memory of his desperate flight into the Somerset marshes. He could not rely upon the existing military system to counter the continuing threat offered by the Danes. If he were to survive and consolidate his hold upon Wessex, he would have to innovate.

And innovate he did. The king's adoption of Danish tactics in the winter of 878, such as his use of strongholds and small mobile raiding parties to harry the lands of his enemies, was forced upon him by the immediate circumstances.[25] Over the next twenty years of his reign, however, he was to revolutionize Anglo-Saxon military practice. Just as King Offa had responded a century earlier to the proliferation of bookland and to the pressures of the first Norse raids by imposing the "common burdens" upon bookland tenure, Alfred answered the Danish challenge by creating an impressive system of fortified boroughs throughout his realm and by reforming the West Saxon fyrd, changing it from a sporadic levy of king's men and their retinues into a standing force. The defensive system that Alfred sponsored, and its extension to Mercia under the ealdorman Æthelred and the lady Æthelflæd, enabled his kingdom to survive and formed the basis for the reconquest of the Danelaw by his son Edward and his grandson Æthelstan.[26]

The Chronicle entry under 891, a long and involved annal that supplies invaluable information about the character of military operations during the last years of Alfred's reign, allows us to glimpse the emergent military system:

> The king had divided his army [his fierd] into two, so that always half of its men were at home, half on service, apart from the men who guarded the boroughs [butan thaem monnum the tha burga healdan scolden].[27]

Passing over for the moment the reference to the burghal system, let us consider Alfred's reform of the fyrd. The division of the fyrd into two rotating contingents was designed to give some continuity to West Saxon military actions. Rather than respond to viking incursions with ad hoc levies which were disbanded when the crisis had passed, the West Saxons would now always have a force in the field. Moreover, Alfred's fyrd, like the Danish heres, was to be composed of mounted warriors possessing the necessary mobility to pursue an enemy known for its elusiveness.[28]

The fyrdmen who waited their turn "at home" also filled a necessary defensive function. It was essential that some king's thegns and their retainers remain behind to guard their lands and those of their neighbors on campaign against sudden raids, if for no other reason than the obvious one that landholders would have been reluctant to leave their estates and families totally undefended.[29] The West Frankish king Charles the Bald learned this lesson in dramatic fashion in the summer of 856 when he summoned a general assembly to deal with a viking invasion of the Seine basin and his magnates refused to attend, fearing to leave their own lands undefended.[30] King Alfred was wise enough not to present his noblemen with that dilemma.

The charter evidence even suggests that a general summons of a shire fyrd in the early tenth century did not require every local landed thegn to serve in the host. Goda, a prominent Kentish thegn, did not join the shire fyrd when King Edward called "all the men of Kent to battle" in 902.[31] He seems to have been excused from serving, for if he had been derelict in his duty to the king, his adversary in a lawsuit over the Kentish estate of Cooling, Queen Eadgifu, would have certainly mentioned it, and she does not.[32] Goda may well have been one of the landowners permitted to remain behind with their warrior-retainers to guard the shire against sudden incursions and to preserve the king's peace.

The warriors who remained home or who had completed their tour of duty appear to have been obliged to join the garrisons of the nearby boroughs on local forays. When Ealdormen Æthelred of Mercia, Æthelhelm of Wiltshire, and Æthelnoth of Somerset raised the forces of the western shires against a viking army that had made a stronghold on the Severn at Buttington in the autumn of 893, they assembled an army from the nearby borough garrisons which included "the king's thegns who were at home [*æt ham*] near the fortifications."[33] The duty of these thegns to defend their localities, rather than the survival of an ancient obligation of all free men to military service, explains the appearance of the *other folc* fighting alongside the London *burwaran* in 895 and identifies the *land leod* who routed the *here* of Northampton in 916.[34]

Alfred also had compelling administrative reasons for his division of the fyrd. The Anglo-Saxons did not draw a rigorous distinction between "military" and "police" actions. The same men who led the king's hosts, his thegns, reeves, and ealdormen, also did justice, a point driven home by Ælfric of Eynsham's choice of the term *gemotman* to gloss the Latin *decurio*.[35] Similarly, the mounted men who were responsible according to Æthelstan's laws for the capture of lawbreakers were the same men who defended the boroughs in war.[36] The thin line between a posse and a fyrd was driven home by Edward the Elder's "expedition" against his cousin Æthelwold's retinue in the winter of 899.[37] In a sense, one could conceive of the fyrd as a posse led by the king himself.[38] It is little wonder, then, that Alfred should require part of his thegnage to serve his interests by remaining "at home." After all, the Danish invasions did not end ordinary criminal activity; on the contrary, from Alfred's treaty with Guthrum it would appear that English lawbreakers could find men among the vikings who were willing to buy their stolen goods and even refuge from West Saxon law.[39] The threat that an invasion of this sort could pose to social discipline is eloquently illustrated by Wulfstan's "Sermon of the Wolf," written under analogous circumstances a century later.[40]

Alfred's innovations did not affect the basic makeup of the fyrd, which remained composed of nobles and their lesser-born followers.[41] Certainly, tenth- and eleventh-century glosses studiously avoid terms connoting social rank when defining words such as *bellator, belliger,* or even *miles.*[42] And the single exception, *miles ordinarius: anlang cempa vel heanra cempa, idem gregarius,*[43] at least suggests that some miles were of humble origin. The Chronicle annals for 895 and 1010 even imply that king's thegns formed a minority of the king's fighting forces.[44] However, it is equally certain that Alfred's fyrds were not thought of as peasant levies. For one thing, Alfred's forces were mounted. The Chronicle consistently has them "riding after the Danes" and at one point reports that the English fyrd besieging a viking army in Chester used the crops in the fields to feed their horses.[45] The "great horse" of the Middle Ages was unknown to the Anglo-Saxons, and even in the eleventh century the heriot of thegns called for "palfreys" (in the Domesday Book scribes' terminology) rather than destriers.[46] Horses, nevertheless, were valuable animals in ninth- and tenth-century England, and their use by the warriors of the fyrd argues strongly for a select rather than a mass levy.[47] Furthermore, the summoning of a fyrd appears to have left ordinary agricultural activities, such as the harvest, largely unaffected. In the autumn of 895 King Alfred encamped the fyrd in the vicinity of London in order to protect the peasants of the area while they harvested their crops. The Danes had established a stronghold on the Lea about twenty miles north of London, and Alfred feared that they would steal or burn the crops. The distinction between those who guarded the fields and those who harvested the crops is quite clear in the Chronicle's account.[48]

Alfred's limitation of military service to a half year could not have been predicated upon agricultural concerns, as some have suggested.[49] If the fyrd had been composed of peasant levies taken from the fields, one would expect to find exemptions for sowing, harvest, and the like, rather than a limitation on the length of service. A more plausible explanation for the limitation to a half-year period would be the difficulty of keeping an army provisioned for a more extended period. Indeed, the Chronicle entry for 893 specifically links logistics with the fyrdmen's term of service. The English fyrd led by Prince Edward had cornered a fleeing viking army on the islet of Thorney, where they besieged them "for as long as their provisions lasted; but they had completed their term of service and used up their provisions."[50] Despite certain victory, Edward's contingent disbanded and returned to their homes, passing King Alfred and their relief on the way.

The king himself drew a clear distinction between those who labored and those who fought. Alfred the Great is the first medieval writer to divide society into the three orders that were later to be popularized by Adalbéron of Laon.[51] In the midst of his rather loose translation of Boethius's *Consolation of Philosophy*, Alfred added a personal observation on statecraft:

> This, then, is a king's material and his tools for ruling with, that he have his land fully manned. He must have men who pray, and soldiers and workmen. Lo, you know that without these materials no king can reveal his skill. Also, this is his material, which he must have for those tools— sustenance for those three orders; and their sustenance consists in land to live on, and gifts, and weapons, and food, and ale, and whatever else these three orders require. And without those things he cannot hold those tools, nor without those tools do any of the things that he is charged to do.[52]

For Alfred, beadsmen (*gebedmen*) prayed, warriors (*fyrdmen*) fought, and workers (*weorcmen*) labored, each a necessary, distinct class. This tripartite classification of society according to function, which was to be repeated with greater elaboration by Abbot Ælfric of Eynsham and Archbishop Wulfstan II of York a century later,[53] tells against the notion of peasant levies and farmer warriors.

This is not to argue that the Alfredian fyrd was composed exclusively of noble landowners and their lesser-born retainers. The law code that Alfred issued sometime around 890 stipulates a double penalty for breaking into the fortified dwelling of a noble (*burhbryce*) or through a ceorl's fence (*ceorles edorbryce*) "while the fyrd is out [in the field],"[54] which implies that some peasant landowners answered the summons to the host. It is questionable, however, whether such landholding commoners, whose fields were probably worked by slaves and geburs, should be characterized as "peasants." On the whole, the evidence leads one to believe that the Alfredian fyrd was made up of landed lords and their military retainers, rather than peasants who exchanged the plough for the sword every half year.

We possess very little evidence concerning the tactical organization of Alfred's armies. If Asser's accounts of Ashdown and Edington are accurate, the tactics used by these armies were relatively simple; in both cases the leaders deployed their troops in a shield-wall, ordered them to close ranks, and advanced on the enemy. Whether these troops were divided into units is unknown. Asser does say that at Ashdown the English split their forces equally between King Æthelred and his brother Alfred and that the two divisions arrived at the battle separately, but this appears to have been an ad hoc decision rather than the usual deployment.[55] We would probably be safe in assuming that Alfred's reformed fyrd continued to consist of the levies of individual shires, but even in this we ought to be cautious, since the Chronicle entries for the period 893–899 do not refer to the shire contingents within the royal host.

The annal for 903, however, does. In the winter of 902 Alfred's son, Edward the Elder, sent a punitive expedition against the Danes of East Anglia, who, induced by the disaffected ætheling Æthelwold, had broken the peace by raiding English Mercia. The fyrd harried the Cambridgeshire fenlands in revenge. Satisfied with the damage that he had inflicted upon his enemies, Edward had it announced throughout the entire army that all the contingents were to set out together for home. The men of Kent, commanded by Ealdorman Sigewulf and Ealdorman Sigehelm, lingered behind against the express orders of the king. They were overtaken by the Danish army at the Holme (probably in southern Essex) and were forced to engage the enemy. "And a great slaughter was made on both sides, but more of the Danes were killed, though they remained in possession of the battlefield."[56] If we are permitted to generalize from the Chronicler's account of these events, each shire within Edward's fyrd retained its own command structure, unit integrity, and a measure of independence. The king's host, then, was a conglomeration of individual shire levies held together by the personal command of the king.

There is no evidence for subordinate tactical units below the shire level until the second half of the tenth century, when the hundred and perhaps the ship-soke make their appearance in the sources. I would tend to agree with Eric John that the hundred possessed military functions from its inception,[57] much like the centenas of Francia, which they resembled, but without positive evidence this must remain speculation. We are on more solid ground when we turn to the warrior retinues of the king and his great magnates. We at least know that they existed.

We do not know, however, how such retinues were integrated into the structure of the army, whether they fought as separate units under their individual lords or whether they were used to form the all-important first rank of the shield-wall. Still, their existence is enough to remind us that the lordship bond remained powerful in ninth- and tenth-century England. One might note in this context that Asser described the fyrd-men who followed Ealdorman Æthelwulf of Berkshire in 871 as "his *sodales*," "his companions," a usage that brings the *Battle of Maldon* to mind.[58]

The Alfredian fyrd was designed to act in tandem with the *burh-waran,* the permanent garrisons that the king settled in the newly con-structed boroughs. The creation of the burghal system as outlined in the early tenth-century document known as the "Burghal Hidage" marks a watershed in the history of Anglo-Saxon governance.[59] Despite formidable obstacles, including the recalcitrance of the native nobility, the West Saxon dynasty of the late ninth and the early tenth century managed to oversee the construction of a vast network of fortified towns, many of which were clearly built to be permanent settlements rather than temporary refuges. These boroughs served both to consol-idate the English kings' hold over the land south of the Thames, the West Saxon patrimony, and to extend their control over areas of Danish settlement. Alfred's son, Edward the Elder, and his daughter, Æthelflæd, "lady of the Mercians," in particular seem to have understood the value of these fortified towns; their conquest of Danish Mercia and East Anglia dotted those lands with burhs.[60] By 918, at the latest, Wessex alone boasted thirty boroughs of varying sizes, nominally manned by 27,071 warriors.[61] In short, Alfred's borough system may have been the most impressive achievement of his reign and the single greatest reason for the survival of his dynasty.

The concept of fortresses was not original to Alfred. A similar system of fortified bridges had been attempted with a measure of success by Charles the Bald in the 860s, and the Danes themselves used strongholds as bases and places of refuge in their raids on England.[62] Nor were the Anglo-Saxons of the day strangers to fortifications. As we have seen, the kings of the Mercian hegemony had imposed the burden of "fortress-work" on those who held bookland under them, and the physical re-mains of their building efforts suggest that they exacted these dues with rigor. The great eighth-century Mercian dykes on the Welsh border, once thought to be lines of territorial demarcation, now appear to have been intended as defensive earthworks not unlike the contemporary structures carved across southern Denmark. Recent archaeological excavations at the sites of two Mercian royal vills, Hereford and Tamworth, have revealed traces of extensive eighth-century ditch and rampart defenses.[63] The pre-Alfredian *enceinte* uncovered at Hereford enclosed 33 acres and boasted a regular internal layout, making it a worthy predecessor and model for Alfred's boroughs.[64] Unique to Alfred's scheme were the scale of the endeavor, the strategic disposition of the boroughs, and the offensive manner in which they were to be used.

Recent work on the Alfredian and Edwardian boroughs has tended to concentrate upon their economic and administrative functions. As interesting and significant as these may be, we must recognize that Alfred intended the burhs to be primarily strongholds, and royal strongholds at that. One might even argue that the commercial functions of the burhs had a military import, for only economically sound foundations could maintain a permanent garrison of the size needed and endure extended sieges. In fact, some of these boroughs sacrificed economic for purely military considerations; both Pilton and Halwell were replaced in the calmer days of the mid-tenth century by the more commercially sited towns of Barnstaple and Totnes.[65] Asser emphasizes how remarkable Alfred's building program was ("What shall I say . . . of the cities and towns to be rebuilt and of others to be constructed where previously there were none?"),[66] and in this he was guilty of no exaggeration. Alfred apparently conceived the grand scheme outlined in the Burghal Hidage, and implemented it with ingenuity and speed. The boroughs were essential to his military strategy. In order to understand how critical they were, we must examine first their geographical distribution and, second, the manner in which they were actually used.

The thirty burhs were distributed widely throughout the West Saxon kingdom and situated in such a way that no part of the kingdom was more than twenty miles, a day's march,[67] from a fortified center. They dominated the kingdom's lines of communication: the navigable rivers, Roman roads, and major trackways (see map 2). In many cases, Alfred reused sites that had previously boasted Roman and Iron Age fortifications; but he did not limit himself to such locations, and did not hesitate to build boroughs on virgin ground. Finally, most boroughs were located near royal vills, evidently to permit the king better control over his strongholds. These royal residences, in turn, were fortified centers that formed an essential part of Alfred's overall defensive network.[68]

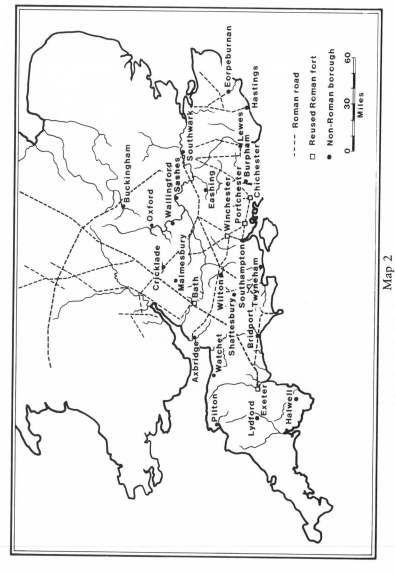

Map 2

The Burghal Hidage; strategic sitings of boroughs

The strategic siting of the burhs is obvious upon even a cursory examination. Portchester, Southampton, and the other boroughs along the southern coast of England guarded the mouths of navigable rivers and the inlets that offered the best harborage in the area. The burhs of Southwark, Sashes, Wallingford, and Cricklade formed a continuous line of defense along the Thames. (Wallingford was not only sited on the river but, as its name suggests, controlled an important ford.) The borough at Wareham was located near the coast of Dorset on a ridge of high ground between the Frome and Piddle rivers, which made it not only a strategic point, guarding access into the interior of Dorset, but also a natural stronghold. Both aspects are demonstrated by the British government's decision to shore up the western bank as a barricade against tanks in 1940.[69] Even an apparent exception such as Lydford, which was planted on neither a river nor a major road, was on a strategic site, a promontory which marked the traditional frontier with Cornwall and guarded the access route up the valley of the Lyd.[70]

David Hinton, who has closely examined the siting of each of the burhs, concluded that "their main intention was obviously to provide refuges, to block rivers and to guard river crossings."[71] That the boroughs were to be places of refuge is undeniable. A charter issued sometime between 889 and 899 by Ealdorman Æthelred even declares that the ealdorman and his lady "ordered the borough at Worcester to be built for the protection of all the people, and also to exalt the praise of God therein."[72] But Hinton's emphasis upon the boroughs' defensive capabilities fails to appreciate the full purpose of this system. The boroughs were meant not only to be static points of defense but were designed to operate in conjunction with Alfred's reformed fyrd, a symbiotic relationship made even more striking by the fact that many of these burhs were built by the fyrd.[73] Neither Alfred's mobile field forces nor his boroughs alone would have afforded a sufficient defense against the vikings; together, however, they robbed the vikings of their major strategic advantages: surprise and mobility.

Alfred had created a network of strong points and a standing, mobile army that together served as the foundation for a military system based on the mutual support between self-contained strongholds and mobile field forces.[74] Alfred's boroughs served not only as places of refuge but also as staging points for offensives directed against enemy forces in the area.

The presence of well-garrisoned boroughs along the major travel routes of Wessex presented an obstacle for viking invaders. Even if a viking *here* avoided the borough forces and successfully raided the interior, the booty-laden army would face borough garrisons as it attempted to return to its ships or stronghold. The ill-fated viking host led by earl Ohter and Hroald in 914 is a case in point. After ravaging the coast of southern Wales and the Severn estuary, they were intercepted by a host from Hereford, Gloucester, and other nearby boroughs, which routed them in the field and then besieged them in their stronghold. When the Danes escaped to Somerset, they faced still another borough garrison, that of Watchet. Their numbers reduced by casualties and starvation, this Danish *here* finally fled to Ireland.[75]

Similarly, the viking hosts that established fortresses at Appledore and Milton Regis in 893 discovered that they could not mount full-scale assaults on the countryside because Alfred had encamped his fyrd between them. They responded with small raiding parties that moved along the fringes of the Weald. These, however, also proved unsuccessful, because of the constant harassment of mounted bands from the boroughs and the fyrd. Although the vikings did capture booty in 893, the Chronicler makes it clear that the fyrd and boroughs combined to limit the free movement of the raiders and eventually impelled them to abandon Appledore entirely. The large amount of loot that they seized as they made their way north to Essex so hindered their progress that they were outflanked by the English army, which routed them at Farnham and recovered the booty. Panic-stricken, the remnants of the viking forces fled across the Thames, without bothering to find a ford, only to be caught once more on the isle of Thorney.[76]

Boroughs could also impede the movement of enemy troops in a more direct fashion. Both Alfred and Edward adopted the Carolingian tactic of controlling movement along a river by building fortifications on both banks and connecting them with bridges.[77] Charles the Bald had pioneered this strategy between 862 and his death in 877. Citing "ancient custom and that of other peoples" (*juxta antiquam et aliarum gentium consuetudinem*), Charles announced to the magnates assembled at Pîtres in 864 that those who were unable to march against the enemy should "come to the defense of their fatherland" by building "new cities, bridges, and crossings over swamps" and by performing guard duty in the marches.[78] This building program was aimed at securing Paris and the Seine basin, and to a remarkable extent it succeeded. Despite the Northmen's capture of the prototype fortified bridge at Pont de l'Arche in 865, Charles persisted in his efforts, and by 870 had succeeded in raising *castella* at strategic points along the Seine, Oise, and Marne rivers. By doing so he gained a measure of security for this vital area. Between 876, when a fleet of 100 viking ships appeared in the Seine estuary, and 885, when the Northmen rowed up the Seine and unsuccessfully besieged Paris, the Seine basin was free of the ravages of the Northmen.[79] The parallels between Charles's defensive measures and those adopted by Alfred in the 890s are striking. Alfred was well-informed about the activities of the vikings on the Continent, and in all likelihood would have known about Charles's military constructions. It is difficult to escape the conclusion that Alfred found the model for his "double-burhs" in West Francia.[80]

The annal of 895 is most instructive on the tactical uses of Alfred's double-burhs. In that year the Danes established a fortress on the river Lea about twenty miles north of London, obviously threatening London's food supply. After the London garrison mounted an unsuccessful attack on the fortress, Alfred led the fyrd to the vicinity of London and encamped while the peasants harvested their crops. Meanwhile, the king rode along the Lea and sought a spot where the river could be obstructed. Here he ordered the fyrd to construct fortifications on both banks. Once raised and connected, this double-burh would block passage on the river; in order to escape by water the Danes would have to risk rowing under a garrisoned bridge. The vikings understood full well the implications of the new construction, and, abandoning both their stronghold and their ships, fled overland, pursued by the mounted English army. The London garrison completed the operation by seizing the abandoned ships.[81]

It was dangerous for the Danes to leave a burh intact behind them, but it was equally dangerous to attempt to take one. Lacking siege equipment, the Danes could not storm burhs defended by a system of ditches, earthworks strengthened by wooden revetments, and palisades.[82] They were reduced to the expedient of starving the town into submission, which gave the fyrd or neighboring garrisons time to relieve the besieged burh. In a number of instances, the hunter became the prey, as the borough garrison and the relief force joined together in pursuit of the enemy.[83] Relief, however, was often unnecessary, as borough garrisons alone could drive off viking raiding parties, as witnessed by the successful resistance offered by Pilton in 893, Chichester in 894, and Bedford and Wingamere in 917. The only success that the vikings enjoyed against a borough, in fact, occurred in 892, when the great *here* stormed a half-made, poorly garrisoned fortress up the Lympne estuary.[84] The security of the Alfredian burhs provides a profound contrast with the dismal fortunes of London and Canterbury in 851, Winchester in 860, and York in 867.

Militarily, these boroughs served a dual function: they provided static strong points affording refuge to the inhabitants of a region and, simultaneously, provided soldiers for offensives directed against nearby enemy bases. Garrisons rarely operated alone. Rather, a West Saxon ealdorman would concentrate his forces by combining troops raised from neighboring boroughs with the fyrdmen who were at home. The expeditions against Buttington in 893 and Tempsford in 917 reveal how successful such expeditions could be. The boroughs thus tactically supplemented the field forces, allowing the latter to pursue the main body of the enemy host without jeopardizing the security of the various localities. The boroughs and fyrds operated, in other words, as integral parts of a well-thought-out defense-in-depth system.[85]

Alfred's borough system was revolutionary in its strategic conception and extraordinarily expensive in its execution. The boroughs, moreover, had not only to be built, but manned and maintained. Without standing garrisons, these fortified towns were worse than useless; they could be taken by the Danes and turned into enemy strongholds.[86] Nothing reveals the genius of Alfred and his children more than their solution to this problem, the creation of a sophisticated and effective administrative system for the maintenance and defense of the boroughs. The Burghal Hidage is once again our primary source for this scheme. It provides a list of thirty-three burhs, thirty of them in Wessex and three in Mercia, and quotes the number of hides "belonging" to each. The text concludes with a statement relating the hidage allotments to the burhs' defenses:

> For the maintenance and defence of an acre's breadth of wall, sixteen hides are required. If every hide is represented by one man, then every pole [i.e., 5½ yards] of wall can be manned by four men. Then, for the maintenance of twenty poles of wall, eighty hides are required by the same reckoning as I have stated above. . . . For the maintenance of a circuit of twelve furlongs of wall, 1920 hides are required. If the circuit is greater, the additional amount can easily be deduced from this amount, for 160 men are always required for one furlong, then every pole of wall is manned by four men.[87]

The theoretical wall lengths obtained by applying this conversion formula to the burhs' stated hidage assessments agree remarkably well with their actual measurements.[88] This suggests that the compiler of the Burghal Hidage had at his disposal detailed information about the defenses of the West Saxon boroughs and lends credence to the supposition that the Burghal Hidage was an official rather than a private document. But what was the purpose of this document? One should observe that the conversion table at the end of the text converts wall lengths to hides, when from the body of the text one would expect just the reverse, since the text gives each burh's allotted hidage, rather than the area of its defenses. Moreover, the conversion formula is stated as a general formula, the tone of which is clearly prescriptive. When one further considers that the hidage allotments for two Mercian boroughs, Worcester and Warwick, are appended to a text concerned specifically with Wessex,[89] it becomes reasonable to view the Burghal Hidage in a Mercian context, as a summary of existing West Saxon practice compiled by Edward the Elder to aid in the extension of the system into Mercia.[90]

According to the Burghal Hidage, the Edwardian boroughs were to be fully integrated into the countryside. Each borough was to be the center of a large district created specifically to serve the needs of the town. On the basis of the prescribed four men for every 5½ yards, the average borough would have required a garrison of about 900 men. The landholders within these "burghal districts" were charged with providing the men necessary to maintain and garrison the burhs, upon the basis of one man from every hide of their land.[91]

While the scale of the service demanded and the systematic manner of exacting it were novel, the scheme itself was not. In essence, the burghal system was an extension of the existing "common burdens" incumbent upon bookland, one of which, it should be recalled, was "the necessary defense of fortifications against enemies," to use the formulation of fortification work that appears in Æthelbald's privilege of 749.[92] Certainly, Asser's description of Alfred's attempt to build and defend fortified towns in Wessex supports this construction:

> What of the cities and towns which he had restored and the others, which he had built where none had been before?. . . And what of the great trouble and vexation . . . he had with his own people, who voluntarily submit to little or no labour for the common needs of the kingdom [*qui nullum aut parvum voluntarie pro communi regni necessitate vellent subire laborem*]?[93]

Indeed, Asser explicitly describes the works demanded by Alfred as "the building of fortresses and the other things for the common profit of the whole kingdom [*id est de arcibus construendis et ceteris communibus communis regni utilitatibus.*]"[94] Expressions such as "labor for the common needs of the kingdom" and "for the common profit of the whole kingdom" have a familiar ring. This is the language of the landbooks, adapted, certainly, to Asser's narrative purposes, but recognizable nonetheless.[95]

It is clear, moreover, from Asser's description of the building of the boroughs that the burden fell upon the landowners of the kingdom:

> But if . . . his [Alfred's] orders were not carried out because of the slackness of the people, or things begun late in time of need were unfinished and of no profit to those who undertook them—for I may tell of fortresses ordered by him and still not begun, or begun too late to be brought to completion—and enemy forces broke in by land or sea, as often happened, on every side, the opponents of the royal ordinances then were ashamed with a vain repentance when on the brink of ruin. . . . But though . . . they are sadly afflicted through this, and moved to tears by the loss of their fathers, wives, children, retainers [ministros], slaves, handmaids, their labours and all their goods, what help is hateful repentance, when it cannot succour their slain kinsmen, nor redeem captives from odious captivity, nor even can it help them sustain themselves, who have escaped, seeing that they have nought with which to sustain their own lives.[96]

The people whose slackness had threatened the kingdom with disaster were Alfred's magnates, the heads of great households, the lords of the lesser thegns. It was such men who, having lost all to the Danes, repented that "they had carelessly neglected the king's orders," and promised "to fulfill with all their strength what they have before refused, that is, with regard to the building of fortresses and the other things for the common profit of the whole kingdom."[97]

Asser's intent seems evident. He was defining the king's demand of labor service for the building of the burhs as one of the "common burdens" incumbent upon the tenures of the West Saxon aristocracy. It is tempting to read this passage as a sermon to the nobility upon the dangers of insubordination to the king. The "folly and obstinacy" of such men, the king's "own people," was their refusal to render to Alfred the legitimate services due from their estates. Their punishment lay appropriately in the loss of those lands.

Asser's account allows us some insight into Alfred's military difficulties. The defense of Wessex depended upon his ability to exact from his nobles the military service owed from their lands. The problem lay in persuading the magnates to submit to the king's commands and perform the services. For even a peripatetic king could not be everywhere at once, and in an age in which travel was difficult and communications poor, royal governance of necessity rested upon the landed aristocracy and the officials whom the king established in the various localities, the very men who led the king's armies.[98] The measure of a good king was his ability "to bring over and to bind to his own will and to the common profit of the whole kingdom his bishops, ealdormen, nobles, and the thegns who were dearest to him, and also his reeves."[99] For without an effective means of coercion, Alfred could rule only "by gently instructing, flattering, urging, and commanding them."[100] Only after all else had failed would the king attempt to punish the obdurate.[101] As Asser emphasized, the true danger to a recalcitrant noble lay not so much in the king's displeasure as in the loss of his lands, family, retainers, slaves, and life to the Danish invaders. Fear of the Northmen, as well as the duty they owed their royal lord, led a hesitant West Saxon aristocracy to obey King Alfred and give him what they had agreed were his, the "common burdens."

Their reluctance to comply with Alfred's demands is not surprising. The cost of building or repairing some thirty burhs, maintaining in them a garrison force of nearly 30,000 men, and keeping a standing army in the field year round must have represented a considerable drain upon the resources of the West Saxon landholding class, especially in light of the devastation wrought by the Danish incursions and the sizable tributes paid to the enemy in the period from 871 through 878.[102] Moreover, fortress work was, as we have seen, the most recent of the "common burdens" in Wessex; it is doubtful that it was more than a generation old at the time. Yet now Alfred was exacting this service on a scale hitherto unknown, unless one is to compare it with the labor expended upon Offa's Dyke in another kingdom and century. In spite of the occasional burh "begun too late in time of need" or destroyed when half built, as was an unfinished fortification in the fens of West Kent,[103] Alfred and his successors managed to ring their kingdoms and the territories seized from the Danes in East Anglia, Mercia, and Northumbria with fortified centers.

The burghal districts of the Burghal hidage were thus the culmination of a royal policy toward land tenure begun in the eighth century. The boroughs that Alfred ordered built against the *pagani*[104] hark back to Æthelbald's edict at the Synod of Gumley in 749 and Offa's "petition and doctrine" to the Kentish churches in 792, that they consent to the three things he "taught," namely, the rendering of "host-service against the pagans, the construction of bridges, and the fortification of fortresses against the pagans."[105] And just as Offa exploited the landed resources of his kingdom to build the great dyke bearing his name as a defensive work against the Welsh threat, Alfred a century later used the same means to create a network of fortified towns unparalleled in the Europe of his day as a bulwark against the Danes.

FOUR

The Growth of Royal Lordship in Tenth-Century England

The creation of the burghal system marks a watershed in the history of Anglo-Saxon governance. Despite formidable obstacles, the West Saxon dynasty of the late ninth and the early tenth century managed to oversee the construction of a network of fortified towns, the street layouts and physical dimensions of which imply permanent settlements rather than mere fortresses. Apparently, Alfred and his children, Æthelflæd and Edward, were able "to bring over and bind their nobility to their own will and to the common profit of the whole nation"; for the boroughs became the centers of territorial districts of considerable size, carved out of the neighboring countryside in order to service the town. Edward the Elder, as we have seen, regarded the burghal scheme as an elaboration upon the "common burdens," specifically, upon fortress work. Hence the landholders within each burghal district were to be held responsible for the burh's maintenance and manning, their liability to service arising from their tenures. By the reign of Edward's son, Æthelstan (924–939), burhbot had become an annual render to be performed "by a fortnight after the Rogation days."[1] The policy of the West Saxon kings transformed the "common burdens" from sporadic levies demanded only in time of need into regular royal exactions.

The scheme outlined in the Burghal Hidage points to a reorganization and enlargement of Anglo-Saxon administration. These newly constructed boroughs were designed to be more than mere fortresses, and the system of "burghal districts" had civil as well as purely military functions. As Chadwick long ago suggested,[2] the "burghal districts" of the Midlands should be regarded as a nascent form of the shire. Stenton, among others,[3] dated the shiring of the Midlands, in fact, if not in name, to the same period as the compilation of the Burghal Hidage, and these new shires were frequently grouped around newly built or reconstructed boroughs, from which they often received their names.[4] Certainly, when one glances at the law codes of Edward the Elder and his sons, it becomes readily apparent how important these boroughs were to the Anglo-Saxon civil administration of the time. They served the king as the sites of royal mints during a period of profound currency reform,[5] as market towns,[6] and as the seats of the king's justice.[7] In short, they were islands of royal power through which the king and his agents, ealdormen, bishops, and reeves, were able to dominate the countryside.

Whether by intention or not, Alfred's boroughs had established a royal presence throughout his realm. After the 890s it became far more difficult for the nobility of Wessex to show contempt for the king's orders or to come to terms on their own with the Northmen. The rulers of England during the first half of the tenth century enjoyed amicable relations with their aristocracy, based upon a farsighted policy of rewarding loyal service with land and jurisdiction. The result was a community of interests between Crown and aristocracy, and a system of governance that depended heavily upon the support and cooperation of local landholders.[8] But if Alfred and his successors held out carrots to the native aristocracy, they also occasionally brandished a stick. And here the boroughs were critically important, for they provided these West Saxon rulers with the institutional coercive power that their predecessors had lacked. And if the burhs were useful for the governance and defense of Wessex, they were essential for controlling the areas that Edward redeemed from viking rule between 909 and 920. Edward's refurbishment of Danish towns such as Huntingdon, Bedford, and Manchester had as its view the same purpose as William the Conqueror's castle-building. Both Edward the Elder and the Conqueror found themselves confronting a subject population which was less than trustworthy. It is significant that Edward did not simply entrust the boroughs to the local Danish leaders who submitted to him. Instead, he settled them with garrisons composed either solely of Englishmen, or, in some instances, of men of both races.[9] It is against a political backdrop of potential revolt that one ought to view the great tenth-century reforms that served to aggrandize royal power.

During the first decades of the tenth century, the West Saxon kings were faced with the problem of securing their conquests and binding the subjugated populations to their will. The boroughs provided them with one tool of governance, but more was needed to guarantee the loyalty of former enemies. Edward chose to use the most powerful social bond known to that society: personal lordship. He himself had felt the power of that bond in the first year of his reign. When Alfred died on 26 October 899, the West Saxon nobility selected Edward as his successor, undoubtedly reflecting the will of the late monarch. One magnate, however, refused to bow down to the new king. As the eldest son of Alfred's predecessor, Æthelred I, Æthelwold's claim to the throne was at least as compelling as Edward's, and having been passed over as a child in favor of his uncle, the ætheling was in no mood to step aside for his cousin. Æthelwold, like so many disappointed royal aspirants before him, chose to rebel rather than submit, and the strength of the lordship bond was such that his followers were willing to back him, their chosen lord, against the new king. Gathering together his retainers, the rebel prince seized two royal estates on the river Allen: Twyneham, a strategically sited burh on the Hampshire coast; and Wimborne, in Dorset, the burial place of King Æthelred I. Æthelwold chose to make his stand in the latter burh, near his father's grave, perhaps to remind his followers and enemies that he too was the son of a king. He barricaded the gates of the burh and, in the best heroic fashion, declared that "he would live or die there." His cousin was more than willing to give him the chance to make good his boast. Edward encamped the fyrd at Badbury Rings, an Iron Age hill-fort about four miles northwest of Wimborne, and made preparations to attack. That evening Æthelwold stole away. The king ordered the fyrd to ride after the rebels, but the chase proved in vain, as the prince and his men crossed the Thames to safety. The viking army in Northumbria received Æthelwold and, according to the "B," "C," and "D" recensions of the Chronicle, "accepted him as king and gave allegiance to him" (the most West Saxon version of the Chronicle, "A," suppressed this, possibly because Edward did not wish to emphasize his cousin's royal pretensions).[10]

The Chronicle's account provides us with a fascinating glimpse of the dynastic tensions within the House of Wessex at the end of the ninth century. It also reminds us that despite the portentous title that Alfred assumed in the latter part of his reign, *Angul-Saxonum rex,* and the exaltation of Christian monarchy by clerical writers, kingship remained a species of lordship. The annal's use of the term *bugan,* "to bow," is striking in this respect. In the first part of the entry we hear of Æthelwold's supporters who *him to gebugon,* who "took him as their lord," while at the conclusion of the "B," "C," and "D" versions we are told that the Danes took the exile as their king and "bowed" to him (*and him to gebugon*). "Bowing" was the way that the Anglo-Saxons described homage, referring to a symbolic act of subordination which accompanied the giving of an oath of fealty.[11] The Danes' choice of Æthelwold as king and their "bowing" to him describe a single event, just as those who swore to live and die with the ætheling in Wimborne had not only chosen him as their lord but had accepted him as their king.

The same Northmen who had "bowed" to Æthelwold in 899/900 were to do homage to Edward in the second decade of the tenth century. The Anglo-Saxon Chronicle describes in some detail the king's great campaign against the Danes of Mercia, East Anglia, and Northumbria. Consistently, the Chronicle informs us that Edward's victory was signaled by the submission to his lordship of the leaders of the "armies" (*heres*) settled in a region:

> [914] And Earl Thurcetel came and accepted him as his lord [*gesohte him to hlaforde*], and so did all the earls and the principal men who belonged to Bedford.[12]

> [917] Earl Thurferth and the holds submitted to him, and so did all the army which belonged to Northampton . . . and sought to have him as their lord and protector [*sohton hine him to hlaforde and to mund-boran*]. . . . And all the army in East Anglia swore agreement with him, that they would wish all that he wished, and protect [*frithian*] all that he would protect, both at sea and on the land. And the army which belonged to Cambridge chose him especially as its lord and protector [*geces synderlice him to hlaforde and to munboran*], and established it with oaths, just as he decreed.[13]

Edward's conquests, and those of Æthelstan and Edmund after him, thus took the form of imposing the king's personal lordship upon the Danish landowners whom the Chronicle characterizes as "the army."[14] Rather than becoming the subjects of an English king, they chose Edward as their *hlaford and mundbora,* their lord and protector, and confirmed this relationship with hold-oaths insisted upon by their conqueror.

Edward's demand for personal allegiance from the Danes was a practice sanctioned by long-established custom. His great-grandfather, Ecgberht, had not only been king of the West Saxons but also "lord of

the East Angles," whose king and people "sought him as their protector."[15] Asser, who ought to have known, tells us that Alfred's lordship
extended over the southern districts of Wales by the early 890s. He had
achieved this hegemony piecemeal over the course of a decade, as the
kings of Gwent and Glywysing sought his lordship and protection as a
hedge against the depredations of Ealdorman Æthelred of Mercia, and
the kings of Dyfed and Brycheiniog submitted to him from fear of their
ambitious neighbor, Anarawd ap Rhodri of Gwynedd. Even Anarawd
eventually sought Alfred's lordship, turning from his viking allies, "from
whom he got no benefit, only a good deal of misfortune," to the English
king. Asser tells us that Anarawd, "eagerly desiring Alfred's friendship"
(*amicitiam regis studiose requirens*), sought the king in person. Alfred
received Anarawd with honor, accepted him as his godson, and show-
ered him with gifts; the Welsh king, in return, bowed to Alfred, sub-
jecting himself with all his people to the West Saxon ruler's lordship
"on the same condition as Æthelred and the Mercians, namely, that in
every respect he would be obedient to the royal will."[16]

The reference to Æthelred and the Mercians reminds us that Alfred's
rule over the Mercians was based on the voluntary acceptance of his
lordship by the native Mercian magnates rather than on hereditary
right.[17] This was equally true of the general submission of "all the Angles
and Saxons" outside the Danelaw that followed Alfred's climactic capture of London in 886. This submission may have represented a cere-
monial recognition of Alfred's leadership in the struggle against the
Danes; it may even have been "regarded (by some) as marking the
emergence among the English of a sense of common identity, under a
common leader."[18] One thing, however, is clear from Asser's account
of the occasion. The "Angles and Saxons" whom Alfred had redeemed
from viking domination took him not as their "king" but as their lord;
they "turned willingly to King Alfred and submitted themselves to his
lordship" (*suo dominio se subdiderunt*), much as Æthelred with his
followers and the Welsh kings with theirs had done before.

Like any other Anglo-Saxon lord of his day, King Alfred demanded
hold-oaths from his commended men, including his advisors and agents.
One ealdorman, Wulfhere, even forfeited his office and inheritance because he had "deserted without permission both his lord King Alfred
[*suum dominum regem Alfredum*] and homeland in spite of the oath
that he had sworn to the king and all his leading men."[19] That Edward
continued this practice seems certain. In his Exeter code Edward used
the language of lordship to remind his *witan* (that is, his prelates, eal-

dormen, and reeves) of their duty to him "to favor what he favors, and discountenance what he discountenances, both by land and by sea."[20] Later in the same code the king referred to a general oath and a pledge to refrain from aiding lawbreakers, which may also have been phrased in the manner of a hold-oath.[21]

This tendency to associate kingship with personal lordship culminated in Edmund's third code, issued ca. 943 at Colyton-on-Axe (Devonshire). Here we find the text of a general oath of fealty, which states explicitly what may have been implied in the laws of Edward:

> In the first place, all [*omnes*] shall swear in the name of the Lord, before whom this holy thing [i.e., the relic] is holy, that they will be faithful to King Edmund, even as a man ought to be faithful to his lord [*sicut homo debet esse fidelis domino suo*], without any dispute or dissension, openly or in secret, favoring what he favors and discountenancing what he discountenances.[22]

What was meant by the term "omnes"? Liebermann argued persuasively that all the king's subjects who were "moot-worthy," that is, qualified to attend the assemblies of hundred, borough, and shire, were to take this oath.[23] VI *Æthelstan*, c. 10 seems to confirm this view, since it strongly implies that such oaths were to be administered by the royal reeves at the shire courts.[24] If so, Edmund was demanding that the middling and great landholders of his realm, nobleman and commoner alike, should pledge fealty to him, just as if he were their personal lord. For by the mid-tenth century only freemen enjoying a certain status, apparently determined by the amount of land they possessed, were deemed "worthy" of acting as suitors. From the pleas recorded in the *Libellus* section of the *Liber Eliensis*, it would seem that only the "best" men of the hundred and shire attended the moots.[25] By the reign of Cnut the phrases "the thegns of the shire" and "the suitors of the shire court" had become synonymous in Mercia and the Danelaw. Thus the shire court described in KCD 755 (S 501) was made up of the thegns of the shire of Hereford, who were asked to "act rightly and like thegns."[26] The Domesday Book description of Fersfield, Norfolk, indicates that in that shire in 1066 only villagers with more than a virgate of land had the right and obligation to pay suit to the hundred.[27]

Although one would hesitate to pronounce that each man who swore this oath became through it a personal retainer of King Edmund,[28] nevertheless, it is undeniable that in form the Colyton oath is nothing more or less than an oath of commendation.[29] Unlike the Carolingian oaths of fidelity upon which Edmund's was probably modeled,[30] there is no implication that a man was promising to be a faithful subject of a king, or that an individual had any positive duties toward the king qua king. Edmund's oath thus has no parallel for the phrase "ad honorem regni sui," which appears in Charlemagne's subject-oath of 802.[31] Instead, it defines what it means for a man to be loyal to his king, and for this it uses the language of commendation.[32]

Sworn on holy relics in the name of the Lord, the Colyton oath drew upon a force more powerful than any wielded by an earthly king, the shared Christian belief that Divine retribution would visit oathbreakers. A supernatural sanction was needed to secure a man's promises in a period when the coercive power of government was so weak. A wrongdoer who did not fear for his spiritual well-being or his reputation in the community could easily break faith with his lord and king and still die in bed.[33] Most tenth-century Englishmen, however, would have paused long before forswearing themselves. The sanctity and efficacy of the solemn oath was taken so much for granted that the entire Anglo-Saxon legal system was founded upon it. A defendant's guilt or innocence did not depend upon an investigation into the facts of the case, as it would in a modern court of law, but upon his willingness to swear before God that he was innocent of the charge and his ability to produce the required number of oath-helpers to attest to his good faith. It is little wonder that Alfred chose to begin his law code with a series of enactments concerned with the breaking of vows. According to these, a man who failed to fulfill a rightful oath—Alfred is careful here to exclude vows of treachery against one's lord, which he declares "better left unfulfilled"—was to submit to incarceration at a king's *tun,* where he was to endure for forty days whatever penance the bishop prescribed for him. If he refused to go, he was to be outlawed and excommunicated; in other words, thrust out of the society of man and God.[34] A man who broke his oath of loyalty to King Edmund thus risked more than his life.

A sanction of this sort was, of course, only compelling to Christians. Fortunately, the Danes who swore their loyalty to Edmund at Colyton shared the faith of their king. Alfred had made conversion a condition of peace in 878, which is not surprising when one considers the problems that Christian kings had in dealing with pagan foes. Because of their blithe contempt for the wrath of the Christian God, the pagan Northmen appeared untrustworthy in the extreme to the English. Just as the Romans had found the Celts of Spain shocking in their lack of *fides,* the English were confounded by a foe to whom oaths seemed mere words, to be honored or broken as the situation required. Alfred even attempted to come to an agreement with the heathens using their own religious strictures to bind them. In 876 the vikings of Cambridge slipped past Alfred's army and seized Wareham, a royal burh in Dorset. The king reacted promptly, laying siege to Wareham, but the best he could achieve was a stalemate and an even-handed agreement: the vikings were to leave Alfred's kingdom, and Alfred was to allow them to depart in safety. To secure this treaty, the two armies exchanged hostages and oaths. Alfred, who seems to have been a practical sort, realized that pagans would have little respect or use for Christian relics, and insisted that the Danes swear instead on an object sacred to them, a "holy ring" associated with the worship of Thor.[35] The king's attempt at ecumenical peacemaking, however, failed miserably. The Danes,

> practising their usual treachery, after their own manner, and paying no heed to the hostages, the oath and the promise of faith, broke the treaty, killed all the [hostages] they had, and turning away they went unexpectedly to another place, called Exeter.[36]

Alfred seems to have learned his lesson. Two years later we find him sitting with his army outside of the burh of Chippenham, starving into submission the remnants of the Danish army that he had defeated at Edington. This time he would not lift the siege and permit the Danes to quit his kingdom until their king, Guthrum, had first promised to give him hostages *and* accept Christianity. Three weeks later the Danish leader and thirty of his most distinguished followers were baptized at Aller, near Alfred's stronghold of Athelney. The viking chieftain returned to East Anglia a Christian monarch, Alfred's own godson, and in the course of a generation, the children of those who had murdered King Edmund had come to venerate the royal martyr as a saint. By 942 the land of the Five Boroughs, the Danelaw between the Welland and Humber, was Christian territory. The poet who described King Edmund's recapture of the Five Boroughs from the Norse saw nothing ironic in depicting it as a redemption of God's people from the "bonds of captivity to the heathens."[37] It was only fitting that these Christians of Danish descent should swear fidelity to their secular redeemer in the name of the Lord and upon holy relics.

Considered as a whole, then, the Colyton oath and its predecessors point toward a redefinition of Anglo-Saxon kingship, one in which the personal link between the king and his subjects was emphasized. By associating royal authority with personal lordship, the tenth-century

English rulers were identifying themselves as the *hlafordas and mund-boran* of all their free subjects, whether Dane or Saxon, noble or commoner. One need not belabor the point that the political events of the tenth century, the absorption of Mercia and the conquest of the Dane-law, necessitated a new, broader conception of kingship.[38] Edmund's oath, which appears to have been introduced soon after the king's redemption of the Five Boroughs in 942, had the effect of unifying the diverse provinces and the peoples over which he ruled by binding each man to him personally, much as Charlemagne's oaths of loyalty had united his crazy-quilt empire in the person of the Frankish king.

Alfred and his successors were not content merely to claim as monarchs the fidelity and obedience due a lord. They went beyond this, asserting their right to regulate the exercise of lordship by those under them. This, again, was not without precedent. As early as the seventh century, Ine, king of the West Saxons, had legislated on matters concerning the dealings of his men with their own dependents. However, in most instances these enactments arose from the king's rights over land and his claim to lordship over the tenants of his nobility.[39] In contrast, the law codes from Alfred through Cnut present the king as standing above the lordship bond. Whereas Ine decreed that a man who left his lord without permission was to be returned and fined sixty shillings payable to the lord,[40] Alfred restated this law two centuries later to emphasize royal authority, declaring that a man could only leave his lord with the cognizance of the king's ealdorman in whose shire he served. If he departed without informing the ealdorman, any lord who accepted his services was liable to a fine of 120 shillings payable to the king.[41] Edward the Elder and his son Æthelstan elaborated upon this by defining the offense as *cynges oferhyrnes,* insubordination to the king.[42] In addition, the latter monarch was responsible for a succession of laws specifying the circumstances under which a man could seek a new lord.[43] In each of these decrees it was the king who guaranteed the rights of lord and man and who determined what these rights ought to be.

The attitude of the tenth-century English rulers toward lordship is perhaps best exemplified by Æthelstan's famous order that every man have a lord or be branded an outlaw.[44] The lordship bond, which had formerly drawn men into opposing the king, as we have seen in the Cynewulf-Cyneheard and Edward-Æthelwold episodes in the Chronicle, and which in practice continued to divide men's loyalties whenever an ætheling, ealdorman, or magnate rebelled,[45] was undergoing a transformation in the Anglo-Saxon law codes. Lordship was now portrayed by the king as a tool of royal governance and social control. Like the chief men of the new tithing and "hundred" associations,[46] a lord was to be responsible for the lawful behavior of his dependents.[47] By Cnut's reign, the king's ascendancy in principle over his magnates' followings was so firmly established that writs began to speak of clienteles as licensed by royal authority: "I inform you that I have granted him that he be entitled to his sake and soke . . . over as many thegns as I have granted him to have."[48] Nor was theory totally divorced from practice. In 1051, for instance, Edward the Confessor attempted to quash the threatened rebellion of Earl Godwine and his sons by transferring the allegiance of their thegns to himself, a measure that proved at least initially successful.[49] And while this may have been the most spectacular example of the king's power over the commendation relationship, it is not the only one that may be adduced.[50]

Edward the Confessor's ability to contest for the loyalty of his rebellious earls' own followers contrasts sharply with St. Aldhelm's adjuration to Bishop Wilfrid's clergy some three hundred and fifty years before to remain faithful to their lord in his dispute with the king and share his exile, as was the duty of all good retainers.[51] This is not to argue that the king-subject relationship had emerged as the primary political bond sometime between the eighth and the eleventh century; Godwine's triumphant return in 1052, due in no small measure to the aid rendered him by his erstwhile thegns,[52] warns us against reading too much into the events of 1051. Nevertheless, it is indisputable that Edward laid claim as king to the loyalty of Godwine's thegns, and that his appeal to them was at least temporarily successful. This is to be attributed in part to the nature of the earl's following. For many of his men were territorial lords in their own right, endowed with bookland and hence as much dependent upon maintaining the goodwill of the king for their fortunes as upon gaining Godwine's favor. The fear of material loss, however, was but one factor. In addition, Edward's initial success can be explained in constitutional terms, since Godwine's thegns had not only commended themselves to him but had sworn an equally solemn oath of fidelity to the king.

The military import of the oaths of fealty exacted by the kings of the tenth and eleventh centuries cannot be overestimated. Because of them, the leaders of Alfred's and Edward the Elder's armies, their ealdormen, reeves, bishops, and household retainers were solemnly bound to love what their royal lords loved and hate what they hated. By the end of Edmund's reign the rank and file of the fyrd had joined their leaders in this pledge. It was not on a whim that Edmund demanded hold-oaths from the suitors to the popular assemblies any more than it was a coincidence that the divisions of the fyrd should be the shire, hundred, and borough.[53] The "judicial" and "military" functions of the state blended together in tenth-century England, subsumed under the general heading of "maintaining the king's peace." As we have observed, an armed action to maintain or restore the king's peace did not differ materially from an expedition against the king's enemies.[54] The pursuit forces of Æthelstan's codes could easily turn into local military levies, especially when confronted with the necessity of opposing overmighty "families."[55] To be "fyrd-worthy" and "moot-worthy" were thus two sides of the same coin.[56]

The hold-oath restored to the fyrd some of the cohesion that had been lost with the evolution of that institution. As we have seen, the spread of book-right had altered the nature and composition of the fyrd, transforming it from the king's retinue arrayed for war into an assembly of landowners and the contingents they owed in respect of their bookland. Thus the bulk of the tenth-century royal hosts need not have stood in an immediate relationship to the king. The imposition of the hold-oath upon all "moot-worthy" men changed this. Now those who attended the royal hosts were obliged to regard the king as if he were their own lord, loving what he loved, hating what he hated. The warriors who served the king and his agents in the fyrd were now bound before God to render their service faithfully, as a man ought to do for his lord.

This dual foundation of military obligation in tenth-century England upon the lordship tie and land tenure helps explain Edward the Elder's policy in the Danelaw. There is reason to believe that Edward not only demanded that the Danes "take him to lord" but required that they submit to him *with their lands*. The *Libellus* portion of the *Liber Eliensis*, which is based upon a pre-Conquest vernacular source,[57] relates the details of a lawsuit of ca. 975 that sheds invaluable light upon Edward's conquest of the Midlands. The sons of Boga, a Dane, claimed some property in Huntingdonshire through their maternal uncle Tope. They argued that the estate of Bluntisham ought to have devolved upon them as Tope's heirs, since the land was properly his by hereditary right. According to their complaint, Tope's grandmother, "then in the flower of her virginity," sought Edward at Cambridge and submitted to him in regard to this property.[58] In view of her submission, they asserted, the land ought not to have been forfeited to the Crown, as it appears to have been.

The jurors of Huntingdonshire rejected this plea on the ground that Tope's grandmother had not sought the king in time. The elder men of the shire remembered that Edward had recovered Huntingdonshire before Cambridgeshire. Hence the woman's acceptance of Edward's lordship at Cambridge would have been a defense for lands belonging to that borough, but not for her Huntingdonshire properties. In short, her submission came too late to save Bluntisham from forfeiture.[59]

If we can generalize from this suit, it would appear that tenurial considerations played an important role in the submission of the southern Danelaw to Edward's lordship. Those who failed to swear the requisite oath of fealty or were tardy in responding to Edward's demands lost their lands to him. When one considers that at the time of the suit Bluntisham was the hereditary property of a thegn bearing the English name of Wulfnoth, Edward's confiscation of these estates appears as part of a deliberate policy of settling the newly acquired territories with men of known loyalties.[60] Those who received Edward as their lord were allowed to retain their lands, or, more precisely, were granted books confirming these properties. Thus it told heavily against the sons of Boga that, having claimed Bluntisham by hereditary right (*iure heredi-tario*), they were unable to produce a charter in support of their plea. As the jurors of the shire declared, "it was more fitting that the one who had the book should also have the land."[61]

Edward's interest in the lands of his Danish subjects undoubtedly stemmed from both fiscal and military concerns. By granting their holdings back to them, Edward was asserting that he enjoyed the same land rights over the estates of his Danish subjects as he had by custom over the English. This would have included the various services and "tribute" (*feorm*) that Edward possessed in Wessex.[62] It is therefore not surprising that the hidation of the Midlands has been traced back to Edward's reign,[63] for the hide, as we shall see, was the basic unit of tax assessment. It is also likely that Edward imposed the "common burdens" upon the tenures of the Danes who sought his lordship, although in the absence of extant charters this, of course, must remain conjecture. One of the few genuine landbooks that has survived from Edward's reign does, however, describe host duty, bridge repair, and fortress work as services "rendered throughout the whole nation" (*swa mon ofer eall folc do*), and it seems less than plausible that the king would have forgiven his Danish subjects what he insisted upon from his English ones.[64] Cer-

tainly, when Mercia submitted to Edward after the death of his sister
Æthelflæd and the deposition of her daughter,[65] the king specifically
distributed the burden of repairing and manning the borough of Nottingham between the Danes and Englishmen of that province. Moreover,
when midland and East Anglian charters do become more abundant
from the mid-tenth century on, they invariably reserve the "common
burdens."[66] A Cambridgeshire landbook of 957, the original of which
has been preserved, even describes the three dues as "common to all"
(*quae omnibus communibus sunt*).[67]

When the viking invasions resumed at the end of the tenth century,
the military system devised by Alfred and elaborated upon by his son
and grandsons formed the basis of Æthelred II's defense of his kingdom.
English resistance thus depended heavily upon the performance of the
"common burdens," the crucial importance of which is underscored by
the appearance for the first time of legislation upon this subject. In two
of Æthelred II's codes we encounter decrees insisting that the military
dues incumbent upon the land be discharged "whenever the occasion
demands, as may be ordered for our common need."[68]

The physical record reveals that one of these, *burhbot,* was not only
demanded but performed. Edward's and Æthelstan's conquests had
brought to a close the great period of military construction begun under
Alfred. England's prosperity and security in the mid-tenth century allowed the development of secondary markets conspicuous for their lack
of defenses. All this changed, however, in the 990s. Under Æthelred II
new fortifications were erected and old ones refurbished. Archaeologists
have excavated three Æthelredian burghal forts over the last two decades, each built on the site of a pre-Roman hill-fort, each boasting
impressive defenses. The late Saxon burh at South Cadbury was one of
these. The fort, erected around A.D. 1010, crowns a 500-foot hill dom-
inating the Foss Way near the Somerset-Dorset border. Its defenses
include a fourteen- to twenty-foot-thick rampart, faced with a wall of
masonry that originally rose to a height of about ten feet. Altogether,
the burh at South Cadbury enclosed about 1200 yards. Despite its mint,
apparently transferred from nearby Ilchester, South Cadbury was a
military rather than an economic center. Archaeologists have found few
buildings on the site and little evidence that it was ever an active market.
Significantly, the burh was abandoned at the end of the Danish wars,
its walls slighted ca. 1020.[69] Similar strongholds were established by
Æthelred at Old Sarum—the juncture of three Roman roads—and at
Cissbury in southern Sussex.[70] In addition, the defenses of pre-existing

burhs were strengthened during this period, stone curtains replacing timber revetments and palisades.[71]

Most tantalizing of all is the case of Goltho Manor in Lincolnshire, a private burh. Despite the dictum that the Normans introduced castles into England, Goltho Manor appears to have been a pre-Conquest castle. Its extensive rampart and ditch defenses were refurbished around the year 1000, making them contemporaneous with Æthelred's building program. Goltho, at present an anomaly, may well prove typical when other aristocratic estates have been excavated.[72] At least one thegn, then, was demanding *burhbot* from his tenants for the defenses of his private residences. One can only speculate whether such "fortress-work" was in fulfillment of the "common burdens" or the result of private enterprise.

Because of changes in the Danes' military organization, the burghal system and territorial fyrd proved far less effective in this new round of wars than it had in the past.[73] To make matters worse, English grand strategy had also changed. The parts of Edward's system remained, but the function of each had been redefined during a generation of peace. The fyrd, for example, reverted to its earlier incarnation as an ad hoc levy summoned to meet crises, a far less expensive expedient than maintaining a standing army. A nation at peace could survive with such levies; a state under siege could not. Nor were Æthelred's defenses integrated into the defense-in-depth system envisioned by Alfred and Edward. No longer used in tandem with the fyrd to launch offensives or defended by permanent garrisons, the burhs now stood merely as places of refuge for the civilian population. As such, they failed to stem the viking invasion. Burh after burh was stormed and burnt by the invaders: London in 982, Watchet in 988, Bamburgh in 993, Exeter and Wilton in 1003, and Wallingford in 1006. The success stories are few. London withstood attack in 994; Lydford may have impeded an advance in the west country in 997, but only after the region had been devastated; Exeter stoutly resisted the *here* in 1001, but the vikings still ravaged Devonshire; Old Sarum, a new fort, held out in 1003 against a viking army that had destroyed Wilton, one of Alfred's boroughs. Both the strengths and weaknesses of Æthelred's boroughs are brought out most clearly in the annal of 1006. After having burned the borough of Wallingford and ravaged Berkshire as far inland as Cuckhamsley Barrow, the Danish army retired to their ships with their booty, boldly marching past the gates of Winchester. The citizens of that town were able to do no more than huddle behind their walls and watch passively as their enemies passed by.[74]

The vulnerability of the boroughs, brought home by these disasters, led Æthelred and his advisors to bolster their naval forces in hope of preventing the Danes from landing.[75] In 1008, as the Chronicle states:

> the king gave orders that ships should be speedily built throughout the whole of England: namely [one large warship to be provided from every] three hundred hides and a cutter [*scegth*] from every ten hides.[76]

There is still a great deal of controversy surrounding these naval districts, or ship-sokes. One cannot be certain, for example, whether they were originally to be units of three hundred hides, as in the "D" version quoted above, or of three hundred and ten hides, as in all other recensions of the Chronicle.[77] Nor can one even maintain with confidence that this arrangement was first instituted in 1008, despite the testimony of the Chronicle, for other evidence suggests that the bishop of Sherborne was supplying a ship from his three hundred hides in Dorset some years before, and one charter of questionable authenticity speaks of ship-sokes in the reign of King Edgar.[78] The nature of the ship-sokes, however, is less open to debate; they were territorial districts responsible for the outfitting and manning of ships, which represented but an extension of the "common burdens" to naval matters.

The holders of tenures would now be responsible not only for the building of fortifications but for warships as well. In the law codes issued by Æthelred in 1008 the outfitting of ships (*scipfyrdunga*) takes its place alongside the repairing of bridges and fortresses and attendance in the king's host (*fyrdunga*).[79] And the sources of the eleventh century will now begin to distinguish between the *landfyrd* and the *scipfyrd,* describing both as "services due from a landowner."[80]

Despite all of the king's preparations and maneuvers, Æthelred's reign was an unmitigated disaster. The Anglo-Saxon Chronicle's dismal account of it, a lament composed after the king's death, may well be colored by defeatism, as Simon Keynes recently suggested.[81] But if the annalist exaggerated Æthelred's failures, he did not invent them. Many of the king's policies were well conceived, but in the final analysis they failed to save his kingdom from conquest, partly because of the strength of his enemies and partly because of the treachery and incompetence of those who led his armies. Æthelred II has been saddled with the punning—and misleading—nickname "Unræd," the "ill-advised." In light of the events of his reign, however, the "ill-served" would be more accurate. If we can trust the Chronicle's account at all, Æthelred suffered constant betrayal at the hands of his ealdormen and magnates. Eadric *Streona* may not have been quite the Judas portrayed by the annalist, an East Anglian with little love for a West Mercian ealdorman, but there can be little doubt that he and others were willing to cut their losses and seek accommodation with Swein and Cnut.[82] For whatever reasons, and many can be cited, Æthelred's nobility was divided and exhibited signs of disaffection with the king.[83]

Under these circumstances it is not at all surprising that Æthelred's later codes should enjoin loyalty to the king. Nor is it surprising that the author of these laws, Archbishop Wulfstan of York chose the language of lordship to remind his audience of their responsibility to the king. V *Æthelred*, c. 35, the first of these appeals, is perhaps the most striking: "And let us loyally support one royal lord, and all of us together defend our lives and our country, to the best of our ability."[84] The term that Wulfstan used was *cynehlaford,* literally "royal lord," a tenth-century coinage that first appears in the extant sources in VI *Æthelstan,* c. 9, § 7. The bishop and reeves belonging to the peace-guild of London called Æthelstan their cynehlaford because it was literally true: they were his commended men. Similarly, bishops, ealdormen, and king's thegns of the mid- and late tenth century often addressed the king as their "royal lord" in their wills.[85] By the end of the century, however, cynehlaford had acquired a new connotation, one which reflected developments in the ideology of kingship. In Æthelred's codes and in the homilies of Ælfric of Eynsham and Archbishop Wulfstan, the king was presented as the cynehlaford, the "liege lord," of all his subjects, a portrayal that harked back to the wording of the Colyton oath and looked forward to Cnut's promise of faithful lordship to the entire nation at the great assembly of 1020.[86]

The other side of the coin was the growing association of treason with *hlafordswicung,* betrayal of one's lord. Archbishop Wulfstan, the man responsible for drafting Æthelred's laws, chose to use precisely this phrase in his "Sermon of the Wolf" (1014) to denounce his countrymen for their habitual disloyalty to their monarchs: "And a great treachery it is also in the world that a man should betray his lord to death, or drive him in his lifetime from the land; and both have happened in this country: Edward [the Martyr] was betrayed and then killed and afterwards burnt, and Æthelred was driven out of his country."[87] A little over two centuries before, in the year A.D. 786, King Ælfwold of

Northumbria and all his chief men, both ecclesiastical and secular, swore to Pope Hadrian's Legates that they would never conspire against the life of a king, not because he was the lord of his people, but because he was the Lord's anointed.[88] A gaping ideological gulf separates these two explanations of the gravity of treason. Hadrian's Legates presented an argument for the sanctity of a king's person that was universal in its application; to conspire against a king was to conspire against God's chosen. Wulfstan's definition of treason is based on the unstated premise that each man owes his king the same loyalty due a lord. In other words, Wulfstan took for granted his audience's acceptance of the royal ideology implicit in the Colyton oath. In addition, the archbishop, who knew the Legates' report and used it elsewhere in his writings, obviously believed that an accusation of hlafordswicung would strike a deeper chord in his secular audience than would a harangue about their betrayal of the Lord's anointed.

As we have seen, the loyalty and disloyalty of ealdormen and other king's men had been expressed through the language of lordship since the days of Bede and probably before. Wulfstan's sermon universalized this concept, extending it to all free Englishmen, no matter who their chosen lord might be. In this, Wulfstan was echoing the laws he had drafted for Æthelred and Cnut, and building upon a foundation laid by Alfred. Alfred, who had reason to fear disloyalty, included in his code a law against devising the death of a king and another against plotting the death of one's lord. The two appear as separate crimes, but they were clearly linked in Alfred's mind, since he placed them in the same chapter and provided the same penalty: death and the loss of property.[89] Both injunctions were repeated in subsequent law codes. Æthelred, in particular, was concerned about the possibility that his subjects might conspire against his life or abandon him in battle, again, reasonable worries for that most unfortunate monarch.[90] His Danish successor, Cnut, made the final connection between high treason and the betrayal of a personal lord. The fifty-seventh clause of his second code—like Æthelred's later dooms, the handiwork of Wulfstan—made a subtle alteration in Alfred's law, conflating the two types of treachery and placing them under the same rubric, *lafordes syrwunge*. Once again the obligations of a subject to his king were clarified by analogy to lordship.

The burghal system, shires, hundreds, and ship-sokes gave the tenth-century English kings something that had been denied their predecessors, an administration sophisticated enough to permit them to control the territorial magnates. In addition, the new conception of kingship implicit in the law codes and the hold-oaths of this century placed royal authority upon a more secure foundation by equating it with lordship. When viewed together, these innovations permit one to gain some insight into the military power of the late Anglo-Saxon rulers. Essentially, these kings had the means of exacting the "common burdens" and punishing those who were reluctant to fulfill their obligations as landholders. Moreover, the theory of royal lordship gave some cohesion to levies no longer connected directly by bonds of commendation. Because the king was the royal lord of all "fyrd-worthy" men, the fyrd became once more his retinue arrayed for battle, but with a great difference: fyrd service for many was now a condition of tenure. In order to trace the further development of these ideas in late Anglo-Saxon England, one must now turn to the most complete source for our knowledge of Old English institutions on the eve of the Conquest: Domesday Book.

FIVE

Fyrd Service and Hidage

Any study of late Anglo-Saxon institutions must inevitably revolve around Domesday Book, yet the difficulties of interpretation associated with this work are notorious and extend to the passages dealing with military matters. Starting from the same texts, scholars have come to radically different conclusions concerning the nature of military obligation on the eve of the Conquest. Some, notably Sir Frank Stenton, have contended that fyrd service was the duty of peasants, that the *expeditio* of the landbooks and Domesday custumals was in fact limited to ceorls recruited territorially. The thegn's obligation, they assert, was completely different in origin, following from his rank. Whether he held fifty hides of land or none was irrelevant, for he was a warrior and a king's man by birth.[1] Others, led by Eric John, have argued that the late Anglo-Saxon fyrd was essentially a "feudal host" of landed aristocrats and thegnly retainers, whose obligation to service derived from their possession of land.[2] A difficulty with all these approaches to the problem of the Anglo-Saxon fyrd on the eve of the Conquest is that they have been taken with an eye toward the future and lie in the shadow of Anglo-Norman feudalism. Consideration of late Anglo-Saxon military obligation in light of the past history of the fyrd may prove more fruitful.

The present inquiry has focused upon the relationship between military obligations and the institutions of lordship and land tenure in Anglo-Saxon England. In the previous chapters we traced the origin and development of the "common burdens," host duty, fortress-work, and bridge-work, which fixed military service to book-right. Domesday Book allows us to examine further the nature of these dues, for it sheds light upon the principle of assessment for fyrd service at the end of the Anglo-Saxon period.

On the whole, Domesday Book is simply unconcerned with detailing the workings of the pre-Conquest fyrd. This is quite understandable if, as has been plausibly suggested, the Inquest was conducted to provide William the Conqueror with a record of his kingdom's wealth and resources at a time when such information was crucial.[3] The making of Domesday Book should be viewed against the backdrop of King Cnut IV of Denmark's threat of invasion in 1085. William responded to the danger by returning from Normandy

> with a larger force of mounted men and infantry from France and Brittany than had ever come into this country, so that people wondered how this country could maintain all that army. And the king had all the army dispersed all over the country among his vassals, and they provisioned the army each in proportion to his land. . . . But when the king found out for a fact that his enemies had been hindered and could not carry out their expedition—then he let some of the army go to their own country, and some he kept in this country over winter.[4]

The Chronicler emphasizes not only the size of the Conqueror's mercenary army but the expense and difficulties of maintaining it. William's solution, charging the soldiers' upkeep to his vassals, each according to his means, was one guaranteed to start the king wondering about the wealth he had distributed among his barons. Shortly afterward, at Christmastime, William decided to find out. Meeting with his council at Gloucester, he discussed with them his desire to learn more about the resources of his kingdom. The upshot was the Domesday Inquest. William ordered commissioners to be sent "over all England into every shire and had them find out how many hundred hides there were in the shire, or what land and cattle the king himself had in the country, or what dues he ought to have in twelve months from the shire."[5] It is thought that William received the completed returns within a year, perhaps as early as 1 August 1086, when he held a great assembly at Salisbury to take oaths of fealty from his tenants-in-chief and their greater vassals. The two volumes of Domesday Book, the thirty-one county surveys that make up "Great Domesday" and the three of "Little Domesday," were rendered into their present form by 9 September 1087, the date of William's death, less than twenty months after the king had ordered the Inquest.[6] The haste with which the commissioners and scribes did their work attests to the Conqueror's seriousness of purpose. The Inquest was not the result of royal whim; nor was it a mere stocktaking after twenty years of rule. Rather, it was fueled by military need, by William's urgent desire to discover what he held personally and what he had granted away, so that he could better exploit these resources in the face of possible invasion. Domesday Book meant that William and his successors would no longer have to wonder how they could afford to maintain the troops necessary to defend England. They now knew.

Domesday Book is essentially a vast land register in which the fiscal and economic elements predominate. Despite V. H. Galbraith's dictum that Domesday Book is "the formal written record of the introduction of feudal tenure and therefore of feudal law into England," the survey is markedly unconcerned with knight service, a puzzling omission in light of the military crisis of 1085/1086, and one that has interesting implications about the relative military value of William's mercenary army and his feudal host.[7] Nor is Domesday Book overly forthcoming about military arrangements "in the time of King Edward" (abbreviated as T.R.E.). The only aspect of the old fyrd that seems to have interested the commissioners was its fiscal side—the customary payments to the king in lieu of such service, and the fines owed the king for failure to answer his summons.[8] Any information about the organization and recruitment of the fyrd that found its way into the survey was purely incidental to the king's financial concern. Nevertheless, the scattered references to *expeditio* in Domesday Book, as ambiguous as each may be, reveal a great deal about the extent of the individual landowner's obligation T.R.E. when taken together. The most explicit of these is a well-known passage that occurs at the beginning of the Berkshire survey, which informs us that

> if the king sent an army anywhere, only one soldier [*miles*] went from five hides, and four shillings were given for his subsistence or wages from each hide for two months. The money, indeed, was not sent to the king, but was given to the soldiers [*militibus*].[9]

Whatever else may have been true of the Berkshire fyrd during Edward's reign, it was not a levy of all able-bodied free men. Rather, a general rule prevailed in the shire that five hides of land were to supply one soldier and his provisions. One is reminded here of the Burghal Hidage and its prescription of one man from every hide for borough work; in both the obligation to serve is stated as belonging to the land. It is reasonable to conclude that the Berkshire Domesday text, like the Burghal Hidage, refers to the "common burdens" of the charters, the former alluding to *ferdsocn* and the latter to *wealgeweorc* or *burhbot*. Having come this far, one can go no further with an analysis of the Berkshire text without encountering difficulties. What exactly did "one *miles* from five hides" mean? Leaving aside for the moment the problem posed by the term "miles", let us consider the meaning of the "hide" in late Anglo-Saxon England.

Hidage is one of the most difficult and technical topics in Anglo-Saxon studies. The amount of attention that it has received over the years well attests its importance.[10] Maitland, writing in 1897, even found it necessary to apologize to his readers for raising once again the "dreary old question" of the hide.[11] Fortunately, we need not be concerned here with the technical problems associated with hidage; it is not essential, for example, to establish whether all hides comprised exactly 120 fiscal acres, as Maitland thought,[12] or whether the size of the hide varied from region to region.[13] It is enough for our present purpose that we define the hide and establish its relationship, if any, to the value of the land. In other words, the question to be answered is whether hidage was based upon the economic resources of an estate or was simply an arbitrary measure.

It is now generally conceded that the hide and its constituent parts, the virgate and the acre, did not simply measure area. What it did measure, however, is far from clear. The word itself is derived from the term *hiwisc,* meaning "family."[14] In the *Historia Ecclesiastica,* Bede rendered "hide" as "the land (or measure) of N families, by the English reckoning [*terra (mensura) iuxta consuetudinem aestimationis Anglorum, N familiarum*],"[15] which has led many scholars to pronounce the hide the tenement of the "normal" ceorl, or a measure that took as its basis the peasant's standard of living.[16] This definition has been preferred by historians who have portrayed early Anglo-Saxon society as a ceorl-centered society, since in this view the fundamental unit of all Anglo-Saxon landholding was the land of a free peasant's household. Others have read Bede's "family" as the household of a warrior noble.[17] If, however, one looks at the evidence of Eddius, who wrote at the beginning of the eighth century, and of the early charters, a third possibility emerges.

In the *Vita Wilfridi,* Eddius expressed "hides" through two phrases, which he used interchangeably: "the land of N *manses*" and the "land of N tribute-payers [*tributariorum*]."[18] The latter formula also appears in a number of early charters, one of which survives in a near contemporary manuscript.[19] To this we might add the evidence of BCS 170, a cartulary copy of an eighth-century charter with a claim to respect, where we read that "a certain piece of land . . . taxed under an appraisal of 10 *manses* [*sub aestimatione .X. mansionum taxatam*]" was granted to Aldhelm, abbot of Malmesbury.[20] Whatever "hide" may have meant during the prehistory of the Anglo-Saxons,[21] by the time of its entry into the written sources it would seem to have been a cadastral unit. Thus when Bede wrote of "the land of N families," he meant neither X areal acres nor a portion of land capable of supporting N number of cierlisc households. Rather, the "hide" was a term of taxation, or tribute; it told the lord how much food-rent, tribute, and service he could expect from his holding. More precisely, a hide referred to the render expected from the holding of a normal *gafolgelda* ("tribute-payer").[22]

Any lingering doubt as to the character of the eighth-century hide is dispelled by the Tribal Hidage, a tribute list compiled for the kings of the Mercian hegemony. A large round number of hides is attributed to every one of the thirty-five people mentioned in this document. In fact, each hidage assessment was a multiple of 100 or 1000. Furthermore, Wessex's 100,000 hides, a figure that has disturbed more than one commentator, cannot represent the kingdom's area, population, or value. It is completely out of line with the other assessments, being more than triple that of the next largest kingdoms, East Anglia and Mercia. The most plausible interpretation of the West Saxon hidage is that it represents the largest possible tribute that the Mercian overlords could exact from their most formidable subject realm.[23]

Despite the punitive appraisal of Wessex in the Tribal Hidage, hidage seems to have been ordinarily determined by a region's area and resources, the latter being the more important factor. We have the testimony of Bede for this. In the *Historia Ecclesiastica*, II. 9, we learn that King Edwin of Northumbria brought the Isles of Anglesey and Man under his sway. Bede goes on to describe Edwin's acquisitions: "of these islands, the southern one, which is the larger and more fertile of the two, measures 960 'families,' according to the English reckoning, while the other measures a bit more than 300."[24] Bede is correct in saying that Anglesey is larger than Man, but only by fifty square miles. Anglesey has an area of 276 square miles, while its companion measures 227 square miles. One can account for the considerable difference between their hidage assessments only by Bede's comment upon their relative prosperity.[25] This inference is supported by the hidage assessments that Bede provides for the isles of Thanet, Wight, and Iona. Iona's six square miles were assessed at only "five families." In contrast, Thanet, seven times the size of Iona, was more than a hundred times its superior in hidage.[26] Similarly, the Isle of Wight is slightly larger than Angseley, being 299 square miles in area, but was rated at over 200 more hides.[27] Obviously, area alone cannot account for these variations in hidage. We are led to conclude that eighth-century hidage represented the number of notional "tribute-payers" that could be supported in a district, and that this in turn was based upon the perceived wealth of that region.

From both Bede's writings and the Tribal Hidage it would appear that hidage was imposed by a king or overlord upon large districts, which were sometimes the settlement areas of whole tribes. These assessments need not have been customary, and could vary considerably over the course of a century, as seems to have been the case with Mercia.[28] In addition, each estate within a particular *regio* or kingdom was also hidated, and again the basis for the assessment appears to have been the anticipated render from the holding's land and its inhabitants. While it would be tempting to relate the hidage of individual estates to that imposed upon the kingdom as a whole, the fragmentary nature of the evidence urges caution here. One must face the possibility that the "hide" of the Tribal Hidage was not equivalent to the "hide" of the early charters, although both were cadastral units.

When Edward the Elder conquered the Midlands, he imposed hidage assessments upon his newly acquired territories,[29] much as the Mercian kings had done more than a century before him. But Edward expected more than "tribute" from the lands that he brought under his control, for he and his successors used hidage as a means of assessing the amount of service owed to a borough from its surrounding countryside.[30] Like the *regiones* of the Tribal Hidage, the borough-districts that they created were assessed in large round figures.[31] And within each of these districts or shires (as they were later to be called) the total hidage assessment was apportioned among territorial units rated at approximately one hundred hides and then divided among the villages comprising these "hundreds." Finally, since many villages were themselves partitioned into a number of different estates, each village distributed its quota of hides among its constituent parts. The owners of these estates would then have been responsible for the payment of tribute and the rendering of service, burdens onerous enough in the mid-tenth century to force even wealthy landholders in the Midlands to sell some of their property in order to pay the taxes on the rest.[32] Although the initial assessment was territorial, subsequent adjustments of hidation took place at the level of the individual holding. This and the fact that landlords rather than royal agents collected the geld gradually changed the character of the levy; its original territorial aspect was all but lost as it became more and more a tenurial render.[33] By the reign of Edgar the Peaceable hidage had become the basis of an extraordinarily efficient system of royal taxation, one that was to be perfected at the beginning of the eleventh century under the pressures of the viking invasions.[34] The hide, along with the carucate in the northern Danelaw, was to remain the most important unit of assessment for taxation throughout the Anglo-Saxon period. This, at any rate, is the accepted and most probable theory concerning the evolution of the hidage system based upon the available sources, the Burghal Hidage, the County Hidage, and Domesday Book.[35]

In 1888, John Horace Round delivered what appeared to be a death blow to the notion that the hide of Domesday Book and its constituent parts, the virgate and the "acre," simply measured area. When Round systematically reassembled the villages of Cambridgeshire from the entries referring to them scattered throughout the Domesday county returns, a remarkable pattern emerged. More often than not, the hidages of their constituent estates added up to five hides or a multiple of that figure. And even those villages that at first sight did not seem to fit into this decimal scheme often could be brought into conformity with it if grouped with their neighbors, a creative if dubious methodological approach.[36] Nor did Cambridgeshire prove unique in this. In many of the hidated shires a decimal basis was found to underlie the village geld-assessments.[37] Such groupings, Round argued, must reflect the basic artificiality of the Domesday hide. With some important exceptions, notably Middlesex,[38] the hide of Domesday Book did not touch directly upon real agrarian arrangements. Thus concealed in the "feudal" arrangement of Domesday Book was, in Round's words, "a vast system of artificial hidation."[39] Round's classic exposition of Domesday hidation came to an unequivocal conclusion which has since been echoed by other researchers:

> I take my stand . . . that the hide assessment was fixed *independently of area or value* [his italics], and that, consequently, all attempts that have been made to discover and establish the relation which that assessment

bore to area, whether in Vill or Manor, have proved not only contradictory among themselves, but, as was inevitable, vain.[40]

In one sense, Round's point is well taken. There is no discernible
mathematical formula through which one can derive a Domesday estate's hidage from the information given about its economic resources
and its stated T.R.E. value.[41] One need only peruse the folios of Domesday Book to be convinced of this. To give but one striking example,
Wilden (DB, i. 209b) and Colmworth (DB, i. 213b), neighboring estates
in Barford Hundred, Bedfordshire, were both rated at five hides in
Domesday Book. The former, however, had an arable capacity of sixteen
ploughs,[42] which was actually worked by ten teams, a population of
twenty sokemen, twelve bordars, and one slave, and was worth twenty
pounds before 1066. The latter had "land for 10 ploughs," 10 teams,
12 *villani*, 13 bordars, and one slave, and was valued at four pounds
T.R.E. The artificial character of the hidage assessment is readily apparent here, and while this example is egregious, it is not exceptional.[43]

It does not follow, however, that Domesday hidage bore no relation
whatsoever to an estate's value, that hidage was a purely arbitrary tax
assessment "fixed independently of area or value." Soon after Round
published his study of Domesday statistics, Maitland challenged his
conclusions about hidage, writing that his own examination of Domesday Book had convinced him "that the distribution of fiscal hides has
not been altogether independent of the varying value of land"; that
"some force, conscious or unconscious, has made for 'one pound, one
hide.' "[44] Maitland, however, did not know what to make of this dis-
covery. He was reluctant to place too much weight on it or to draw
out its implications. It not only contradicted Round, whose scholarship
he genuinely admired and whose notorious acerbity he found daunting,
but it also failed to explain why estates of the same value often bore
widely divergent hidage assessments. As befits a legal scholar, Maitland
resolved the contradictions judiciously. He neither repudiated the "equitable element" as a statistical chimera nor presented it as the underlying regulatory principle of hidation. Instead, he saw it as a rough rule
of thumb used by the king and his *witan* to distribute hides to the
various hundreds, a force less powerful in the practical determination
of tax liability than those of privilege and favoritism.[45]

Maitland's diffidence about linking hidage to value was natural
enough under the circumstances. His approach to Domesday statistics
was highly impressionistic. Looking over the tables of hides and values
that he had compiled for the various shires, he believed that he could

discern a pattern, but a pattern that seemed to grow increasingly faint as he moved from the level of the shire to that of the individual manor. Given the state of the discipline of statistics in the late nineteenth century, Maitland could take his work no further. Fortunately, modern statisticians can. Unsurprisingly for those familiar with his work, Maitland's intuition proved remarkably sound.

Regression analysis is a measurement of the strength of association between two or more variables, or, more precisely, of covariance. Such analyses performed on the "hides T.R.E." and "value T.R.E." of individual estates in the counties constituting the south midland Domesday circuit consistently produce statistically significant results.[46] As tables A1–A5 demonstrate, hidage in each shire of this circuit was so closely related to the value of the assessed property in 1066 that more than seventy-five percent of the variation in hidage assessments from estate to estate can be accounted for by the differences in their pre-Conquest values. To be precise, log-linear regressions of value on hidage in the shires of Bedford, Buckingham, Cambridge, Hertford, and Middlesex produce Pearson product-moment coefficients (Pearson's r) that range from .87 to .93 with corresponding coefficients of determination (r^2) that exceed .75.[47] These results are statistically significant at a .001 confidence level; in other words, there is less than one chance in a thousand that hides and values T.R.E. are unrelated in these shires. Preliminary testing in the other six Domesday circuits has produced correlations on the same order of magnitude (see tables A6–A12). In the south midland Domesday circuit, then, and possibly in the others, hidage assessment followed valuation.

This analysis can be taken even further. When the slopes of these regression lines are examined, one discovers that a pound's worth of land tended to be assessed at one hide in three of the five south midland counties. In both Cambridgeshire and Hertfordshire, on the other hand, the ratio of an estate's hidage to its pre-Conquest value stood more in the neighborhood of 3:5. (The curvature of the regression lines is so slight in all cases that it really does not affect these generalizations.) This implies that the value of a hide differed among Domesday counties, which would seem to confirm the traditional hypothesis that the original unit of hidation was the shire rather than the vill or the individual estate. The precise relationship between hidage and valuation, indeed, could vary dramatically from shire to shire. Sussex, for example, had a total of 3474 hides in 1066 that were valued at 3467 pounds, while Leicestershire had 2500 hides worth only 491 pounds.[48] These correlations, coupled with the results of regression analyses performed in sample shires representing the other Domesday circuits, suggest that prior to 1066 "one pound, one hide" was a general rule subject to local exceptions, and that the exact relationship between hidage and valuation was established at the shire level, with some shires being more heavily taxed than others.

If a land's hidage was indeed tied to its value, why have researchers found it impossible to discover an exact formula that would convert the one into the other? Perhaps one might better ask why scholars have expected to find such an equation. Even if "one pound, one hide" had once been true for all shires (or borough-districts), it would have been at best a rough guideline, limited by the king's ability to obtain accurate information about the value of the land in his realm. Furthermore, over time the fluctuations of value and the tendency of hidage to grow custom-bound would have caused the two to diverge even more markedly—unless, of course, tenth- and eleventh-century Anglo-Saxon monarchs were able to adjust hidage on a regular basis, which would have required a staggeringly efficient administration.[49] To demand mathematical precision from the Anglo-Saxon system for geld assessment is to ask more than some modern governments are capable of achieving. Throughout much of the United States today the assessed value of property bears only a marginal resemblance at any one time to real market value, and yet the two are, at least nominally, related. Similarly, we should not assume that because Domesday estates assessed at the same number of hides were often markedly different in value, hides and *valuits* were therefore totally independent quantities.

Historians have also been misled by the existence of "beneficial hidation," especially on the great estates held by the king and his magnates, episcopal and lay, which in some cases meant that properties which brought in more than £20 a year for their owners paid less than estates worth a tenth as much.[50] That larger estates tended to be taxed at a lower rate is apparent from an analysis of geld liability in the Bedfordshire survey, where holdings valued at £15 T.R.E. or less were likely to be assessed at the rate of one hide per pound, while greater estates tended to owe half as much tax on the pound. Similarly, the inclusion of royal manors in the regression analyses reduces both the significance of the coefficient of determination and the slope of the regression line (see table A6a). An examination of the scattergrams formed by plotting hidage against *valuits* (figs. A1–A11) and an analysis of residuals for Buckinghamshire (table A1a) reveals that the relationship between tax assessment and value was actually *linear* for estates worth £15 or less. The curvilinear form suggested by the statistical analyses of data for all properties seems to be due to a handful of anomalous larger estates whose hidage assessments were far less closely related to their economic productivity.

What are we to make of these results? While the larger and more prosperous estates did pay, on the average, a larger total tax than their more modest neighbors, their tax rate in many instances was not fully proportional to their value. This does not mean that late Anglo-Saxon England had a sophisticated system of regressive taxation, complete with various tax brackets and the administrative machinery that that would imply. A simpler and more historically plausible explanation—and one must never fall into the trap of mistaking statistical models for historical reality—is that many magnates and prominent king's thegns were able to obtain special favor from the king. That this should have been so is quite understandable. For those who benefited most from such favorable assessments were the class upon which the governance of the realm depended. The decision to tax royal estates lightly, for example, proved especially profitable to the shire-reeves who farmed them, the men responsible for the collection of the king's revenues.[51] In effect, then, the Confessor and his advisors were offering the great landowners and the more important royal agents a quid pro quo: a lighter tax burden in return for their willing cooperation in the running of government. This, of course, is only a general conclusion, and many prominent landowners did pay their fair share and more in terms of taxes (the case of Leofwine Cilt of Bedfordshire and Hertfordshire comes immediately to mind).[52] Statistics, in fact, fail to help us understand the tax assessment borne by any particular great estate. In order to do that one must inquire into its tenurial history and its recent owners' standing with the Crown.

"Beneficial hidation" was real enough, but it affected relatively few estates in the south midland circuit. In most instances, an estate received its assessed hidage largely on the basis of its economic productivity, and not as a result of some private bargain struck by the landowner with the king or his agents. What was true in the south Midlands was equally true in Berkshire, where it would also seem that the recruitment of fyrd warriors was grounded firmly in agricultural realities: the more valuable an estate or village, the more warriors it could afford to provision and send on campaign (see table A6). If the "Berkshire rule" or some similar principle relating service to hidage could be detected in the other shires, one would then be justified in concluding that by the mid-eleventh century the Anglo-Saxon kings had devised a system of national defense that systematically utilized the economic resources of their kingdom by rooting the fyrd in land tenure.

But how prevalent was the five-hide rule? Stenton warned that it may have been merely a local custom limited to Berkshire. On Stenton's view, Berkshire was a peculiar county from which it is dangerous to generalize. Not only was this region so far from the sea that it was geographically protected from the ravages of the vikings, but its hide was "small," composed of forty fiscal acres rather than 120.[53] Hollister, on the other hand, considered the five-hide recruitment rule to have been "universal" in the hidated regions of England. In addition to explicit evidence for its existence in Wiltshire and Devon, the latter being anything but a safe inland region with small hides, Hollister pointed to the prevalence of five-hide groupings in virtually every hidated shire, from Staffordshire in the northern Midlands to Devon in the southwest and Essex in the east.[54] He concluded from this that in every one of these shires five hides of land produced one warrior for the king's expeditions. Similarly, the carucated shires of the northern Danelaw seem to have been assessed on a duodecimal pattern, for their reconstructed villages often fall into six-carucate units or multiples thereof.[55] If five-hide groupings suggest a five-hide recruitment rule, Hollister argued, then six-carucate groupings should, by analogy, point to a six-carucate recruitment rule in these shires.[56]

Hollister's reasoning in this matter is open to question. From the most ancient times, hidage was primarily a unit of assessment for the king's food-rent. In the eleventh century, hidage was most conspicuously used to determine an estate's geld liability. At the usual rate of 2s. on the hide, collection of the geld would have been greatly facilitated by five- and ten-hide blocks of land. Thus the mere existence of such groupings of land need not imply anything about late Anglo-Saxon military arrangements. Fiscal rather than military concerns may have determined the decimal groupings found in much of hidated England.

That the positive evidence for the universality of the five-hide rule is circumstantial and inconclusive is hardly surprising in light of the paucity of the sources. Proof for the existence of a national five-hide rule has been sought both in Æthelred II's ship-sokes and in the so-called "promotion laws" found in two early eleventh-century texts associated with Archbishop Wulfstan, *Gethynctho* and the *Northleoda laga*. The arguments fashioned from these, however, are tenuous.

Let us begin with the ship-sokes. The sources do present them as a national system for the construction of ships, and if one grants that each district was precisely three hundred hides and that every vessel outfitted by a ship-soke had a crew of sixty warriors raised from that district, then one could argue that the five-hide rule was the basis of recruitment for the late Anglo-Saxon *scypfyrd* and, a posteriori, for the *landfyrd*. But these are large "ifs," since neither the hidage of the sokes nor the size of the ships is certain. The ship-sokes of the 1008 annal may well have consisted of three hundred hides, as the Oswaldslow and Sherborne evidence would suggest, but one cannot be confident about this in light of the 310-hide figure that appears in every recension of the Chronicle except for "D."[57]

The complement of the "typical" English warship of the late tenth and early eleventh centuries is no more easily determined. Certainly, some ships of this period had sixty-man crews; the celebrated Chronicle entry for 896 which tells of Alfred's creation of a fleet is decisive on this point: "Then King Alfred had 'long ships' built to oppose the Danish warships. They were almost twice as long as the others. Some had sixty oars, some more."[58] Apparently, the sixty-oared long ship was only one type of vessel in Alfred's new navy. In the early eleventh century, Archbishop Ælfric of Canterbury drew up a will in which he left his best ship to the king, along with sixty helmets and sixty coats of mail.[59] Most historians have assumed that the archbishop's ship was manned by sixty rower-warriors, a reasonable enough inference, but far from certain in light of the Gokstad ship's sixty-four shields and thirty-two oarholes.[60] A few years after this, Ælfric's contemporary, Ælfwold, bishop of Crediton, made a bequest to the king of a *scegth* with sixty-four oars. Harmer, who gathered most of the evidence for sixty-man ships, felt that the figures given in the Chronicle (s.a. 1040 and 1041) for the total money levies by Harthacnut for his sailors' wages, the amount that each seaman received, and the total number of ships in the royal fleet, clinched the matter, for her calculations revealed that each ship was manned by a crew of approximately sixty-four men.[61] More recently, M. K. Lawson looked at these same figures with dramatically different results. Following the researches of Stewart Lyon, Lawson took the Chronicle's mark as 10s. 8d. instead of the 13s. 4d. that Harmer assumed, and arrived at an average ship's complement of seventy-nine rowers and one steerman.[62] This would bring it into line both with the eighty-man ship that Godwine gave to Hardacnut in 1040 as a peace-offering for the murder of the ætheling Alfred and with the eleventh-century warship excavated in Roskild fjord.[63] To complicate matters even further, we possess an undated document, probably of the early eleventh century, which strongly implies that the Bishop of London owed only forty-five sailors from his ship-soke,[64] a figure reminiscent of the "twenty-benchers" that were the standard levy ships throughout eleventh- and twelfth-century Scandinavia.[65] Some of the warships that defended Edward the Confessor's England were even smaller than that. The forty ships that Dover and Sandwich provided the king in return for their privileges each had a crew of only twenty-one men.[66] Finally, we must accept the possibility, as inequitable as it might seem, that there was no "typical" levy ship in late Anglo-Saxon England. The ship-sokes may have in fact produced vessels unequal in size and quality. At any rate, there is no proof that levy ships were constructed according to strict royal specifications.

The early eleventh-century "promotion laws" afford no surer foundation for a universal five-hide rule. From these we learn that a ceorl who prospered, so that he accumulated five hides of land assessed to the king's service (*fif hida to cynges utware*), was entitled to the legal status of a thegn.[67] This can be taken to refer to the five-hide rule only if one is willing to assume that a thegn by definition owed personal armed service in respect of his land. To use these documents to establish the universality of the five-hide rule and at the same time to prove that thegns were expected to serve for their holdings is, of course, to argue in circles.

That England had a number of methods for military recruitment in 1066 is not inconceivable; certainly, it possessed a number of different ones before this. Nothing conclusive can be said about the military quotas demanded by English kings in the eighth and ninth centuries, but the one piece of evidence that we do possess, a memorandum drawn up in 801 endorsing a Mercian landbook issued some thirty years before, declares that the holder of a thirty-hide estate in Middlesex, a gesith named Pilheard, was to supply King Coenwulf with "only five men in the necessity of an expedition" (*in expeditionis necessitatem vires .v. tantum mittantur*).[68] In other words, one man was to go from every six hides (this in a shire whose villages were clearly assessed on a decimal basis in the eleventh century). Whether the amount of military service demanded from this land was fixed according to hidage or was the result of a private bargain struck between king and magnate is an unanswerable question. Still, it seems curious that the only evidence we have for quotas before the tenth century fails to support the five-hide rule.

For that matter, the five-hide rule is not supported by the tenth- and early eleventh-century sources either. At the beginning of the tenth century, when the West Saxon dynasty was engaged in the Reconquest, the Crown demanded far more than one warrior from every five hides. The Burghal Hidage, as we have already seen, stipulated that each hide attached to a borough was to supply one man for garrison duty (which, of course, may have been distinct from fyrd service). A decade or so later, Æthelstan decreed in a law issued at Grately, Hampshire, that "every man shall provide two well-mounted men for every plough."[69] In context this seems to refer to the military obligation of burgesses, an extraordinarily heavy burden if the "plough" of Æthelstan's day was anything like its Domesday descendant, an agricultural or cadastral unit roughly equivalent to one hide.

Finally, the Chronicle entry for 1008 describes not only Æthelred's attempt to extend the ship-sokes throughout England but also reports the king's order that every *eight* hides provide a byrnie and a helmet. There is much that is cryptic about this annal. One cannot be certain whether each eight-hide unit was to provide war gear or a warrior. Furthermore, this emergency measure, like so much else undertaken by Æthelred, may have been better in conception than execution, since evidence for its practice is lacking. Still, its existence along with the tenth-century recruitment rules warns us that the military demands of Anglo-Saxon kings need not always have taken the form of one soldier from each five hides or six carucates.

To entertain the notion that a single rule was practiced throughout England in the late Saxon period is to overestimate the uniformity of that society. The author of the *Rectitudines Singularum Personarum*, an early eleventh-century treatise on the rights, duties, and ranks of people on a large West Saxon estate, twice warned his readers against generalizing too readily from his survey, since in his day the customs of shires were various and estate-law was fixed on each estate.[70] We would be well-advised to be as cautious about the five-hide rule. The Confessor's England was precocious in the uniformity of its governance, but even so, its legal and financial organization reflected diverse local customs and traditions. The West Saxons, Mercians, and Danes each boasted their own laws—to say nothing of the customs of the Welsh who dwelled under English rule in the marches.[71]

Although royal taxes were levied throughout England, the methods employed by the Crown to assess and collect its renders exhibited regional peculiarities. As students of Domesday Book well know, the names and meanings of the cadastral units change as one progresses through its folios. The shires of Wessex, Mercia, and the southern Danelaw paid geld according to hides. The northern Danelaw was assessed by carucates; Kent, by sulungs; and East Anglia, by "leets" and "hundreds." Northumbria, about which we know little, seems to have retained elements of an ancient arrangement, perhaps Celtic in origin, by which food-rents were paid into royal manors.

Military arrangements and customs were no less influenced by regionalism. Fyrdwite varied from shire to shire, as did the heriot payments owed to the king.[72] The boroughs present their own problems, for while many were integrated into the military organization of the shire, a number, most prominently the ports of Dover, Sandwich, Romney, and Hythe, seem to have struck individual bargains with the king defining the military service due from them.[73] As is evident from the examples just cited, the location of a borough was an important consideration in determining its fyrd obligation. The burgesses of Hereford and the Welshmen of Archenfield thus bore a considerably heavier military burden in 1066 than did their counterparts in Malmesbury or Exeter, a sensible arrangement in light of the endemic warfare visited on the Welsh border.[74] This regional diversity does not make a universal rule for military recruitment impossible. It does, however, make it unsafe to generalize from the customs of one or two neighboring shires, especially if those shires happened to belong to the same ancient kingdom. In light of the available evidence, it is most reasonable to conclude that one soldier usually served for five hides in the West Saxon shires of Berkshire, Wiltshire, and Devon, and that a similar fyrd arrangement may have obtained elsewhere. Even this would have made England far more uniform in its military organization than most kingdoms of the early Middle Ages.

Although the universality of the five-hide rule in late Anglo-Saxon England cannot be established beyond a reasonable doubt, the assessment of the "common burdens" by hides and carucates can. In Cheshire, for example, the "one hide, one man" principle laid down in the Burghal Hidage for *burhbot* survived into the reign of Edward the Confessor.[75] And while the ship-sokes and the "promotion laws" may not prove the existence of a five-hide rule, they do suggest that the amount of military service one owed the king from one's land was determined by the cadastral rating of that property.[76] This inference is supported by the charter evidence and by Domesday Book. In the second half of the tenth century Bishop Oswald stated explicitly that those who held loanland from the Church of Worcester were obliged to fulfill the service owed to the king from their benefices (*beneficia*), according to the "quantity of land that each possessed" (*secundum . . . terrarum quas quisque possidet quantitem*).[77] The individual leases themselves leave little doubt that by royal service Oswald meant the "common burdens," the *cynges utwaru* of the "promotion laws."[78] If we compare Oswald's *læns* with those granted in the mid-eleventh century by Ealdred, his successor in the see of Worcester, it becomes quite clear that the phrase *quantitas terrarum* of Oswald's letter meant in fact the hidage of the leased land.[79]

Certain passages in Domesday Book suggest that military service was customarily assessed in terms of hides and carucates (and sulungs?), even in those counties in which the five-hide rule cannot be shown to have existed. Bedfordshire provides a good example of this. The borough of Bedford was never hidated for the geld, but whenever the king went on campaign, whether by land or by sea, the town "defended itself for a half hundred" (*pro dimidio hundredo se defendebat*), that is, it was required to send and provision as many men as an honor of fifty hides.[80] On its face, this text does not seem very helpful. Certainly, it cannot be used to prove that Bedfordshire had the five-hide rule, unless one wishes to draw a questionable inference from the fact that fifty hides comprise ten five-hide units. Nevertheless, the passage does reveal something about the basis of fyrd service in that shire. In mid-eleventh-century Bedfordshire, the statement that a holding acquitted itself on the king's campaigns for fifty hides had a meaning for contemporaries. In other words, this shire must have had some standard rule, similar to that practiced in Berkshire. Furthermore, this rule must have been so well established that the jurors for Bedford and the Domesday commissioners responsible for the south Midlands felt that it was unnecessary to define it.

Attention should also be paid to the wording of the Bedford entry. "Pro N hidis se defendit" is one of the standard formulae employed by the Domesday scribes to express the number of hides (or carucates) belonging to an estate.[81] Although this phrase has often been thought to refer to geld liability,[82] its use in the Bedford passage implies that it had wider connotations. One might in fact argue that the Domesday term "geld" meant more than merely "danegeld," subsuming, in fact, all the obligations owed to the king from a holding. In other words, it expressed the *cynges utwaru*. We need not rely solely upon the Bedford entry for this. In the Lincolnshire Domesday survey we read that "the royal borough of Stamford gave geld T.R.E. for twelve-and-a-half hundreds for expeditions by land and by sea and for danegeld."[83] Surely, the phrase "dedit geldum T.R.E. pro .xii. hundredis et dimidio" has the same meaning as "pro .xii. hundredis et dimidio se defendit," and both ought to be translated as "it acquitted itself for twelve-and-a-half hundreds."

The notion that the common Domesday formula, "pro N hidis se defendit," referred to military obligations as well as to geld liability is supported by the wording of a law issued by King Cnut (an important piece of evidence to which we will return in the next chapter):

> He who with the cognisance of the shire has performed the service de-
> manded from a landowner on expeditions either by sea or by land [*se
> the land gewerod haebbe on scypfyrde and on landfyrd*] shall hold [his
> land] unmolested by litigation during his life.[84]

The word *werian* corresponds exactly to the Domesday term *defendere:* both mean "to defend" and, by extension, to acquit of an obligation.[85] From the use of *werian* in this doom, it would appear that in the early eleventh century a landowner primarily "defended" his property by rendering the military services due the king from it. If this usage of "defend" also obtains in Domesday Book, as the Bedford and Stamford passages suggest, then one would have to conclude from the appearance of the formula "pro N hidis defendit" in the Domesday surveys of the south Midland counties and elsewhere that fyrd service was regularly levied upon the basis of hides or some other cadastral unit.[86] Hence fyrd service "in the time of King Edward" was conceived to be a type of royal taxation which, like the danegeld, varied according to an estate's value.

The use of the term "geld" for military service should not surprise us; fyrd service comprised not only armed service but fiscal renders, as the Domesday custumals constantly remind us. Fyrdwite is the most obvious of these, but hardly the only one. The Berkshire customs stipulate not only the extent of service, but the amount of provisions that must be supplied to a warrior,[87] and a number of other boroughs in the time of Edward the Confessor either supplemented or commuted their military service for cash.[88] Nor should we be misled by the sacrosanctity of the "common burdens" in the landbooks; fyrd service may have been universal, but it need not have taken the form of sending armed contingents to the king's host. Ely Abbey, for example, acquitted its lands of *fyrdinge* through the payment of 10,000 eels a year to the king,[89] and the scattered references in Domesday Book to lands that "aided in the king's expeditions" imply that lesser landowners T.R.E. made similar, if less interesting and eccentric, arrangements with the Crown. In context, these passages seem to denote fiscal aid rather than armed service. This would explain how a man could hold only six bovates of land and still "aid in the host." Even more to the point, when Domesday Book does define what "aid" was expected, it takes the form of payments in cash or kind. The inhabitants of Maldon in Essex thus "aided in the host" by finding a horse for the army (*inuenire caballum in exercitu*) and providing money toward the construction of a ship.[90] The financial profits accruing from the fiscal renders associated with the fyrd might explain why landowners were so anxious to receive expeditio from their lands.[91]

Whether or not the fyrd in 1066 was recruited through a national system based on units of five hides and six carucates, we can be fairly certain that military service was levied on the basis of cadastral units that reflected real economic conditions. Once again one is reminded that William conquered a realm that was far more sophisticated administratively than most of the duchies and kingdoms of western Europe. England's Carolingian-style government was not only capable of taxing its subjects and creating a unified currency but was also able to exploit the wealth of the kingdom systematically for its defense.

SIX

Book-Right and Military Obligation

If military service in late Anglo-Saxon England was indeed "rooted in the soil," was the obligation to render it territorial, tenurial, or personal? To put it another way, who served and why? The answer to this question forms the very heart of the dispute between the followers of Stenton and those of Eric John.[1] Fragmentary as the sources are, the answer they give is clear. The obligation to serve in the royal host rested in the eleventh century upon a dual foundation of land tenure and lordship. On the one hand, those who possessed land in book-right were obliged to render the military service due from their holdings, just as they owed the payment of geld. On the other hand, those thegns who were personally commended to the king were expected to attend him on campaign if so ordered. The attempt to characterize these duties as "Germanic" or "feudal" is fruitless. Military obligation had evolved and changed as the king's need for and ability to exact armed service from his subjects had changed. Just as English law on the eve of the Conquest was a hodgepodge of archaic custom and royal innovation that varied according to locale, thus preserving if not the reality then at least the memory of independent kingdoms and peoples, so the defense of the realm depended upon a system that had developed organically over the centuries and which reflected the military history of England. In a sense, late Anglo-Saxon military obligation looked back both to the seventh-century fyrds of King Oswiu and the reforms of Alfred and his successors. This is quite apparent when we examine the relationship between fyrd service and bookland.

As we have seen, fyrd service as a burden upon the land was an outgrowth of the king's attempt to retain control over the land that he had granted out in book-right and over the men who held it. The legal compilations of the early eleventh century attest to the success of this royal policy. By the reign of Cnut bookland was conceived as land for which one performed *fyrdfæreld*. Thus II *Cnut*, c. 79, quoted in the previous chapter, stipulates that if a landowner had "defended his land on campaign either by sea or land" (*se the land gewerod hæbbe on scypfyrde and on landfyrde*), he was both to hold the land undisturbed by litigation during his days and to have the right to dispose of it as he pleased upon his death.[2] Although this text does not use the term "bocland," its language leaves no doubt as to the type of tenure acquitted by attendance in the fyrd, for free disposal forms the very essence of book-right. One may infer from this, then, that a landholder's title to land possessed in book-right obliged him to "defend" it in person on the king's campaigns. Conversely, we learn from other laws and the charters that one who deserted the royal host or broke the king's peace while in the field forfeited his land.[3] All land that he held on loan reverted to the lord who had granted it to him, and all his bookland passed back into the king's hand.[4]

The *Rectitudines Singularum Personarum,* a work attributed to the early eleventh century, affords further insight into the relationship between bookland and fyrd service. This tract sets forth the rights and obligations of the lord of an estate (probably in Wessex) and of the various groups of men who dwelled upon it under him.[5] The text begins with the holder of the tenure, termed here a "thegn":

> Thegn's law. The law of the thegn is that he be entitled to [*wyrthe*[6]] his book-right, and that he shall contribute [*thæt he . . . do*] three things in respect of his land: armed service [*fyrdfæreld*], and the repairing of fortresses [*burhbote*] and work on bridges [*brycegeweorc*]. [§ 1] Also in respect of many estates, further service [or land-dues: *landriht*] arises on the king's order [or summons: *cyninges gebanne*] such as service connected with the deer fence at the king's residence, and equipping a guard ship [*frithscip*[7]], and guarding the coast [*sæweard*], and guarding the lord [*heafodweard*], and military watch [*fyrdweard*], almsgiving and church dues, and many other things.[8]

Military service was thus the fundamental obligation of the thegn (in

Wessex, at any rate). But the *Rectitudines* does not connect such service to the "freedom" of the thegn. Rather, the lord of the estate owed the performance of the "common burdens" as a condition of holding his land in book-right. Morever, he owed this service not to some abstract "state" or "folk" but to his *lord,* the king. While the three "common burdens" may have been the most prominent services due from a thegn's bookland, they hardly constituted all the service that the king could require from his thegn in respect of his land. If we examine the duties enumerated in chapter 1, § 1 and compare them with those owed by the *geneat,* enumerated in chapter 2, we find that the relationship between the king and his thegn paralleled in some respects that which existed between the thegn and his tenant, the *geneat.*

> Geneat's right. Geneat-right is various according to what is fixed in respect of the estate: in some he must pay rent and contribute a pasturage swine a year, ride and perform carrying service and furnish means of carriage [*ridan & auerian & lade lædan*], work and entertain his lord, reap and mow, cut deer hedges and keep up places from which deer may be shot, build and fence the lord's house, bring strangers to the village, pay church dues and alms money, act as guard to his lord [*heafodwearde healdan*], take care of the horses and carry messages far and near wheresoever he is directed [*horsewearde, ærendian fyr swa nyr, swa hwyder swa him mon to tæcth*].[9]

If the geneat had to "keep up places from which deer may be shot," his lord had to provide similar services at the king's residence;[10] and while the thegn was responsible for guarding the king's person and providing military watch in his lands, his geneat was obliged to perform the same duties on his behalf.[11] It would seem that the author of the *Rectitudines* viewed bookland as a privileged but still dependent form of tenure. The thegn was the lord of the estate, but he held his land *de rege,*[12] rendering service to the king for it, just as his own man, the geneat, held of and rendered service to him.

The *Rectitudines* asserts that a thegn was to "do three things in respect of his land." It would be rash, however, to assume from the use of "do" in the text that thegns were expected to acquit the "common burdens" through their own labor. Presumably, wealthy thegns would not have repaired fortresses and bridges with their own hands or personally discharged their obligations at the king's deer hedge or kept watch on the seacoast. Rather, they would have been responsible for such services. The third chapter of the *Rectitudines,* which enumerates the duties of the cottar, a free tenant endowed with five or more acres, supports this view. The cottar, we are told, must "acquit his lord's demesne [*werige his hlafordes inland*], if so ordered, by keeping watch on the seacoast [*sæward*] and by working at the king's deer hedge [*æt cyniges deorhege*] and such things according to his condition [*æt swilean thingan, swilc his maeth sy*]." We hear an echo of this last clause in the Lancashire Domesday's description of the inhabitants and customs of "the land between the Ribble and Mersey Rivers." The thegns of this locality, king's men of modest wealth, each living on a hide or so of royal land, were obliged to "build the king's lodges, and whatever pertained to them, fisheries, woodland enclosures, and stag-beats, just as if they were villagers [*sicut villani*]."[13] "Sicut villani" can only mean that thegns ordinarily did not perform such menial labor but could be required to do so by local custom. We are led to conclude from these and similar passages in Domesday Book that thegns and peasants rendered different sorts of service.[14] Although men of thegnly rank sometimes labored at deer hedges and performed other such manual labor in the service of the king, they were not ordinarily expected to do so. All but the most humble of thegns would have dispatched peasant tenants, cottars and geburs, to take care of these tasks.

Was the labor necessary for the upkeep of fortresses and bridges also performed by peasants? One would assume so, but here the *Rectitudines* proves to be of little value, since the upkeep of neither appears among the obligations of its cottars and geburs. The text simply states that the bookholder was responsible for maintaining the bridges and fortifications in his neighborhood; it does not specify who was to perform the actual work. Once again Domesday Book must be called on to fill the gap. The Domesday survey of Chester relates that the royal reeve was wont in the time of King Edward to call up one man from each hide of that shire for the repair of the city walls, and that the lord of that man was responsible for his appearance. If someone failed to appear, a 40s. fine was to be paid, not, however, by the delinquent peasant but by his lord.[15] Apparently, the thegns of Cheshire "did" burhbot in respect of their land by making sure that their peasants answered the reeve's summons, much as the thegn of the *Rectitudines* acquitted himself of his obligation at the king's deer hedge. The Cheshire custumal suggests that while the lords of bookland may have owed burhbot and the related service of *brycegeweorc* as a condition of their tenure, their peasant tenants actually performed the necessary labor.

The third "common burden," *fyrdfæreld*, was different. Bookholders were not only responsible for supplying troops to the king, they acquitted their land personally in his host. If the *Rectitudines* is ambiguous on this point, Cnut's laws are not. As we have seen, II *Cnut,* c. 79 states explicitly that landholders defended their land "on ship-fyrd and on land-fyrd," and that such service was to be done in full view of the shire. Of course, it is possible that the "defended" (*gewerod*) of this doom meant no more than "acquitted the land of its military obligations," but such a possibility seems unlikely in light of the other two laws in this series. Taken together, II *Cnut,* caps. 77 through 79 draw a picture of a fyrd manned by landholders, in which commended men fought at the side of their lords. Thus if a warrior were to desert his lord out of cowardice while on campaign, he was to lose his life and property (II *Cnut,* c. 77). But if a man were to distinguish himself in battle by falling by the side of his lord, his lord was to remit the payment of his heriot and his heirs were to succeed to his landed estate (II *Cnut,* c. 78). In view of this and the distinctly martial connotation of the word "thegn" in the texts of the tenth and eleventh centuries, one may reasonably assume that the first requirement of the "thegn's law" of the *Rectitudines* was that he serve in the fyrd "in respect of his land."

The later law codes lend support to our construction of the nature of bookland in the *Rectitudines,* indirectly suggesting that bookland was a dependent tenure held directly of the king. According to the dooms, the possession of such a tenure placed a man into a special relationship with the king. In effect, they represented the king as the landholder's own *landhlaford.* For just as a territorial lord was to be responsible for the good behavior of those who dwelled under him and entitled to the fines incurred by them,[16] so I *Æthelred,* c. 1, § 14 represents the king as possessed of the exclusive right to amerce those who held bookland.[17] The holder of the book was, in fact, so closely associated with the king that he could not be forced to pay compensation or answer for a crime unless a king's reeve was present.[18] What makes this piece of legislation all the more remarkable is how well it dovetails with III *Æthelred,* c. 11, which states that no one but the king should have jurisdiction [*socne*] over a king's thegn.[19] While neither the law codes nor Domesday Book explicitly describes the king as the personal lord of every bookholder,[20] nevertheless, the two laws cited above strongly suggest that the holder of such tenure enjoyed a relationship to the king analogous to the one created by the act of commendation.

Even the interposition of some other lord between the king and the bookholder did not affect the royal interest and rights over his book. The king continued to assert and exercise his authority over such land, exacting from it the *utwaru* owed him. And just as land held on loan from some lord reverted to that lord if his man made forfeiture,[21] so all bookland passed back into the king's hand, no matter whom the landholder claimed as his mediate lord.[22]

Once the connection between bookland tenure and royal lordship is understood, certain difficulties in the Domesday passages concerning fyrd service are resolved, and the basis of military obligation in late Anglo-Saxon England becomes far clearer. Without any doubt, the Worcestershire Domesday survey provides the most complete evidence for a study of this topic.[23] The customs of this county read:

> When the king goes against the enemy, should anyone summoned by his edict remain, if he is a man so free that he has his soke and sake, and can go with his land to whomever he wishes, he is in the king's mercy for all of his land. But if the free man of some other lord has stayed away from the host and *his lord has led [duxerit] another in his place,* he will pay 40s. to his lord who received the summons. But if nobody at all has gone in his place, he himself shall pay his lord 40s., but his lord shall pay the entire amount to the king[24] [emphasis added].

Although this passage is primarily concerned with the king's fiscal interests in the fyrd, that is, with the forfeitures that he could claim if someone failed to fulfill his military service,[25] it also illuminates the nature of the obligation to serve the king on campaign and the organization of the royal host. The text identifies two separate categories of free men who attend the king on expedition. The first is clearly composed of men of considerable rank, for they are described as "so free" that they not only hold their lands by book-right, indicated in the text by the stock formula for the right of free disposal,[26] but also enjoy rights of jurisdiction, sake and soke, over those who dwelled upon their estates. Let us label this group A. The second category of fyrdmen in this shire, B, is also made up of free men, and this is not at all surprising when one remembers that to be "fyrd-worthy," one had to be free.[27] But all similarity between the two groups ends here. In almost every other respect, they seem to differ. The text speaks of A as being summoned to the fyrd by the king's edict; B apparently receives no such summons. If a man from group A fails to respond to the king's call, all of his land may be lost to the king; one of group B, on the contrary, faces no more than fyrdwite, a money fine of 40 shillings, for neglecting the host, and this money is given not to the king, but to the man's lord. And while the text makes a point of defining the tenurial privileges enjoyed by A, it never specifically mentions B's rights over the land, a silence that eloquently attests to B's lesser freedom.

In fact, while A is identified by his free tenure, B seems to be identified more on the basis of lordship. For this group is introduced in the text with a cryptic statement concerning commendation: they are the free men of "some other lord" (*cuiuscunque alterius domini*). But other than whom? The Domesday jurors have handed us a puzzle. The difference in lordship was deemed both worthy of mention and yet so obvious that it called for no further elaboration. To comprehend its meaning one must know who the lords of A and B were. It is reasonable to surmise that the lord of group A was in fact the king himself. This would explain why it was unnecessary to name him explicitly in the text; the Worcestershire customs, after all, were royal customs set forth by the local jurors upon the demand and for the benefit of the king. Nor need we rest this identification solely upon the logic of this argument. Rather, one should ask who would have been the lord of a man who possessed not only his lands in book-right but the perquisites of justice as well. The answer, of course, is the king, for only he could book land and confer franchises of immunity. Indeed, II *Cnut*, c. 12 describes a grant of jurisdiction as a special honor that a king would bestow upon a favored subject.[28]

The fyrdmen of group B were therefore the men of lords other than the king. The text itself gives some reason to believe that they were in fact commended to members of group A, for their lords are described as the recipients of the king's summons, and this, as one may remember, is a characteristic of the fyrd warriors of group A. The Domesday Book survey of this shire and "Hemming's Cartulary," a work concerned with the lands of the Church of Worcester and ascribed to an English monk of the late eleventh century,[29] lend support to this thesis. When one peruses the folios of the Worcestershire Domesday and the eleventh-century charters relating to the county, at least one great lord stands out: the bishop of Worcester, the lord of the triple hundred of Oswaldslow.[30] In the eleventh century the bishop exercised regalian authority within Oswaldslow, and among the services that he demanded from his tenants was the performance of armed service upon the king's expeditions, whether by land or by sea.[31] While technically this service belonged to the *cyninges utwaru*, the bishop held his lands "so freely" that he alone answered for the royal service owed from them. As Domesday Book stated:

The Church of St. Mary of Worcester has one hundred called Oswaldslow, in which lie 300 hides. From these the bishop of the same church has by a constitution of ancient times [*a constitutione antiquorum temporum*][32] all the profits of jurisdiction [*redditiones socharum*] and all customary dues pertaining therein to the demesne support and to the king's service [*regis servitium*] and his own, so that no sheriff [Hemming's *indiculum* adds here "or *exactor* of royal service"[33]] can have any claim there for any plea or any other cause. Thus the whole county witnesses.[34]

The landholders of Oswaldslow thus "defended" their land to the bishop rather than to the king or to one of his agents. The exclusion of the sheriff meant that the bishop himself would have been responsible for bringing his complement of fyrd-warriors into the field, and indeed, in 1066 we find that the bishop had a tenant named Eadric, whom Hemming describes as "the pilot of the bishop's ship and the leader of the same bishop's military forces owed to the king's service [*ductor exercitus eiusdem episcopi ad servitium regis*]."[35] Undoubtedly, the bishop of Worcester should be numbered among the lords of the fyrd-men of group B.

Although the bishop of Worcester's position in the shire was exceptional, there were others "so free that they had their soke and sake and could go with their land to whomsoever they wished." Three other churches, Evesham, Pershore, and Westminster, held between them the lordship of four hundreds.[36] St. Peter's of Westminster possessed its lands "as quit and free of all claims as King Edward held in his demesne,"[37] and all enjoyed the pleas of their free men and most forfeitures that they might make.[38] As Domesday Book put it in its description of Pershore, the abbot "has the forfeitures from his 100 hides as he ought to have from his own land . . . and all others enjoy the same from their lands."[39] The implication seems to be that in Worcestershire book-right ordinarily carried with it sake and soke over the inhabitants of the estate. If this is correct, then a king's thegn such as Beorhtwine who, in Hemming's words, had his land "freely by inheritance, having, that is, the power of giving it to whomsoever he wished, since it was his paternal inheritance, for which he owed service to no man but the king" would also have had jurisdictional rights and, consequently, would have been responsible for the fyrd service arising from the lands of his tenants.[40] These pre-Conquest grants of liberty had in fact alienated so much of the profits of royal justice that the sheriff was provoked to complain in the shire return: "In this county there are twelve hundreds;

seven are so quit, the shire says, that the sheriff has nothing in them, and therefore he [the sheriff] says that he loses much in farm [*in firma*]."[41] And if we can generalize from the triple hundred of Oswaldslow, the sheriff had also been deprived of his military command in these seven hundreds. The Worcestershire military customs, concerned as they are with the money fines arising from neglect of the fyrd, can only be fully appreciated if read in light of this county's jurisdictional arrangements.

An analysis of the Worcestershire customs thus suggests that there were two distinct grades of fyrdmen in this shire. On the one hand, there were the great landowners, the king's prelates, agents and thegns, all of whom held privileged tenures and seignorial rights over the lands of other free men. These were the men to whom the king addressed his summonses and writs.[42] On the other hand, there were lesser fyrdmen drawn from the lower rungs of free society, 200-shilling men who were commended to and sometimes held their land under the jurisdiction of the local magnates.[43] (In practice, of course, these two groups were not so distinct as the shire customs suggest, since thegns in this county and others occasionally held land not only by book-right but also as tenants of the great churches or of greater lords. The Domesday Book custumals, one must remember, present only a simplified paradigm of how royal administration *was supposed* to operate. They were not concerned with anomalies, which must have been dealt with on an ad hoc basis.)

The gulf between the social and legal status of the two groups of warriors in Worcestershire helps explain the discrepancy in the penalties they faced for neglect of military service. The fyrdmen of group A stood in an especially close relationship to the king. They held their land by book-right, which made them the king's justiciables; they themselves possessed by royal favor rights of jurisdiction; and they were the king's own men. This threefold tie to the king aggravated their offense. Although the law codes regard simple neglect of the "common burdens" as emendable by the payment of a *wite*,[44] the fyrdmen of group A were guilty of more than mere neglect. They had received a personal summons to attend their royal lord in battle, and their failure to respond was willful disobedience.[45] Loss of their property was appropriate punishment. As king's thegns they were entitled to their bookland, to use the language of the *Rectitudines*, but their rank also obliged them to "do three things in regard to their land," one of which was the performance of fyrd service.[46] Both the refusal to acquit his land as he ought and his despite of the king's just command called into question a thegn's "worthiness" to hold the book.[47] It is not surprising that the king should have regarded it as having been forfeited into his hands.[48]

The situation of the fyrdmen of group B was entirely different. They held their tenures either by loan from a lord other than the king, from whom they "could not recede" (that is, whose permission was needed if they wished to place this land under the protection of another lord),[49] or under his seignory. A fyrdman of this sort was obligated to serve his lord, not the king, and his lord was the one responsible for the *cynges utwaru* arising from the tenement. Simply put, the king demanded a certain number of fyrd warriors from a certain number of hides. Whoever held an estate "freely" or possessed jurisdiction over it was answerable for those soldiers, the precise identity of whom was a matter of little consequence to the king. A lord was thus quit with the king if he brought his full quota of provisioned warriors on campaign. If one of the fyrdmen whom the magnate expected to go remained behind, the lord was expected to find a suitable replacement. The absentee, for his part, was amerced forty shillings, payable to the man he had wronged, his lord. The king, having received the required complement of warriors from the magnate's lands, stood outside this transaction. But if the lord for some reason was unable to secure a substitute, and the king received less than his due, the lord owed the king compensation for his dereliction. Hence the forty shillings that the nobleman exacted from the absent fyrdman were turned over by him in full to the king, which meant, in practice, to the sheriff. The failure of the lesser fyrdman to accompany his landhlaford was viewed simultaneously as the fault of the lord, for which *wite* had to be paid to the king, and an injury to the lord, for which he was compensated by the wrongdoer.[50]

In a number of ways the Domesday customs of Berkshire resemble those of Worcestershire. The Berkshire text reads in full:

> If the king sent an army anywhere, only one soldier [*miles*] went from five hides, and for his provision or pay [*eius uictum uel stipendium*], four shillings were given him from each hide for his two months of service. The money, however, was not sent to the king but given to the soldiers [*militibus*]. If anyone summoned to serve in an expedition failed to do so, he forfeited all his land to the king. If anyone for the sake of remaining behind promised to send another in his place, and nevertheless, he who should have been sent remained behind, his lord [*dominus eius*] was freed of obligation by the payment of 50 shillings.[51]

Both this and the Worcestershire custumal are concerned with *royal* expeditions and the penalties to be assessed against one who fails to fulfill his obligations to the king. In both shires the penalty varied according to the gravity of the offense. Those who ignored personal summonses to attend the host forfeited all their land to the king. If, however, the man of some lord promised to send another on campaign in his place, and that substitute failed to appear, the lord of the defaulter was liable for a *wite* of fifty shillings, but once this money was tendered to the king, the lord was quit.

The major difficulty presented by the Berkshire passage is in reconciling the "five-hide rule" with the king's summons. Stenton argued that every landed thegn received a personal summons to battle because of his rank. In addition, each had the entirely distinct responsibility to see that "the free men upon his estate served in accordance with local custom," that is, with the "five-hide rule."[52] In Berkshire, then, according to Stenton, a landed thegn was obligated to see that one peasant warrior appeared in the host from every five hides of land that he possessed. Hollister countered by asserting that "the entire Berkshire passage should be regarded as a self-consistent unit which refers neither to thegns exclusively nor to peasants exclusively but rather to warrior-representatives of five-hide districts, whether thegn or peasant."[53] In Hollister's view, the summons was sent to an important lord, who in turn summoned the "warrior-representatives" from each of the five-hide military units on his estate.[54] The text itself is vague enough to permit either interpretation. All it says is: "If anyone summoned to serve in a expedition failed to go, he forfeited all his land to the king." Nothing in this implies that every Berkshire thegn received a personal summons from the king. Nor is there any clear indication of the relationship, if any, that existed between the milites who served for five hides and those summoned to attend the fyrd.

Is it then possible to identify these landholders and relate their obligation for military service to the "five-hide rule"? The most fruitful approach to this problem lies in examining the Berkshire customs in light of those of Worcestershire. The Berkshire survey, unlike Worcestershire's, is silent about the types of tenures forfeited by those who failed to heed the king's ban. However, since only bookland and royal loanland could be forfeited into the king's hand, it is reasonable to conclude that those who received summonses to serve in the Berkshire hundreds of the royal fyrd held their land either by book-right or on loan from the king. In other words, the primary responsibility for defending the king in battle fell in this shire upon the lords of bookland—the same sort of men summoned in Worcestershire—and the king's own demesne thegns. The identity of the former is known from the various entries in the Domesday survey; the existence of the latter may be inferred from the Berkshire customs themselves. The customs describe the *heriot*, or "relief," as the Norman scribe termed it, due from "the demesne thegns or soldiers of the king" (*taini uel milites regis dominici*) in this shire, and it is quite possible that such men were king's retainers maintained on the royal lands.[55] For what it is worth, their heriot consisted of all their weapons along with two horses, one saddled and the other unsaddled. Whatever their obligation to serve may have been, these men at least possessed the accoutrements of fyrd warriors.

The Berkshire thegn with five hides of land, then, was responsible for the appearance of one soldier in the host and ordinarily would have served as the fyrd warrior himself. (One might add here that in the case of royal expeditions, especially during the troubled reign of Æthelred II, the unexcused absence of a great thegnly landholder from the king's fyrd would have been cause for extreme suspicion and perhaps an accusation of treason.) If for reasons of health or sex the bookholder was unable to discharge the obligation in person, he or she would have had to send an acceptable replacement to the sheriff along with, I would expect, a plausible explanation for the substitution. A lord whose estates were rated at more than five hides had to find additional warriors upon the basis of one soldier from every five hides. If he failed to produce the requisite number of fyrdmen, he, like his counterpart in Worcestershire, would have had to compensate the king with money. If, however, he ignored the summons entirely, his land would then have been at the mercy of the king.

In actual practice, of course, landholdings did not always fall neatly into the schema described in the Berkshire customs. The small landowner with fewer than five hides may have had to enter into some arrangement with his neighbors to acquit his land of its military obligations,[56] not unlike the military recruitment system instituted by Charlemagne in the early ninth century, whereby free men endowed with three or four manses were to equip themselves and serve in the host, while those with less land were to combine to arm and provision one of their number.[57] A second complication arose due to the fact that some ecclesiastical tenants were men of considerable local or even national prominence, holding from the church for political rather than economic reasons. (In this regard, the Confessor's and the Conqueror's England were not dissimilar.) Thus the same individual could have at times served in the fyrd as a bookholder and other times as a subtenant, depending upon the particular tenure for which he was answering. It is even possible that local magnates who held thegnland would have found themselves answering royal summonses to the fyrd personally while acquitting their obligations as subtenants through stipendiary warriors. What is to be emphasized here, however, is that the Berkshire customs describe a *tenurial* service owed to the Crown by those who held immediately of the Crown. This service was the "common burden" termed *fyrdfæreld* in the charters of the period. The customs merely define the obligation as it existed in this particular shire on the eve of the Conquest.

The proposed characterization of fyrd service in the Berkshire and Worcestershire Domesday custumals as a tenurial due normally discharged by the landholder himself receives strong support from two entries in the Lincolnshire Domesday survey. The first crops up in the description of a "manor":

> In Covenham [Ludborough Wapentake] Alsi and Chetel and Turuer had 3.5 carucates of land [assessed] to the geld [*ad geldum*]. . . . Chetel and Turuer were brothers, and after their father's death they divided the land, in such wise however that when Chetel was doing the king's service he should have his brother Turuer's aid.[58]

The second is found in the *clamores* section appended to the account of the shire:

> Siwate and Alnod and Fenchel and Aschil divided their father's land amongst them equally, share and share alike, and held it in such wise that if a royal campaign was necessary [*ita tenuerunt ut si opus fuit expeditione regis*], and Siwate could go, the other brothers assisted him [*alii fratres iuuerunt eum*]. After him [Siwate], another went, and Siwate with the others assisted him; and thus with respect to them all. Siwate, nevertheless [*tamen*], was the king's man [*homo regis*].[59]

Both of these are concerned with bookland held "in parage" and reveal how such holdings were acquitted of the king's utware.[60] While the exact arrangement whereby the king was provided with a fyrd warrior appears to have been private, the military service was clearly the responsibility of the landholder(s). The use of such phrases as "they divided the land in such wise" or "they held it in such wise" shows that the Domesday jurors conceived of fyrd service as a necessary condition of tenure. Thus all the brothers owed personal service in the king's host in respect of their land. Because estates held in parage were deemed to constitute a single holding for purposes of the king's utware regardless of how many individuals enjoyed an interest in the property, only one of the owners was required to attend the fyrd.[61] Those who remained at home would assist the one who went, presumably with arms, provisions, and salary.

We do not possess a sufficient amount of evidence to explain with any certainty why one individual holding in parage was chosen over another to serve the king in arms. There were probably a multiplicity of reasons, and each arrangement may well have been unique. In the case of Siwate and his brothers, the personal commendation of the fyrdman may have been a crucial factor in the decision. The text's emphasis upon Siwate's status as a homo regis suggests that he was doubly obliged to follow the king into battle, first as a king's man and second as a bookholder. Of the four brothers, he was therefore the natural candidate to serve as the fyrdman for their joint lands, since he would have had to render such service anyway. A calculus of this sort probably took place whenever kinsmen held bookland jointly.

In Lincolnshire, as in Worcestershire and Bedfordshire, the lords of bookland personally discharged the military service due from their holdings. And this seems to have held true for both large and small landowners. While Chetel and Turuer may have held fewer than three-and-a-half carucates between them,[62] Godwine, Siwate's father, may have possessed as many as twenty carucates of land, worth approximately twelve pounds per annum.[63] Furthermore, we know from the claims advanced by their Norman successors, the bishop of Durham and Eudo fitz Spirewic, that Siwate and his brother held their lands with sake and soke.[64] Apparently, they were men of some standing in the shire.

The fyrd service described in the Berkshire and Worcestershire customs is thus best understood as a tenurial obligation arising from book-right. Stenton's attempt to contrast the personal duty of each thegn to serve the king in arms with his responsibility as a landowner to see that the peasants on his estates and those under his jurisdiction fulfilled *their* obligation to serve in the territorial fyrd, an obligation that derived from the ancient duty of all free men to defend the nation,[65] involves a strained reading of the relevant texts. And although Hollister's interpretation is on the whole more convincing, he too places insufficient emphasis upon the tenurial aspect of military service. His insistence upon the phrase the "territorial fyrd,"[66] while accurately representing the organization of the host by hundred and shire under local royal agents, underplays the crucial fact that the obligation to serve lay not so much upon the land as upon the landholders, and then only upon those who held by book-right or by royal loan.

On one crucial point I agree with Stenton: territorial lords endowed with jurisdictional rights not only acquitted their own bookland of the "common burdens" but were also responsible for the military service of the sokemen, liberi homines, radcnihts, and other fyrd-worthy land-holders whose soke belonged to them. In some instances this involved lords assuming the military responsibilities and powers of the sheriff within their franchises, which for all practical purposes became private hundreds. We have already examined in some detail the workings of this system in Worcestershire and Berkshire, and it is likely that a similar situation prevailed throughout most of eastern and northern England. The Domesday surveys of the Danelaw shires reveal a region charac-terized by a well-developed system of territorial soke, possibly older than the tenth-century hundreds and wapentakes, in which a privileged lord administered justice and collected renders from several outlying villages and holdings attached to a central manor.[67] The Domesday soke-districts of the northern and eastern Danelaw resemble in many respects the centena-like districts that formed the basis of royal admin-istration in pre-viking Wessex, East Anglia, and Northumbria.[68] Whether they are relics of this age, as some have thought, or products of the viking period is difficult to ascertain.[69] What is certain is that these franchises were based upon regalian rights. The lords of the Dane-law sokes, whose names are carefully listed in the Domesday surveys of Lincolnshire, Yorkshire, Derbyshire, and Nottinghamshire,[70] enjoyed not only sake and soke and toll and team over their men but also "royal customs," which probably comprised both services and fiscal renders that ordinarily supported the king and his agents. Such rights could only be legitimately bestowed by royal gift (although in practice they were sometimes usurped). It seems likely that those so endowed exer-cised the same military powers within their franchises that the bishop of Worcester did within his.

The whole subject of territorial soke remains obscure, in large part because of Domesday Book's cavalier and often haphazard treatment of socage.[71] The Norman conquerors apparently placed a greater em-phasis upon personal commendation than on soke-rights, and this has left its mark on the Inquest. Hidden within its folios is a vast system of territorial/jurisdictional lordship that may be impossible to recon-struct from its presentation in Domesday Book. Researchers who have attempted to do so have been stymied from the start by the text's inconsistent use of the very term "soca," which might mean "belonging to the soke of an estate" or might merely denote that the holding was "sokeland," that is, land attached to a manor by the commendation of the sokeman who held it.[72] The difference was crucial to the Anglo-Saxons, whose conception of lordship could well accommodate a man being commended to one or more lords, while belonging to the soke of still another. Much remains to be done on the problem of soke-rights. For the purposes of the present study it is enough to know that sake and soke played an important part in the organization and recruitment of the fyrd, and that such rights were a source of military obligation in England on the eve of the Conquest.

Those who held great estates or soke-districts could not acquit their military obligations through personal service alone. The king required such men to send to the host a contingent of warriors, the size of which was to be determined by the cadastral assessment charged against their property. Preferably, the lord of the estate would lead his men himself, but because some landowners were incapable of bearing arms, the king willingly accepted the services of capable substitutes. But who were these fyrdmen, these "milites" of the Berkshire customs, and why did they follow the landholder into battle? Although the available evidence precludes a definitive answer to these questions, one thing at least seems clear: fyrd-warriors were not peasants who alternated between the plough and the sword.

SEVEN

The Anglo-Saxon Milites

As we saw in chapter three, the division of society into three orders—those who labored, those who fought, and those who prayed—goes back to Alfred's reign. By the first decade of the eleventh century this social classification had become so firmly established that the two most distinguished clerical writers of the age, Abbot Ælfric of Eynsham and Archbishop Wulfstan of York, presented it in their works as the proper and necessary ordering of a Christian polity.[1] Both, moreover, conceived each order as exclusive in its functions. Thus Ælfric writes in his *Treatise on the Old and New Testaments:*

> The throne stands on these three supports: laborers [*laboratores*], soldiers [*bellatores*], beadsmen [*oratores*]. Laborers are they who provide us with sustenance, the ploughmen and husbandmen [*yrthlingas and æhte men*], *devoted to that alone* [emphasis added]. Beadsmen are they who intercede for us to God . . . *devoted to that alone* for the benefit of us all. Soldiers are they who guard our boroughs and also our land, fighting with weapons against the oncoming army; as St. Paul, the teacher of the nations, said in his teaching: *Non sine causa portat miles gladium et cetera*[2]—"The *cniht*[3] beareth not the sword without cause. He is God's minister [*Godes thegn*] to their profit."[4]

Wulfstan, the recipient of a letter from Ælfric upon this very topic,[5] incorporated the idea of a tripartite society into his *Institutes of Polity,* and, like Ælfric, portrayed each order as performing a specific function for the sake of the "entire nation" (*for ealne theodscipe*).[6]

Ælfric's and Wulfstan's conception of society does not sit well with Stenton's reconstruction of the late Anglo-Saxon fyrd. If we are to take seriously the words of these writers, at least one of whom, Wulfstan, was a man as comfortable in worldly as in spiritual affairs, then those who tilled the fields were not those who defended them. For Ælfric, the line of demarcation was absolute: the average peasant cultivator was no more a warrior than was the typical woman or child. When he wished to impress his audience with the immensity of the Exodus from Egypt, the abbot explained that "six hundred thousand men were in that host [*fyrde*], as Moses wrote, six hundred thousand warriors [*wigendra manna*], not including peasants [*ceorlfolce*], children, and women."[7] This is a rather free translation of what "Moses" actually wrote; the passage that he paraphrases, *Exodus* 12.37–38, simply says, "The sons of Israel set out from Ramses on the way to Succoth, about six hundred thousand men on foot, not counting the little ones [*parvulis:* perhaps "dependents"].[8] Ælfric has added a martial flavor to the text in the Vulgate[9] and has glossed it by dividing the Israelites into those who fought and those who did not, the latter consisting of women, children, and ceorlfolc.

Ælfric, in fact, was so insistent upon each order adhering strictly to its own function that he used this sentiment to climax his *Colloquy*, a conversation-piece composed for the benefit of his students. Here Ælfric has a character called the "wise counselor" (*sapiens consiliarius*) resolve a heated debate over the relative importance of the various secular professions by declaring, "Whoever you are, whether priest or monk, or peasant or warrior,[10] exercise yourself in this, and be what you are; because it is a great disgrace and shame for a man not to want to be what he is, and what he has to be."[11] Clearly, Ælfric believed that in a properly run society peasants ploughed and warriors fought.[12]

That Ælfric's and Wulfstan's theory of the three orders was a literary simplification is undeniable. It conceals the complexities of a geographically varied society in which the aristocracy included not only earls and magnates but thegns endowed with modest holdings of one or two hides, and sometimes even less, and in which the ceorlisc class embraced both the *gebur*, a man "trembling on the verge of serfdom,"[13] and the *geneat*, a commoner without a trace of servility, who served his lord mainly as a riding man.[14] One need only glance at the Domesday surveys for eastern England, with their thousands of sokemen and freemen, lords of estates stocked not only with cattle but with slaves, cottars, and villani, to realize how much is ignored by Wulfstan's and Ælfric's conception of the social order. Even more to the point, some Anglo-Saxons of humble birth did fight in Ælfric's day. The evidence for cierlisc warriors is too strong to be ignored; not only did commoners serve in the fyrds of pre-viking England, as we have seen, but the sources suggest that they fought in the late Saxon armies, taking part in campaigns up to and including the Battle of Hastings.[15]

What then is the value of Ælfric's and Wulfstan's schema for the study of Anglo-Saxon military obligation? Simply put, it challenges the widely held assumption that early eleventh-century fyrds were primarily levies of free peasants. For these two churchmen the armies of Æthelred II were, at least ideally, professional forces, composed of warriors rather than peasant cultivators, just as the great fyrd of Moses had been. Turning to Domesday Book, we find that the evidence of the Berkshire custumal also militates against armies made up of ploughmen-warriors. Once again the customs state:

> If the king sent an army anywhere, only one *miles* went from five hides, and for his upkeep or pay, four shillings were given him from each hide for his two months of service. The money, however, was not sent to the king but given to the *milites*.[16]

The first point to be made about this passage is that it characterizes the Berkshire fyrdman as a *miles*. But what should we make of the term "miles" as used here? The customs' mixed parentage presents us with an obvious initial difficulty, for they express conditions that pertained under the Confessor in terms familiar to the Conqueror. When, for instance, the Berkshire jurors explained that the heriot of a "king's demesne thegn or *miles*" consisted of all his weapons, together with two horses, one with a saddle and the other without, the Domesday commissioners took them to be speaking of "relief."[17] Our task, then, is twofold: first we must determine what the Norman royal legates understood by the term "miles," and then we must decide whether they interpreted the Anglo-Saxon jurors' testimony correctly.

What precisely did the eleventh- and early twelfth-century Normans mean when they spoke of *milites?* The term is used in the sources of this period to describe a bewildering variety of men. Those accustomed to reading "knight" whenever they come across the word *miles* will have no difficulty in recognizing Eudo Dapifer,[18] Roger Bigod,[19] and Rodulf of Warenne, father of William,[20] as milites. Each was a man of wealth and rank, an influential feudal tenant who also held a considerable estate in chief.[21] But such knights formed but a single stratum, and a small one at that, of a multilayered order. The vast majority of Domesday Book's milites were much humbler men, possessed of subtenancies that on average were smaller than two hides,[22] and deemed to be so inconsequential that the Domesday scribes often did not bother with their names. The economic and social position of such "knights" may have been comparable to that of the pre-Conquest sokemen and "free men." Thus in the Middlesex manor of Harmondsworth a sokeman held two hides T.R.E., which at the time of the Inquest were in the possession of a miles, and at Pirton, Hertfordshire, a pre-Conquest sokeman continued to hold his tenement T.R.W. as an "English *miles.*"[23] In a number of instances we even discover milites ensconced among the personnel of their lord's manor, squeezed between the villagers and the bordars without any clear indication that they enjoyed what we assume they had, a more privileged tenure and a higher social status than their peasant neighbors.[24] Milites of this sort are also to be found in a number of pre-Conquest Norman ducal charters, where they are regarded as mere appurtenances to a manor, a source of revenue for the landholder not unlike the estate's demesne, its church, or its mill.[25]

Domesday Book even affords a few examples of landless milites. In addition to his "enfeoffed men" (*feudati homines*),[26] Abbot Baldwin maintained some thirty-four "French and English *milites*" within the town of Bury St. Edmunds.[27] Similarly, Gilbert Crispin, abbot of St. Peter's of Westminster, set aside twenty-five houses near the monastery for his resident "*milites* and his other men [*homines*]."[28] For obvious reasons these are exceptional entries. Domesday Book and its satellites were land surveys. It is not in the least surprising that so few household men should appear in them. Nevertheless, there is much evidence to suggest that in the early years of the Conqueror's reign milites without landed fiefs outnumbered those who possessed them. It is even possible that some of Domesday's lesser milites were actually household knights with *fief-rentes* to supplement their lords' other presents.[29]

St. Anselm's well-known allegory of the warriors allows us some insight into the maintenance of mercenary soldiers in the late eleventh century. Anselm warned his monks not to expect material rewards for their service to God, using a simile derived from the secular world to drive his point home. According to him, a prince retains three sorts of milites: those who serve for the fiefs they hold from him, those "who bear arms and toil on his behalf for pay" (*pro stipendiis in militaribus armis sibi desudant*), and those who labor in the hope of regaining an inheritance forfeited by their parents. The first resemble the angels who minister to God, and the last are like his elect. Many Christians, however, serve as mercenaries (*solidarios milites*), faithful in the midst of their possessions, abandoning God in times of trouble.[30] That Anselm equated the stipendiary miles with the ordinary "Christian" suggests that the mercenary warrior must have been a common figure in Anselm's day. Indeed, two of the three milites he described were landless retainers.

Eleventh- and early twelfth-century Anglo-Norman literary sources agree on the practical military importance and ubiquity of stipendiary warriors. Orderic Vitalis's *Ecclesiastical History*, in particular, is filled with references to military households and mercenary troops. His anecdote about the siege of Bridgnorth shows that, Anselm's disparagement aside, hired soldiers could serve their lords as loyally as any feudal retainer. When Robert of Belleme, earl of Shrewsbury and head of the powerful Montgomery family, rebelled against Henry I in 1102, he entrusted the defense of his castle at Bridgnorth to "milites stipendiarii," placing them under the command of a number of feudal knights. After a brief siege, Robert's feudal vassals surrendered the stronghold without bothering to ask the advice or consent of the mercenaries, who became quite upset at what they considered treachery. As these mercenaries rode out through the besieging forces, they loudly lamented their fate—and undoubtedly their prospects for future employment—calling "on the whole army to witness the tricks of the plotters, so that their downfall might not bring contempt on other mercenaries."[31]

Robert of Belleme was not exceptional in his use of milites stipendiarii; every Norman magnate, lay or ecclesiastical, seems to have employed them,[32] none with more effect than the Conqueror himself. Many of the troops with which he won England had been non-Norman mercenaries, drawn to his cause, according to William of Poitiers, by the duke's "well-known generosity."[33] William, in fact, hired troops for all his major campaigns on the continent. We may even owe the creation of Domesday Book to William's reliance upon mercenaries; the Anglo-Saxon Chronicle seems to associate the Conqueror's decision to hold the Inquest with his need to billet and maintain the stipendiary troops he had assembled to counter the threatened invasion of his Danish rival, Cnut IV.[34]

Sally Harvey, who studied the problem of the Domesday milites in detail, concluded from this diversity that there were two distinct levels of milites at the time of the Inquest: the "middling"[35] well-connected knights and the professional serving men.[36] The tenancies of the former offered their lords political and social advantages[37] as well as a means of discharging a portion of their military obligation to the king, the so-called *servitium debitum*.[38] In the words of Abbot Baldwin's "Feudal Book," these "middling" knights held their fiefs in return for a number of milites to serve the monastery.[39] And they discovered the warriors they needed among their social inferiors. Some they maintained within their own households; others were supported through grants of a hide or two of the fief that they were retained to acquit. Milites of this sort were professional fighting men who earned their modest tenements and wages by bearing arms in the service of their patrons. Such "active" knights may well have constituted the bulk of the early Anglo-Norman feudal levies; they certainly constituted the lion's share of Domesday milites.

What bridged the social chasm that lay between a miles of the first rank such as Ralph de Tosny and the unnamed *probati milites* who held in Walter of St. Valery's manor of Isleworth?[40] What was it that allowed men of such unequal wealth and prestige to be lumped together under the rubric of "milites"? The answer must be sought in the one thing shared by all these men, a common function. For each miles, from the great feudal vassal to the lowly man-at-arms, was considered to be a mounted military retainer, that is, one who received some form of maintenance from his lord in return for fealty and armed service. As the literary sources make clear, the Anglo-Norman use of the term "miles" implied both vassalage and the profession of arms.[41]

The milites of the Berkshire customs were in fact men of this sort, military tenants and domestic warriors retained by the holders of book-land to acquit their estates of *fyrdfæreld*. As we have already seen, the idea of a military retainer was anything but foreign to the Anglo-Saxons. On the contrary, literary sources from *Beowulf* to *The Battle of Maldon* insist that a man's primary obligation was to defend and avenge his lord.[42] Armed service was deemed to be so essential an element in the commendation relationship that a retainer's duties found tangible expression in his payment of heriot (*heregeatu*, literally "war-gear"), a death-due that appears to have originated in the return of the arms with which the lord had outfitted his man.[43] Although the character of the heriot was evolving throughout the period, becoming increasingly associated with problems of tenurial succession,[44] the nobility often continued to pay this impost in kind, with weapons, byrnies, and horses,

up until the Conquest.[45] This resistance of the heriot to money com-
mutation bears witness to the military flavor of lordship in late Anglo-
Saxon England.

Nor would the Norman use of "miles" have struck their English
contemporaries as odd. To be sure, the Old English vocabularies tended
to gloss miles with *cempa*, "warrior,"[46] but, from Bede's day on, miles
also connoted a retainer who served his lord with arms.[47] The charters
of the tenth century thus use *miles regis* and *minister regis* interchangeably to render the vernacular *cynges thegn*,[48] and it is not unheard of
for the same individual to be designated as someone's minister in one
charter, his *fidelis* in a second, and his miles in still a third.[49] The
unknown Flemish cleric who composed the *Encomium Emmae* clearly
expected his English audience to understand miles as "vassal," since his
portrayal of Godwine's heinous treachery toward the ætheling Alfred
hinged precisely upon the earl's false oath to be that young man's
miles.[50] In similar fashion, the anonymous author of the *Vita Ædwardi
Regis* relates how certain Northumbrian noblemen, chafing under the
heavy yoke of Tostig's justice, stormed the absent earl's home and killed
those of "his *milites* who were surprised and could not get away."[51]
When we turn to the Chronicle's versions of this story, we discover that
the Anonymous' milites were in fact Tostig's *huskarlas* or *hiredmenn*,
in other words, the earl's military household.[52]

One may object that the *Encomium Emmae* and the *Vita Ædwardi*
are of Flemish provenance, even if composed for English courts, and
consequently are of doubtful relevance to the Anglo-Saxon use of miles.
No similar suspicion, however, can be cast upon the works of Ælfric
of Eynsham or the anonymous *Vita Oswaldi, Archiepiscopi Eboracensis*, written by a monk of Ramsey between 995 and 1005.[53] Ælfric
found no difficulty in equating the "warrior [*bellator*] who defends our
boroughs and land" with the biblical miles "who carries the sword."[54]
Even more striking is Ælfric's choice of words to render miles into the
vernacular, *cniht*.[55] For *cniht* bore a technical meaning in the late tenth
and the early eleventh century, denoting the retainer of some lord,
usually a member of his household.[56] We should not take this association
of the miles with the cniht as an eccentricity of Ælfric's. One need only
recall Alcuin's division of Archbishop Eanbald II's secular household
into his high-born milites and their commended men, described as *ignobiles milites*, for a suitable precedent.[57]

The author of the *Vita Oswaldi* employed miles in a similar, though
far narrower, sense. For him a miles was an aristocratic retainer, a thegn

of the king or of some great magnate. This comes out most clearly in his narrative treatment of the murder of Edward the Martyr. He relates that the king was slain by certain milites who dwelled with Queen Æthelfryth. Who were these men? If we take the author at his word, the murderers were noble retainers, ministri, of the king's brother, Æthelred.[58] King Edward, moreover, was vulnerable to their treacherous attack only because, trusting to God and fearing no man, he chose to visit his brother with but a small retinue, or to use the language of the *Vita*, with "very few *milites* of his own."[59]

The term "miles" appears elsewhere in the *Vita* as a title of honor, equivalent to *cynges thegn*.[60] This usage recalls the chivalric flavor sometimes given this term by eleventh- and twelfth-century Norman historians.[61] We ought not to take this, however, as proof that all Anglo-Saxon milites were of noble blood, for the *Vita Oswaldi* itself hints at the existence of lesser milites,[62] although the biographer was not concerned with men of this sort. What is to be emphasized is that the author of the *Vita*, like Ælfric, regarded miles as a term connoting service.

Finally, there is the evidence of the Bayeux Tapestry, a work that bridges the Norman and Anglo-Saxon milieux, having been commissioned by William's half-brother Odo, bishop of Bayeux and earl of Kent, and designed by English artists.[63] The investigations of scholars such as Sir Francis Wormald, M. Forster, and R. Lepelley have established the Tapestry as Anglo-Saxon in its style, design, and orthography.[64] Nor should we assume that the Tapestry is English merely in its formal elements. Nicholas Brooks, for instance, made an exhaustive study of the weapons and armor depicted in this work. From the artist's careful and consistent portrayal of hauberks with mail trousers, armor more suited to foot soldiers than to mounted warriors, Brooks concluded that the Tapestry is a more dependable source for the military equipment of the English than of the Normans.[65] In addition, the Bayeux Tapestry seems to tell its story from an Anglo-Saxon point of view. For it departs from the Norman version of the Conquest in certain crucial respects, most notably in its portrayal of the Confessor's displeasure over Harold's oath to King William[66] and its emphasis upon Harold's legitimate succession to the throne.[67] In light of this it would be reasonable to assume that the Tapestry's latinity was also influenced by contemporary English usage. If so, then one would conclude that the Anglo-Saxons of the Conquest era thought a miles to be both a warrior with byrnie[68] and a retainer. The term is clearly used in the latter sense in plate 2, which depicts Harold and "his *milites*" riding unarmed to

Bosham Church. Everything about the scene points up the peaceful character of the mounted company, from the falcon on Harold's wrist to the hunting dogs that run ahead of the troop.[69] Plate 2 represents an Anglo-Saxon earl's entourage, his chosen retainers; that such men should be titled *sui milites* tells us much about the connotations of this phrase.

The pacific nature of plate 2 should not mislead us, however. In every other plate that mentions them in its title, milites appear as heavily armored men. The Domesday jurors of Cambridgeshire seem to have shared this conception of the miles, since the phrase, "the arms of one *miles*," was so clear to them that they felt no need to define it more precisely. The jurors explained that it was the custom of the borough for a "lawman"[70] to pay the sheriff as a heriot (*harieta*) "eight pounds, one palfrey, and the arms of one *miles*."[71] In light of II *Cnut*, c. 71, this would seem to imply that in Cambridgeshire the ordinary miles was armed with a helmet, coat of mail, sword, spear, and shield; in other words, with the weapons borne by the milites of the Bayeux Tapestry.[72] The reference to the palfrey is also of interest, since the Tapestry consistently places its milites on horseback. Not that the Anglo-Saxons were chevaliers who charged the enemy with lance couched.[73] The Norman Domesday commissioners knew full well the difference between a palfrey and a destrier, and were careful to include only the former in the heriot of the Cambridgeshire lawmen. From the time of Alfred's reforms, however, the fyrd was essentially a mounted troop that rode to battle and pursued the defeated enemy on horseback. And as Stenton pointed out long ago, the native English population readily identified the horse soldiers of the Norman conquerors with the *cnihtas*, or "knights," of their English predecessors.[74] The miles of the Bayeux Tapestry, then, was a retainer who served his lord not only in peace but in war. He may be thought of as a professional warrior.

The Berkshire custumal itself lends support to the view that its miles was a military dependent of some lord. We may begin once more with the word itself. Miles is used not only to describe the fyrdmen who served for each five hides but also appears later in the customs in a passage concerning the payment of heriots. When a "demesne" thegn or miles of the king (*tainus uel miles regis dominicus*) lay dying, he was obliged to send all of his weapons to the king as a "relief" (*pro releuamento*), along with two horses, one of which was to be saddled, and his hunting animals, if the king wished to have them.[75] As in the pre-Conquest charters, miles here translates the Anglo-Saxon word *thegn*.[76]

But what does it mean to say that the Berkshire milites were "thegns"? Some have leaped from this to the supposition that the Berkshire fyrd was a purely aristocratic levy.[77] This ignores the ambiguity of the term "thegn." Although it is quite true, as H. R. Loyn reminds us, that the thegns of the tenth- and eleventh-century lawbooks must be understood as members of an aristocratic class,[78] the term "thegn" itself does not denote nobility but service.[79] The word takes on an aristocratic patina only when attached to the modifier *cynges* or when such an attachment is understood.[80] The nobility of late Anglo-Saxon England were known as *thegnas* and enjoyed *thegnriht* precisely because they formed a class that had the right and duty to serve the king.

The basic obligation of the late Anglo-Saxon thegn was to perform service to the king in respect to his bookland, the "thegn's law" of the *Rectitudines Singularum Personarum*. Similarly, a ceorl could attain thegnship if he managed to accumulate five hides of land assessed to the king's service, according to the early eleventh-century compilations on status known as *Gethynctho* and the *Northleoda laga*.[81] Scholars have too often concentrated exclusively upon the figure of five hides in these provisions. The references to royal service seem to me at least as important. The *Northleoda laga* thus emphasizes that the five hides must be land upon which the erstwhile ceorl discharges the king's dues, while *Gethynctho* ties the promotion in rank even more securely to royal service, declaring:

2. And if a *ceorl* prospered, that he possessed fully five hides of his own [*fullice agendes landes,* an apparent reference to book-right],[82] a church and kitchen, bell-house and *burh*-gate, *a seat and a special office in the king's hall,* then he was entitled to the rights of a thegn.

3. And the thegn who prospered that he *served the king and rode in his household band* [*in his hirede*], on riding errands, if he himself had a thegn who served him, possessing five hides on which he had discharged *the king's dues,* and who had attended his lord *in the king's hall, and had thrice gone on his errand to the king*—then he [the thegn's thegn] was afterwards allowed to represent his lord with a preliminary oath.[83]

The thegns described in these provisions are both aristocratic land-owners and servants. To be a thegn meant to be at the king's disposal—hence the reference to "the seat and special office in the king's hall"—although a thegn could be personally commended to some greater thegn. Rank was thus determined in part by an individual's service to the king.

The author of *Gethynctho,* probably Wulfstan,[84] used the term *thegn* to indicate service rather than noble rank in the preface to the compilation:

> Once it used to be that people and rights went by dignities, and councillors of the people were then entitled to honor, each according to his rank, whether noble or commoner [ge eorl ge ceorl], retainer or lord [ge thegen ge theoden].[85]

This is a reminder that the ministerial sense of "thegn" was never lost. It dominates in the Alfredian translations and was preserved in the verb, *thegnian*, "to serve."[86] Furthermore, it is found in Domesday Book. While the *taini regis* who held T.R.E. were undoubtedly noblemen, the post-Conquest *Taini Regis* whose tenures are described at the end of each Domesday county survey are best thought of as Englishmen holding of the king in sergeanty.[87] In Wiltshire, for example, we find ensconced among these "King's Thegns" four huntsmen, a group of royal foresters, a royal purveyor, a king's beadsman, a goldsmith, and a female artisan, who, we are told, "used to make and still makes gold fringe for the King and Queen."[88]

The Berkshire customs seem to reflect both senses of the term "thegn" in their use of miles. While the "demesne thegn, or *miles*, of the king" mentioned in the heriot provision may well have enjoyed the privileges and wergild of a nobleman, there is no reason whatsoever to suppose that the milites of the fyrd regulations were in fact king's thegns. Rather, the jurors' use of the term "miles" tells us only that they expected these fyrdmen to be the military retainers of some lord.

This argument need not rest solely upon semantic inference. The Berkshire custumal itself supplies certain invaluable clues as to the identity of its fyrd-warriors. Two conclusions about these men emerge from a careful reading of the text: first, they received wages from the holders of the tenure for which they served; second, these milites were commended to lords who were responsible to the king for their appearance in the fyrd. The size of the Berkshire miles' salary argues against identifying him as a peasant who tilled his lord's field for part of the year, only to abandon his plough for a spear whenever the king raised a host. A miles was to receive four shillings from each of the five hides, that is, one full pound from the land he defended to cover his wages and provisions for his two months of campaigning.[89] A pound was far from a negligible sum of money in 1066. If we may trust the statistics of Domesday Book, it represented the ordinary annual revenue expected from one hide of land.[90] Only the more prosperous sokemen, liberi homines, geneats, and radcnihts were blessed with tenures of this size; most commoners had to content themselves with far less.[91] Indeed, the holdings of unnamed Norman milites in Domesday Book averaged only one-and-a-half hides, which provided a yearly income of one pound, seventeen shillings.[92] The four pence per diem afforded the Berkshire milites was even comparable to the wages paid to Anglo-Norman stipendiary knights throughout the twelfth century.[93] If the Berkshire milites were men of humble birth—geburs, cottars, and the like—their military service with its attendant rewards certainly raised them above others of their class.

Not that the eleventh-century fyrd was composed exclusively of thegns. As we have seen in the previous chapters, commoners had fought in the fyrds of Alfred and his predecessors, and despite Ælfric's schema, such men continued to bear arms in the late tenth and the eleventh century. In fact, the majority of the Englishmen identified in Domesday Book as having fought at Hastings were liberi homines, men of that intermediate stratum of society that occupied a place between the thegnly aristocracy and the economically dependent peasantry.[94] The Domesday survey of Hampshire thus records that of the three liberi homines who held manors in Tytherley, two died at Harold's side. Both apparently held by book-right, since the text describes them as having possessed their property in *alodium de rege*. Because the three estates were consolidated after the Conquest, only the combined hidage and value are given: four hides, one virgate, worth 50s. If this was all that the two deceased fyrdmen held, a dangerous assumption given their anonymity, they were of modest means, their lands bringing them probably less in a year than the 20s. a Berkshire miles received for two months of service.[95] Three other "free men" are known from Domesday Book to have died at Hastings: Breme, a "free man" of King Edward, who held one-and-a-half carucates in Suffolk worth 60s.; a nameless tenant of St. Edmund's in Suffolk, who possessed only twelve acres worth 16p.; and Eadric "the Deacon," who held property in Cavendish, Suffolk, and was "a free man of Harold . . . who died with him in battle."[96] Admittedly, a sample of five is small, far too small to serve as justification for broad generalizations about the personnel of the fyrd at Hastings. But, then again, as Freeman declared in his characteristic and inimitable style: "few indeed . . . are the men whom we know by name as having joined in the great march and fought in the great battle. Still there are a few names which should sound like the call of the trumpet in the ears of every man of English birth."[97] And it seems significant that alongside abbots, sheriffs, housecarls, and the thegns of Abingdon and Ramsey, we should find five ordinary liberi homines.

One might be tempted by the appearance of such men in the roll of the dead at Hastings to return to the idea that Harold's fyrd had been a general levy of all able-bodied free men. This temptation is to be resisted. Despite the common description of sokemen, liberi homines, radcnihts, censarii, and geneats as free peasants or the peasant elite, such men were "peasants" only in the broadest sense of the word. They were not "rural cultivators whose surpluses [were] transferred to a dominant group of rulers that uses the surpluses to underwrite its own standard of living,"[98] except in the sense that they either paid rent or owed services for their tenures, which would also have been true of thegns who had ecclesiastical læns or the lesser thegns of south Lancashire. Even if the "free men" of Tytherley who fell at Hastings held less than 50s. worth of land between them, they were, nevertheless, lords in their own right, the seignors of the two villagers and twenty-two bordars who dwelled in Tytherley and worked its lands. Breme's estate in Suffolk was not only stocked with bordars, villagers, and slaves, but he himself held the commendation of another "free man," who had eleven acres in that same village.[99] In this context it is interesting to observe that in Pirton, Hertfordshire, a sokeman managed to retain his tenure by becoming the *miles Anglicus* of Ralph of Limesy.[100]

Breme and others of his status fit uncertainly into the neat "1200-shilling and 200-shilling man" classification of Anglo-Saxon society presented in the legal texts of the early eleventh century, which were, after all, antiquarian in flavor and simplistic in their presentation of the social orders. As is well known, sokemen and their ilk were obliged to render an assortment of services, notably two that required a horse, "inward" (guard-duty) and *avera* (carrying-duty). They also owed suit in the hundred courts (possibly the origin of the name "sokeman"), paid taxes to the king, and provided labor services, such as hewing deer hedges, and mowing and reaping on their lord's lands, which may have actually been performed by their dependents.[101] That some of these men owed fyrd service in addition to their other duties is not surprising. Sokemen and other fyrd-worthy men were entitled to serve in arms. That some actually did does not hark back to an ancient time when all free men were called upon to defend the nation. Rather, sokemen, like thegns, attended the king's host either to discharge their own tenurial obligation or that of their landlord.[102]

Domesday Book stipulates that the money collected from each hide was to be paid directly to the Berkshire milites rather than sent on to the king. At first glance, this is a puzzling provision, for we have learned to read the Domesday custumals as records of royal rights and dues. Why did the Domesday jurors and commissioners bother to record the wages of the Berkshire milites if the king himself was never to see any of this money? How was it in the king's interest that the landowners of the shire remunerate their fyrd-warriors at this rate?

The answer is suggested by the level at which these wages were set. The salary provision defined the quality, as opposed to the quantity, of military service demanded by the king from the holders of bookland in Berkshire. The customs of Oxford, Warwick, and Malmesbury all have fyrd regulations which allow these boroughs the option of sending a specific number of warriors on campaign with the king or of commuting this obligation at the rate of one pound per warrior.[103] According to the Malmesbury account, this money was to be used to provision the king's *buzecarles*, that is, his mercenaries. It would appear, therefore, that one pound was deemed to be the amount of money needed to hire and support a stipendiary warrior during a campaign.[104] By setting the Berkshire milites' wages at one pound, the king was in effect guaranteeing that he would receive professional warriors rather than poorly paid and provisioned peasants. Conversely, by stipulating that these milites were to be paid directly, the Berkshire landowners were protecting themselves from any possible chicanery on the king's part. The king could not treat fyrdfæreld as a means of raising money; he could not call out the fyrd, collect the money raised for the warriors' wages, and then dismiss the host, as William Rufus appears to have done in 1094.[105]

The Berkshire miles, however, was not merely a stipendiary warrior whose obligation to service rested solely upon his acceptance of wages. The shire customs make it clear that he was either the commended man of the lord who paid his salary or belonged to his soke. As we may recall, in Berkshire, as in Worcestershire, if an owner of bookland failed to answer the king's summons in person,[106] he forfeited his property, because he had neglected to acquit it of its fyrdfæreld. If, however, one of the lesser fyrd-warriors or his substitute failed to appear in the host, the king held *his lord* accountable.[107] The natural conclusion to be drawn from this is that the Berkshire miles was precisely what his title implied, a military retainer of one who held bookland. Thus the miles was obliged to serve his immediate lord rather than the king, and his failure was perceived as the failure of the man who retained him.

EIGHT

Lords and Retainers in the King's Host

LANDED RETAINERS AND HOUSEHOLD WARRIORS

If the suggested reading of the Berkshire and Worcestershire custumals is accepted, then the late Anglo-Saxon fyrd should be viewed as a royal levy composed of privileged landowners and their own retainers, reinforced by the king's military household and stipendiary troops. The landowners bore arms in the king's service as a consequence of their bookland tenure. The retainers' obligation was primarily to their own lords and arose from the hold-oaths they had sworn and the wages they had accepted. In essence, the holders of bookland fought for the king, while their retainers fought for them, the king being, of course, the beneficiary of the retainers' service.

A similar conception of the fyrd is implicit in the literary and legal sources of the early eleventh century. The poem of the battle of Maldon (991) is the single extant source containing an extended description of the fyrd in action.[1] Scholars of the last generation were prone to accept this work as a historical source for the battle, and less than a decade ago Eric John was able to declare that "everyone agrees that the poem is nearly contemporary."[2] That statement could not be made today. Recent scholarship has moved the date of composition forward to ca. 1020 and has revealed the poem to be a literary creation that fits comfortably into an established genre.[3] One author has gone so far as to question whether the poet had any idea what a real battle was like.[4]

In the face of this criticism it would be unwise to rely upon the poem for details of the death of Ealdorman Byrhtnoth and his men or for the tactics employed in the battle. But it is one thing to acknowledge *The Battle of Maldon* to be a piece of imaginative literature, a work of art rather than of history, and quite another to dismiss it completely as a source for the period. After all, it was written for an audience of aristocratic warriors, who were undoubtedly familiar with the organization of the fyrd. Even granting the poet's deliberate archaism and his addiction to literary conventions, it is more than likely that the poem presents an idealized, but essentially accurate, portrayal of an early eleventh-century Anglo-Saxon host, one that would not have struck its audience as too far removed from the reality they knew.[5]

As Chadwick recognized many years ago, the poem is suffused with the ideals of lordship.[6] Consider the speech of Ælfwine, a Mercian of noble descent, urging on his companions after Byrhtnoth had fallen:

Remember the times when often we spoke at the mead-drinking, when on the bench we uttered boasting, heroes in hall, about hard strife. Now he who is brave may show it in the test. . . . Thanes shall not reproach me among the people, that I wish to leave this army [*fyrd*], to seek my home, now my prince lies low, hewn down in battle. That is the greatest of griefs to me; he was both my kinsman and my lord.[7]

Consider also the poet's condemnation of the cowardly sons of Odda, one of whom precipitated a mass flight by fleeing the battle upon the slain earl's own horse:

Godric fled from the battle and left the valiant one who had often given him many a steed; he leaped on the horse which his lord had owned, on the trappings, as was not right, and both his brothers . . . galloped with him. . . . They fled to the fastness and saved their lives, and more men than was at all fitting, if they had all remembered the rewards which he [Byrhtnoth] had given them for their benefit. Thus erstwhile Offa once said in the meeting-place, that many spoke bravely there who would not endure the stress.[8]

This is the language of the comitatus. The poet's attitude toward the behavior of the English troops at Maldon was shaped by his conception of the duties owed a lord by his men. For him, it was the commendation bond that cemented Byrhtnoth's fyrd. The ealdorman himself is thus described as King Æthelred's thegn, and the author is careful to represent him as defending his royal lord's honor and land.[9] As we have seen, Alfred and his successors had exacted hold-oaths from their ealdormen and reeves, making the treason of such men an especially heinous crime. The poet's Byrhtnoth plays "Beowulf" to Eadric Streona's "Heremod"; his fidelity to Æthelred is the obverse side of the coin to the treacheries bemoaned by the Chronicler and denounced by Wulfstan. Similarly, the poet links every warrior whom he mentions, even those who seem to have been local landowners,[10] to Byrhtnoth by ties of personal lordship. Many, in fact, are said to have been members of the ealdorman's household.[11] Thus, after Byrhtnoth had fallen and defeat had become inevitable, the English fought on, not to protect their homeland against the viking menace, not even to fulfill their duty to King Æthelred, who, interestingly, is not mentioned again after the death of his ealdorman, but precisely to avenge "their beloved lord [winedrihten], and work slaughter upon their foes."[12]

The principle of lordship governs the fyrd of *The Battle of Maldon*. This much is certain. But how accurate was the perception of the poet? Was his portrayal of the East Saxon fyrd as Byrhtnoth's comitatus merely a literary conceit, a deliberate archaism? Although the poet has presented us with an ideal rather than a real fyrd, his emphasis upon the obligations of lordship as the unifying principle of this army was no artistic fancy. The ealdormen of the late tenth century exercised delegated regalian powers over their extensive territories. None of them, not even Æthelstan "Half King," created a lasting dynasty, but this does not alter the reality of their viceregal authority. Byrhtnoth was more than an agent of the king to the nobility of Essex; he was, in a very real sense, their cynehlaford, the beneficiary of the oaths of loyalty that they had sworn to a distant king. Such ealdormen may have been recruited from cadet branches of the royal family, but in the course of the tenth century they had developed territorial roots. The historical Byrhtnoth, for example, possessed through marriage and inheritance extensive holdings in the shires that he governed. His patronage of the great religious houses of the fenlands and of East Anglia may have earned him the enmity of local landholders dispossessed by the monastic reformers, but it also guaranteed him the loyal support of the heads of these houses and their thegns.[13]

It is naive to believe that all those who followed Byrhtnoth into battle at Maldon had bowed to him and chosen his will. The poet's vision of the fyrd as an ealdorman's war band, nevertheless, does contain a kernel of truth. Because of his landed possessions and office, many Essex landowners undoubtedly sought Byrhtnoth as their lord and protector, and together with the ealdormen's military household, such men would have naturally formed the core of Byrhtnoth's army.

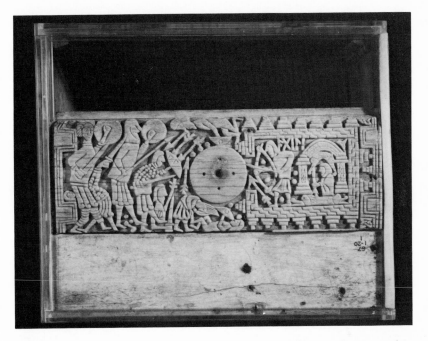

Figure 1. Lid panel of the Franks Casket. This whalebone casket, carved in Northumbria in the first half of the eighth century, is eclectically decorated with scenes from the Bible, Germanic mythology, and Roman legend and history. The lid panel, which depicts Egil the Archer's defense of his home, is a vivid portrayal of warfare in the time of Bede. The armor and weapons borne by the attackers, including mail coats, helmets, swords, spears, and round shields, represent the type of arms possessed by aristocratic warriors of the period. (Bargello Museum, Florence; British Museum photo)

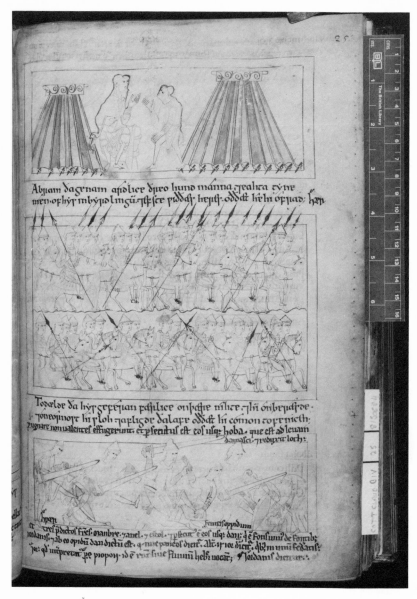

Figure 2. Abram and his armed servants rescue Lot, from the Canterbury Hexateuch (St. Augustine's, second quarter of the eleventh century). The illustration provides interesting insight into Anglo-Saxon military practice in the early eleventh century. In depicting Abram's warriors as mounted, the artist was following the Old English text rather than the Vulgate's treatment of the rescue. Note that the Hebrew warriors pursue Lot's captors on horseback (middle strip), but engage them on foot (bottom strip). (British Library, MS/Cotton Claudius B.iv, 25R)

Figure 3. Earl Harold rides to Bosham with his military retainers (*milites*), from the Bayeux Tapestry (Wilson, ed., plate 2). The scene emphasizes the peaceful character of the mounted company, from the falcon on Harold's wrist to the hunting dogs that run ahead of his entourage. This is the only scene in the Tapestry in which *milites* appear without armor. (Town of Bayeux; photograph courtesy of *National Geographic Magazine*)

Figure 4. A scout tells King Harold about Duke William's army, from the Bayeux Tapestry (Wilson, ed., plate 56). Harold and the English scout wear the same armor and carry the same weapons as the Norman soldiers portrayed in the previous panels. Harold is shown on horseback, with a lance (or spear) in his left hand, a kite-shaped shield on his left arm, and a sword girded to his side. His feet, adorned with spurs, are planted in the stirrups. Only Harold's prominent mustache distinguishes him from a Norman warrior. (Town of Bayeux; photograph courtesy of *National Geographic Magazine*)

Figure 5. The Normans attack the English shield-wall, from the Bayeux Tapestry (Wilson, ed., plates 61–62). With the exception of the lone English archer, who wears only a tunic, the soldiers on both sides are armed with mail-shirts, kite-shaped shields, and conical helmets with nose-guards. The English are drawn into a tight formation, the so-called shield wall, and oppose the Norman horsemen with spears, which they use both as missiles and thrusting weapons, battle-axes, and arrows. The artist emphasizes the aristocratic and professional character of both armies. (Town of Bayeux; photograph courtesy of *National Geographic Magazine*)

Figure 6. Battle scene, from the Bayeux Tapestry (Wilson, ed., plates 65–66). The defensive work of sharpened stakes on the right hand side of the panel belongs to the next scene. (Town of Bayeux; photograph courtesy of *National Geographic Magazine*)

Figure 7. French horsemen attack English defenders on a hill, from the Bayeux Tapestry (Wilson, ed., plates 66–67). Because the English warriors in this panel lack body armor, some commentators have viewed them to be local peasant levies called up in support of the "select fyrd." One should note, however, that the defenders of the hill are well armed—one swings a battle-axe and has a sword girded to his side, while three others bear kite-shaped shields—and fight fiercely against the charging French horsemen. The sharpened stakes depicted in the previous plate belong to this scene and indicate that the Anglo-Saxons had deployed on the hill before the battle rather than retreated to it. (Town of Bayeux; photograph courtesy of National Geographic Magazine)

Figure 8. The Normans pursue the defeated English, from the Bayeaux Tapestry (Wilson, ed., plate 73). The English survivors, four of whom are on foot, and one on horseback, are shown armed only with maces. Their social status, however, can not be determined from this, since even aristocrats would have discarded their armor in flight. (Town of Bayeux; photograph courtesy of *National Geographic Magazine*)

A more prosaic source, Cnut's second code, affords us another glimpse of the organization and composition of an early eleventh-century fyrd, and what we see supports the *Maldon*-poet's portrayal. A series of laws, clauses 77 to 79, deal with the behavior of fyrdmen on campaign. We have already examined the last of these in some detail in our discussion of the tenurial basis of military obligation; the argument need not be repeated here.[14] The first two laws, however, deserve to be quoted in full:

> 77. Concerning the man who deserts his lord. And the man who, through cowardice, deserts his lord or his comrades on a military expedition, either by sea or by land, shall lose all that he possesses and his own life, and the lord shall take back the property and the land which he had given him. [§ 1] And if he has bookland it shall pass into the king's hand.

> 78. Concerning the man who falls before his lord. And the heriot of the man who falls before his lord during a campaign [*on fyrdunge*], whether within the country or abroad, shall be remitted, and the heirs shall succeed to his land and his property and make a very just division of the same.[15]

Apparently, the drafter of these provisions, presumably Wulfstan, believed that the warriors of the king's host would fight at the side of their own lords, to whom they would be accountable for their behavior in battle. Thus if a man abandoned his lord or his companions (*geferan*) in a peace-guild in the midst of battle, he was deemed guilty of betraying not only the king but his lord. Any land he held on læn returned to the lord whom he had wronged, and any bookland that he may have possessed was forfeited to the king.[16] Conversely, if one were to die a heroic death, defending one's lord in the fyrd, the lord would be obliged to remit his fallen man's heriot and see that his lands and property passed to his heirs in accordance with legal custom. If, as seems distinctly possible, c. 78, like c. 77, is concerned with lænland, then death in battle guaranteed that the lord's gift would remain in the possession of the dead man's family.

II *Cnut*, c. 77 implies that some warriors held lænland from the lords whom they attended in the fyrd. Other sources give us some reason to believe that this practice was not at all uncommon in the eleventh century. References to thegns endowing their commended men (*cnihtas*) with precarious tenures or converting such existing tenures into bookland occur in a number of the surviving wills of the period.[17] In addition, Domesday Book records many dependent holdings T.R.E., characterized by the general formula: "X held this *manerium* [or *terram*] from [or under] Y, and could give or sell [it] without the license of his lord."[18] In the majority of these cases, it is impossible to tell from Domesday Book alone whether a tenant was the commended man of the landowner. Fortunately, a few Domesday satellites are still extant, and when we compare, for example, the Exchequer Domesday description of dependent tenures in Cambridgeshire with the corresponding entries in the *Inquisitio Cantabrigiensis,* a remarkable pattern emerges. Where the former describes a man as merely holding from or under another, the latter consistently characterizes this relationship in terms of personal commendation.[19] The ideas of lordship and dependent tenure apparently were becoming more and more intertwined in late Anglo-Saxon England, a process that can be seen most clearly in the relationship between ecclesiastical lords and their tenants.

Bishop Ealdred of Worcester (1046–1062) made the equation explicit when he made a lease conditional on the recipient and his heirs acknowledging "the lordship of whoever is bishop at the time."[20] Some of Ealdred's contemporaries even went further, and enriched their churches by asking a donation of land in return for their lordship. One East Anglian thegn in the time of Edward the Confessor, Ælfric Modercope, gave land to the monasteries of Bury St. Edmunds and Ely, received these estates back as life-tenancies, and performed homage to the abbots.[21] As both Harmer and Douglas have observed, it is highly unlikely that Ælfric's bequests and acts of homage were unrelated.[22] The medieval chronicler of Abingdon Abbey relates a similar story about a certain magnate named Thorkill, who "did homage for himself to the Church of Abingdon and to Abbot Ordric with his estate at Kingston." The chronicler hastens to explain that "in those days, it was allowed every free man to act thus, so that dominion of the aforesaid vill lay under the perpetual right of the Church."[23] Almost in confirmation of this we read in the *Inquisitio Eliensis* that a "liber homo" of Ely commended himself in such wise that he could not sell his land outside the Church.[24]

Occasionally, the sources permit us a glimpse into the nature of the relationship between a lay landowner-lord and his tenant-retainer. In at least two known secular leases the tenants were the lord's milites. Domesday Book thus shows five thegns holding the manor of Feckenham T.R.E. from (*de*) Earl Edwin with the right of free disposal; under them (*sub se*) we find four milites "who were as free as they were."[25] A Kentish charter of 1050, KCD 1338 (S 1502) reveals a thegn, Æthelric Bigga,[26] as maintaining two of his men upon property that he had granted to them as *precaria*.[27] Æthelric, it seems, wished to make a bequest of his estates at Bodesham and Wilderton to St. Augustine's. At the time that the charter was drafted, Æthelric's miles Wade "sat" at the former and Leofwine Freirage at the latter. The thegn's agreement with the abbey included a proviso to protect the interests of his men: as long as they should live, Wade and Leofwine would be entitled to the full beneficial enjoyment of the lands. Only after their deaths would the estates pass to the Church.[28] Finally, we have an interesting notice in Domesday Book concerning a Gloucestershire "free man" (*liber homo*) who held two hides of land in the royal hundredal manor of Cirencester, in return for 20s. a year in rent and performing "service to the sheriff throughout the whole of England"—a possible reference to fyrd service.[29]

No detailed account of land issued by a nobleman to a retainer has survived. This, however, ought not to be taken as proof that such endowments were rare; the evidence cited above shows otherwise. Probably most transactions of this sort went unrecorded, a written instrument being deemed unnecessary for a precarious tenure.[30] If by some chance a document was drawn up, the odds are good that it would not have long survived its beneficiaries, for with their demise the charter would have lost its reason for being. In view of the lack of evidence, one cannot even begin to speculate about the possible terms involved in the establishment of these læns. Whether a miles such as Wade promised his lord specific services in return for his tenement or merely continued to render the faithful service that had earned him his reward in the first place—the single most common reason given in Bishop Oswald's leases for the creation of a læn—cannot be ascertained.

Fortunately, we are on far more solid ground when we turn from the aristocratic to the ecclesiastical læns of the tenth and eleventh centuries. The vast majority of Anglo-Saxon charter material, the diplomas, writs, wills, and memoranda, is concerned with grants made to and by religious establishments. It is not necessary to seek abstruse reasons for this. Quite simply, the monastic and episcopal chapters of England weathered the Conquest without too much damage while most of the Anglo-Saxon aristocracy foundered in that great storm.[31] Since these religious houses based their titles to many of their possessions upon pre-Norman donations, the monks and canons took care to store their Anglo-Saxon muniments, thus guarding against possible encroachments by powerful neighbors and their own tenants.[32] Even the records of læns granted to men long dead were preserved on occasion as evidence of the community's ancient ownership of the estates mentioned in the documents. Hence many of these leases found their way into the various medieval cartularies.

Which brings us to what may well be the most famous series of texts in Anglo-Saxon diplomatics: the leases and memoranda issued by Oswald, bishop of Worcester (961–992) and archbishop of York (972–992).[33] Seventy-six leases bearing Oswald's name have been preserved in the two great eleventh-century cartularies of the see of Worcester, which are traditionally known as "Hemming's Cartulary."[34] Forty-nine of these were to men characterized as the bishop's ministri (28), fideles (7), thegns (3),[35] homines or men (3), milites (3),[36] cnihtas (3), cliens (1), and amicus (1). Hence almost two-thirds of the tenants named in these "lænbooks" can be identified unequivocally as the bishop's own retainers. In only a single instance, in fact, do we find a man holding of Oswald who is known to have been the client of another lord.[37]

Oswald's leases typically conveyed to the grantee and to two successive heirs life interests in a modest estate carved out of the Church's demesne.[38] If we accept the charters at face value, they represent highly privileged tenures. The most common service demanded was the performance of the "common burdens" assessed upon the land, mentioned in twenty-two of the texts. The only other render mentioned with any regularity is the payment of church-scot. In fact, thirty charters attach no terms whatsoever to the tenures expressed in them.

Whether we take Stenton's position that each of these leases "must have been governed by its own set of explicit understandings"[39] or John's that the lænbooks imposed only the services they actually claimed,[40] it is certain that most tenants of Bishop Oswald would have been expected to render more than church-scot for their land. Further insight into the terms of tenure for Worcester's thegnland is afforded by the much discussed letter or *indiculum* from Bishop Oswald to King Edgar in which he explained what was expected of "faithful men subjected to him" (*fidos mihi subditos*) whom he had provided with loans of three lives:

> I have granted the land to be held under me [*sub me*] to be held on these terms, to wit, that every one of these men shall fulfill the whole law of riding as riding men should, and that they shall pay in full all those dues which of right belong to the church, that is to say, *cirisceott* . . . and all other dues of the church . . . and shall swear that so long as they possess the said land they shall be humbly obedient to the commands of the bishop. What is more, they shall lend their horses, they shall ride them-

selves and be ready to build bridges and do all that is necessary in burning lime for the work of the church; they shall erect a hedge for the bishop's hunt and shall lend their own hunting spears whenever the bishop shall need them. And further, to meet many other wants of the lord bishop, whether for fulfillment of the service due to him or that due to the king [*ad suum servitium sive ad regale explendum*], they shall with all humility and subjection be obedient to the domination and to the will of the chief commander [*archiductor*] who presides over the see, in consideration of the benefice [*beneficium*] which has been loaned to them and according to the quantity of the land that each of them possesses.[41]

The duties described by Bishop Oswald's letter form a miscellaneous list ranging from bridge-building and service in the hunt to the much discussed "law of riding ... which pertains to riding men" (*equitandi lex ... quae ad equites pertinet*). In crucial respects they recall equally the "thegn's law" and the "geneat's law" of the eleventh-century *Rectitudines Singularum Personarum*.[42] What is to be emphasized here, however, is the nature of the relation between the bishop and his lessees. They have been endowed with land because they had shown themselves to be the bishop's "faithful subjects";[43] they are obliged to swear that "so long as they possess the said land they shall be humbly subject to the commands of the bishop"; they are to be obedient with all humility to the domination and will of the archiductor who presides over the see in consideration of the benefice lent to them (*beneficium quod illis prestitum est*). It is obvious that Oswald's tenants did not merely lease the Church's land in return for rent and service, but did fealty to him as well, undoubtedly confirming in many cases an existing relationship.[44] Indeed, as we have seen, one of Oswald's eleventh-century successors, Bishop Ealdred, required a tenant of the Church "to be submissive and obedient and acknowledge the lordship of whoever is bishop at the time."[45] Any defection from obedience, so the charter continues, would result in the immediate forfeiture of the land. Thus the lessee's tenure is made contingent upon his act of homage and his continued fidelity.[46]

As Stenton reminds us at length, the memorandum never explicitly stipulates military service as a condition of tenure.[47] Nevertheless, it strongly implies it. The bishop's tenants, we read, are to be obedient to him as archiductor in order to meet his wants "for the fulfillment of the service ... due to the king." The phrase *servitium ad regale explendum*, when taken in conjunction with the bishop's role as archiductor, clearly must refer to the performance of the "common burdens." This reading is supported by the qualification that follows: the royal burdens are to be acquitted "according to the quantity of land that each of them possesses." If we again turn to Ealdred's lease to Wulfgeat, we learn that the holder of the tenure was to "discharge the obligations on these 1½ hides at the rate of one, for three lives," upon the king's summons (to cinges banne).[48] Read in the light of the *Rectitudines* and of II *Cnut*, c. 79, this would seem to indicate the defense of the property in the fyrd, although it is impossible to determine whether actual armed service or a money payment is intended. We would not be reading too much into the memorandum to see in it an insistence upon the tenant's acquittal of his tenure in the royal host.

One should observe, however, that the bishop's tenants are not obliged directly to the king for these services, but rather to their "lord bishop." Indeed, it is *his* "work" (*opus est domino antistiti*) they do when they discharge royal service. A straightforward reading of this text would lead one to conclude that Oswald's tenants were required, by and large, to serve under him, their archiductor, in the king's fyrd in satisfaction of the see's military obligation to the king arising from its enjoyment of book tenure.[49]

This interpretation is supported both by Domesday Book and by "Hemming's Cartulary." Thus the lands of St. Mary's of Worcester are prefaced in Domesday Book by an account of the bishop's great immunity of Oswaldslow.[50] The Domesday commissioners recorded the "ancient customs" regarding the bishop's rights over his triple hundred. We learn from this *indiculum*, as it is called in the survey, and from a slightly longer version inserted in "Hemming's Cartulary" that the bishop often lent (*prestitum*) portions of the Church's demesne for three lives in return for service to him and the Church. Moreover, the bishop himself was responsible to the king for all royal dues attached to these 300 hides, for no sheriff or, as Hemming put it, no "exactor of royal service,"[51] had any claim in any matter there.

When we examine the individual Domesday entries for the Church's holdings, we discover that the bishop's tenants were a mixed lot, who ranged from the Wulfric who held one hide at Huddington "as a rustic doing service"[52] to great lords such as Beorhtric Ælfgarson[53] and Bishop Beorhtheah's own brother, Æthelric.[54] Most of the larger holdings, those of two or more hides, and the smaller tenures held by the bishop's great tenants are expressly said to have provided "the bishop with whatever he owed to the king's service."[55] Thus four "free men" held ten hides at Bishampton from the bishop, rendering sake and soke, church-scot, fees for burials, attendance at the pleas of the hundred, and service on military campaigns by land and sea (*expeditiones et nauigia*).[56] Beorhtric himself held but one hide from the bishop, for which he paid an annual rent. Nevertheless (*tamen*), he rendered to "the bishop's soke [*ad socam episcopi*] whatever he [the bishop] owed to the king's service" from this land.[57] At Croome d'Abitot we find that Bishop Wulfstan endowed one of his miles, presumably the Englishman, Sigeweard, who held this subtenancy T.R.W., with a five-hide estate on the express condition that he marry the daughter of the late tenant, support her mother, and serve the bishop (*seruiret episcopo*) for the holding.[58] Five more hides of the bishop's demesne were held by a thegn named Eadric, described in Domesday Book as *stirman* and by Hemming as "the helmsman of the bishop's ship and leader of his military forces for the king's service in the days of King Edward." According to the Survey, Eadric held the manor of Hindlip and "performed service, with other services belonging to the king and to the bishop."[59]

It would be unwise to assume from this that every Worcester tenant described in Domesday Book as responsible to the bishop for the performance of royal service actually attended the fyrd himself. In at least one instance we may be certain that the holder did not, for the bishop's tenant at Knightwick was the nun Ealdgyth.[60] If we are to believe the Domesday customs of the shire, many who owed fyrd service found substitutes to discharge their military duties to their lords.[61] This ought not to surprise us, any more than the idea that post-Conquest mesne tenants often acquitted their military service to their lords through the mediacy of lesser milites. Both before and after the Conquest, military service constituted only one of the reasons that religious houses created subtenancies. Bishops and abbots sought influential tenants for political, economic, and social reasons. St. Benedict's of Ramsey could expect a number of benefits other than fyrd service from having the sheriff of Huntingdonshire, Ælfric, as its tenant in that shire T.R.E., and the same can be said for Sheriff Godric's tenancy upon an Abingdon estate in his shire of Berkshire.[62] Prelates sometimes had personal reasons for creating læns. Even saints such as Bishop Oswald were not above loaning their Church's land to kinsmen. One of the Confessor's abbots, Wulfric of Ely, saw the lands of his monastery as fuel for his brother's matrimonial ambitions.[63] Be that as it may, it is likely that many of those who held in Oswaldslow did serve the bishop in arms in partial return for their holdings.[64]

Such was the case with Sigmund, Worcester's tenant at Crowle. The Domesday entry for Crowle is reticent about the precise terms of Sigmund's tenure, stating simply that he held five hides *de episcopo* T.R.E. and rendered "all service and geld" to the bishop for them.[65] If we had to rely upon the Domesday entry alone, we could not even classify Sigmund among the bishop's tenants who owed service to the king. Fortunately, however, Hemming chose to describe the history of Crowle. According to him, Sigmund was a Danish *miles* of Earl Leofric, who held one half of the vill of Crowle, the other half belonging, of course, to St. Mary's. "Like others of his race," Sigmund was greedy and not too particular about how he obtained what he wanted. What he wanted in this case was the other half of Crowle, and after failing to convince the monks to give it to him, he decided to use force. The result was the devastation of Crowle, followed immediately by a lawsuit. The intervention of Earl Leofric on behalf of his man led to a compromise solution. Sigmund was to receive a life interest in the Church's property, but in return for his tenure he had to agree to perform service to St. Mary's on military campaigns, whether by land or by sea. Hemming, who lived within a generation of Sigmund, added parenthetically that the Dane not only promised to serve the Church in arms but in fact he often did so.[66]

Hemming and Domesday Book both agree that Sigmund owed his service to the Church of Worcester. In entry after entry of the survey we read that the tenant's service, whether it be to the Church or to the king, belonged to the "bishop's soke."[67] As we suggested in a previous chapter,[68] the Oswaldslow evidence fits in well with the Domesday customs of Worcestershire. The bishop is obviously to be numbered among those who received a personal summons to the fyrd, which Wulfstan II (1062–1095) appears to have answered through a surrogate, and his tenants are just as plainly the warriors who helped to satisfy the bishopric's military burdens. From the language of the surviving charters it is clear that, as the Worcester customs imply, the bishop's tenants were his commended men, serving him just as he served his lord, the king.

According to his memorandum to Edgar, Bishop Oswald assessed the amount of service he expected from his lessees in proportion to the quantity of land they received as benefices. The same idea appears to underlie Bishop Ealdred's grant of the manor of Ditchford to Wulfgeat, for an assumption of this sort is necessary if one is to make sense of the statement that Wulfgeat was to discharge the obligation on these one-and-a-half hides at the rate of one.[69] It would not be altogether safe to argue from these examples that the Domesday landholders in

Oswaldslow likewise owed service to the bishop at a fixed rate dependent upon the hidage assessed against their tenements. A generalization of this sort goes beyond the evidence, although it is tempting to believe that it may hold some truth.

When we turn from the Worcester documents to those of the other religious houses, we find that the military burdens imposed upon a tenure were not necessarily pegged to its size. Indeed, not all dependent tenures need have owed military service. The bishop of Winchester's great manor of Taunton (Somerset) is a case in point. Three lists of the dues pertaining to Taunton have come down to us. One appears in the Exchequer Domesday,[70] a second in the Exeter Domesday Book,[71] and the third in a twelfth-century cartulary from Winchester Cathedral, the *Codex Wintoniensis*.[72] The last purports to be an Old English record of the customs of this manor "on the day that King Edward was quick and dead," and from its witness list, which includes such Anglo-Saxon notables as Wulfward White, Abbot Ælfsige of Bath, and Abbot Wulfgeat (of Athelney?), it can be ascertained that it was drawn up some time prior to the other two.[73] In all three records, the various estates appended to Taunton are represented as owing fiscal payments and judicial dues. The extent of these burdens differed slightly from estate to estate, some owing more, some less. Of special interest is the treatment of military obligations, represented in the Old English memorandum by the tenant's liability to the bishop for fyrdwite and in the two Domesday versions by the statement that certain manors "ought to go on military expeditions with the men of the bishop."[74] The memorandum, for instance, states that only the "bishop's men" holding at Nynehead Flory and Hele were liable for fyrdwite, while Domesday expands this list to include all of Taunton's appendages except Bagborough and Stoke St. Mary. What is certain is that military service was incumbent upon certain tenures and not upon others. Thus the *biscopes mann*[75] Dunna had to pay suit in the bishop's court but was not obligated to serve with the bishop's contingent in the fyrd, while another of the bishop's men, Ealdred, who held but a single hide of Taunton's land at Hele,[76] was so obliged.

We are left with a riddle. Why did certain tenants of Taunton owe military service to the bishop of Winchester, while others did not? Moreover, why are military burdens incumbent upon certain estates in the two Domesday accounts when the same estates are free of these obligations in the Old English memorandum? As with so many of the questions that arise from the study of Anglo-Saxon institutions, the available evidence is more patient of conjecture than of conclusive answers. It is possible, maybe even probable, but hardly provable, that each tenant struck his own bargain with the bishop in order to determine which of the customary dues would attach to his particular tenure. This interpretation has the merit of explaining how estates such as Oake and Tolland could acquire the burden of military service between the Confessor's death and the compilation of Domesday Book. Dunna, the bishop's man and tenant in these lands T.R.E., had, like so many of his fellow countrymen, suffered the loss of his lands some time before 1086.[77] Is it not possible that the Norman who replaced Dunna came to a new understanding with the bishop when he took up the tenancy?

Finally, we come to an obscure, largely ignored, yet extremely interesting document that appears to describe how the bishop of London recruited men from his estates in Essex, Middlesex, Surrey, and the neighboring shires in order to raise a crew for the king's hipfyrd.[78] The difficulties of interpretation presented by this text are formidable. It is in the form of a list of estates, each followed by a number, and is headed by a single explanatory word: (s)cipmen. The memorandum names thirty-two separate lands in all, which totaled somewhere in the vicinity of 350 hides—if we can rely on the Domesday assessments[79]—and produced all told some forty-five men. Nowhere in it do we find mention of either the bishop of London or the community at St. Paul's. However, there is a strong presumption in favor of such an association. Twenty-four of the estates named in the text can be shown to have belonged either to the bishop or to the cathedral chapter, and the manuscript itself was originally stored with the muniments of St. Paul's. It is thus reasonable to believe that we have preserved in this document a description of the arrangements made by the see of London to acquit its lands of its obligation in Æthelred's scypfyrd. If this reading is accepted, then one would be led to conclude that the bishop of London had adopted an entirely different tack toward the "common burdens" than had his brethren in the see of Worcester. For there is no discernible relationship in this list between the size of a particular tenement and the extent of its military obligation to the landowner. Thus both the thirty-hide manor of Clapham (Surrey) and the fifty-six hides held by the bishop of London at Stepney and Islington (Middlesex) furnished two scypmen.[80] One finds an even more dramatic example among the Essex estates. St. Osyth, assessed in Domesday Book at seven hides, contributed four men, while Tillingham, a manor of twenty hides and six acres, supplied only two men.[81] Evidently, the service demanded by the bishop had some basis other than the quantity of land held by his tenant.[82] What this principle was, however, one cannot say.

No doubt many lay and ecclesiastical lords settled their military retainers upon loanland in the tenth and eleventh centuries. But it is questionable whether this was in fact the most common form of maintenance at the time. It is likely that many English magnates, like their Norman successors,[83] preferred to keep military dependents closer at hand, maintaining for that purpose armed household men who could render immediate aid if the need arose. Certainly, the reference to salaried warriors in the Berkshire customs suggests that stipendiary retainers were far from rare on the eve of the Conquest. This inference is amply borne out by the other sources for the period.[84]

In our discussion of the composition of the late Anglo-Saxon fyrd, we noted Ælfric's translation of the miles "who bears the sword" as *byrth se cniht his swurd*.[85] We said then, and it bears repeating here, that the term *cniht* (literally "boy") was often used with a possessive to denote a household retainer. Although *cnihtas* served their lords in civilian occupations,[86] it was their military character that seems to have most impressed the men of the mid- and late eleventh century. For, as Stenton himself observed, the English word *cniht*, "knight," rather than the French word *chevalier*, came to represent the Norman warriors of William and his successors, constituting a "most remarkable exception to the general prevalence of French social nomenclature in England."[87] The Anglo-Saxon Chronicle bears witness to this, for when its continuators sought a word to describe the mounted retainers who rode with the great Norman lords, they decided upon *cniht*, apparently identifying these new military entourages with those familiar to them from before the advent of the Normans.[88]

Escort and hunting service probably constituted a major portion of the peacetime service rendered an Anglo-Saxon lord by his household retainers.[89] It was not only socially proper but necessary for a nobleman to surround himself with a large and impressive retinue when he either itinerated through his estates or made some other journey. For the forests and roads were infested by bands of robbers and outlaws,[90] and in those uncertain times even the most innocent mission could suddenly erupt into violence, as kings Cynewulf and Edward the Martyr discovered to their dismay some two centuries apart.[91]

Even one's home provided no refuge. From its frequent appearance in the Anglo-Saxon law codes, forcible entry, *hamsocn*, must have been among the more common crimes of the tenth and eleventh centuries.[92]

Consequently, a military household was a desirable precaution against the incursions of one's enemies. This is illustrated vividly by a late tenth-century charter, which professes to describe "the crimes by which Wulfbold ruined himself with his lord [i.e., the king]."[93] After a lifetime of wrongdoing, the thegn Wulfbold died, leaving a disputed inheritance. Among his crimes, which seem to have been directed mainly against his own kinsmen, was the seizure of an estate known as Bourne from his uncle Brihtmær. Brihtmær's kinsman, Eadmær, a king's thegn, immediately took possession of this land by force. But he did not enjoy his tenure long, for Wulfbold's son led his following to Bourne and laid siege to the estate. Eadmær and all fifteen of his men died in the ensuing battle.

Similar disaster visited the household of Earl Tostig in 1065. As we may recall,[94] rebellious Northumbrian thegns stormed Tostig's residence in York while the earl was in Wiltshire hunting with King Edward. Catching Tostig's household men unprepared, the rebels slaughtered all they could find. The various accounts of the uprising describe the victims as the earl's milites, huskarlas, and hiredmen, that is, his domestic military retainers.[95] It is obvious that Tostig, a harsh and unpopular ruler, maintained a large military contingent within his household, although it may be doubted whether all two hundred of the viros ex curialibus illius whom Florence of Worcester says were massacred by the rebels were professional warriors. Finally, there is the occasional reference to household warriors serving their lords in the fyrd. In 1054 Earl Siward of Northumbria raided Scotland with a large force of men. The northern recension of the Chronicle, the "D" version, celebrated Siward's great victory, boasting that the earl "routed the king Macbeth, and killed all the best in the land, and carried off a large amount of plunder such as had never been captured before."[96] The Chronicler, however, also took note of the heavy losses sustained by the English, and it is interesting to observe that among those who fell were a number of the earl's housecarls, i.e., his household warriors, and those of the king.[97] Domesday Book mentions the housecarls of earls Harold, Leofwine, Ælfgar, and Waltheof, in addition to those of King Edward,[98] and we can be fairly certain that these individuals represent but the tip of the iceberg. The only housecarls who found their way into the Inquest were those who had made the transition from household to landed retainers, and most housecarls were probably not so fortunate.[99] Each of the Confessor's earls probably maintained his own company of housecarls, whose main duty was to act as his bodyguard and hearth-troop.

According to the poem of the battle of Maldon, a major portion of Byrhtnoth's forces consisted of his household retainers. Certainly, those who are represented as having borne the brunt of the fighting after the death of Byrhtnoth were members of his *hired*.[100] Nor should we take this metaphorically. Offa, one of the more prominent warriors in the poem, is explicitly said to have dwelt with his lord the earl:

> Quickly was Offa hewn down in the battle; yet he had accomplished what he had promised his prince, as erstwhile he boasted with his giver of rings, that they should ride to the *burh,* unscathed to *their* home [emphasis added], or fall amid the host, perish of wounds on the field of battle. Near the prince he lay low, as befits a thane.[101]

If we take the poem on its face, Earl Byrhtnoth maintained a large and heterogenous entourage that included the grandson of a Mercian ealdorman, young warriors of high birth, and at least one "simple ceorl."[102] Even if the poem must be regarded as fictitious in detail, there is no reason to doubt that the poet accurately represented the composition of an earl's military household in the early eleventh century.

KING'S MEN AND MERCENARIES

The king himself, as the greatest lord in Anglo-Saxon England, enjoyed the largest military household in the realm. The imposition of the "common burdens" had added something new to the king's military resources, the thegn who served in respect of his bookland. But a more ancient element within the fyrd, the king's personal entourage, retained its importance throughout the period. From the thegns who fell at Cynewulf's side to the "vassals" who followed Alfred into the swamps of Somerset, royal retainers had played a key role in warfare, serving as the dependable core of the king's armies.

According to the traditional view, the early eleventh century witnessed a radical transformation of the king's armed retinue that left it a more highly organized and formidable fighting force. Cnut's triumph had resulted in the establishment of a new body of royal followers, a military guild not unlike the Byzantine Varangian guard, the company of royal housecarls. The historians of the last generation were certain about this. The consensus that developed about the housecarls, and which only recently has been challenged, made them out to be a professional military body, maintained within the royal household of the Anglo-Danish rulers of England and paid set wages at regular intervals to supplement their daily fare. In this view, the housecarls constituted a warrior elite, whose preeminence in battle was reflected by the weapons they bore. Cnut, we are told, required his warriors to possess "splendid armor," including a double-edged sword with a gold-inlaid hilt, as a condition of acceptance into his military entourage. Although a foot-soldier, a housecarl would also have owned a horse to carry him to battle and in pursuit of the defeated enemy, and a variety of defensive and offensive weapons, including a mail-shirt, helmet, shield, javelin, and, of course, the "massive and bloodthirsty two-handed axe" that characterizes him in the popular imagination.

Historians have generally viewed the king's housecarls as a corporate entity governed according to its own regulations and capable of acting as a judicial body whenever it became necessary to discipline one of its members, including the king himself. The laws supposedly governing their brotherhood, the so-called *Vederlov,* stress that each housecarl owed fidelity and aid to his fellows and, above all, to his lord, King Cnut. One's place in court was determined by a combination of merit and seniority. To refuse a comrade his rightful seat at the mess was deemed a grave breach of etiquette, since it showed contempt for one's sworn brother, and an offender was to be himself demoted at table to reflect his loss of honor. Honor and discipline were the ruling principles in the housecarls' guild-regulations, reflecting Cnut's concern with the proper deportment of his household men. Just as the viking brotherhood of Jómsborg had been bound by iron laws to maintain peace among themselves, so the housecarls, their putative offspring, were to behave in the king's court with dignity and sobriety. Cnut wanted his military retainers to be more than ferocious warriors; he wanted them to be a disciplined, military brotherhood. And they were. In battle after battle, including Stamford Bridge and Hastings, the king's housecarls spearheaded the fyrd and stiffened its ranks of amateurs. In short, the king's housecarls were both a law-bound guild and a paid, standing army.[103]

Unfortunately, this neat and convenient reconstruction has been erected on an eroding foundation. Our understanding of the housecarls has advanced by subtraction in recent times. The late twelfth- and thirteenth-century literary sources upon which M. K. Larson, Johannes Steenstrup, and others depended have increasingly been subjected to criticism, and much that was once "known" about the housecarls is now questionable. The *Jómsvikinga Saga* and the *Lex castrensis* of Cnut are cases in point. The similarities between Cnut's legislation for his military household and the regulations governing the pirate brotherhood of Jómsborg have often been pointed out.[104] Twenty-five years ago it would have been unthinkable to write about Cnut's housecarls without acknowledging the influence of the Jómsvikings upon their organization. After all, as Stenton repeatedly observed in his magisterial survey, Thorkell the Tall's own brother commanded Jómsborg, and many of Cnut's housecarls must have come from that warrior community.[105] The excavation of a great circular fortress at Trelleborg in the 1930s and 1940s, followed by the uncovering of similar fortifications at Aggersborg and Fyrkat, seemed to give historical substance to the late twelfth-century *Jómsvikinga Saga*. If the magnificent barracks-camp of Jómsborg existed, and surely it must have in light of these findings, then the Jómsvikings were historical. Furthermore, archaeologists placed the construction of the Danish circular fortresses around 1000, which made perfect sense to historians, who saw them as barrack-camps for the training of the great army that Swein and Cnut led to England. It followed logically that Cnut's housecarls had passed through one of these camps and had received military training and lessons in discipline not unlike those recorded in the *Jómsvikinga Saga*.

Present-day scholars are less impressed with the authority of the *Jómsvikinga Saga*. Critics have pointed out that Jómsborg is first mentioned in written sources around 1200, two centuries after the brotherhood was supposedly destroyed. Despite considerable effort, moreover, archaeologists have found no trace of this fortress. Wollin, a small town in Poland, has been suggested as a possible site, but even if it proved to be the historical Jómsborg it would not rehabilitate the saga, since Wollin was a Danish market town that bore as much resemblance to the saga's citadel as Kansas does to Oz.[106] Even Gwyn Jones, whose sympathy for the literary sources is pronounced, is unwilling to come to the defense of the *Jómsvikinga Saga*'s "dreams and folktales": "It is difficult, indeed impossible, to accept saga notions of Jomsborg as a warrior community of men between the ages of 18 and 50, their services for sale to the highest bidder, bound by iron laws to keep peace among themselves and avenge each other's death." Such tales, he concedes, were "the misconceptions and pseudo-heroic (which means romantic) embroidery of a later age."[107] Others are not so charitable; Lauritz Weibull, for example, finds no historical basis whatsoever for either Jómsborg or its viking brotherhood.[108] In short, the adventures of Palna-Toki and his celibate warrior band seem to be nothing more than a good yarn, a medieval tall tale that modern historians starved for sources have swallowed too greedily.

The case of the *Lex castrensis sive curie*, the main source for the traditional conception of Cnut's housecarls, is not nearly so clear-cut. Three related versions of "Cnut's" household regulations have come down to us. Two are embedded in the late twelfth- or early thirteenth-century Danish histories of Sven Aggeson and Saxo Grammaticus; the third is a vernacular text, also ca. 1200. The earliest and most complete of these appears in Sven Aggeson's *Brevis historia regum Dacie*. According to Sven, a minor Danish nobleman, Cnut's regulations had only recently been written down. Archbishop Absalon, concerned that the traditional rules governing the royal household were in danger of being forgotten, had prepared a vernacular text of Cnut the Great's *Witherlogh* ("penalties" or "regulations") in consultation with his former pupil Cnut VI (1182–1202) a few years before.[109] Sven subsequently rendered this text into Latin.

As has been pointed out recently, Absalon was a firm supporter of royal power who had every reason to "dignify and consolidate current arrangements [in the royal household] by tracing them back to a legislative act by a great ruler of the past."[110] The royal housecarls of twelfth-century Denmark formed the central administrative institution of that kingdom, and as a corporate body possessed judicial authority as well as military power. If a king was to rule effectively, he had to maintain control over his military household, and Absalon's work should be seen as part of a program designed to promote royal authority at the expense of this unruly aristocracy of service. Saxo's use of the *Lex castrensis* leaves little doubt about Absalon's intent, since Saxo explicitly compares the good order maintained in Cnut the Great's court with the "undisciplined and rebellious" behavior of the young warriors of his day.[111]

Absalon thus had reason to improve, if not forge, Cnut's *Lex castrensis;* which does not prove that he did. But even if the archbishop wished to produce a faithful record of Cnut's household laws, it is doubtful whether he could have. The laws he compiled would have been based upon oral traditions that were then a century-and-a-half old, traditions that, as Sven put it, were in danger of being forgotten. The studies of anthropologists on the transmission of oral traditions have taught us to be cautious about accepting ancient lore uncritically. Finally, Sven's and Saxo's explanation of the purpose of the *Lex castrensis* is at odds with the texts they present. Both authors tell us that Cnut issued these laws to maintain discipline over the vast throng of soldiers who had flocked to his court. The *Lex castrensis* could not have been used effectively for this purpose. Whatever one might believe about its antiquity, the code's character seems clear enough: it was designed to regulate an immediate following rather than the 3000 house-carls of Sven's account. All things considered, it would be unwise to rely too heavily upon the *Lex castrensis*.

Nevertheless, these laws ought not to be dismissed out of hand. Some of the details in Sven's text do echo genuine eleventh-century practices. Cnut's purported insistence that each housecarl own a sword with a gilded hilt recalls both Earl Godwine's peace-offering to Harthacnut of a ship and its crew of eighty warriors, each of whom also had "a sword with a gilded hilt fastened round his loins," and the *Northleoda laga*'s pronouncement that even if a ceorl "prospers so that he possesses a helmet and a coat of mail and a gold-plated sword, if he has not [5 hides of] land, he is a ceorl all the same."[112] According to Sven's account, a housecarl who repeatedly showed contempt for a comrade by usurping his seat at the king's table was to be pelted with meat bones by his fellows, which well describes Archbishop Ælfheah of Canterbury's un-sanitary martyrdom in 1012.[113] At the time that Sven wrote, throwing food apparently was already looked upon askance by the better sort, for Saxo chose to substitute ostracism, a penalty borrowed from the Rule of the Templars, in his *Lex castrensis*.[114] Even if Absalon or Sven knew of this incident, it is hardly likely that they would have wished to hold it up as a model for the behavior of Cnut VI's retainers.

If nothing else, Absalon's efforts suggest that the Danish court of his day believed that Cnut's housecarls had been constituted into a law-bound guild. That Cnut would have organized his household in this manner is far from implausible, since guilds seemed to abound in tenth- and eleventh-century England. Some years before Cnut established his rule in England, for example, the thegns of Cambridge had promulgated their own guild regulations, in which they swore to one another an "oath of true loyalty," and undertook to protect their guild-brothers in blood-feuds and arrange for their proper burial. Any thegn who failed to observe all the rules faithfully was to be fined by his fellows, which surely suggests a court of some kind. And just as Cnut supposedly reserved his housecarls' ultimate fealty, so a thegn of the guild was to obey his chosen lord and attend to his "necessary business" even at the expense of his guild-brothers' needs.[115] Landowners of the "district of London" had formed themselves into a "peace-guild" in the days of Æthelstan, in order to comply better with royal decrees. Led by a king's reeve, guild members were to gather their commended men and ride against "any kindred so strong and large . . . that they refuse us our rights and stand up for a thief."[116] The military connotations are unmistakable. The thegns of Cambridge, the London landowners of Æthelstan's code, and the "cnihtas" of London, whose association survived the Conquest, all belonged to law-bound guilds in Cnut's day and before. Is it so difficult to believe that the king's housecarls would have followed suit? Indeed, there may even be an oblique reference to guilds fighting as units in II *Cnut,* c. 77.[117]

We are forced back to the contemporary sources, and here we are confronted with a familiar problem. When we exclude the romantic fictions of the sagas and the questionable laws preserved in later histories, we are left with only a few scattered references to housecarls in charters, chronicles, and, oddly enough, Domesday Book. Those who have studied the history of the vikings in their native lands will not be surprised to learn that tenth- and eleventh-century Scandinavian sources provide little enlightenment on the nature of this institution. The word *huskarl* itself is Norse and literally means "household man," that is, a dependent who was maintained in his lord's household in return for daily service.[118] The word, if not the institution, may have originated in Cnut's England, since individuals who would have been called housecarls in the English sources are termed *hemthægar,* "home-taken," or *hirthman,* "member of the household," on tenth-century Danish runestones.[119] The term, however, soon spread throughout the Norse world, and we find it used on a number of eleventh-century Swedish runestones, most of them too cryptic to be of much use for our purposes. One, at least, does shed some light on the connotation of "housecarl" in mid–eleventh-century Sweden. The Turinge stone in Södermanland was raised to commemorate vikings who had fallen on campaign in Russia. It reads in part:

> Ketil and Bjorn raised this stone for Thorstein their father, Onund for his brother, *and the housecarles for their peer,* and Ketillaug for her husband. These brothers [comrades?] were the best of men, at home and afield with a host. They kept their housecarles well.[120]

The emphasis is obviously upon the housecarls' dependent status and military service. Throughout the northern world of the eleventh century, in fact, the term "huskarl" tended to denote a retainer of a magnate. This does not mean that all housecarls resided with their lords. If Klavs Randsborg's interpretation of the Danish runestones is correct, a number of Harald Gormsson's *hemthægar* made the transition from household retainers to landed lords, and by doing so aided their royal lord's establishment of a territorial state in western Denmark.[121] Similarly, some of Cnut's and his successors' housecarls in England became landowners in their own right, receiving from their royal lords grants of bookland. We cannot assume that a housecarl was necessarily a domestic follower.

The company of king's housecarls first appears in England during the reign of the Dane Cnut. The origins of this body remain obscure, although it seems certain enough that it was a royal creation, and it has been reasonably suggested that the first housecarls were the crews of the forty ships that Cnut kept with him in 1018 when the bulk of his fleet returned to Denmark. The inspiration for the housecarls has been credited variously to the Jómsvikings, to the old Norse bodyguard known as the "bearsarks,"[122] and to the existing royal household that Cnut inherited from his Anglo-Saxon predecessors.[123] As we have just seen, the Jómsvikings may not have existed at all. Both the Norse and the Old English royal households are plausible candidates, and, in all likelihood, both helped shape the institution as it developed in England.

Housecarls, whether of a king or a magnate, could expect food, lodging, clothing, and weapons. If Cnut's housecarls numbered in the hundreds, let alone the thousands, the cost of maintaining them must have been considerable. Undoubtedly, the Anglo-Danish kings raised the needed revenues through the levying of *heregeld,* although such monies were used not only to maintain housecarls but also to purchase more purely mercenary forces. By 1066 some of the Crown's regular annual revenues were earmarked for the support of the king's housecarls. The Domesday Book survey of Dorset states that four boroughs, Dorchester, Bridport, Wareham, and Shaftesbury, owed annual payments for the upkeep of housecarls (*ad opus huscarlium*).[124] The four-and-a-half marks of silver a year thus raised could have supported no more than a handful of men, four if the king's housecarls were paid at the same rate as the Berkshire milites. Obviously, Edward must have had other regular sources of income, including, presumably, a portion of the geld, to pay for his household. The Dorset borough customs may not have provided Edward with much cash, but they do supply the historian with valuable evidence for the existence of the housecarls as a corporate body on the eve of the Conquest.

If, as seems probable, housecarls received wages, they were stipendiary troops. According to the *Lex castrensis,* Cnut not only saw to his household troop's daily needs but paid each man a monthly wage.[125]

That Cnut paid his followers wages is beyond serious doubt, whatever one might think about the historicity of the *Lex castrensis*. English monarchs both before and after Cnut certainly did so. Alfred the Great, for example, reserved one-sixth of his annual revenue from taxation (i.e., his *feorm*), for the wages of the fighting men (*bellatores*) he maintained in his court, and distributed these funds annually at Eastertide.[126] Alfred's military following appears to have been organized into some sort of hierarchy, since the £200 the king left them in his will was to be divided unequally, "to each as much as will belong to him according to the manner in which I have just now made distribution to them."[127] We have no reason to believe that Cnut, whom the scalds knew as "the gracious giver of mighty gifts," was any meaner than Alfred toward his men.[128] (It seems significant in this context that Florence of Worcester, writing in the early twelfth century, should have chosen *solidarius* to translate *huskarl*.)[129]

Acceptance of pay did not make the housecarls a "mercenary army." The distinction between "stipendiary soldier" and "mercenary" may seem oversubtle to a modern reader raised in a capitalistic society. To the northern world of the early Middle Ages it was basic. As the author of the vernacular *Lex castrensis,* the *Vederlov,* explained: "The king and other leading men who have a *hird* should show their men favour and good will and give them their proper pay. In return men should give their lord loyalty and service and be prepared to do all his commands."[130] This is the same reciprocity that shaped the world of the *Beowulf*-poet: "I repaid in war the treasures that he [King Hygelac] gave me—with my bright sword . . . There was no need for him . . . to buy with treasure a worse warrior."[131] Cnut's housecarls would have well understood Beowulf's boast. Their obligation to serve in arms arose from the lordship bond rather than the cash nexus. In this they probably differed from their contemporaries, the mysterious *lithsmen* and *butsecarls* of the coastal boroughs,[132] who seem to have sided with the highest bidder, and certainly from the shipmen whom Edward the Confessor paid off and dismissed from his service between 1049 and 1050.[133] Like all dependents, housecarls expected to be maintained according to their deserts. *Swerian,* an Anglo-Saxon hold-oath dating from the middle of the tenth century, even makes this an explicit condition of the lordship contract.[134] But the rewards that housecarls and other retainers earned were incidental to the service they rendered. Thus wages were an accident rather than the essence of a housecarl's service. If we were to seek the ideal housecarl we would find him in Byrhtnoth's heroic thegn

Offa or in the young Beowulf rather than in the great mercenary captain Thorkell the Tall.

Not all housecarls dwelled in the royal court and accompanied the king on his peregrinations. Like other free dependents, housecarls served in hope of suitable rewards, the greatest of which would be a grant of bookland, and a number of them succeeded in making the leap from domestic serving man to landed retainer.[135] Most were probably not so fortunate. Many undoubtedly did live with the king and serve him as escorts, companions, and bodyguards. Some may have lived outside of the court, on fiscal land set aside for their use. As Stenton noted long ago, there is a tantalizing reference in the Berkshire Domesday survey to fifteen acres that the king had in Wallingford on which his housecarls used to dwell (*in quibus manebat huscarles*).[136] Wallingford was a strategic ford across the Thames,[137] and Stenton was prepared to read this passage as referring to garrison duty. The idea is tempting, but the evidence is far too fragile for conclusions. Like the Dorset borough customs, the Wallingford notice raises questions that cannot be answered on the basis of the extant evidence.

Hollister was surely correct when he pronounced the housecarls "a unique, closely-knit organization of professional warriors who served the kings of England from Cnut to Harold Godwineson and became the spearhead of the English army."[138] Their military value was demonstrated on at least two occasions. In 1041 two of Harthacnut's housecarls were killed by the citizens of Worcester while attempting to collect a particularly noisome tax. The king responded much as Edward the Confessor was to react a decade later when the citizens of Dover killed some of Eustace of Bologne's troops; he decided to ravage the entire shire. According to "Florence of Worcester," a reliable source for local events, Harthacnut dispatched the forces of five earls and "almost all his housecarls" to teach his new subjects a lesson in obedience.[139] In 1054 King Edward ordered Earl Siward of Northumbria to launch a full-scale invasion of Scotland, with the intention of replacing a hostile king, Macbeth, with one friendlier to the English, the exile Malcolm. In order to insure victory, Edward provided his earl with a large supply fleet, a logistical necessity in light of the unhospitable character of the Scottish countryside,[140] and a contingent of his own housecarls. The king entrusted both these fyrds to his earls rather than lead them himself. Nevertheless, his housecarls took an active part in the fighting. We cannot leap from this to a declaration that the housecarls formed a substantial, paid standing army. All versions of the Chronicle emphasize the ferocity of Siward's battle with Macbeth, and the northern recension, "D," identifies the most noteworthy of the casualties: the earl's son and nephew, some of his housecarls, and also some of the king's. This seems to underscore the status enjoyed by both comital and royal housecarls and to suggest that their numbers were small enough that the loss of a few was worthy of notice. One might infer from the Chronicle evidence that royal housecarls formed a small military elite, whose participation in a fyrd was not conditional upon the king's presence. In other words, they fought as a tactical unit in addition to serving as the king's personal bodyguard.

In their contractual relationship with the king and in their corporate identity, the royal housecarls may have owed much to Scandinavian antecedents. But in their role as the king's armed household, his personal retainers, they differed little from the retinues that surrounded earlier Anglo-Saxon kings. Like their thegnly predecessors, housecarls served their royal lords in peace as well as in war. They appear in the sources as tax collectors, witnesses to royal charters, recipients of land grants, and donors of land.[141] One might best characterize them as a group of ministers and attendants upon the king who specialized in, but were not limited to, war. Thus we find the same man described as a *cynges huskarl* in one charter and a *minister regis* in another.[142] Similarly, the Domesday survey of Buckinghamshire designated Burgheard of Shenley as a *huscarle regis Edwardi* in one entry and as a *teignus regis Edwardi* in the very next.[143] It was precisely this ministerial aspect which most struck the Norse writers on this period. For they knew the English king's housecarls not by the Scandinavian term "huskarls," but as *thing-amen,* an Anglo-Saxon loan word derived from *thegnung,* "service," and related etymologically to *thegn.*[144] It is tempting to say that the housecarls introduced an element of professionalism into the king's household, that they differed from their thegnly predecessors by their rigid discipline and sophisticated organization. But even this goes beyond the evidence. Reading Asser's *Life of King Alfred,* one is struck by how much Alfred's military household resembles Cnut's. Both were corporate bodies of household retainers whose members served the king in both military and ministerial capacities. Cnut's housecarls thus stand firmly rooted in the tradition of Anglo-Saxon lordship. They would not have looked particularly out of place feasting in a hall such as Heorot, boasting over their drink about the great deeds they had performed for their lord and the still greater ones that they would do to repay him for his generosity.

The royal burgesses of Hereford and the king's Welshmen in the Archenfield district of Herefordshire on first glance seem to have little or nothing in common with King Edward's housecarls. First impressions, however, are misleading. The Welsh marches was a region characterized by raiding and warfare during the later years of Edward the Confessor's reign, so much so that Domesday Book reveals a ribbon of wasteland in 1066 that stretched along the frontier from Cheshire to Gloucestershire, an Offa's Dyke of destruction. From 1046 to 1065 the Anglo-Saxon Chronicle records ten major raids, either by English forces into Wales or by Welsh armies against the border shires. The chronicles leave the reader dizzy with images of rapine and pillage, of the heads of Welsh chieftains and kings being borne to Edward the Confessor, of the exiled Earl Ælfgar and his Welsh ally King Gruffydd ap Llewellyn ransacking a cathedral, killing the canons who tried to defend it, and burning down the borough of Hereford.[145] That the burgesses and landholders settled in this no man's land should have been burdened with especially heavy military obligations is not in the least surprising.

In 1066, according to Domesday Book, 103 men dwelled in Hereford "inside and outside the wall," all of whom apparently owed military service to the king.[146] The borough customs explain that "if the sheriff went into Wales with an army, these men went with him. But if anyone was ordered to go and did not go, he paid a fine of 40s. to the king."[147] The implication is that, theoretically, all 103 burgesses were obliged to follow the sheriff, the king's agent, on an offensive expedition, but that in practice only some of these men would receive a summons to go. This, of course, would have been a practical precaution. Hereford had been sacked and burned in 1055, and it would have been foolhardy to have left the town undefended against raids. Even if only half of these men were called, Hereford bore an extraordinarily heavy burden in comparison with other Domesday boroughs. Malmesbury, in Wiltshire, for example, was required to send only one man to the fyrd or pay 20s. for the upkeep of the king's *butsecarls*.[148] Oxford, which may have had as many as 5000 inhabitants in 1066, and was certainly one of the largest and most prosperous towns in the Midlands, sent 20 men to the fyrd, or compounded this service for £20.[149] The Devonshire boroughs provide an even more startling contrast. Exeter, which had at least 335 houses in 1066, three times as many as Hereford had, served in the fyrd for but five hides, sending in all probability a single man. Its neighbors, Barnstaple, Lydford, and Totnes, were reckoned as five hides together, although Lydford alone was about the same size as Hereford.[150] One could go on with this list, but the results would be the same. The only borough in Domesday Book that can match Hereford's military burden is Shrewsbury, in Shropshire, also in the Welsh marches.[151]

Like the lesser fyrdmen of neighboring Worcestershire, a burgess who failed to answer the summons was fined 40s., which was to be paid directly to the king. There is no mention of any intermediate lord between the king and these burgesses.[152] I would suggest that the reason for this was that there was no intermediate lord. That the 103 burgesses were king's men comes out clearly in the Hereford customs, which in parts resemble the duties owed by the king's thegns and drengs between the Ribble and Mersey rivers.[153] The miscellany of services included cash payments, agricultural labor, stalling of game for the king's hunt, and escorts for the king and his court. Such services were incumbent upon everyone who held property in the city. Although a man could leave the borough, he could not sell his tenement without obtaining the reeve's consent and a promise from the prospective buyer that he would assume all the services due the king. If one was unable to fulfill his obligations due to poverty, his house was taken without payment by the reeve, "who ensured that the house did not remain empty and the king was not without service."[154] The king is thus represented as the burgesses' landlord. He may also have been their personal lord, for the burgesses of Hereford owed the king their heriot. A burgess "who served with a horse" was obliged to give the king his horse and arms upon his death.[155] A lesser burgess or his heir paid a mere 10s. All these payments and services were rendered directly to the king or to his local agent, the sheriff. It seems clear that the obligations defined in the Domesday customs of this borough derive from a combination of tenure on royal land and personal lordship, the two so intertwined by 1066 that it would be difficult to separate them. The military customs of the borough should be understood within the context of military settlement. The burgesses of Hereford or of Shrewsbury, who owed similar dues, did not follow the sheriff into Wales because they were free men defending their homeland; they served because they were king's men, royal dependents, settled on fiscal land. They were, in effect, English "king's freemen."

The same was true of their Welsh neighbors in Archenfield. This border district, known to the Welsh as Erging, had long been contested by the English and Welsh. In the tenth century it appears to have become part of the English kingdom, but a tenuous part at best. There is even some suggestion that Gruffydd ap Llewellyn managed to reclaim Archenfield in 1055 and hold it until his death in 1063.[156] Certainly he ravaged it. According to Domesday Book, the Welsh king and his brother devastated the region, probably in 1055 when Gruffydd and his ally Earl Ælfgar led an army of vikings and Welshmen in a truly impressive *chevauchée*.[157]

The Domesday commissioners could not obtain information about the value of the land before 1066, but they did write down Archenfield's peculiar local customs, the laws under which an English king ruled Welshmen. The military arrangements for his district are especially interesting. We are told:

> Anyone who does not go when ordered by the sheriff to go with him into Wales is fined the same [2s. or 1 ox to the king]. But if the sheriff does not go, none of them goes. When the army advances on the enemy, these men by custom form the vanguard and on their return the rear-guard.[158]

To this the entry for Archenfield two folios later adds some information about conditions in 1086 that helps to illuminate the pre-Conquest military customs: "They do not pay tax nor other customary dues, except that they march in the king's army if they have been ordered [*pergunt in exercitu regis si jussum eis fuerit*]." The "they" of the latter passage does not refer to everybody in Archenfield, or even to all able-bodied free men, but to the "100 men, less 4" who were *king's* men. (The text is explicit about their status.) These king's men seem to have enjoyed a status equivalent to the sokemen and liberi homines of the eastern Midlands and East Anglia. They were lords in their own right, with peasants who dwelled on their lands, but enjoyed only modest wealth; combined, they and their men possessed a grand total of 73 ploughs.[159] The liberi homines of Archenfield, like the king's horsemen of Hereford in 1066, owed the king a heriot consisting of a horse and weapons. The men of Archenfield summoned to war by the sheriff, like those who followed the sheriff in Hereford, were king's men obliged to respond by ties of lordship. The military institutions of the Welsh marches are not generally applicable to the more tranquil areas of late Anglo-Saxon England. They are the customs of military colonists and native king's men on a troubled frontier.

The king's stipendiary retainers, his housecarls, are the most striking reminder that royal lordship continued to play a crucial role in the organization of the late Anglo-Saxon fyrd. But the principle of royal lordship reached deeper than this. All the king's higher officers, most notably the earls, the stallers, and the sheriffs, were obliged by their oaths of personal commendation to serve him in arms, leading the local and regional contingents of the royal host. Moreover, if we can place any weight at all upon the heriot provisions of Cnut's laws and Domesday Book, it would seem that king's men were at least theoretically obliged to lend their royal lord military support if the need arose. For it was precisely the gift of horse, sword, and armor that symbolized the bond created by the commendation ceremony.[160] There is no reason to believe that the king did not expect from his men what other lords expected from theirs.

In the case of the king's thegns, the tenurial obligation did not so much supersede as reinforce and define more exactly an existing personal duty. It would be rash indeed to attempt to disentangle the various strands of obligation and self-interest that led Earl Harold to accept command of the punitive forces that King Edward sent into Wales in 1055 and 1063.[161] The military obligation of one of Harold's stature was overdetermined, arising in part from his office, in part from his commendation, and in part from his possession of vast tracts of land. The king expected his great magnates, lay and ecclesiastical, to answer his summons to battle, and their estate demanded that they come with a suitable armed following. The military obligation of the landed aristocracy did not end there, however. They also owed contingents of warriors in respect of their lands. These fyrdmen would have fought as units, under the command of a sheriff, or a captain appointed by the nobleman, if they belonged to a private hundred, or the magnate himself. This dual obligation also characterized the service of the king's lesser retainers. The burgesses of Hereford and the king's Welshmen in Archenfield followed the sheriff into Wales because they dwelled on the royal fisc and owed such service for their tenures and because they were king's men answering the summons of their lord.

Even when a warrior-landowner had "bowed" to a lord other than the king, the very fact that he held his property by book-right made him, in some sense, a king's man; for it placed him in a special relationship with the king, one akin to *landhlafordscipe*. Nor must we forget that Anglo-Saxon monarchs from the time of Edward the Elder had been studiously promoting the idea that the king was the lord and protector of all his moot-worthy subjects. It is no coincidence that the later lawbooks, which so stress this aspect of kingship, demanding oaths of fealty from the suitors of the hundred and shire courts, should treat desertion from a fyrd under the king's personal command as tantamount to *hlafordswicung,* the bootless crime of betraying one's own lord.[162]

A NATION IN ARMS?

If late Anglo-Saxon armies were composed of lords and their personal followings, and if the basis of military obligation was lordship and land tenure, what then of the "nation in arms"? The question is particularly pertinent, since the notion has become firmly entrenched in the secondary literature that two distinct types of military obligation coexisted in the Confessor's England. The first, we are told, was the ancient universal military duty of all free men to serve in the "nation in arms," a duty largely limited by 1066 to the massing of local forces for emergency defense. Led by local royal agents and king's thegns, these levies of poorly armed and ill-disciplined free peasants defended the coastal areas against the sudden incursion of pirates and the interior localities against the raids of small, mounted bands of vikings. Generally, their success was limited. The second, according to the accepted view, was a territorial obligation, in some instances defined as one warrior from every five hides of land, used to assemble select armies of trained or semitrained soldiers. Because England's enemies in the tenth and eleventh centuries were such that successful defense depended upon well-disciplined and mobile forces of manageable size, this limited, territorial obligation gradually supplanted the universal duty of able-bodied free men. At battles such as Stamford Bridge or Hastings, the English army consisted largely of select troops levied from the entire realm, buttressed by stipendiary troops and by the free men of the immediate vicinity.[163]

This vision of the fyrd nicely reconciles the evidence for limited military obligation with the assumption that in early Germanic societies all able-bodied free men were obliged by their status to defend the homeland. Such a reconciliation, however, would be unnecessary if no universal military obligation existed in Anglo-Saxon England. Its proponents have generally assumed its existence and, relying upon its purported antiquity, have placed the burden of persuasion upon those who would deny its survival into the eleventh century. However, as we have already seen, the arguments advanced for a general military obligation of all free men in early England are not persuasive. The sources, fragmentary and ambiguous as they are, support instead the conclusion that the fyrds of pre-viking England were royal war bands cemented by the bond of lordship. What, then, is the evidence for Anglo-Saxon *leveés en masse* on the eve of the Conquest?

Our discussion properly begins with the critical Chronicle annal of 1016. The fortunes of the English were at their nadir in this year. King Æthelred, who had been restored to the throne in the spring of 1014, was facing his second defeat. Cnut and his ally Eadric Streona, the perfidious ealdorman of Mercia, were celebrating Christmas by ravaging Warwickshire; the king's son, Edmund Ironside, had in the previous year publicly flouted his father's authority by marrying the widow of an executed Danelaw magnate; and the West Saxons had recently submitted to Cnut, giving him hostages and furnishing his army with horses and supplies.[164] On top of this, the king may have been in ill health, since he was to die in April of that year. If there was any time that the "nation in arms" should have been raised, it was in the winter of 1015 and spring of 1016. The Chronicler, unsurprisingly for those who believe in a general military obligation, says explicitly that Edmund called out "the entire English nation" (*ealla Engela theode*) not once but five times that year.[165] The Chronicler used even more specific language about the second fyrd raised in 1016, saying that it was summoned "on pain of the full penalty, every man to go forth who was capable of service" (to give Whitelock's translation of "tha bead man æft fyrde be fullum wite, thæt ælc man the fere wære forth wende").[166] The conclusion seems inescapable: the "nation in arms" saw action in 1015/ 1016.

This interpretation, however, presents some problems. First, as has been pointed out a number of times, the "entire English nation" seems to have been mounted on at least two of these campaigns. One need not belabor the point that horses were expensive in the eleventh century and only the well-to-do could afford them. (One need only glance at the Domesday customs of Hereford to see what a difference the possession of a horse could make to a man's status.[167]) Second, the phrase "ælc man the fere wære forth wende" raises more questions than it answers. If *fere* indeed meant "capable of service," as Whitelock translates it, Edmund called up every able-bodied man, noble, commoner, and slave in 1016. An army of this size is as credible as Xerxes' expeditionary force as recorded by Herodotus.[168] Even if we infer that "every man capable of service" really meant all healthy, adult sokemen, *liberi homines*, and other "free" peasants—realizing, of course, that by calling only such men free we are robbing the geburs, cottars, and their ilk of whatever freedom they may have enjoyed—we would still be confronted with the spectacle of ten thousand Lincolnshire sokemen assembling and marching to a common meetingplace, a logistical nightmare that would have been repeated throughout East Anglia and the eastern Midlands. Finally, we must consider the economic implications of calling out all able-bodied free men. In 1016 the fyrds met only for brief periods, coming together for a battle or campaign and then dispersing. A decade earlier, however, Æthelred had called out the "whole nation from Wessex and Mercia" and kept that army in the field from late summer "throughout the autumn."[169] If the fyrd of 1006 indeed consisted of all the free peasants of Wessex and Mercia, the year's harvest would have rotted in the ground. As it was, Æthelred's decision to summon the forces of Wessex and Mercia produced a great deal of economic hardship for the peasants who came into contact with that army. In the words of the Chronicle: "and the English levy caused the people of the country every sort of harm, so that they profited neither from the native army nor the foreign army."[170]

One obviously cannot take the language of these texts too literally. But if that is the case, what are we to make of them? What did the Chronicler mean when he spoke of an army of "the entire English people"? The solution lies in the area of recruitment rather than in the sort of individual called. In 1016 Edmund Ironside sent summonses, probably in his father's name, throughout *all* the shires. Rather than raising the forces only of Wessex, or Mercia, or the Danelaw, or of a select number of shires within these regions, the ætheling assembled "national" armies.[171] These forces were undoubtedly larger than most English armies, but differed only in the number of shires involved, not in the personnel called forth. The phrase "be fullum wite, ælc man the fere wære" emphasized the seriousness of Edmund's intentions. The first fyrd that the ætheling had summoned in 1016 had dissolved almost immediately, the West Saxons and Mercians refusing to join with the men of the Danelaw because the king and the London contingent had stayed away. There is no indication in the Chronicle that the fyrdmen who went home had been punished for their dereliction of duty, if it really was dereliction.[172] Consequently, Edmund threatened his father's subjects with legal penalties if they failed to respond to his second summons, and the only excuse that he would accept was ill health. This does not mean, however, that he sent a summons to every man; only that those who were obliged to go would be held to their obligation. One, thus, cannot use the Chronicle references to armies of "the entire nation" to demonstrate the existence of a general military obligation.

In the words of Warren Hollister, "we can perhaps conclude that 'all the English people' is merely loose phraseology and that only the select fyrd was called to duty on these campaigns."[173]

Nor does the military organization of the Welsh marches in 1066 reveal traces of an earlier system of universal military obligation. The Domesday customs of the Welsh marches represent instead the peculiar arrangements of a particularly violent region. The king's men in Hereford, Shrewsbury, and Archenfield were duty-bound to follow the sheriff *into* Wales; that is, to go on offensive expeditions against the enemy. It is not immediately obvious how this duty relates to a military obligation that we are told was defensive in nature and limited in its geographical scope. One must also ask why the customs were presented as incumbent upon two boroughs and a border district rather than upon the free men of Herefordshire and Shropshire. Is it not more plausible to read these texts as the customs of military colonists, king's men, settled on royal land on a troubled frontier?

The sieges of Exeter in 1001 and 1067 have also been offered in evidence.[174] On first glance the argument is persuasive. Exeter, as we learn in Domesday Book, answered to the fyrd for five hides, which probably meant that it owed only one fyrdman.[175] Nevertheless, in 1001 the citizens of that borough "stoutly resisted" a viking army, saving the town, if not the surrounding countryside, from being pillaged.[176] In 1067 Exeter again showed that it could be a formidable opponent. For eighteen days the town held out against the forces of William the Conqueror, only opening its gates when the new king promised to renew its ancient privileges.[177] That the citizens of Exeter and other boroughs defended the walls of their towns is beyond question. But what does that tell us about the military *obligations* of these townspeople? The natural incentive to defend one's hearth and life does not necessarily imply a duty to king or country, or even to shire. (In 1067 the thegnage of Devonshire seems to have joined William *against* the townspeople.) The citizens' defense of Exeter may have had no more to do with military obligation than had had the armed resistance of the burgesses of Worcester to the collection of Harthacnut's geld in 1041 or Dover's rough treatment of Eustace of Bologne and his knights in 1051.

The Bayeux Tapestry indicates that poorly armed soldiers fought at Hastings,[178] and some have seen this as a pictorial representation of peasant levies. Even granting that these men were peasants, it does not necessarily follow that Harold's army at Hastings consisted of a select force of professional or semiprofessional warriors and a mass levy of amateurish local peasants. As we have seen, "free men" (liberi homines) did fight, and fall, at Hastings, but these men came from as far away as Suffolk, hardly the immediate locale of the battle.[179] Since we have no idea what constituted the minimally acceptable equipment of a fyrd-man, we cannot say that because a man lacked a hauberk—and one of those "poorly armed" warriors of the Bayeux Tapestry is seen wielding a sword, while others are found fleeing on horses—that he was therefore a local peasant obliged by his free status to stand by his king.

In short, the available evidence supports the existence of a general military obligation of free men on the eve of the Conquest only if one is already convinced that the "nation in arms" was a reality. No source says explicitly that the Anglo-Saxons raised mass levies against their enemies or that all free Englishmen were obliged to defend their home-land. Some historians have explained this scarcity of evidence as an indication that the so-called "Great Fyrd" was an anachronism in 1066. But there is another explanation: such a force never existed. The only armies that defended the Confessor's England were the so-called "se-lect" fyrds described by the Domesday custumals. The "nation in arms," like the Anglo-Saxon peasant commonwealth so dear to Victorian schol-ars, is a historical myth.

A NOTE ON THE STRUCTURE AND ORGANIZATION OF LATE SAXON ARMIES

C. Warren Hollister's analysis of the units constituting the select fyrd, Eric John's pioneering work on the military functions of the hundred and on the importance of private lordship in the ship-sokes, and Michael Powicke's useful, though perhaps overfine, distinction be-tween royal, provincial, and county armies have deepened our under-standing of Anglo-Saxon military organization on the eve of the Con-quest.[1] For each of these scholars, the "nation in arms" was an anachronism in 1066, a vestige of England's primitive Germanic past that had long since ceased to be of practical military value. Because of this, all three have concentrated on the select armies of the Domesday Book custumals. The picture that has gradually emerged from their researches is of a military system that consisted of national armies and local levies, with the local levies making up some of the units of the national armies. Under this schema, tenth- and eleventh-century select fyrds were organized by shire and perhaps hundred, and reinforced by the king's mercenaries and housecarls. This reconstruction is essentially correct. Its details, however, can be brought into sharper focus by a careful study of the sources in light of what we have learned about the nature of Anglo-Saxon military obligation.

As has been noted a number of times, the eleventh-century sources speak of both local and national armies. These forces seem to have shared personnel and systems of recruitment. They differed, however, in their theaters of operation and, of course, in size. Essentially, a local fyrd was the military force of a shire or of a number of neighboring shires, led by royal agents entrusted with the administration of that region. Such fyrds could represent the forces of an ealdordom or earldom (depending upon the time period), or of individual shires. The latter appear in the Chronicle largely in a defensive posture, guarding the shire or the region against the incursion of pirates. They were also employed on occasion as offensive forces, notably in the Welsh marches. In 1056, for example, the moustached warrior-bishop, Leofgar of Hereford, and the sheriff of Herefordshire, Ælfnoth, led the men of that shire in a disastrous campaign against Gruffydd ap Llewellyn.[2] That such sorties into Wales were not exceptional is suggested by references in Domesday Book to the obligation of the burgesses of Hereford and Shrewsbury and the king's Welshmen of Archenfield to follow the sheriff into Wales when he went on campaign. Earls and ealdormen similarly defended their regions and waged offensive wars with forces levied throughout their provinces. The invasions of Scotland by Earl Siward in 1045 and 1054 and of Wales by Earl Swein Godwineson in 1046 are examples of the latter.[3]

The independent military power of the great ealdormen of Æthelred II and the earls of Edward the Confessor is striking and attests to their viceregal authority over the regions entrusted to their care. When, for example, the Danes ravaged and burned Norwich in 1004, Ulfkell Snilling, who had not had time to gather his forces, decided to purchase peace from the enemy. Ulfkell, the ealdorman of East Anglia in fact if not in title, did not seek the king's consent for this truce, but acted on his own initiative with the advice of his East Anglian advisors. When the Danes violated the treaty by pillaging and burning the borough of Thetford, Ulfkell gathered his forces as quickly and secretly as he could, and attempted to surprise the enemy. Interestingly, in the three weeks that separated the assaults on Norwich and Thetford, Ulfkell apparently never contacted the king for orders, aid, or consent for his policies. Nevertheless, the Chronicler did not include him in his gallery of the disloyal.[4]

During the darkest days of Æthelred II's reign the king's ealdormen controlled the military forces of their provinces so completely that they were able to transfer their allegiance from one king to another. Thus King Swein's triumphant march through England in the late summer and autumn of 1013 was punctuated by the submissions of Earl Uhtred "and all the Northumbrians" and of Æthelmær, the ealdorman of Wessex beyond Selwood, and the "western thegns."[5] Three years after this, Earl Uhtred again demonstrated his independence by switching allegiance from Æthelred II and Edmund Ironside to Swein's son Cnut, abruptly halting his harrying of Shropshire on behalf of the latter in order to rush north and save his earldom from the further depredations of the Danes.[6] Cnut apparently regarded Uhtred's shifting loyalties with suspicion, since he ordered the earl killed soon afterward. Uhtred was a model of fidelity in comparison with his notorious contemporaries, Eadric Streona of Mercia and Ælfric Darling of Hampshire, who apparently were able to offer their masters not only their own services but the military power of their ealdordoms.[7]

This is not to argue that late Anglo-Saxon England was a federation of ealdordoms and earldoms rather than a unified kingdom. The last years of Æthelred II's reign show only that ealdormen could behave like kings if the king himself was unable or unwilling to do so. In theory, and most often in practice, the authority of every ealdorman and earl was delegated to him by the king. Ealdormen, like bishops and sheriffs, were the king's *heretogan*, his generals, and under a reluctant warrior-king such as Æthelred II or a positively pacific one such as Edward the Confessor, these royal agents served not only as the leaders of their shires' forces, but were given command of the national armies.[8] As Ælfric wrote in reference to biblical times but with an eye for his own day: "Then the kings set ealdormen under them, to aid themselves, and they often sent them to many battles . . . and the ealdormen defeated the attacking enemies."[9] This is an accurate description of Harthacnut's employment of his earls in 1041, when the new king sent an army into Worcestershire to ravage that shire in revenge for the deaths of the two housecarls whom he had sent there as tax collectors.[10] It also describes Æthelred II's military policy, and was perhaps meant to do so.[11]

The structure of the national fyrd reflected its sources of obligation: royal lordship, personal lordship, and land tenure. A national landfyrd such as the five that were called in 1015/1016 would have consisted of the following components: the forces of the ealdordoms, shires, hundreds (private and royal), private sokes, and various companies of stipendiary troops and personal retainers brought by the king and his great magnates. Similarly, a shipfyrd would have included royal warships, manned by the king's butsecarles and lithsmen, perhaps the private ships of his earls, vessels supplied and manned by the ship-sokes, and, by 1066, the ships owed in lieu of other royal renders by the boroughs that were to become known as the Cinque Ports.[12]

We need not rehearse the overwhelming evidence for the shire as a tactical unit in the late Anglo-Saxon fyrd. The researches of Hollister and others have established this beyond any reasonable doubt.[13] Below the shire level, however, matters become less clear. Much is obscure about the lesser tactical units of the fyrd, but it seems certain that just as shires were subdivided into hundreds for judicial and administrative purposes, so the shire levies of the fyrd consisted of hundred contingents. Ealdorman Æthelweard, who wrote his Latin translation of the Chronicle sometime between 975 and 998, thus characterized a shire fyrd as "Ealdorman Weohstan with the hundreds of the people of Wiltshire [centuriis populi provinciae Vuilsaetum]."[14] We might also note in this context that Ælfric of Eynsham and other late tenth- and early eleventh-century writers regularly translated "centurion" as "hundredes ealdor." This may simply be an attempt to render the Latin literally, but it is difficult to believe that Ælfric, who undoubtedly appreciated the martial flavor of "centurion," would have chosen "hundredes ealdor" if it did not connote a military command.[15]

A previously neglected passage in the Huntingdonshire Domesday survey clinches the matter: "The men of the shire testify that King Edward gave Swineshead [Kimbleton hundred] to Earl Siward with soke and sake, and so Earl Harold had it, except that they [either the men of Swineshead or its hides; it is unclear which is intended] paid geld in the hundred and went with them against the enemy."[16] Apparently, the fyrd service owed from an estate (or a borough[17]) was rendered in the hundred unless the king favored the landowner with an exemption. The military character of the hundred ought not to surprise us. The hundred, after all, was the insular version of the continental centena, and in the latter the military function predominated.[18] It is probable that from its inception the hundred was a unit of the fyrd. This does not necessarily mean, however, that Anglo-Saxon armies were customarily made up of twenty-man squads, since the five-hide rule may not have been universally practiced. The hundreds of Domesday Book, moreover, differed in the number of hides they contained, although they tended to be approximately one hundred hides.

Swineshead apparently did not render fyrd service in Kimbolton Hundred until 1055, when Earl Harold succeeded Siward as its owner.[19] This hundred was itself probably a recent creation, a territorial soke of twenty hides that had been carved out of Leightonstone Hundred for the benefit of the Northumbrian earl. Presumably, Siward had enjoyed Kimbolton and its appendages, including Swineshead, with full sake and soke, which included not only the perquisites of justice but also the right to exact military service and collect fyrdwite from those who held under him. If we take the Domesday jurors at their word, Harold succeeded to the property, but the sheriff recaptured the land for geld and expeditio, and he rather than Harold's ductor was to lead its men into battle.

The case of Swineshead brings us to the matter of private lordship and the fyrd. As is well known, the bishop of Worcester held his triple hundred of Oswaldslow with full military command. On the eve of the Conquest one of the bishop's tenants served as captain of his troops, fulfilling a role that ordinarily would have belonged to the bishop himself, and which, apparently, had belonged to Bishop Ealdred in the 1050s. Nor was the bishop of Worcester alone in his privileged state. In 1066 seven hundreds in the shire were in private hands. It is certain that the sheriff could not levy troops in Oswaldslow—that role belonged to the bishop and his *ductor exercitus ad servitium regis,* Eadric—and probable that he was similarly excluded from the hundreds held by Evesham, Pershore, and Westminster abbeys. As Helen Cam demonstrated some years ago, private hundreds were far from uncommon in late Anglo-Saxon England.[20] The hundredal manor of Tewkesbury in Gloucestershire seems to have been one such franchise held in the time of King Edward by a mere king's thegn, Beorhtric, son of Ælfgar.[21] According to Domesday Book, Tewkesbury and its members combined for ninety-five hides, forty-five of which were in demesne. The estate was exempt from all royal service and geld, except for the service that the lord of the manor, Beorhtric, owed the king.[22] Although this statement of immunity is not as clear as one might hope, it does seem to imply that Beorhtric alone was responsible for the "common burdens," and that the sheriff had to go through him to collect them, rather than exact them himself. It is reasonable to infer that, like the bishop of Worcester, Beorhtric was responsible for levying troops from his lands.

The lords of private hundreds were, in effect, royal officers, and it is not surprising that they should have been held responsible for the military service due from the lands that lay within their franchises.

Private lordship may have played an even greater role in the structure of the fyrd. Both the Swineshead entry and the customs of Worcestershire suggest that those who held land with sake and soke were responsible for the military service owed from their franchises.[23] This system, or a variation of it, may well have prevailed over much of England. In all probability, Earl Siward had enjoyed military jurisdiction not only over his holdings in Huntingdonshire but in Northumbria as well. The great territorial sokes of East Anglia and the northern Danelaw, and the small "shires" of Northumbria bear more than a passing resemblance to continental centenas, and it is tempting to see them, along with the private hundreds of Wessex and Mercia, as forming military districts.[24] Finally, Cnut's laws imply that fyrdmen ordinarily fought at their lord's side. If so, lordship helped structure even the forces raised from royal hundreds. In short, lords and their retainers played a crucial part in the composition of shire fyrds on the eve of the Conquest, the tactical units of which may very well have resembled the *conrois* of the later Middle Ages.[25]

Conclusion

Throughout the Anglo-Saxon period, from the days of Ine to those of Harold Godwineson, lordship played a crucial role in the military organization of the state. In the seventh and eighth centuries royal hosts were essentially royal war bands, composed of the king's retainers and their own followers. Each warrior fought not as a free man defending the nation or the "folk," as many have assumed, but as a commended man serving his lord. Land entered into this system only obliquely. Although military obligation arose from the demands of lordship rather than land tenure, the acceptance of an estate did oblige a man, according to the mores of the time, to requite the gift with faithful service. Moreover, such tenure was precarious. Consequently, both the gift of land and the gift of service were open-ended, each reinforcing and confirming the other.

The introduction of bookland tenure by the churchmen of the seventh century combined with the pressures of the viking invasions to alter this system. Unlike the earlier endowments of royal warriors, bookland was hereditary. Once bookland had been given to the Church or to one of the king's lay followers, the king's proprietary interest in the estate was severely curtailed. Because commendation was not hereditary, a king could not be certain that those who succeeded to a book would be as firm in their devotion to him as the grantee had been. The spread of bookland tenure thus meant that the kings of the period were gradually granting away the land that had been traditionally used to attract and maintain warriors. Therefore, it became necessary to forge a bond between the possession of bookland and the performance of military service. The solution reached by the kings of the Mercian hegemony was the imposition of certain burdens—bridge-work, fortress-work, and attendance in the fyrd—upon land held by book-right.

Under the pressure of the Danish invasions that wracked England in the late ninth and the early tenth century, the kings of the West Saxon dynasty, Alfred and his successors, perfected this new arrangement, redefining "fortress-work" to include the building and maintenance of a system of boroughs, and expanding fyrd service into the manning of a standing army. Alfred's son, Edward, and his grandsons, Æthelstan and Edmund, gradually imposed the duty of attending the fyrd, along with its concomitant fiscal obligations, upon all who held by book-right in their kingdom, whether West Saxon, Mercian, or Dane. The specific amount of military service demanded of a landholder was based upon the hidage assessed against his land. In turn, hidage was apparently determined in the majority of cases by the value of the estate, the general assumption being that one pound's worth of land ought to be assessed at one hide, although the precise relationship between the value of a property and its hidage appears to have varied from shire to shire and even within a single shire.

The evidence suggests that those who held bookland T.R.E. were expected to "defend" their property in person in the royal host. A thegn who held a great estate, upon which the fyrdfæreld lay so heavily that more than a single warrior was required to discharge the duty, would have been obliged to lead one or more other warriors to the fyrd. How the landowner might obtain the necessary fyrdmen was not the concern of the king, so long as these soldiers were suitably competent. In some instances bookholders exchanged a lifetime, or multi-life, interest in a parcel of land for their tenant's armed service. In others they fulfilled their obligation to the king by maintaining fighting men within their own households. Whatever course a magnate chose, he would ordinarily guarantee the loyalty of his warrior-representatives by binding them to himself through commendation. Lordship and land tenure thus provided the twin pillars upon which the military organization of late Anglo-Saxon England rested. In a very real sense, the royal host never ceased being the king's following arrayed for war. In this lies one of the keys to the turbulent politics of the late tenth and of the eleventh century.

Statistical Appendix

TABLES FOR 12 REGRESSION ANALYSES
OF HIDES ON VALUE T.R.E. 11 FIGURES
PLOTTING HIDES AGAINST VALUES

TABLE A1
BUCKINGHAMSHIRE HOLDINGS
[DB i. 143–153]
n = 359

Statistics	Variable y (hides T.R.E.)	Variable x (value T.R.E.)
Mean	5.7	£5.1
Standard deviation	5.9	5.6
Median	4.0	3.0

Log-linear regression analysis

function: $y = \alpha x^\beta$
linear form: $\ln y = \ln \alpha + \beta \ln x$
Regression equation: $y = .264 + .894x$
Standard deviation of y about the regression line: $S = .44$

$R^2 = 84.5\%$, adjusted for 357 d.f.
$F_{(1, 357)} = 1946$

Note: n represents all Buckinghamshire holdings, excluding incomplete entries and royal holdings in 1066. *Terra regis* has been omitted from these calculations because of (1) the difficulties in estimating their values, which often include renders in kind; and (2) their tendency to be either beneficially hidated or not hidated at all.

TABLE A1a

BUCKINGHAMSHIRE HOLDINGS VALUED AT OR LESS THAN £15
[DB i. 143–153]
n = 343

Statistics	Variable y (*hides* T.R.E.)	Variable x (*value* T.R.E.)
Mean	5.0	£4.1
Standard deviation	4.7	3.5
Median	3.5	3.0

Linear regression analysis

function: $y = \alpha + \beta x$
Regression equation: $y = .171 + 1.18x$
$R^2 = 76.6\%$, adjusted for 341 d.f.
$F_{(1.341)} = 1121$

F-test for heteroskedasticity using dummy variables for value

n = 343
k = 9
R^2 (with original and dummy variables) $= 74.1\%$, adj. for 334 d.f.
$R_1^2 =$ (with original variables) $= 76.6\%$, adjusted for 341 d.f.
$F = (R^2 - R_1^2/k) / [(1 - R^2) / (n - k - 1)]$
$F_{(9.331)} = -3.5$

NOTE: n excludes royal holdings in 1066

TABLE A1b

BUCKINGHAMSHIRE VILLAGES
[DB i. 143–153]
n = 215

Statistics	Variable y (*hides* T.R.E.)	Variable x (*value* T.R.E.)
Mean	9.8	£8.6
Standard deviation	6.8	6.4
Median	10.0	7.0

Log-linear regression analysis

function: $y = \alpha x^{\beta}$
linear form: $\ln y = \ln \alpha + \beta \ln x$
Regression equation: $y = .393 + .863x$
Standard deviation of y about the regression line: $S = .41$
$R^2 = 72.1\%$, adjusted for 213 d.f.
$F_{(1, 213)} = 552$

TABLE A2

HERTFORDSHIRE HOLDINGS
[DB i. 132–142]
n = 339

Statistics	Variable y (hides T.R.E.)	Variable x (value T.R.E.)
Mean	3.3	£5.6
Standard deviation	5.0	7.7
Median	2.75	1.5

Log-linear regression analysis

function: $y = \alpha x^{\beta}$
linear form: $\ln y = \ln \alpha + \beta \ln x$
Regression equation: $y = -.201 + .747x$
Standard deviation of y about the regression line: $S = .65$
$R^2 = 76.6\%$, adjusted for 337 d.f.
$F_{(1, 337)} = 1106$

NOTE: n represents all Hertfordshire holdings, excluding royal holdings in 1066.

TABLE A3

BEDFORDSHIRE HOLDINGS
[DB i. 209–218]
n = 362

Statistics	Variable y (hides T.R.E.)	Variable x (value T.R.E.)
Mean	5.1	£3.6
Standard deviation	3.3	4.6
Median	1.8	2.0

Log-linear regression analysis

function: $y = \alpha x^{\beta}$
linear form: $\ln y = \ln \alpha + \beta \ln x$
Regression equation: $y = .116 + .79x$
Standard deviation of y about the regression line: $S = .48$
$R^2 = 83\%$, adjusted for 360 d.f.
$F_{(1, 360)} = 1766$

NOTE: n represents all Buckinghamshire holdings, excluding incomplete entries and royal holdings in 1066.

TABLE A4
MIDDLESEX HOLDINGS
[DB i. 126–131]

n = 92

Statistics	Variable y (*hides T.R.E.*)	Variable x (*value T.R.E.*)
Mean	9.5	£9.9
Standard deviation	15.4	14.8
Median	5.0	5.0

Log-linear regression analysis

function: $y = \alpha x^{\beta}$
linear form: $\ln y = \ln \alpha + \beta \ln x$
Regression equation: $y = .257 + .844x$
Standard deviation of y about the regression line: S = .45

R^2 = 85.8%, adjusted for 90 d.f.
$F_{(1, 90)}$ = 551

NOTE: n represents all Middlesex holdings with information on T.R.E. valuation, excluding royal holdings. Variable y represents geldable hides.

TABLE A5
CAMBRIDGESHIRE HOLDINGS
[DB i. 189–202]

n = 384

Statistics	Variable y (*hides T.R.E.*)	Variable x (*value T.R.E.*)
Mean	2.9	£5.0
Standard deviation	3.1	6.2
Median	1.75	2.9

Log-linear regression analysis

function: $y = \alpha x^{\beta}$
linear form: $\ln y = \ln \alpha + \beta \ln x$
Regression equation: $y = .171 + .759x$
Standard deviation of y about the regression line: S = .52

R^2 = 84.1%, adjusted for 382 d.f.
$F_{(1, 382)}$ = 2026

NOTE: n represents all Cambridgeshire holdings with information on T.R.E valuation, excluding royal holdings.

TABLE A6
BERKSHIRE HOLDINGS
[DB i. 56–63]
n = 278
Representative Shire from the South-Eastern Circuit
(Stephenson no. 1)

Statistics	Variable y (*hides T.R.E.*)	Variable x (*value T.R.E.*)
Mean	7.9	£6.8
Standard deviation	9.1	6.7
Median	5.0	5.0

Log-linear regression analysis

function: $y = \alpha x^\beta$
linear form: $\ln y = \ln \alpha + \beta \ln x$
Standard deviation of y about the regression line: S = .51
R^2 = 77.1%, adjusted for 300 d.f.
$F_{(1,300)}$ = 934

Linear regression analysis

function: $y = \alpha + \beta x$
regression equation: $y = -.05 + 1.17x$
Standard deviation of y about the regression line: S = 4.8
R^2 = 73.2%, adjusted for 300 d.f.
$F_{(1,\ 300)}$ = 756

NOTE: n represents all Berkshire holdings with information on T.R.E. valuation, excluding royal estates. The functional form for the regression line is between log-linear and linear.

TABLE A6*a*

BERKSHIRE HOLDINGS
[DB i. 56–63]
n = 302

Statistics	Variable y (*hides* T.R.E.)	Variable x (*value* T.R.E.)
Mean	8.3	£8.3
Standard deviation	9.6	9.7
Median	5.0	5.0

Linear regression analysis

function: $y = \alpha + \beta x$
regression equation: $y = 2.85 + .658x$
Standard deviation of y about the regression line: $S = 7.15$

$R^2 = 44.4\%$, adjusted for 300 d.f.
$F_{(1, 300)} = 241$

NOTE: n represents all Berkshire holdings with information on T.R.E. valuation, including royal estates.

TABLE A7

WILTSHIRE HOLDINGS
[DB i. 64–74]
n = 485
Representative Shire from the South-Western Circuit
(Stephenson no. 2)

Statistics	Variable y (*hides* T.R.E.)	Variable x (*value* T.R.E.)
Mean	7.7	£6.6
Standard deviation	12.1	11.6
Median	4.0	3.0

Log-linear regression analysis

function: $y = \alpha x^\beta$
linear form: $\ln y = \ln \alpha + \beta \ln x$
Regression equation: $y = .4 + .856x$
Standard deviation of y about the regression line: $S = .54$

$R^2 = 81\%$, adjusted for 483 d.f.
$F_{(1, 483)} = 2065$

NOTE: n represents all Wiltshire holdings, excluding incomplete entries and royal holdings in 1066.

TABLE A8

OXFORDSHIRE HOLDINGS
[DB i. 154–161]
n = 77
Representative Shire from the Midland Circuit
(Stephenson no. 4)

Statistics	Variable y (*hides* T.R.E.)	Variable x (*value* T.R.E.)
Mean	5.7	£4.8
Standard deviation	6.8	5.3
Median	3.5	3.0

Log-linear regression analysis

function: $y = \alpha x^{\beta}$
linear form: $\ln y = \ln \alpha + \beta \ln x$
Regression equation: $y = .315 + .885x$
Standard deviation of y about the regression line: $S = .37$
$R^2 = 83\%$, adjusted for 75 d.f.
$F_{(1, 75)} = 372$

Linear regression analysis

function: $y = \alpha + \beta x$
Regression equation: $y = -0.0763 + 1.2x$
Standard deviation of y about the regression line: $S = 2.3$
$R^2 = 88.5\%$, adjusted for 75 d.f.
$F_{(1, 75)} = 587$

NOTE: n represents a random sample of entries for 1066 from which royal holdings have been excluded. (The RAND Corporation, *A Million Random Digits,* Glencoe, Ill., 1955, pp. 1–3.) The form of the regression line is between linear and log-linear.

TABLE A9

SHROPSHIRE HOLDINGS
[DB i. 252–261]
n = 404
Representative Shire from the Western Circuit
(Stephenson no. 5)

Statistics	Variable y (hides T.R.E.)	Variable x (value T.R.E.)
Mean	2.8	£2.3
Standard deviation	3.9	4.0
Median	2.0	1.0

Log-linear regression analysis

function: $y = \alpha x^{\beta}$
linear form: $\ln y = \ln \alpha + \beta \ln x$
Regression equation: $y = .582 + .564x$
Standard deviation of y about the regression line: $S = .58$

$R^2 = 56.1\%$, adjusted for 411 d.f.
$F_{(1,\,402)} = 517$

Linear regression analysis

function: $y = \alpha + \beta x$
Regression equation: $y = 1.05 + .774x$
Standard deviation of y about the regression line: $S = 2.4$

$R^2 = 62.6\%$, adjusted for 402 d.f.
$F_{(1,\,402)} = 675$

NOTE: n represents all holdings in Shropshire, excluding royal holdings and waste in 1066. The form of the regression line is between linear and log-linear.

TABLE A10
HUNTINGDONSHIRE HOLDINGS
[DB i. 203–208]
n = 112
Representative Shire from the Northern Circuit
(Stephenson no. 6)

Statistics	Variable y (*hides* T.R.E.)	Variable x (*value* T.R.E.)
Mean	5.8	£6.6
Standard deviation	4.8	7.2
Median	5.0	4.0

Log-linear regression analysis

function: $y = \alpha x^\beta$
linear form: $\ln y = \ln \alpha + \beta \ln x$
Regression equation: $y = .884 + .821x$
Standard deviation of y about the regression line: $S = 1.83$
$R^2 = 70.6\%$, adjusted for 110 d.f.
$F_{(1, 110)} = 268$

NOTE: n represents all Huntingdonshire holdings, excluding incomplete entries and royal holdings in 1066.

TABLE A11
DERBYSHIRE HOLDINGS
[DB i. 272–278]
n = 206
Representative Shire from the Northern Circuit
(Stephenson no. 6)

Statistics	Variable y (*carucates T.R.E.*)	Variable x (*value T.R.E.*)
Mean	2.4	£2.5
Standard deviation	2.4	2.7
Median	2.0	2.0

Log-linear regression analysis

function: $y = \alpha x^{\beta}$
linear form: $\ln y = \ln\alpha + \beta\ln x$
Regression equation: $y = .131 + .725x$
Standard deviation of y about the regression line: $S = .57$
$R^2 = 59.7\%$, adjusted for 204 d.f.
$F_{(1.204)} = 302$

Linear regression analysis

function: $y = \alpha + \beta x$
Regression equation: $.571 + .718x$
Standard deviation of y about the regression line: $S = 1.31$
$R^2 = 69.3\%$, adjusted for 204 degrees of freedom
$F_{(1.204)} = 464$

NOTE: n represents all Derbyshire holdings, excluding incomplete entries and royal holdings in 1066. The functional form of the regression line appears to be closer to linear than log-linear.

TABLE A12
ESSEX HOLDINGS
[DB ii. 1–108]
n = 678
Representative Shire from the Eastern Circuit
(Stephenson no. 7)

Log-linear regression analysis

funtion: $y = \alpha x^{\beta}$
linear form: $\ln y = \ln\alpha + \beta\ln x$
Regression equation: $y = 2.41 + .709x$
$R^2 = 64.2\%$, adjusted for 676 d.f.
$F_{(1, 676)} = 1216$

SOURCE: John McDonald and G. D. Snooks, "Tax Assessments," p. 368.

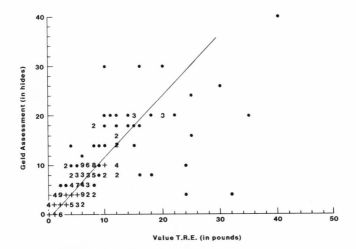

* One observation at that point
4 Four observations at that point
+ More than ten observations at that point

Regression equation for all properties T.R.E. valued at £15 or less: y = .171 + 1.18x

Fig. A1. Geld Assessment–Annual Value Relationship for Properties in Buckinghamshire in 1066

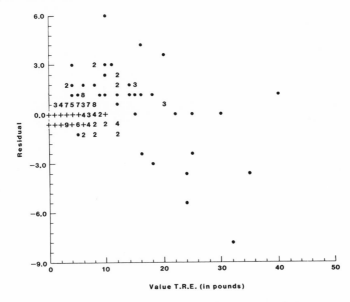

Fig. A1a. Plot of Standardized Residuals against Value for all Buckinghamshire Properties in 1066

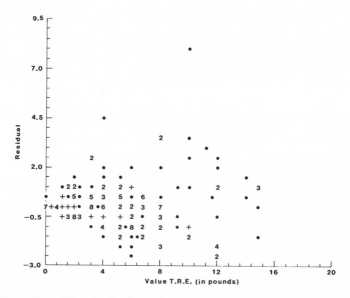

Fig. A1*b*. Plot of Standardized Residuals against Value for all Buckinghamshire Properties worth less than £16

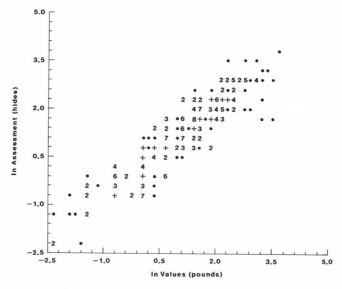

Fig. A1*c*. Plot of Logarithmic Transformation of Hides and Values T.R.E. for Buckinghamshire

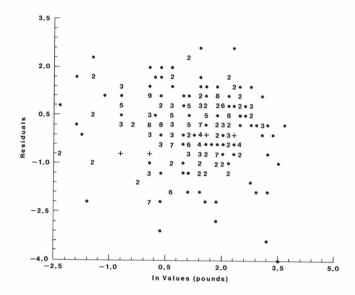

Fig. A1*d*. Plot of Standardized Residuals against ln Values for Logarithmic Transformation of Hides and Values for Bucks

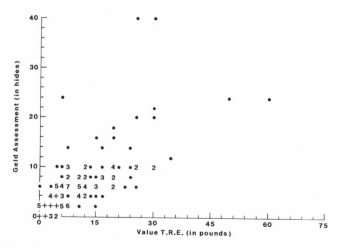

Fig. A2. Geld Assessment–Annual Value Relationship for Properties in Hertfordshire in 1066

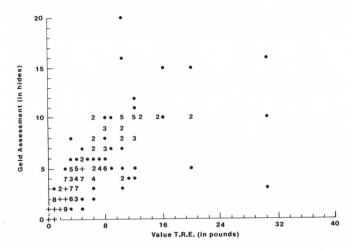

Fig. A3. Geld Assessment–Annual Value Relationship for Properties in Bedfordshire in 1066

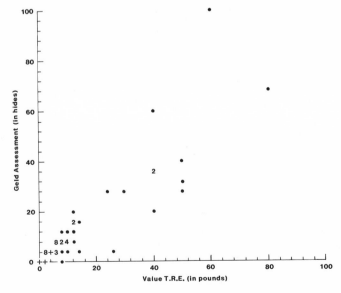

Fig. A4. Geld Assessment–Annual Value Relationship for Properties in Middlesex in 1066

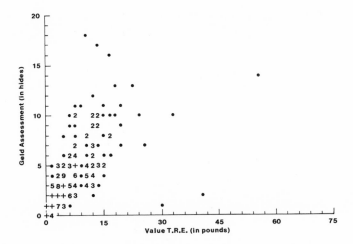

Fig. A5. Geld Assessment–Annual Value Relationship for Properties in Cambridgeshire in 1066

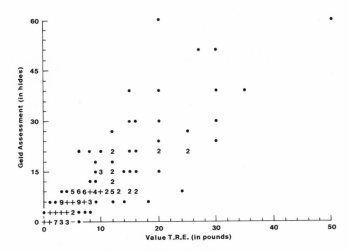

Fig. A6. Geld Assessment–Annual Value Relationship for Properties in Berkshire in 1066 (all royal estates excluded)

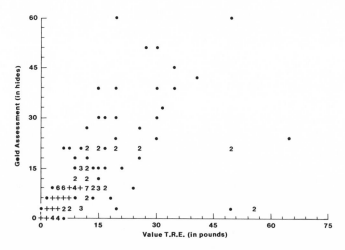

Fig. A6a. Geld Assessment–Annual Value Relationship for Properties in Berkshire in 1066 (including royal estates)

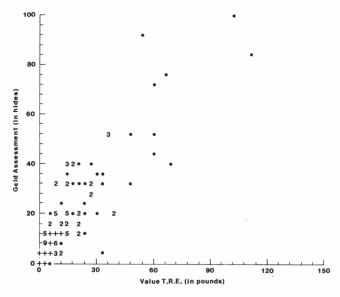

Fig. A7. Geld Assessment–Annual Value Relationship for Properties in Wiltshire in 1066

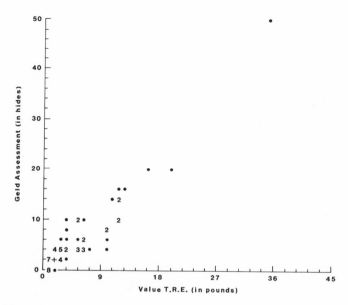

Fig. A8. Geld Assessment–Annual Value Relationship for Properties in Oxfordshire in 1066 (random sample)

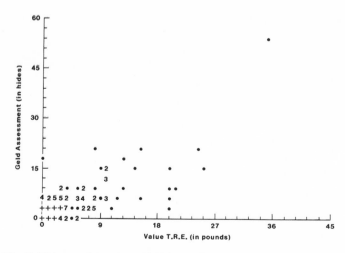

Fig. A9. Geld Assessment–Annual Value Relationship for Properties in Shropshire in 1066

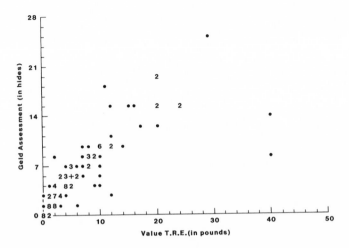

Fig. A10. Geld Assessment–Annual Value Relationship for Properties in Huntingdonshire in 1066

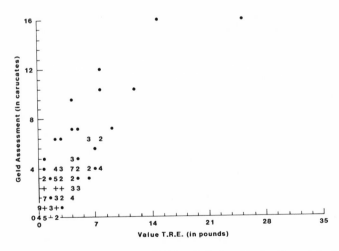

Fig. A11. Geld Assessment–Annual Value Relationship for Properties in Derbyshire in 1066

Notes

INTRODUCTION

1. *ASC,* s.a. 975 D(E), trans. and ed. Dorothy Whitelock, David C. Douglas, and S. I. Tucker; *The Anglo-Saxon Chronicle: a revised translation,* 2d imp., corr. and rev. Whitelock (London, 1965), reprinted in *EHD* I:228. Annals are cited by the date given in the recension of the manuscript used followed in parentheses by the actual date of the events described as ascertained by Whitelock in *EHD* I and II.

2. F. W. Maitland, *Domesday Book and Beyond* (1897; reprint New York, 1966), p. 156.

3. Among the most important representatives of this school are J. H. Round, "The Introduction of Knight Service into England," *EHR* 6 and 7 (1891, 1892), in idem, *Feudal England* (London, 1895); Helena M. Chew, *The English Ecclesiastical Tenants-in-Chief and Knight Service* (London, 1932); Frank M. Stenton, *The First Century of English Feudalism: 1066–1166* (1932; 2d ed., Oxford, 1961), pp. 115–162; David C. Douglas, "The Norman Conquest and English Feudalism," *Economic History Review* 9 (1939): 128–143, reprinted in idem, *Time and the Hour* (London, 1977); idem, *William the Conqueror* (Berkeley and Los Angeles, 1964), pp. 273–280; R. Allen Brown, *The Normans and the Norman Conquest* (New York, 1968), pp. 217–224; idem, *The Origins of English Feudalism* (New York, 1973).

4. Most notably, Edward Freeman, *The History of the Norman Conquest of England,* 6 vols. (Oxford, 1867–1879), I: 1–6; V: 334–336, 336ff.; Marjory Hollings, "The Survival of the Five-Hide Unit in the Western Midlands," *EHR* 63 (1948), 453–487; Eric John, *Land Tenure in Early England* (Leicester, 1960), pp. 113–161; idem, *Orbis Britanniae* (Leicester, 1966), pp. 128–153; idem, "The End of Anglo-Saxon England," in James Campbell, ed., *The Anglo-Saxons* (Ithaca, New York, 1982), pp. 236–237; Frank Barlow, *William I and the Norman Conquest* (London, 1966), pp. 117–120; D. J. A. Matthew, *The Norman Conquest* (London, 1966), pp. 117–120; John Gillingham, "The Introduction of Knight Service into England," *Anglo-Norman Studies* 4 (1982) 53–64.

5. The characterization of the fyrd as an "institution" is itself questionable. The term is best rendered as "an expedition" or "a military force." In the sources, *fyrd, here, exercitus,* and *expeditio* are used interchangeably. On the problems associated with using "fyrd" as a technical term, see C. Warren Hollister, *Anglo-Saxon Military Institutions* (Oxford, 1962), pp. 7–8; idem, "Military Obligation in Late-Saxon and Norman England," *Ordimenti Militari in Occidente Nell'Alto Medioevo,* Settimane di Studio del Centro Italiano di Studi Sull'Alto Medioevo 15 (1968): 175–176.

6. The early historiography of "the feudal revolution" is reviewed by David

C. Douglas, *The Norman Conquest and British Historians* (Glasgow, 1946), reprinted in idem, *Time and the Hour.*

7. Stenton, *English Feudalism,* pp. 117–119. Cf. idem, *Anglo-Saxon England,* 3d ed. (Oxford, 1971), pp. 290–291. Stenton's views on the fyrd evolved over his long career. See Hollister, *Military Institutions,* p. 2, and references.

8. On this putative "Wehrpflicht der Freien," see G. Waitz, *Deutsche Verfassungsgeschichte,* pt. 2, 3d ed. (Berlin, 1882), II:205ff.; H. Fehr, "Das Waffenrecht der Bauern im Mittelalter," *Zeitschrift der Savigny-Stiftung für Rechtsgeschichte (germanistische Abteilung)* 35 (1914): 118ff.; H. Brunner and C. von Schwerin, *Deutsche Rechtsgeschichte,* 2d ed. (Leipzig, 1928), 2:269–279; H. Mitteis, *Lehnrecht und Staatsgewalt* (Weimar, 1933), p. 178; Hermann Conrad, *Der Gedanke der allgemeinen Wehrpflicht in der deutschen Wehrverfassung des Mittelalters, Wehrrechtliche Abhandlungen,* 4 (Berlin, 1937).

9. Maitland, *Domesday Book,* pp. 156–161; Paul Vinogradoff, *English Society in the Eleventh Century* (Oxford, 1908), pp. 22–38, 74–89.

10. Maitland, *Domesday Book,* p. 160.

11. H. Munro Chadwick, *The Origin of the English Nation* (Cambridge, 1907), pp. 158–162.

12. John, *Land Tenure,* pp. 138–139; idem, *Orbis Britanniae,* pp. 128–153.

13. Vinogradoff, *English Society,* pp. 88–89.

14. Hollister, *Military Institutions,* chaps. 2–5.

15. Nicholas Hooper, "Anglo-Saxon Warfare on the Eve of the Conquest: A Brief Survey," *Anglo-Norman Studies* 1 (1979):87–88.

16. Hollister, *Military Institutions,* p. 25.

17. Hooper, "Anglo-Saxon Warfare," pp. 87–88.

18. Michael Powicke, *Military Obligation in Medieval England* (Oxford, 1962), pp. 1–25; Cf. R. H. Hodgkin, *History of the Anglo-Saxons,* 3d ed. (Oxford, 1953), 2:590–598.

19. P. H. Sawyer, *Anglo-Saxon Charters: An Annotated List and Bibliography,* Royal Historical Society Guides and Handbooks, 8 (London, 1968). In my references to charters I have cited them first to the editions of Birch and Kemble (abbr. "BCS" and "K"), then to their numbers in Sawyer's handlist (abbr. "S").

20. On the problems of charter criticism, see H. D. Hazeltine, "On Anglo-Saxon Documents" (1931), in A. J. Robertson, ed. and trans., *Anglo-Saxon Charters,* 2nd ed. (Cambridge, 1956), pp. xiii–xvii; Frank M. Stenton, *The Latin Charters of the Anglo-Saxon Period* (Oxford, 1955), pp. 1–13; Nicholas Brooks, "Anglo-Saxon Charters: The Work of the Last Twenty Years," *Anglo-Saxon England* 3 (1974):211–231; *EHD* I:369–384.

21. H. G. Richardson and G. O. Sayles, *Law and Legislation in England, from Æthelberht to Magna Carta* (Edinburgh, 1964), pp. 15–24; Patrick Wormàld, "*Lex Scripta* and *Verbum Regis:* Legislation and Germanic Kingship from Euric to Cnut," in P. H. Sawyer and Ian Wood, eds., *Early Medieval Kingship* (Leeds, 1977), pp. 113–114; Whitelock, *EHD* I:362. The codes characterize the laws simply as *domas cyninges* without regard to their source. See the preambles to the codes of Æthelberht, Hlothhere and Eadric, Wihtræd, and

Ine. Occasionally the term *ald reht* ("old law") is used, but in at least one instance it is applied to a law that cannot be more than two generations old. See *Wihtræd,* c. 5; F. L. Attenborough, ed. and trans., *The Laws of the Earliest English Kings* (1922; reprint New York, 1974), pp. 24–25, 180–181. The fullest edition of Anglo-Saxon legal texts remains Felix Liebermann, ed., *Die Gesetze der Angelsachsen.* 3 vols. (Halle, 1903–1916) [Vol. I: Texts; Vol. II: Glossary and Commentary; Vol. III: Introduction and Notes to Texts].

22. *Alcuini Epistolae,* no. 86, in W. Wattenbach and E. Dummler, eds., *Monumenta Alcuiniana,* Bibliotheca Rerum Germanicarum, ed. P. Jaffe, 6 (1873; reprint Darmstadt, 1964), 370–371. See also BCS 73 (S 12) (Oswine, king of Kent, A.D. 689): "ad cujus etiam conformationem, pro ignorantia litterarum signum sanctae crucis expressi, et testes ut subscriberent rogavi." Cf. BCS 86 (S 15), 90 (S 16), 98 (S 21). Asser relates that those who rendered justice under Alfred, his *comites, præfecti,* and *ministri,* were commanded to learn to read on pain of losing their offices. Apparently, Alfred intended his law code to be used. *Asser's Life of King Alfred,* ed. W. H. Stevenson (Oxford, 1904), chap. 106, pp. 92–95; Simon Keynes and Michael Lapidge, eds. and trans., *Alfred the Great: Asser's "Life of King Alfred" and Other Contemporary Sources* (Harmondsworth, Middlesex, 1983), pp. 109–110.

23. See the preambles to the early Kentish and West Saxon codes and, especially, *Wihtræd,* c. 1, § 1.

24. Wormald, *"Lex Scripta,"* p. 134. Cf. David Dumville, "Kingship, Genealogies, and Regnal Lists," in P. H. Sawyer and Ian Woods, eds., *Early Medieval Kingship* (Leeds, 1977), pp. 72–104. Dumville argues that the Anglo-Saxon genealogies must be understood as royal propaganda. A genealogy could be a legal title and a political weapon, justifying the rule of a king. Genealogies therefore changed to accommodate changes in the social and political structure, and consequently cannot be taken at face value as statements of ancestry. See also K. Sisam, "Anglo-Saxon Royal Genealogies," *Proceedings of the British Academy* 39 (1953): 287–348.

25. *Bede's Ecclesiastical History of the English People,* ed. and trans. Bertram Colgrave and R. A. B. Mynors (1969; reprint Oxford, 1972) [abbr. "*H.E.*" with book and chapter number], II. 5 (pp. 150–151); J. M. Wallace-Hadrill, *Early Germanic Kingship in England and on the Continent* (Oxford, 1971), pp. 37–44; Wormald, *"Lex Scripta,"* pp. 125–138.

26. As witnessed by the recent controversies over the dating of *Beowulf* and *The Battle of Maldon.* On the former, see chap. 1, n. 1. On the historical value of the poem on the Battle of Maldon, see the works cited by Dorothy Whitelock in *EHD* I:142.

ONE: LORDSHIP, LAND TENURE, AND THE EARLY ANGLO-SAXON FYRD

1. *Beowulf,* 3d ed., ed. F. Klaeber (Lexington, Mass., 1950), ll. 4–11. E. Talbot Donaldson, trans., *Beowulf: A New Prose Translation* (New York, 1966), p. 1. The dating of *Beowulf* has been among the liveliest controversies in recent Anglo-Saxon studies. The scholarly consensus that assigned the poem

to the period ca. 650–800 has evaporated over the last few years; in fact, the majority of the papers presented at the Toronto Conference on the dating of *Beowulf* in 1980 argued for a possible post-viking date of composition. See Colin Chase, ed., *The Dating of Beowulf* (Toronto, 1981). Although it is likely that the poem was revised in the course of the tenth century, it still seems to me that in substance it is a work of the late eighth or early ninth century. The absence of Danish linguistic influence would be exceedingly odd in a poem supposedly composed for an Anglo-Danish audience of the tenth century. Moreover, the poem's failure to mention bookland is telling. The author obviously knew enough to realize that chartered grants would have been anachronistic in the heroic world of the poem, and I doubt whether a poet of the mid-tenth century would have demonstrated so nice a historical sensibility. Finally, the names of the secondary characters in the poem are archaic: only eight of the sixty-nine proper names used by the poet are also found in Domesday Book, and even fewer can be found in tenth-century charters. I would tend to agree with Patrick Wormald that the poem should be dated to ca. 675–875. Patrick Wormald, "Bede, *Beowulf* and the conversion of the Anglo-Saxon aristocracy," in *Bede and Anglo-Saxon England: Papers in Honour of the 1300th Anniversary of the Birth of Bede,* ed. Robert T. Farrell, British Archaeological Reports, British Series, 46 (Oxford, 1978): 94–95; Campbell, *The Anglo-Saxons,* p. 252. Eric John provides an interesting analysis of the tenurial arrangements described in *Beowulf* and offers a cogent argument for an early date of composition. John, "*Beowulf* and the Margins of Literacy," *Bulletin of the John Rylands University Library of Manchester* 56 (1974): 388–422. The best piece on the historical background of *Beowulf* remains Dorothy Whitelock, *The Audience of Beowulf* (Oxford, 1951). Her suggestion of the Age of Offa for the composition of the poem (pp. 58–64) continues to be an attractive possibility. At least two names in *Beowulf,* Offa and Wiglaf, are associated with the Mercian royal family in the late eighth and early ninth centuries.

2. *H.E.,* III. 11, 12.

3. *H.E.,* III. 18.

4. *Beowulf,* ll. 20–25.

5. The word itself derives from the verb *faran* via its alternative form, *feran,* "to go" or "to journey," and its original meaning, "a journey," was preserved in Old Norse *ferth.* See Attenborough, *Laws,* p. 190.

6. For an example of its military connotations in the eighth century, see W. Lindsay, ed., *The Corpus, Epinal, Erfurt and Leyden Glossaries* (London and New York, 1921), E 504: *expeditionibus, ferdun.* For the appearance of the term in the legal sources and full discussion of its meanings, consult Liebermann, *Gesetze,* II, § 1, s.v. *fierd* and *expeditio,* and II, § 2, s.v. *Heer.*

7. Attenborough, *Laws,* pp. 36–61 (text with English translation); *EHD* I:398–407 (translation only); Liebermann, ed., *Gesetze,* I:88–123. David Dumville has recently voiced doubts about the trustworthiness of Ine's code as historical evidence for late seventh-century West Saxon society. Dumville believes it likely that Alfred altered the laws he used to make them more timely. Dumville, "Alfred, Ine, Kindred and Lordship," presented at the AHA Centennial Meeting, Chicago, December 1984. While Alfred undoubtedly preserved

only those laws of Ine which suited his purpose, I am not convinced that the laws of Ine appended to his code were significantly altered in their meaning. Dumville seems to ignore the fact that Alfred's laws occasionally contradict those of Ine. As Liebermann noted some time ago, this is especially true for those clauses that deal with the authority of the king. E.g., *Ine*, c. 39. Cf. *Alfred*, c. 37, § 1. See also Whitelock's comments on Ine's laws in *EHD* I:358.

8. H. R. Loyn, *The Governance of Anglo-Saxon England, 500–1087* (Stanford, 1984), pp. 50–53. See also Stenton, *ASE*, pp. 277–314; T. M. Charles-Edwards, "Kinship, Status and the Origins of the Hide," *Past and Present* 56 (1972): 3–33. Continental archaeological evidence offers little support for this view. On the contrary, early–Iron Age Jutland seems to have been characterized by a highly stratified society dominated by an aristocracy. Pearson, "Economic and Ideological Change: Cyclical Growth in the Pre-state Societies of Jutland," in *Ideology, Power and Prehistory*, ed. Daniel Miller and Christopher Tilley (Cambridge, 1984), pp. 69–90.

9. See the discussions by T. H. Aston, "The Origins of the Manor in England," *TRHS*, 5th Series, 8 (1958): 59–83, esp. 69–71; and H. P. R. Finberg, "Anglo-Saxon England to 1042," in idem, ed., *The Agrarian History of England and Wales*, pt. 2 (Cambridge, 1972), I: 432–433, 440–441, 445–448. See also the excursus at the end of this chapter.

10. For slavery in seventh-century England, see Finberg, *Agrarian History*, pp. 430–431, 435–438, 443–448 (note especially the evidence he cites from Theodore's *Penitential* on p. 435). Cf. Stenton, *ASE*, p. 314.

11. See, e.g., Hollister, *Military Institutions*, pp. 25–37. Cf. Hooper, "Anglo-Saxon Warfare," p. 87.

12. Bernard S. Bachrach, *Merovingian Military Organization, 481–751* (Minneapolis, 1972), pp. 68–69. For the Roman influences on Merovingian military organization, see ibid., pp. 15–17, 34, 71–73.

13. E.g., Stenton, *ASE*, p. 290; Loyn, *Governance*, p. 32.

14. John, *Orbis Britanniae*, pp. 135–136. Cf. Chadwick, *Origin*, p. 161; Finberg, *Agrarian History*, p. 443.

15. Wormald, "*Lex Scripta*," pp. 105–138. Cf. Hermann Nehlsen, "Aktualität und Effektivität der ältesten germanischen Rechtsaufzeichnungen," in Peter Classen, ed., *Recht und Schrift im Mittelalter,* Vorträge und Forschungen, 23 (Sigmaringen, 1977), 449–502, on the scope of the *Lex Salica*.

16. Attenborough, *Laws*, pp. 36–37.

17. The text of Aldhelm's letter is preserved in William of Malmesbury, *De Gestis Pontificum Anglorum*, ed. N.E.S.A. Hamilton, Rolls Series, 52 (1870; reprint Wiesbaden, 1964), 337–339; *EHD* I:794.

18. *EHD* I:176–177. On the sources for this annal, see Charles Plummer, ed., *Two of the Saxon Chronicles Parallel*, 2 vols. (1892–1899; reprint Oxford, 1952), 2:xx; *EHD* I:122. Cf. Simeon of Durham, *Historia Regum*, s.a. 796, 798, 799, in *EHD* I:274–275, for rebellion, loyalty, and revenge in late eighth-century Northumbria.

19. E.g., "The Fight at Finnsburgh," ll. 37–40 (ed. Klaeber, *Beowulf*, p. 247); *Beowulf*, ll. 1068–1159, 2373–2376, 2631–2660, 2863–2874; *Widsith*, ed. K. Malone (London, 1935), ll. 94–98. On the relative claims of lordship

and kingship in the tenth century, see the interesting mistranslation of this annal by Æthelweard, *The Chronicle of Æthelweard,* ed. A. Campbell (London, 1962), p. 24. Cf. Simeon of Durham, *Historia Regum,* s.a. 798, in *EHD* I:275, on the rebellion of ealdorman Wada. Cf. *EHD* I:847, Charlemagne's letter to Æthelheard, archbishop of Canterbury, and Ceolwulf, bishop of Lindsey, in which the king asks the prelates to intercede with King Offa of Mercia on behalf of a band of English exiles at the Frankish court whose exiled lord, Hringstan, had died, and who now wished to return to England.

20. *Beowulf,* ll. 2631–2660. Cf. Ælfwine's speech in *The Battle of Maldon,* ll. 212–224.

21. E.g., *ASC,* s.a. 774, ed. Plummer, *Saxon Chronicles,* 1:51; *EHD* I:178: "The Northumbrians drove their king from York at Easter and took as their lord [*genamon . . . to hlaforde*] Ethelred, Moll's son, and he reigned for four years." Theodor Mayer's work on the personal nature of the early medieval polity, which he terms a *Personenverbandstaat,* is relevant to this argument. See his "Die Entstehung des 'modernen' Staates im Mittelalter und die freien Bauern," *Zeitschrift der Savigny-Stiftung für Rechtsgeschichte (germanistische Abteilung)* 57 (1937): 210–288.

22. H. M. Chadwick, *Studies in Anglo-Saxon Institutions* (Cambridge, 1905), pp. 302–303. Cf. D. H. Green, *The Carolingian Lord* (Cambridge, 1965), pp. 220–221, 346–349; John, *Orbis Britanniae,* pp. 140–141.

23. The epithets for king in *Beowulf* include: "guardian of warriors" (*wigendra hleo:* ll. 899, 1972, etc.) and "lord" (*hlaford,* ll. 267, etc.; *dryhten,* ll. 1484, etc.). In at least two passages the "nation" is equated explicitly with the king's retainers and hearth-companions (ll. 1228–1231, 3170–3179: "swa begnornodon Geata leode / hlaf-ordes hyre heorth geneatas"). In no passage is a king presented as anything other than a lord.

24. See, e.g., the career of the young St. Guthlac. *Felix's Life of St. Guthlac,* ed. Bertram Colgrave (Cambridge, 1956), chaps. 16–18 (pp. 80–83). Cf. the careers of the exiled æthelings Æthelbald of Mercia (ibid., chap. 49, p. 149) and Cædwalla of Wessex, discussed below.

25. *Poenitentiale Theodori,* IV. 6, in Arthur W. Haddan and William Stubbs, eds., *Councils and Ecclesiastical Documents* (1871; reprint Oxford, 1964), 3:180, cited by Dorothy Whitelock, *The Beginnings of English Society,* rev. ed. (1972; reprint Baltimore, 1977), p. 37.

26. III *Edmund,* c. 1, in A. J. Robertson, ed. and trans., *The Laws of the Kings of England from Edmund to Henry I* (Cambridge, 1925), pp. 12–13. See discussion in chap. 4 below.

27. Attenborough, *Laws,* pp. 56–59. On this series of laws, see T. M. Charles-Edwards, "The Distinction Between Land and Moveable Wealth in Anglo-Saxon England," in P. H. Sawyer, ed., *Medieval Settlement* (London, 1976), pp. 185–187.

28. See T. H. Aston, "Origins of the Manor," pp. 65–68; John F. McGovern, "The Meaning of 'Gesette Land' in Anglo-Saxon Land Tenure," *Speculum* 46 (1971): 589–596. One could take this a step farther and read *gesett land* as the land held by "housed" tenants, if *Ine,* c. 67 indeed belongs to the series 63–68. Chapter 67 distinguishes between tenants who have accepted

dwellings from their lords, and have therefore bound themselves to the tenancy, and those who have not, and consequently may abandon their holdings if the lord should increase the services due from them. The term "gesett land" does not appear in this clause, but the phrase does appear in the other laws of this series, and it is possible that *Ine*, c. 67 has provided us with a definition of the unstated term. One might note in this context that the primary meaning of *gesette* is "establishment" or "foundation." See Joseph Bosworth and T. N. Toller, *An Anglo-Saxon Dictionary* (1898; reprint Oxford, 1972), s.v. *gesetnes*.

29. For a peasant pursuing a feud, see *ASC*, s.a. 757, where a herdsman avenges the murder of his lord by killing the evil King Sigeberht.

30. Attenborough, *Laws*, pp. 52–53. The use of the terms "ham" and "inhiwan" in this text suggests that the nobleman was a *landhlaford*.

31. Cf. *Ine*, c. 22.

32. Cf. *Wihtræd*, c. 5. This Kentish law, which is contemporaneous with Ine's code, also asserts that a lord shall collect the fines assessed against his men in accordance with "old right."

33. *Ine*, caps. 19, 33. The "cyninges horswealh" can mean either an unfree horse servant (*wealh* = slave) or a "Welsh horseman." The latter seems more probable, since the preceding chapter is concerned with the blood prices of various grades of Welshmen. See *EHD* I:402, n. 5.

34. *Ine*, c. 6, § 3. Cf. *Hlothhere and Eadric*, c. 14. The terms "gafolgelda" and "gebur" seem to describe different ranks of cierlisc men. The former is the vernacular equivalent for *tributarius* ("tribute-payer"), a common term in the early Latin charters for the holder of a hide or, by extension, for the hide itself. See, e.g., BCS 144 (S 43). A comparison of *Ine*, c. 23, § 3 with c. 32 reveals that the Welsh gafolgelda and the Welshman who held a hide of land enjoyed the same wergild. The gebur ("gebur" from "bur," meaning "house") was probably a peasant cultivator who held a virgate of land and, perhaps, a house given to him by his lord. See Chadwick, *Institutions*, p. 87, n. 1; Finberg, *Agrarian History*, pp. 413, 440–441, 510, 513–514.

35. E.g., T. Wright and R. P. Wülcker, eds., *Anglo-Saxon and Old English Vocabularies* (London, 1884), 1:204 (1. 12): *Caesarium tributum, id est regalis, tributum;* A. S. Napier, ed., *Old English Glossses*, Anecdota Oxoniensis, Mediaeval and Modern Series, 11 (1900; reprint Hildesheim, 1969), p. 39: *fiscale, cynelic; fiscale, gafollic;* and p. 177: *tributum, gaval*. The king's claim to lordship over those who dwelled on fiscal land, whether the land was in the immediate possession of the king or had been lent to one of his gesiths, might provide the key to *Ine*, caps. 63–67.

36. H. P. R. Finberg, *Lucerna* (London, 1964), pp. 144–160.

37. *H.E.*, IV. 13. Cf. *Vita Wilfridi*, c. 41, ed. B. Colgrave, *The Life of Bishop Wilfrid by Eddius Stephanus* (Cambridge, 1927), p. 82. Cf. also BCS 64 (S 232). For further discussion, see John, *Land Tenure*, pp. 8, 13; Finberg, *Agrarian History*, p. 436, n. 5.

38. *Æthelberht*, c. 6. The use of the term *drihtinbeage* to describe the offense of killing a "free man" implies that the victim was a retainer of the king. See Attenborough, *Laws*, p. 175. Cf. K. P. Witney, *The Kingdom of Kent* (London, 1982), pp. 97–98, 242.

39. *Æthelberht,* caps. 13, 14.
40. *Æthelberht,* caps. 6, 8.
41. *Æthelberht,* caps. 9, 27–29.
42. A. K. G. Kristensen, "Danelaw Institutions and Danish Society in the Viking Age," *Mediaeval Scandinavia* 8 (1975): 34–42, provides a useful summary in English of the findings of the Königsfreiheit school and a convenient bibliography. Cf. H. Schulze, "Rodungsfreiheit und Königsfreiheit," *Historische Zeitschrift* 219 (1974): 529–550, for a more critical assessment. Franz Staab, "A Reconsideration of the Ancestry of Modern Political Liberty: The Problem of the So-Called 'King's Freemen,' " *Viator* 11 (1980): 57–69, contends that most of the *ingenui* of the capitularies were neither "king's free" peasant settlers nor folk-free peasants, but noblemen of modest means. He further distinguishes the *ingenui* who held fiscal land from the semi-servile *fiscalini*. Staab does concede that the *liberi homines,* or *ingenui,* always enjoyed a special relationship with the king.
43. H. Dannenbauer, "Die Freien im Karolingischen Heer," in *Aus Verfassungs- und Landesgeschichte: Festschrift für Theodor Mayer* (Lindau, 1954), 1:53–56. Cf. K. Bosl, *Frühformen der Gesellschaft im mittelalterlichen Europa* (Munich, 1964), pp. 212–214; Kristensen, "Danelaw," p. 39.
44. Kristensen, "Danelaw," pp. 42–73. Cf. R. H. C. Davis, *The Kalendar of Abbot Samson,* Camden, 3d Series, 84 (1955): xxxii–xlvii; idem, "East Anglia and the Danelaw," *TRHS,* 5th Series, 5 (1955): 23–39; J. E. A. Jolliffe, *Pre-Feudal England: The Jutes* (1933; reprint London, 1962), pp. 32–39. For parallels with early Northumbrian land tenure, see G. W. S. Barrow, *The Kingdom of the Scots* (New York, 1973), pp. 7–68.
45. Dannenbauer, "Die Freien," pp. 53–56; Kristensen, "Danelaw," pp. 39–40. Cf. Jolliffe, *Jutes,* pp. 32, 65; Davis, *Kalendar,* p. xlvi.
46. H. Dannenbauer, "Hundertschaft, Centena, und Huntari," *Historisches Jahrbuch* 69 (1949): 155–219; Bachrach, *Merovingian Military,* pp. 32–33; Kristensen, "Danelaw," pp. 37–42.
47. The phrase was coined by Helen Cam to describe this early administrative arrangement. Helen Cam, "Manerium cum Hundredo: The Hundred and the Hundredal Manor" (1932), in idem, *Liberties and Communities in Medieval England* (Cambridge, 1944), pp. 64–90. On the early "king's *tuns*" and the "hundreds" attached to them, see Jolliffe, *Jutes,* pp. 40, 119; Davis, "East Anglia," pp. 23–39; Barrow, *Scots,* pp. 8–27; G. R. J. Jones, "Multiple Estates and Early Settlement," in P. H. Sawyer, ed., *Medieval Settlement* (London, 1976), pp. 15–40; and P. H. Sawyer, "The Royal *Tun* in Pre-Conquest England," in *Ideal and Reality in Frankish and Anglo-Saxon Society,* ed. Patrick Wormald with Donald Bullough and Roger Collins (Oxford, 1983), pp. 272–299. Cf. H. P. R. Finberg, ed., *The Early Charters of Wessex* (Leicester, 1964), no. 398 (A.D. 794: King Beohtric): "ut libertatem habeat omnium fiscalium negotiorum et operum regalium et omnium rerum que ad villam regiam pertinent."
48. *Vita Wilfridi,* chap. 41, ed. Colgrave, p. 82; *H.E.,* IV. 13; BCS 64 (S 232).
49. Hanna Vollrath-Reichelt, *Königsgedanke und Königtum bei den An-*

gelsachsen bis zur mitte des 9 Jahrhunderts (Cologne, 1971), pp. 202–203, 220–221; Kristensen, "Danelaw," pp. 60–63. But cf. Nicholas Brooks, "The Development of Military Obligations in Eighth- and Ninth-century England," in *England Before the Conquest,* ed. Peter Clemoes and Kathleen Hughes (Cambridge, 1971), p. 70, n. 5. Cædwalla's attempt to exterminate the native population of the Isle of Wight so that he could resettle it with West Saxons may be an example of such military colonization. See *H.E.,* IV. 16.

50. Franz Irsigler, *Untersuchungen zur Geschichte der Frühfränkischen Adels,* Rheinisches Archiv, no. 70 (1969): 186–220; Walter Schlesinger and J. Werner, "Über den Adel im Frankenreich," in *Siedlung, Sprache und Bevölkerungsstruktur im Frankenreich,* ed. F. Petri (Darmstadt, 1973), pp. 545–551; E. Ennen and W. Janssen, *Deutsche Agrargeschichte* (Wiesbaden, 1979), pp. 105–110, 121, 125–127; Edward James, "Merovingian Cemetery Studies and Some Implications for Anglo-Saxon England," in *Anglo-Saxon Cemeteries 1979. The Fourth Anglo-Saxon Symposium at Oxford,* ed. Philip Rahtz, Tania Dickinson, and Lorna Watts, British Archaeological Reports, British Series, 82 (1980), 35–55, esp. 37–39. Cf. Michael Parker Pearson's interpretation of the archaeological evidence for social hierarchy in early–Iron Age Jutland. Pearson, "Economic and Ideological Change," pp. 69–90.

51. See especially the pioneer study by D. H. Green, *The Carolingian Lord.* See also W. Schlesinger, "Herrschaft und Gefolgschaft in der germanisch-deutschen Verfassungsgeschichte," *Historische Zeitschrift* 176 (1953): 225–275, trans. and repr. in *Lordship and Community in Medieval Europe,* ed. Frederic Cheyette (New York, 1975), pp. 64–99.

52. Irsigler, *Frühfränkischen Adels,* pp. 48–82, 221–255 (the latter pages are translated in *The Medieval Nobility,* ed. Timothy Reuter [Amsterdam, 1978], pp. 105–136); Karl Bosl, "Adel und Freiheit, Gefolgschaft und Herrschaft," in *Gebhardts Handbuch der deutschen Geschichte,* ed. H. Grundmann (Stuttgart, 1970), 1:693–729.

53. *Vita Wilfridi,* chap. 42; *H.E.,* IV. 12, 15; *ASC,* s.a. 685.

54. *ASC,* s.a. 676.

55. *H.E.,* IV. 15. Bede terms Cædwalla's war band an "army" (*exercitus*): *H.E.,* IV. 12, 15, ed. Colgrave and Mynors, pp. 368, 380.

56. Interestingly, Centwine is depicted in the Chronicle as a powerful king who "drove the Britons as far as the sea." *ASC,* s.a. 682. Aldhelm, who ought to have known, confirms this portrayal. See G. H. Wheeler, "The Genealogy of the West Saxon Kings," *EHR* 36 (1921): 165.

57. Thus the term for noble used in Ine's code is *gesith,* "companion." Liebermann takes this to mean that gesiths were "royal companions." *Gesetze,* 2:428–429: s.v. *Gefolgsadel* (§ 3).

58. Alcuin characterizes the king as a *rector* "super principes populi sui." *Monumenta Alcuiniana,* Epistola, no. 80 (p. 352).

59. A by-product of such an "election" was the creation of noble exiles, the unsuccessful claimants to the throne. Early Anglo-Saxon history is thus littered with exiled æthelings such as Cædwalla, Cyneheard, and Ecgberht of Wessex; Guthlac and Æthelbald of Mercia; Sigeberht of East Anglia; and Edwin, Oswald, Oswiu, and Aldfrith of Northumbria. Each exiled ætheling, moreover,

was accompanied by his noble followers. See, e.g., Felix, *Life of St. Guthlac,* chaps. 42, 50; Aldhelm's !etter to Wilfrid's clergy, *EHD* I:93–94.

60. Chadwick, *Institutions,* pp. 357–360; Green, *Carolingian Lord,* pp. 218–225; Vollrath-Reichelt, *Königsgedanke,* pp. 54–63; Kenneth Harrison, *The Framework of Anglo-Saxon History* (Cambridge, 1976), pp. 87–92.

61. *Beowulf,* ll. 39–41. Cf. Simeon of Durham, *Historia Regum,* s.a. 796–799, in *EHD* I:274–275, for the "prowling of the hungry æthelings" in late eighth-century Northumbria.

62. Chadwick suggested that the *gesithcundmen landagende* of Ine's day were not ordinarily king's men, basing his argument upon *Ine,* c. 45, which places the landholding gesith below both the ealdorman and the *cynges thegn. Institutions,* p. 346. But, as Chadwick himself pointed out, *Ine,* c. 45's "king's thegn" is the "distinguished councillor" of *Ine,* c. 6 (*gethungena wita*). The higher position accorded the "king's thegn," then, may have been due to his office in the king's household, rather than to any difference in personal commendation. See, e.g., Asser, *Life of King Alfred,* chaps. 100–101. Certainly, *Beowulf* reveals a hierarchy among the landholding king's men who feasted in *Heorot,* with precedence given to Hrothgar's court officials, Wulfgar and Æschere (ll. 348, 360, 1323, 1329, 1420).

63. *Ine,* c. 45.

64. *Ine,* c. 6, § 2. On the relationship between the king and his *witan* in early Anglo-Saxon England, see Chadwick, *Institutions,* chap. 9; Peter Hunter Blair, *An Introduction to Anglo-Saxon England,* 2d ed. (Cambridge, 1977), pp. 214–222.

65. *Ine,* c. 6, §§ 2 & 3.

66. *Ine,* caps. 64–66.

67. When Ine's laws speak of the inheritance of ancestral seats (*frumstolas*), it is the ceorl rather than the gesithcund man who is represented as the heir. *Ine,* c. 38. A number of historians have interpreted the term "folcland" to refer to the hereditary familial estates held by nobles and commoners. Some, following Vinogradoff, have seen it as land held under *folcriht;* others, notably Stenton, have suggested that it was land subject to the rents and services by which the whole people had traditionally maintained the king. Eric John has taken a radically different approach to "folkland." Observing that the original meaning of "folk" was army, John proposed that "folkland" was fiscal land lent by the king to his warriors. See Stenton, *ASE,* pp. 309–312; John, *Orbis Britanniae,* pp. 64–127. I myself lean toward John's interpretation, although in light of the scanty and ambiguous nature of the evidence—*folcland* is mentioned only six times in the whole Anglo-Saxon corpus and is never defined—the only thing certain about *folcland* is that it was a form of tenure that contrasted in some way with *bocland.* One certainly cannot use the few references to it as evidence for hereditary familial estates.

68. John, *Land Tenure,* pp. 49–50.

69. BCS 35 (S 13). Cf. BCS 40 (S 14), 42 (S 10), 45 (S 8), 141 (S 1180), 148 (S 23), and 160 (S 24). All these charters are authentic or at least possess a genuine substratum.

70. BCS 218 (S 63) and 278 (S 148). Both charters deal with the same

property, three "cassati" (or hides) at *Huntenatun* (Gloucestershire?). H. P. R. Finberg, *The Early Charters of the West Midlands* (Leicester, 1961), no. 21, pp. 37–38. The first of these charters purports to be a grant by Ealdred and Uhtred, "sub-rulers" of the Hwicce, with the consent of their overlord, Offa of Mercia, to their *comes*, the *præfectus* (BCS 183 [S 55]) Beornheard. The latter charter, BCS 278, is dated 796 and records the grant of this property by Ecgfrith, King of Mercia, to "his faithful *princeps*" Æthelmund, son of Ingeld (BCS 202 [S 58], 203 [S 59]). It would be difficult to account for BCS 278 if BCS 218 represented a grant of land in book-right. But if we examine BCS 218, we find that the charter contains no reference to the power of bequest or to the eternality of the concession. In this it contrasts sharply with the other authentic Hwiccean charters of this period. E.g., BCS 187 (S 56), 202 (S 58), 203 (S 59), and 232 (S 57). It is quite possible, therefore, that BCS 218 was intended to be only a *læn* and that with the death of Beornheard it returned to the royal fisc to be granted out once more.

71. *Ine*, c. 36, § 1.

72. *Gesith* renders the text's *comes* in the Old English translation of the *Historia. The Old English Version of Bede's Ecclesiastical History*, ed. Thomas Miller, Early English Text Society, vols. 95, 96, 110, 111 (Oxford, 1890–1898), 95:326.

73. *H.E.*, IV. 22, ed. Colgrave and Mynors, pp. 400–403. The degree to which the ethos of the feud penetrated the concept of war is strikingly revealed by *Beowulf*, ll. 2024–2069. Cf. *H.E.*, IV. 21, ed. Colgrave and Mynors, pp. 400–401, on the terms of peace agreed upon by Mercia and Northumbria following the Battle of the Trent: "no further lives were demanded for the death of the king's [Ecgfrith's] brother [who fell in the battle] but only the usual money compensation which was paid to the king to whom the duty of vengeance belonged."

74. *H.E.*, IV. 22, ed. Colgrave and Mynors, p. 402: "A quo interrogatus qui esset, timuit se militem fuisse confiteri; rusticum se potius et pauperem atque uxoreo uinculo conligatum fuisse respondit, et propter uictum militibus adferendum in expeditionem se cum sui similibus uenisse testatus est."

75. John, *Orbis Britanniae*, p. 137. Cf. Chadwick, *Origin*, pp. 159–160.

76. *H.E.*, V. 23, ed. Colgrave and Mynors, p. 560.

77. *H.E.*, I. 22, ed. Colgrave and Mynors, pp. 66–68: "Attamen recente adhuc memoria calamitatis et cladis inflictae seruabant utcumque reges, sacerdotes, priuati et optimates suum quique ordinem." Cf. Gildas, *De Excidio Britanniae*, chap. 26, ed. and trans. Michael Winterbottom, *Gildas' The Ruin of Britain and Other Works* (London, 1978), p. 99: "Et ob hoc reges, publici, privati, sacerdotes, ecclesiastici, suum quique ordinem servabant." On the *nobiles* as *publici*, see Vollrath-Reichelt, *Königsgedanke*, pp. 50–54.

78. Elsewhere in the *Historia* Bede uses *plebs* (II. 14; III. 30), *mediocres* (III. 27), and *ignobiles* (V. 7) in parallel construction with *nobiles*. The Alfredian translation rendered *tam nobiles quam priuati* as *ge æthele ge unæthele*. Miller, *OE Bede*, 95:480. Cf. Wright and Wülker, *Vocabularies*, 1:95 (l. 16). See also Bosworth and Toller, *OE Dictionary*, s.v. *unæthele*.

79. *Vita Wilfridi*, chap. 2, ed. Colgrave, pp. 4–7.

80. Entry into the religious life is often represented in the early Anglo-Saxon sources as entering the service of the king. It was deemed necessary that a kingdom have its own bishop if it were to be defended properly. See *H.E.*, II. 2; III. 7; ed. Colgrave and Mynors, pp. 140–141, 236–237. Cf. Wallace-Hadrill, *Germanic Kingship*, chaps. 2–4.

81. *Vita Wilfridi*, chap. 2, ed. Colgrave, p. 7.

82. *Beowulf*, ll. 247–250, trans. Donaldson, p. 5.

83. Fosterage was a common practice among the aristocracy of early Northumbria. See, e.g., *Vita Wilfridi*, chaps. 21, 47. Cf. *Vita Sancti Cuthberti Auctore Anonymo*, II:7; *Vita Sancti Cuthberti Auctore Beda*, chap. 14 (both in *Two Lives of Saint Cuthbert*, ed. Bertram Colgrave [Cambridge, 1940], pp. 121, 201).

84. *Vita Wilfridi*, chap. 21.

85. Ibid., chap. 2, ed. Colgrave, p. 6: "arma et equos vestimentaque sibi pueris eius adeptus est, in quibus ante regalibus conspectibus apte stare posset." Note the use of the singular form "posset." Cf. *Beowulf*, ll. 247–250.

86. Green, *Carolingian Lord*, p. 100.

87. E.g., Gregory of Tours, *Historia Francorum*, V. 3, ed. W. Arndt and Bruno Krusch, *MGH, Scriptores rerum Merovingicarum*, 1 (1885; reprint Hannover, 1961). Cf. the equivalent use of *pueri* and *liberti* in *Lex Salica*, c. 78, ed. K. A. Eckhardt (Weimar, 1953). For further discussion of the Merovingian *pueri* and their social status, see M. Deloche, *La Trustis et L'Antrustion Royal* (Paris, 1878), pp. 71–79; P. Guilhiermoz, *Essai sur L'Origine de la Noblesse en France au Moyen Age* (Paris, 1902), pp. 51ff.; Bachrach, *Merovingian Military*, p. 52. On the evolution of the meaning of *puer* from "boy" to "servant," see H. Kuhn, "Die Grenzen der germanischen Gefolgschaft," *Zeitschrift der Savigny-Stiftung für Rechtsgeschichte (germanistische Abteilung)* 73 (1955): 57. Cf. Green, *Carolingian Lord*, pp. 100–106.

88. See *H.E.*, I. 27 (eighth *responsio*), ed. Colgrave and Mynors, p. 98. Cf. *1 Samuel*, 21:5–6.

89. *Vita Wilfridi*, chaps. 13, 48, ed. Colgrave, pp. 26, 98.

90. *Monumenta Alcuiniana*, Epistola no. 174 (pp. 623–624); *EHD* I:865–866.

91. Ibid., p. 623, *EHD* I:864, 865.

92. Cf. *Vita Wilfridi*, chap. 24, ed. Colgrave, p. 48, on Bishop Wilfrid's "countless followers arrayed and armed like a king's retinue."

93. Charles Plummer, ed., *Venerabilis Baedae Opera Historica*. 2 vols. (Oxford, 1896), 1:405–423. The passage relevant to this discussion appears on pp. 414–417, and is translated in *EHD* I:804–806. Cf. Chadwick, *Institutions*, pp. 367–377; John, *Land Tenure*, pp. 44–46, 73–74, and idem, *Orbis Britanniae*, pp. 80–83.

94. Plummer, *Baedae Opera*, 1:415–416. This is one of the earliest references to bookland tenure.

95. Ibid., p. 414.

96. Ibid., p. 415. *Beowulf*, ll. 2493–2496 attests to the prevalence of mercenaries in the early Anglo-Saxon period. One mark of a successful chieftain

was his ability to attract followers from other "peoples." Cf. *H.E.,* III. 14; Felix, *Life of St. Guthlac,* chap. 17. The role of mercenaries in early Anglo-Saxon England deserves fuller treatment than it has hitherto received.

97. Charles-Edwards, "Land and Moveable Wealth," pp. 183–184. Cf. John, *Orbis Britanniae,* pp. 64–127.

98. *Ine,* c. 38. Cf. *Beowulf,* ll. 2606–2608 and *Widsith,* ll. 94–96.

99. I follow Vollrath-Reichelt, *Königsgedanke,* pp. 51–54, here.

100. Cf. BCS 159 (S 27), a Kentish charter issued by King Eadberht in 738. The king had seven of his "companions" (*comites*) attest, and they in turn called upon their own comites to subscribe the grant. For an example of an ecclesiastical magnate granting land to his followers, see *Vita Wilfridi,* chap. 63. Cf. BCS 192 (S 1182), an eighth-century charter recording how a thegn endowed a monastery with land then held by another layman (presumably as a læn).

101. Bede, *Historia Abbatum,* chap. 1, in Plummer, *Baedae Opera,* 1:364–365.

102. *Widsith,* ll. 89–96, ed. Malone; R. K. Gordon, trans., *Anglo-Saxon Poetry* (London, 1967), p. 69: "Then the king of the Goths treated me well; he, prince of the city-dwellers, gave me a ring. . . . I gave it into the keeping of Eadgils, my protecting lord, when I came home, as reward to the dear one because he, the prince of the Myrgings, gave me land, my father's dwelling-place."

103. J. R. Clark Hall and C. L. Wrenn, trans., *Beowulf and the Finnsburg Fragment* (London, 1950), p. 131; *Beowulf,* ll. 2196–2199 (Klaeber, p. 82): "Him waes bam samod / on tham leodscipe lond gecynde, / eard ethelriht, othrum swithor / side rice tham thaer selra waes." Cf. John, "Beowulf," pp. 409–410.

104. Notions of *freondscipe* and *feondscipe,* gift-giving and feud, permeate *Beowulf.* See, e.g., ll. 20–25, 150–158, 2144–2199, 2490–2494, 2633–2660. The offer of a gift and its acceptance morally obliged the recipient to requite the favor. Gifts thus created social bonds as well as serving as economic rewards and incentives. See P. Grierson, "Commerce in the Dark Ages," *TRHS,* 5th Series, 9 (1959): 123–140; Green, *Carolingian Lord,* pp. 391–395; Charles-Edwards, "Land and Moveable Wealth," pp. 180–187. Its implications for Germanic land-law are brought out by E. Levy, *West Roman Vulgar Law* (Philadelphia, 1951), pp. 164–168.

105. Liebermann, *Gesetze,* 2:269, 428–429, s.v. *Adel* (§ 3b) and *Gefolgs-adel* (§§ 3–5); H. R. Loyn, "Gesiths and Thegns in Anglo-Saxon England from the Seventh to the Tenth Century," *EHR* 70 (1955): 533–540. "Cund," the second element in *gesithcund* (e.g., *Ine,* c. 51), indicates hereditary status. It is clear from the early law codes (e.g., *Ine,* c. 34, § 1) and saints' lives (e.g., Felix, *Life of St. Guthlac,* chaps. 1–3) that nobility was heritable in the seventh and eighth centuries.

106. See, e.g., the references to liberality in *Beowulf,* collected by Klaeber, *Beowulf,* p. 270. Cf. *Beowulf,* ll. 1719–1720, on Heremod's niggardliness. For other references see "The Wanderer," ll. 22, 34, 44, in G. P. Krapp and E. V. K. Dobbie, eds., *The Exeter Book* (New York, 1936); *Widsith,* ll. 55ff.,

90ff.; Blanche C. Williams, ed., *Gnomic Poetry in Anglo-Saxon* (New York, 1914), pp. 121–122, 127. *H.E.,* III. 14 (on the generosity of King Oswine). See also *H.E.,* Ill. 14; Asser, *Life of King Alfred,* chaps. 76, 80, 81.

107. Marcel Mauss, *Essai sur le don, forme archaïque de l'échange* (1925), trans. I. Cunnison, *The Gift* (Glencoe, Ill., 1954), is the seminal anthropological work on the meaning and function of gift-giving in primitive societies. See also Bronislaw Malinowski, *Argonauts of the Western Pacific* (1922; reprint London, 1950), pp. 97ff., 173ff.; H. A. Powell, "Competitive Leadership in Trobriand Political Organization," *J. of the Royal Anthropological Institute* 90 (1960): 118–145; Marshall Sahlins, "On the Sociology of Primitive Exchange" (1965), reprint in idem, *Stone Age Economics* (Chicago, 1972), pp. 149–183. Interesting parallels may be discerned between the Anglo-Saxon and Trobriand societies. Cf. also reciprocity in early Welsh "heroic" society. Wendy Davies, *Wales in the Early Middle Ages* (Leicester, 1982), pp. 68–71.

108. *Swerian,* c. 1, ed. Liebermann, *Gesetze,* 1:396–397. Cf. *Beowulf,* ll. 1068ff., 2490ff., 2633ff.; *Genesis B,* 1. 164.

109. Mauss, *The Gift,* p. 3, points out that in primitive societies prestation and counter-prestation often take place under a voluntary guise, although they are actually obligatory. Thus the *Beowulf*-poet stresses the king's moral duty to enrich his retainers. *Beowulf,* ll. 70–81, 1718–1719, 1749–1750.

110. *Beowulf,* ll. 2490–2496, trans. Donaldson, p. 44.

111. Bede, *Historia Abbatum,* chap. 1, Plummer, *Baedae Opera,* 1:364–365.

112. *Deor,* ll. 35–42, in Klaeber, *Beowulf,* p. 286.

113. *Geoguth,* "youth," was often used in Old English poetry in its substantive sense and, as such, was often paired with *duguth* ("manhood," and by extension, "proved warrior"). E.g., *Beowulf,* ll. 160, 621, 1674. Cf. the anonymous *Life of St. Oswald* in *EHD* I:914, where Earl Brihtnoth addresses the army/council as "veterans and young men." In *Beowulf,* ll. 1189–1190, the geoguth are depicted as sitting apart from Hrothgar's other retainers; Beowulf sits among them between the king's two sons. The phrase used here to describe them, *hæletha bearn,* recalls the phrase that Bede used to denote the landless Northumbrian warriors in his letter to Ecgberht, *filii nobilium ac emeritorum militum,* just as the word "geoguth" itself finds its parallel in Bede's *Historia* as *iuuentus* and *iuuenis. H.E.,* III. 1; IV. 22. See Chadwick, *Institutions,* pp. 33–54.

114. It is not coincidental that Hygelac's gift-giving is preceded by a passage, ll. 2183–2189, that tells of Beowulf's inglorious youth, when he appeared "sluggish" and consequently had received few gifts in the mead-hall. If one takes the literal meanings of geoguth and duguth seriously, one might be able to see here a passage from youth into manhood.

115. Bede, *Historia Abbatum,* chap. 1, in Plummer, *Baedae Opera,* 1:364; *Beowulf,* ll. 2195–2199.

116. Charles-Edwards, "Land and Moveable Wealth," p. 182, suggests that emeriti milites should be regarded as the Latin equivalent of duguth. Chadwick, *Institutions,* p. 347, n. 3, argued that comites were duguth. On the possible distinction between comites and "tried warriors," see ibid., pp. 339–340.

117. *Anonymous Life of St. Cuthbert,* IV. 3, 7; Bede, *Life of St. Cuthberht,* chaps. 15, 25, 29; *Historia Abbatum Auctore Anonymo,* chap. 34; *H.E.,* V. 4, 5. The holders of these estates were obliged to provide hospitality to their lord and his followers if they should chance to be in the neighborhood. *Historia Abbatum Auctore Anonymo,* chap. 34; *Vita Wilfridi,* chap. 2.

118. Imma is introduced as "de milita eius [Ecgfridi] iuuenis." *H.E.,* IV. 22, ed. Colgrave and Mynors, p. 400.

119. For Alfred's attempt to systematize this attendance, see Asser, *Life of King Alfred,* chap. 100.

120. *H.E.,* I. 34, ed. Colgrave and Mynors, pp. 116–117; *ASC,* s.a. 603 E.

121. *H.E.,* II. 12, ed. Colgrave and Mynors, pp. 180–181. Cf. *ASC,* s.a. 617 E.

122. *H.E.,* I. 34.

123. *H.E.,* III. 14, ed. Colgrave and Mynors, pp. 256–257.

124. *H.E.,* III. 2, 24; *Vita Wilfridi,* chaps. 19, 20.

125. *Ine,* caps. 63–66; Bede, *Historia Abbatum,* chap. 1.

126. *H.E.,* IV. 22, ed. Colgrave and Mynors, p. 400.

127. Attenborough, *Laws,* p. 190. The term "gesith" also derives from a word meaning "journey," *sinthaz.* See H. Beer, *Führen und Folgen, Herrschen und Beherrschtwerden im Sprachgut der Angelsachsen* (Breslau, 1939), p. 218.

128. Even when the possibility of danger seemed remote, the Anglo-Saxon lord did not travel alone, but was attended by an armed, although possibly small, retinue. See, e.g., *ASC,* s.a. 757. The greater the danger, the greater the moral obligation of a retainer to accompany his lord. *Beowulf,* ll. 2631–2660, 2860–2883. Whether ordered to or not—and we should remember that Beowulf explicitly ordered his thegns to remain behind when he went to slay the dragon—the warrior-retainer was obliged to share his lord's peril. On the difference between "fidelity" and "obedience," see Mitteis, *Lehnrecht,* pp. 531–533; Green, *Carolingian Lord,* pp. 74–76. Cf. *Andreas,* chap. 4, ed. K. R. Brooks, *Andreas and the Fates of the Apostles* (Oxford, 1961).

129. Cf. *Lex Baiuvariorum,* IV:23, which defines a *heriraita* as a band of men numbering at least forty–two. Theodore John Rivers, trans., *Laws of the Alamans and Bavarians* (Philadelphia, 1977), p. 133.

130. *ASC,* s.a. 449 (E), 477, 495, 501. See Leslie Alcock, *Arthur's Britain: History and Archaeology, A.D. 367–634* (Harmondsworth, Mddlx., 1971), p. 335. Michael Jones recently reviewed the archaeological and literary evidence for the Anglo-Saxon invasions, and concluded that they indicate "a migration characterized by small numbers, a multiplicity of small landings and a movement heavily dominated by military elements." Michael Jones, "The Logistics of the Anglo-Saxon Invasions," in *Naval History: The Sixth Symposium of the U.S. Naval Academy,* ed. Daniel Masterson (Wilmington, Delaware, 1987), pp. 62–69. The ship types available to the Angles and Saxons of the fifth and sixth centuries lacked true keels capable of supporting masts and sails. Such rowboats could not have supported a folk migration. Michael Parker Pearson, "Economic and Ideological Change," pp. 86–87, notes that the late third- or early fourth-century votive deposit of weapons at Ejsbol in Jutland suggests a hierarchically structured war band that numbered approximately 200 men.

131. *H.E.*, I. 15. Cf. Nennius, *British History and the Welsh Annals,* ed. and trans. John Morris (London, 1980), chaps. 31, 37.

132. *ASC*, s.a. 784 (recte, 786).

133. *H.E.*, IV. 12, 15, ed. Colgrave and Mynors, pp. 368, 380.

134. Felix, *Life of St. Guthlac,* chaps. 16–18, ed. Colgrave, pp. 80–81.

135. *Vita Wilfridi,* chap. 60, ed. Colgrave, p. 132.

136. Brian Hope-Taylor, *Yeavering,* Dept. of the Environment Archaeological Reports, 7 (1977): 161.

137. *The Goddodin: The Oldest Scottish Poem,* trans. K. H. Jackson (Edinburgh, 1969), B 20 (and notes). See discussion by Alcock, *Arthur's Britain,* pp. 336–337, on the numbers in the poem. See also Wendy Davies, *Wales,* pp. 199, 209–210, on the date and historical value of the poem.

138. P. H. Sawyer, *The Age of the Vikings,* 2d ed. (New York, 1971), chap. 6.

139. *H.E.*, IV. 13, ed. Colgrave and Mynors, pp. 372–373.

140. J. M. Wallace-Hadrill, "War and Peace in the Earlier Middle Ages," *TRHS,* 5th Series, 25 (1975): 162, 165–166.

141. Green has stressed the Anglo-Saxon adaptation of the vocabulary of warfare and the comitatus to the religious vocation. *Carolingian Lord,* pp. 287–321. See also Wallace-Hadrill, "War and Peace," pp. 168–169. Felix's *Life of St. Guthlac,* chaps. 27, 29, provides a particularly striking example of this.

EXCURSUS ON THE "FREEDOM" OF THE CEORL

1. E.g., Bosworth and Toller, *OE Dictionary,* s.v. *ceorl.* Cf. Liebermann, *Gesetze,* 2 (pt. 2), s.v. *Bauer* and *gemeinfrei;* H. R. Loyn, *Anglo-Saxon England and the Norman Conquest* (Oxford, 1962), pp. 166–170; Stenton, *ASE,* p. 314.

2. H. Schabram, "Bezeichnungen für 'Bauer' im Altenglischen," in R. Wenksus, H. Jahnkuhn, K. Grinda, eds., *Wort und Begriff "Bauer,"* Abhandlungen der Akademie der Wissenschaften in Göttingen, Philologisch-Historische Klasse, 3d Series, 80 (1975): 80.

3. E.g., *Beowulf,* ll. 1590 and 2972 (where it is applied to King Ongentheow). Cf. BCS 178 (S 92): "aldceorl"; BCS 447 (S 322). In BCS 451 (S 298) we find the word used as a proper name for a nobleman. Cf. Finberg, *Charters of Wessex,* nos. 566–567; *ASC,* s.a. 851.

4. The eighth-century Corpus Glossary pairs *ceorl* and *uxorius.* Lindsay, ed., p. 187. Cf. Napier, *OE Glosses,* p. 131: *maritum, ceorl.*

5. For the primary source references, see Frank M. Stenton, "The Thriving of the Anglo-Saxon Ceorl" (1958), in Doris M. Stenton, ed., *Preparatory to Anglo-Saxon England, Being the Collected Papers of Frank Merry Stenton* (Oxford, 1970), pp. 383–393.

6. Aston, "Origins of the Manor," p. 70. Cf. John, *Orbis Britanniae,* p. 133; Finberg, *Lucerna,* pp. 144–145; R. I. Page, *Life in Anglo-Saxon England* (London, 1970), p. 78.

7. For the oath-worthiness of the ceorl in early Kent and Wessex, see

Wihtræd, c. 21, and *Ine*, caps. 30, 54. One interesting distinction drawn between the slave and the ceorl in the early codes is that the latter was compensated for insults offered to his honor and person. See *Æthelberht*, c. 24; *Alfred*, c. 35, §6.

8. *Ine*, caps. 23, § 3; 24, § 1; 74, §§ 1–2.

9. *Willelmi Articuli Retractati*, c. 15, § 1 = *Leges Henrici Primi*, c. 78, § 1. Liebermann, *Gesetze*, 1: 491, 594. The ceremony is recorded only in these two twelfth-century texts, but its resemblance to the manumission rituals practiced in other early barbarian kingdoms suggests that its roots may be found in pre-Conquest England.

10. H. P. R. Finberg pointed out that Ine's code does not state the value of a ceorl's wergild. *Agrarian History*, p. 440. But a comparison of *Ine*, caps. 34, § 1, 51, and 70, with *Alfred*, caps. 26–28; *Alfred and Guthrum*, c. 2; and VI *Æthelstan*, c. 8, § 2, suggests that the West Saxon ceorl's blood-price in the seventh century was the same as it was in the late ninth century, namely, 200 shillings. In both Mercia and Northumbria in the early eleventh century the wergild of the ceorl was also reckoned at 200 shillings. See *EHD* I: 469, 470.

11. Cf. *Mircna laga*, caps. 1; 1, § 1; *EHD* I:470.

12. *EHD* I:70; Liebermann, *Gesetze*, 1:464.

13. E.g., *Ine*, caps. 14, 30. Cf. *Ine*, c. 51.

14. *Ine*, caps. 18, 37.

15. *Ine*, caps. 23, § 3; 24, § 2; 32; 33.

16. *Ine*, c. 6, § 3. Cf. *Alfred*, c. 39.

17. See, e.g., Finberg, *Agrarian History*, pp. 435, 437–438, and references there. See especially *H.E.*, IV. 13, and *EHD* I:794–795 (Brihtwold, archbishop of Canterbury, to Frothhere, bishop of Sherborne, on the redemption of a captive, A.D. 709 X 731). See also D. Pelteret, "Slave Raiding and Slave Trading in Early England," in *Anglo-Saxon England*, 9 (1981): 99–114; W. G. Runciman, "Accelerating Social Mobility: The Case of Anglo-Saxon England," *Past and Present* 104 (1984): 11–12.

18. The translation was long thought to be the work of Alfred himself, but Janet Bately recently demonstrated that this is unlikely. *The Old English Orosius*, ed. Janet Bately, Early English Text Society, Supplementary Series, 6 (Oxford, 1980), pp. lxxiii–xciii.

19. *Orosius*, IV. iii, ed. Bately, p. 87. I follow H. P. R. Finberg's analysis here. *Lucerna*, p. 146, and *Agrarian History*, p. 451.

20. *Alfred and Guthrum*, c. 2; Attenborough, *Laws*, pp. 98–99. Bately suggests that the translator of the OE *Orosius* never meant to equate a ceorl with a freedman, but was merely following Isidore's definition of libertinus in the *Etymologies* (= "son of a freedman"). OE *Orosius*, p. 274. Although her argument is plausible, it ignores the equation drawn between West Saxon ceorls and Danish freedmen in this contemporary treaty. For a different interpretation of this clause, see Keynes and Lapidge, *Alfred the Great*, p. 312, n. 3.

21. *Ine*, c. 39.

22. *Ine*, c. 3, § 2.

23. *Ine*, c. 67. See discussion of this clause at n. 28.

24. BCS 594 (S 359); Robertson, ed. and trans., *Anglo-Saxon Charters*, no.

110. See the commentary by Finberg, *Lucerna,* pp. 131–143. But cf. Maitland, *Domesday Book,* pp. 330–331.

25. Wright and Wülcker, *Vocabularies,* 1:115.

26. See A. Berger, *Encyclopedic Dictionary of Roman Law* (Philadelphia, 1953), s.v. *peculium.* It is interesting to note that the term "peculium" is used in the Visigothic laws to denote the hereditable property of slaves and freedom. *Lex Visigothorum,* XII, c. 2, §§ 13–14, ed. K. Zeumer, *MGH, Leges, Sectio I,* I (Hannover, 1902); S. P. Scott, trans., *The Visigothic Code* (Boston, 1910).

27. Dorothy Whitelock, ed. and trans., *Anglo-Saxon Wills* (Cambridge, 1930), no. 3. Cf. David Herlihy, "The Carolingian Mansus," *Economic History Review* 18 (1960): 79–89. Herlihy concludes, p. 89, that the Frankish *mansus* was "an accommodation of two distinct moral or legal titles to a tenure, the one, to permanent use, put forward by the settler by right of the labor he or a predecessor expended upon it, the other by the seigneur, who claimed the ownership, the *dominium,* over it."

28. Whitelock, *Wills,* nos. 19, 21.

29. *Æthelberht,* caps. 4; 6; 9; 13; 15; 24; 26; 75, § 1; 85; *Hlothhere and Eadric,* caps. 1 and 3; *Wihtræd,* c. 8. See discussions of early Kentish society by Finberg, *Agrarian History,* pp. 430–436; P. H. Sawyer, *From Roman Britain to Norman England* (London, 1978), pp. 172–174; K. P. Witney, *Kent,* pp. 96–102, 242–243.

30. *Wihtræd,* c. 8.

31. *Æthelberht,* c. 25.

32. F. E. Harmer, ed., *Select English Documents of the Ninth and Tenth Centuries* (Cambridge, 1914), no. 2 (=S 1482), pp. 3–5 and comments, pp. 40–42.

33. See the discussions by Chadwick, *Institutions,* chap. 3 (esp. pp. 91–98); Peter Hunter Blair, *An Introduction to Anglo-Saxon England,* 2d ed. (Cambridge, 1977), pp. 260–261 (cf. his treatment of the problem in the first edition); Sawyer, *Roman Britain,* pp. 172–173; Witney, *Kent,* pp. 100–102, 243. On the composition of early Kentish and West Saxon currency, see Chadwick, *Institutions,* pp. 13–18, 113–114; Attenborough, *Laws,* p. 191; and Stewart Lyon, "Some Problems in Interpreting Anglo-Saxon Coinage," *Anglo-Saxon England* 5 (1976): 177–178.

34. *Æthelberht,* c. 15. Cf. *Ine,* c. 6, § 3.

35. The evidence for the status of the ceorl in pre-viking Northumbria and Mercia is scanty. We do, however, possess information about the structure of these societies in the early eleventh century. See *EHD* I:468–476. We know even less about the social structure of the other kingdoms in early England. See the discussion by Finberg, *Agrarian History,* pp. 436–437, 442–448.

36. R. I. Page, *Life in Anglo-Saxon England,* p. 78.

TWO: BOOKLAND AND THE ORIGINS OF
THE "COMMON BURDENS"

1. Plummer, *Baedae Opera,* 1:405–423.

2. Kinship obligations, which also played an important role in early Anglo-

Saxon warfare, fall outside the scope of the present inquiry. Further research, however, should be undertaken on the influences of kinship upon the lordship bond. In the early Anglo-Saxon period, at any rate, "wars" and "feuds" were not clearly distinguished, and kinship terminology was often used to denote the retinues of kings and war bands of nobles. See *Beowulf*, ll. 387, 729 (*sibbe-gedriht*); ll. 1068, 1710, 2475 (*eaferan*); l. 65 (*wine-megas*). Cf. Green, *Carolingian Lord*, pp. 314–316. For an introduction to kinship obligations in Anglo-Saxon England, see Whitelock, *Beginnings*, chap. 2. The question of kindred structure and the existence of lineage groups in pre-Conquest England remains a subject of controversy, on which see H. R. Loyn, "Kinship in Anglo-Saxon England," in *Anglo-Saxon England*, 3(1974):197–201. Cf. Charles-Edwards, "Kinship, Status, and the Origins of the Hide." See also the anthropological discussion of kinship and political terminology by Elman Service, "Kinship Terminology and Evolution," *American Anthropologist* 62 (1960): 747–762.

3. *Beowulf*, ll. 2195–2199, 2606–2608 (*folc-rihta gehwylc, swa his fæder ahte*).

4. See, e.g., *Ine*, caps. 24, § 2; 32; *Gethynctho*, c. 2; *Northleoda laga*, c. 9. Cf. Charles-Edwards, "Kinship, Status, and the Origins of the Hide"; idem, "Land and Moveable Wealth."

5. See, e.g., *Beowulf*, ll. 3111–3113, in which warriors are equated with householders (*bold-agendra*) and leaders of the tribe (*folc-agende*, literally "owners of the folk").

6. *Widsith*, ll. 93–96. Cf. *Beowulf*, ll. 2197ff., 2606–2608.

7. BCS 600 (S 398). See Stenton, *Latin Charters*, p. 61, n. 1. See also Harmer, *Select Documents*, no. 10. Cf. BCS 248 (S 125), A.D. 786, which describes how King Offa of Mercia endowed one of his thegns and his sister with land that had once been held by their father. Cf. KCD 616 (S 1336). Cf. John, *Land Tenure*, p. 62. It is likely that the king's thegns expected that their sons would follow them both in their service to the king and in their tenures.

8. *Vita Wilfridi*, chap. 21. Cf. *Felix's Life of St. Guthlac*, chaps. 16–19, 34.

9. Plummer, *Baedae Opera*, 1:414–415. Bede's concern is also evident in *H.E.*, V. 23, ed. Colgrave and Mynors, pp. 560–561.

10. The nature of bookland has generated a good deal of controversy, on which see Maitland, *Domesday Book*, pp. 254–258; P. Vinogradoff, "Folkright," *EHR* 8 (1898): 1–17; Chadwick, *Institutions*, pp. 371–374; Stenton, *ASE*, pp. 306–312; John, *Land Tenure*, pp. 1–63; Vollrath-Reichelt, *Königsgedanke*, pp. 65–68, 192–225.

11. John, *Land Tenure*, p. 1; Stenton, *Latin Charters*, pp. 31–33; W. Levison, *England and the Continent in the Eighth Century* (Oxford, 1946), pp. 224–233. The earliest surviving West Saxon charter that commands respect, BCS 197 (S 1163), is from the episcopate of Hlothhere (or Leutherius), A.D. 670 X 676, and shows Frankish influence. See Levison, op. cit., pp. 226–228.

12. Stenton, *ASE*, p. 307; idem, *Latin Charters*, p. 33.

13. John, *Land Tenure*, pp. 2–63. On the meaning of "vulgar law," see Ernst Levy, *Vulgar Law*, pp. 2–12.

14. Levy, *Vulgar Law*, pp. 43–49, 90–94.

15. See, e.g., BCS 187 (S 56): "cum campis silvis pratis pascuis cum omnibus se pertinentibus"; BCS 194 (S 33): "cum omni tributo quod regibus inde dabatur"; BCS 254 (S 128): "cum omni tributo quod regibus ante debetur."

16. BCS 88 (S 17).

17. BCS 96 (S 18).

18. See, e.g., BCS 35 (S 13), 36 (S 7), 40 (S 14), 42 (S 10), 85 (S 53), 140 (S 92), 146 (S 85), 149 (S 86), 179 (S 258), 180 (S 259), 182 (S 100), etc.

19. BCS 86 (S 15) is representative of the Kentish or "Theodore" charters: "[T]eneas possideas, dones, commutes, venundes, vel quicquid exinde facere volueris liberam habeas potestatem." Cf. BCS 45 (S 8): contemporary text. BCS 154 (S 89), an original charter, provides an example of the Mercian or "Wilfrid" formula: "[I]ta ut quamdiu vixerit potestatem habeat tenendi ac possidendi cuicumque voluerit vel eo vivo vel certe post obitum suum reliquendi." Cf. BCS 153 (S 95), 157 (S 94). The West Saxon charters are similar to the Mercian in form. See, e.g., BCS 72 (S 235), 107 (S 1164), 225 (S 264), 396 (S 282), 426 (S 287). BCS 78 (S 45), a late seventh-century South Saxon charter, follows the Kentish model. Cf. Levy, *Vulgar Law,* p. 66, for Roman vulgar law formulas.

20. E.g., *ius ecclesiasticum:* BCS 42 (S 10: *jure aecclesiastico ac monasteriali*), 123 (S 64), 154 (S 89), 163 (S 101), 165 (S 99), 182 (S 100), 202 (S 58), 203 (S 59), 230 (S 114), 232 (S 57); *ius monasteriale:* BCS 35 (S 13), 36 (S 7), 157 (S 94).

21. Plummer, *Baedae Opera,* 1:415.

22. BCS 34 (S 1165), 35 (S 13), 36 (S 7), 40 (S 14), 41 (S 11), 42 (S 10), 45 (S 8), 139 (S 84), 57 (S 1167), 60 (S 70), 67 (S 59), 72 (S 235), 73 (S 12), 74 (S 252), 78 (S 45), 80 (S 1173), 81 (S 1171), 85 (S 53), 86 (S 15), 88 (S 17), 90 (S 16), 91 (S 22), 97 (S 19), 98 (S 21), 99 (S 20), 107 (S 1164), 111 (S 65), 122 (S 1177), 123 (S 64), 128 (S 1253), 132 (S 42), 137 (S 102), 140 & 178 (S 92), 141 (S 1180), 146 (S 85), 148 (S 23), 149 (S 86), 150 (S 87), 152 (S 88), 153 (S 95), 154 (S 89), 156 (S 1429), 157 (S 94), 159 (S 27), 160 (S 24), 163 (S 101), 164 (S 103), 165 (S 99), 166 (S 1254), 171 (S 98), 175 (S 30), 177 (S 91), 179 (S 258), 180 (S 259), 181 (S 96), 182 (S 100), 1221 (S 255).

23. BCS 230 (S 114). See Maitland, *Domesday Book,* p. 243. Cf. BCS 254 (S 128), a contemporary diploma recording a Kentish land grant by King Offa of Mercia to his minister Osberht.

24. BCS 230 (S 114).

25. E.g., BCS 1040 (S 677), 1042 (S 675), 1101 (S 717), 1176 (S 738), 1196 (S 747), 1305 (S 794). In these and other charters issued by Edgar, royal grants to laymen are introduced by pious poems and protected by anathema.

26. E.g., BCS 36 (S 7). The Kentish charters use the formula *pro remedio animae meae,* while the eighth-century Mercian landbooks ordinarily use *pro redemptione animae meae.* See, e.g., BCS 137 (S 102), 139 (S 84), 140 (S 92), 146 (S 85). The early West Saxon charters agree with the Kentish formula. E.g., BCS 72 (S 235), 74 (S 232).

27. E.g., BCS 34 (S 1165), 35 (S 13), 141 (S 1180), 149 (S 86), 182 (S 100), 187 (S 56), 1331 (S 255).

28. P. Jobert, *La notion de donation, convergences: 630–750,* Publications

de l'Université de Dijon (Paris, 1977), pp. 139–225, especially pp. 207–225. The idea of a *donatio pro anima* was not limited in England to gifts of bookland to the Church. The laws of Ine are also presented as a gift for the remedy of the king's soul. The formula used, *be thære hælo urra sawla and be tham stathole ures rices* ("for the salvation of our souls and the stability of our kingdom"), translates into Anglo-Saxon a phrase that first appears in Merovingian diplomas around 630: *pro regni stabilitate vel remedium animae nostrae.* Attenborough, *Laws,* pp. 35–37; Jobert, *La notion,* p. 216, n. 3.

29. E.g., BCS 40 (S 14), 41 (S 11), 86 (S 15), 90 (S 16), 140 (S 92), 150 (S 87).

30. E.g., BCS 34 (S 1165).

31. *Beowulf,* ll. 2144ff., 2985ff.

32. *Beowulf,* ll. 2884–2886.

33. Keynes and Lapidge, *Alfred the Great,* p. 139; *King Alfred's Old English Version of St. Augustine's Soliloquies,* ed. H. L. Hargrove, (New York, 1902), p. 2 (preface).

34. See, e.g., *ASC,* s.a. 823 (recte, 825), where Ealhstan, bishop of Sherborne, commands a fyrd sent by King Ecgberht against Kent.

35. See, e.g., BCS 348 (S 177), a contemporary text of a grant by King Coenwulf of Mercia in 814, which declares that the estate in question is to be free "ab omni vi saeculari servitutis . . . sicut a primordio Christianae religionis territorias et proprias possessiones orthodoxi et eruditi statuerunt." St. Boniface's letter to Æthelbald, king of Mercia, in 746/747 implies that ecclesiastical estates in both Mercia and Northumbria were not burdened with secular dues until the beginning of the eighth century. *EHD* I:820; M. Tangl, ed., *S. Bonifatii et Lulli Epistolae,* in *MGH, Epistolae,* I, 2d ed. (Berlin, 1955), p. 152, n. 73.

36. *H.E.,* III. 24, ed. Colgrave and Mynors, pp. 292–293.

37. *Epistola ad Ecgbertum,* chap. 12, ed. Plummer, *Baedae Opera,* I1:, 415, where the "abbots" of the spurious monasteries are said to be *liberi exinde a diuino simul et humano seruitio.* Brooks, "Military Obligations," p. 74, nn. 1 & 2. Cf. John, *Land Tenure,* pp. 73–74. If one assumes with Brooks that the eighth-century fyrd was a nation in arms, Bede's expression of concern for the defense of the homeland is difficult to explain. It is more reasonable to read this passage as saying that because the "abbots" were freed from secular duties, neither they nor their men attended the king's hosts. Cf. Archbishop Hincmar of Rheims' assertion that in his day (857/858) "military services are not rendered from those [English] regions, but [instead] the costs of rewarding those who fight are allocated from public resources." Quoted in Janet Nelson, "The Church's Military Service in the Ninth Century: A Contemporary View?" *Studies in Church History* 20(1983):15. Hincmar was undoubtedly wrong about conditions in mid–ninth–century England, but his information may have been a generation or two old.

38. The voluntary nature of early commendation comes out clearly in the *Vita Wilfridi,* chaps. 2 and 21, and is presupposed in Bede's letter to Ecgberht. See also Liebermann, *Gesetze,* 2:506–507 (s.v. *Herrensuche*). Even in the tenth century lords wrestled with the problem of rewarding their followers with hereditary tenures in an age of voluntary commendation. Thus BCS 814 (S

508), a twelfth-century copy of an apparently genuine mid–tenth-century charter, explains that King Edmund granted land at Weston, Somerset, to his faithful minister Æthelhere "eatenus ut vita comite tam fidus mente quam subditus operibus mihi placabile obsequium praebeat. Et post meum obitum cuicunque amicorum meorum voluero eadem fidelitate immobilis obediensque fiat. Sicque omnes posteriores praefatam terram possidentes in hoc decreto fideliter persistant sicuti decet ministro" ("on condition that he should show himself to be my acceptable follower through a faithful mind and obedient actions as long as he should live. And after my death, let him be unshaken and obedient in the same fidelity to whomsoever of my friends that I should wish. And let all his successors who shall possess the aforesaid land persist faithfully in this decree as befits a thegn"). Cf. BCS 600 (S 368).

39. Liebermann, *Gesetze*, 3:6; Attenborough, *Laws*, p. 3.

40. BCS 99 (S 20), authenticated by Brooks, "Military Obligations," p. 75, n. 1. Cf. BCS 90 (S 16); BCS 141 (S 1180).

41. BCS 99 (S 20): "Mihique et posteris meis talem honorem vel oboedientiam exhibeant qualem exhibuerunt antecessoribus meis regibus sub quibus eis justitia et libertas servabatur." Nicholas Brooks reasonably suggests that Wihtræd was concerned with retaining the highly profitable rents and payments from monastic estates as well as their loyalty, respect, and prayers. Brooks, *The Early History of the Church of Canterbury* (Leicester, 1984), pp. 183–184.

42. *H.E.*, IV. 26, ed. Colgrave and Mynors, p. 430.

43. *H.E.*, III. 7, ed. Colgrave and Mynors, p. 236. When a king conquered a people, he would place one of his men over the subject kingdom as its bishop. *H.E.*, II. 6; IV. 12, 15. Cf. *Vita Wilfridi*, chaps. 2, 19, 20, 21.

44. *Vita Wilfridi*, chap. 42; Felix, *Life of St. Guthlac*, chaps. 49, 52.

45. *H.E.*, II. 2, ed. Colgrave and Mynors, p. 140. Cf. *ASC*, s.a. 605 E (the battle appears to have actually taken place between 613 and 616).

46. *Vita Wilfridi*, chap. 13.

47. *H.E.*, III. 24.

48. *Vita Wilfridi*, chap. 42, ed. Colgrave, pp. 84–85: "For the holy bishop of Christ helped the exile, who was often in difficulties, assisting and supporting him in various ways, and strengthened him until he was powerful enough to overcome his enemies and to get the kingdom." Cf. also Felix, *Life of St. Guthlac*, chaps. 49, 52, on the relationship between the exiled Æthelbald and St. Guthlac.

49. *Vita Wilfridi*, chap. 24. See Eric John, "The Social and Political Problems of the Early English Church," in *Land, Church and People: Essays Presented to Professor H. P. R. Finberg*, ed. Joan Thirsk (Leicester, 1970), pp. 39–63; Michael Roper, "Wilfrid's Landholdings in Northumbria," in *Saint Wilfrid at Hexham*, ed. D. P. Kirby (Newcastle-upon-Tyne, 1974), pp. 61–79.

50. *Vita Wilfridi*, chaps. 15, 51; John, "Social and Political Problems," p. 51.

51. "Letter of Boniface and Seven Other Missionary Bishops to Æthelbald, King of Mercia, Urging Him to Reform (746–747)," trans. in *EHD* I:820.

52. By A.D. 732 some undefined "royal right" was exacted from all ecclesiastical estates in Kent. BCS 148 (S 23): "Et jus regium in ea deinceps nullum

repperiatur omnino, excepto dumtaxat tale quale generale est in universis ec-
clesiasticis terris quae in hac Cantia esse noscuntur." See comment by Brooks,
"Military Obligations," p. 75. Brooks assumes that the reserved "jus regium"
was military service, but nothing in the charter requires this supposition.

53. BCS 148 (S 23) is the earliest authentic Kentish landbook with an
immunity clause. Immunity clauses also appear in Mercian charters during the
730s. See, e.g., BCS 165 (S 99), a grant by King Æthelred of Mercia in 737 X
740 to his faithful minister Osred. Cf. BCS 152 (S 88).

54. E.g., BCS 241 (S 1257), 293 (S 155: contemporary text; EHD I:510–
511), 319 (S 1259), 332 (S 1264, contemporary text). The last three texts refer
to Offa's quashing of a book held by Christ Church, Canterbury, on which see
Brooks, Church of Canterbury, pp. 321–322. Cf. Vollrath-Reichelt, Königsgedanke, pp. 163–166. Cf. also BCS 184 (S 260), a letter from Pope Paul I to
Eadberht, king of Northumbria (ca. 757 X 758), trans. in EHD I:830: "The
religious Abbot Forthred . . . reported to us that three monasteries had been
granted to him by a certain abbess . . . and your Excellency took these monasteries from him by force and gave them to a certain 'patrician.' "

55. Alfred's Version of Augustine's Soliloquies, preface. Cf. Alfred, c. 41; I
Edward, c. 2, § 1. The king's magnates also seem to have been pressured by
their own followers for bookland in the middle of the ninth century. See Richard
Abels, "The Devolution of Bookland Tenure in Ninth-century Kent: A Note
on BCS 538," Archaeologia Cantiana 99 (1983): 219.

56. Plummer, Baedae Opera, 1:415. Cf. BCS 67 (S 9), 122 (S 1177), 141
(S 1180), 146 (S 85), 148 (S 268), 282 (S 268). See also BCS 201 (S 106,
endorsement; trans. in EHD I:501), which shows a comes of the Mercian king
Coenwulf purchasing certain privileges ("with 200 shillings, and afterwards 30
every year") for land which he already owned. (The reservation clause of BCS
201 is interesting in its own right, since it limits the burden of expeditio to
sending "but five men." See discussion chap. 5, n. 68.)

57. The military charges of bridge-work, fortress-work, and service upon
military expeditions are often referred to as the trinoda necessitas, a phrase
found only in a forged charter, BCS 50 (S 230). See W. H. Stevenson, "Trinoda
Necessitas," EHR 29 (1914): 689–703. Cf. Brooks, Church of Canterbury, p.
317, who demonstrates upon diplomatic grounds that this charter is a fabrication of the mid-tenth century. Cf. George Dempsey's unconvincing attempt
to rehabilitate BCS 50, "Legal Terminology in Anglo-Saxon England: The Tri-
moda Necessitas Charter," Speculum 57 (1982): 843–849. John suggested the
phrase the "common burdens" as an alternative. Land Tenure, p. 64. Cf. Brooks,
"Military Obligations," p. 75. It has the merit of being based upon the actual
language of the charters, a number of which refer to these burdens as "commonly" owed. See Stevenson, op. cit., p. 689, n. 3.

58. BCS 140 and 178 (S 92), the latter being the more reliable of the two
texts. Brooks, "Military Obligations," p. 76, n. 1, observes that the charred
fragments of the original charter are preserved as BM Otho A. 1, fol. 7; enough
survives of the original to authenticate BCS 178. On BCS 178 and its importance
for the development of the "common burdens," see John, Land Tenure, pp.
67–71; cf. Brooks, "Military Obligations," pp. 76–78.

59. BCS 178 (S 92): "Concedo, ut monasteria et aecclesiae a publicis vectigalibus, et ab omnibus operibus, oneribusque, auctore Deo, servientes absoluti maneant, nisi sola quae communiter fruenda sint, omnique populo edicto regis facienda jubentur, id est instructionibus pontium, vel necessariis defensionibus arcium contra hostes non sunt renuenda. Sed nec hoc praetermittendum est, cum necessarium contat aecclesiis Dei."

60. See, e.g., the immunity charter issued for the episcopal see of Metz in 775, *MGH, Diplomata Karolinorum*, 1, ed. Engelbert Mühlbacher (Hannover, 1906), no. 91, p. 132, which exempts the *homines ingenui* from "de tribus causis—hoste publico, hoc est de banno nostro, quando publicitus promovetur, et wacta vel pontos compenendum." Brooks, "Military Obligations," p. 69, n. 5. For bridge-building as one of the *munera* in the Roman Empire, see *Codex Theodosianus*, ed. Krueger, Mommsen, Meyer (Berlin, 1905), 2:15 (15.3, 6). Marjorie Boyer, *Medieval French Bridges* (Cambridge, Mass., 1976), pp. 16–20. The most recent and provocative work on Frankish fortified bridges is by Dr. Carroll Gillmor. I am grateful to her for allowing me to read her unpublished paper, "The Mobilization of a Work Force on the Fortified Bridges of the Seine, 862–886" (presented at the Third Annual Meeting of the Haskins Society, Houston, Texas, 10 November 1984).

61. Richard Hodges, *Dark Age Economics: The Origins of Towns and Trade* A.D. *600–1000* (New York, 1982), pp. 43–45, 111–113.

62. In Mercian charters of the first half of the ninth century a fourth burden is often reserved: *angilde* or *singulare pretium*, technical terms referring to the money compensation that a victim of a crime is entitled to receive, as opposed to the fine payable to the king or one of his officers. Stevenson, *"Trinoda Necessitas,"* p. 698, n. 44; Maitland, *Domesday Book*, pp. 274, 290–292.

63. Brooks, "Military Obligations," pp. 81–82; M. Biddle, "Towns," in *The Archaeology of Anglo-Saxon England*, ed. D. M. Wilson (London, 1976), pp. 120–122. This excludes royal vills, which seem to have been fortified with either wooden barricades or earthen walls. Hope-Taylor, *Yeavering*. Cf. *ASC*, s.a. 722, 755 (recte, 757). Cf. also *Beowulf*, ll. 2957–2960, on earthen-wall defenses.

64. *H.E.*, V. 23, ed. Colgrave and Mynors, p. 538. Cf. the title given Æthelbald in BCS 154 (S 89, contemporary): "King not only of the Mercians but also of all the kingdoms that are known by the general name South English." He attests the same grant as "Aetdilbalt rex Britanniae." Cf. BCS 157 (S 94), 163 (S 101), 164 (S 103), 181 (S 96). See F. M. Stenton, "The Supremacy of the Mercian Kings," *EHR* 33 (1918): 433–452; John, *Orbis Britanniae*, pp. 8, 17–23; Vollrath-Reichelt, *Königsgedanke*, pp. 133ff.

65. Stevenson, *"Trinoda Necessitas,"* p. 698: "The liability to military service and to aid in the construction and repair of fortresses are such primitive requirements of any organized state that it is unlikely that they were suddenly imposed in the eighth century." It is questionable, however, whether one can accurately characterize the Anglo-Saxon kingdoms of the seventh and eighth centuries as organized territorial states. The "Tribal Hidage," for example, assesses the liabilities of groups and peoples rather than of geographical units. See W. Davies and H. Vierck, "The Contexts of Tribal Hidage: Social Aggregates

and Settlement Patterns," *Frühmittelalterliche Studien* 8 (1974): 228–229, 240. Davies suggests that we ought to view the early kingdoms as "fluid groups who inhabit an elastic area with a fluctuating band of territory between them." Ibid., p. 228. This tallies well with recent studies of Anglo-Saxon settlement, and especially with the phenomenon known as "settlement drift," the tendency of settlements to shift position. Christopher Taylor, *Village and Farmstead: A History of Rural Settlement in England* (London, 1983), pp. 122–123. The proliferation of land held by book-right may be seen as part of a movement toward the establishment of territorial states in early England.

66. S 58 and S 59. Cf. Brooks, "Military Obligations," p. 78.

67. Æthelmund, son of Ingeld, became one of Offa's ealdormen, and was killed while leading the Hwicce on a raid of Wiltshire. BCS 272 (S 146), 273 (S 146), 289 (S 153, contemporary text), 293 (S 155, contemporary text); *ASC*, s.a. 800 (recte, 802).

68. BCS 274 (S 139): "[P]reter expeditionalibus causis et pontium structionem et arcium munimentum quod omni populo necesse est ab eo nullum excussatum esse."

69. Brooks, "Military Obligations," pp. 78–79, on BCS 848 (S 134). Brooks argues that Offa imposed only bridge- and fortress-work in 792. *Expeditio*, he claims, had been exacted from Kentish bookland since before 733. This assumes that the jus regium reserved in BCS 148 (S 23) was in fact host duty, a supposition without any perceivable basis. Apparently, Brooks was influenced by his acceptance of the immunity clause in BCS 1331 (S 255), an eleventh-century text that purports to record a West Saxon grant of 739. The immunity clause, however, is tacked on to a lengthy English bounds, unheard of in a charter of this period. Both are probably later interpolations (if the charter is itself genuine). See Whitelock's comments, *EHD* I:455–456. The reservation itself uses the language of BCS 1074 (S 692), a charter attributed to the reign of King Edgar (A.D. 961).

70. BCS 848 (S 134). The reservation clause stresses the novelty of the demand: "Nisi expeditione intra Canciam contra paganos marinos cum classis migrantibus vel in australes Saxones si necessitas cogit ac pontis constructionem et arcis munitionem contra paganos itemque intra fines Cantwariorum set, et *hec est in ea petitio atque doctrina ut hec tria consentiatis que doceo* ut eo stabilior hec mea libertas permaneat. Si vestra spontanea voluntate hoc non negatis" [emphasis added].

71. E.g., BCS 332 (S 1264, a contemporary text).

72. Brooks, "Military Obligations," pp. 79–80, 84.

73. Offa's ambitions and authority may be gauged by the extensive currency reform that took place during his reign. C. E. Blunt, "The Coinage of Offa," in *Anglo-Saxon Coins*, ed. R. H. Dolley (London, 1961), pp. 39–62. As is well known, Offa also had his son anointed king, which may have been an attempt to create a stronger ideological foundation for kingship. Stenton, *ASE*, pp. 218–219; Wallace-Hadrill, *Early Germanic Kingship*, pp. 113–115. Cf. John, *Orbis Britanniae*, pp. 27–34. For a contemporary assessment of Offa's reign, see Alcuin's letter to Ealdorman Osbert (797), *EHD* I:854–856.

74. Stenton characterized Offa's dyke as "the greatest public work of the

whole Anglo-Saxon period." *ASE,* p. 212. The dyke consisted of a six-foot ditch surmounted by a twenty-four-foot rampart to the east, which together measured approximately sixty feet across. It may once have extended over the entire 150-mile frontier. Eighty miles of earthwork are still visible today. Patrick Wormald estimates that Offa could "hardly have used fewer than 5,000 workmen" to construct the dyke, and may, in fact, have conscripted tens of thousands. "The Age of Offa and Alcuin," in *Anglo-Saxons,* ed. Campbell, p. 122 (see also his general discussion, pp. 119–122). Cyril Fox's seminal study of the dyke, *Offa's Dyke* (London, 1955), has recently been challenged by the researches of David Hill. For a discussion of recent scholarship, see Frank Noble, *Offa's Dyke Reviewed,* ed. Margaret Gelling, British Archaeological Reports, British Series, 114 (1983).

75. Stenton, *ASE,* pp. 526–527; Brooks, *Church of Canterbury,* pp. 22–25.

76. J. Radley, "Excavations in the Defences of the City of York: An Early Medieval Stone Tower and the Successive Earth Ramparts," *Yorkshire Archaeological J.* 44 (1972): 38–64; Biddle, "Towns," p. 117.

77. Asser, *Life of King Alfred,* chap. 27, trans. Keynes and Lapidge, *Alfred the Great,* p. 76.

78. Biddle, "Towns," p. 117.

79. *Two Lives of St. Cuthbert,* ed. Colgrave, pp. 122, 242–244.

80. This conjunction of charter and archaeological evidence has been noted by Finberg, *Charters of Wessex,* p. 188, and Brooks, "Military Obligation," pp. 81–82. The results of the digs at Hamwih and Winchester are reviewed by M. Biddle, "Towns," pp. 107–109, 112–115.

81. The sack of Hamwih in 842 is noted by Nithard, *EHD* I:342. The archaeological evidence for Hamwih's decline is presented by Philip Holdsworth, "Saxon Southampton: A New Review," *Medieval Archaeology* 20 (1976): 30, 60. Richard Hodges, "State Formation and the Role of Trade in Middle Saxon England," *Antiquaries J.* 58 (1978): 442; idem, *Dark Age Economics,* pp. 45, 156, 158, argues that the viking raids on Hamwih merely assisted an ongoing process of decay, which can only be understood through a systems analysis of the international economics and politics of the period.

82. Biddle, "Towns," p. 107, 114–115, 127.-130; Hodges, "State Formation," p. 442.

83. BCS 268 (S 135), 300 (S 270a), 389 (S 273), 390 (S 270, 1403), 391 (S 275), 393 (S 276), 395 (S 271), 398 (S 284), 420 (S 286), 426 (S 287), 852 (S 279).

84. Finberg, *Charters of Wessex,* pp. 118–120 (no. 338). See Brooks's comments on the authenticity of this charter. "Military Obligations," pp. 79–80. In addition to Brooks's arguments, one might also note that the charter's *arenga* resembles those of BCS 195 (S 105) and 224 (S 263), as well as BCS 505 (S 335) and 508 (S 336). The *verba dispositiva* shows similarities to BCS 258 (S 269), an authentic charter issued by the same Beorhtric.

85. This feature, however, is not fatal to its authenticity. Cf. BCS 225 (S 264), a contemporary text recording a grant by King Cynewulf of Wessex (778), which is similar in form to Æthelney 62. BCS 225 begins: "Hoc signum su-

prascriptum sacrosanctae crucis Christi . . . ego Cynewulf rex Saxonum propria manu expressi ad confirmandum donationem munificentiae meae quam dedi Bican comiti meo ac ministro."

86. Finberg, *Charters of Wessex,* p. 120: "Ut libertatem habeat omnium fiscalium negotiorum et operum Regalium, et omnium rerum quae ad Villam Regiam pertinent, nisi aquam [for *unquam*] expeditione sola, quae omnes Comites ad tutelam totius Provinciae, et maxime Ecclesiarum Dei, adire debent."

87. *ASC,* s.a. 787 (recte, 789), 836 (recte, 839).

88. *ASC,* s.a. 787 (recte, 789).

89. The problem of purveyance for the king's campaigns has too often been ignored. It is quite possible that what is termed "expeditionales causae" included a render either in kind or money for the royal commissariat. *The Anonymous Life of St. Cuthbert* hints at the difficulties of supplying an army in the field. *Two Lives of St. Cuthbert,* ed. Colgrave, p. 72.

90. BCS 848 (S 134): "hec est in [m]ea peticio atque doctrina ut hec tria consentiatis que deceo ut eo stabilior hec mea libertas permaneat."

91. BCS 348 (S 177, a contemporary text).

THREE: ROYAL LORDSHIP AND MILITARY INNOVATION IN ALFREDIAN ENGLAND

1. The Tribal Hidage, which has been variously attributed to King Wulfhere (by Wendy Davies) and to King Offa (by Cyril Hart), lists the peoples subject to Mercia during its hegemony, ca. 665–802. In all, the Tribal Hidage names thirty-five tribes and/or political units. See Cyril Hart, "The Tribal Hidage," *TRHS,* 5th Series, 21 (1971): 133–157. Cf. Davies and Vierck, "Tribal Hidage."

2. *EHD* I:193; Plummer, *Saxon Chronicles,* 1:71.

3. *Folc* sometimes renders *exercitus* in the Old English Orosius. *OE Orosius,* ed. Janet Bately, pp. 26, 33, 45, 46. Cf. the use of the term *theod* ("nation") in *ASC,* s.a. 1006 and 1016.

4. *ASC,* s.a. 800 (recte, 802).

5. *Æthelweard,* ed. Campbell, p. 42; Asser, *King Alfred,* chap. 54, trans. Keynes and Lapidge, pp. 83–85; *ASC,* s.a. 878.

6. Simeon of Durham, *Historia Regum,* s.a. 759, 769, 780, 798; *EHD* I:266–275.

7. Asser, *King Alfred,* chap. 54, ed. Stevenson, p. 43, trans. Keynes and Lapidge, p. 84.

8. *ASC,* s.a. 784 (recte, 786), 901 (recte, 900).

9. E.g., *ASC,* s.a. 823 (recte, 825), 874, 901 D, E (recte, 900), 921 A (recte, 918); II *Edward,* c. 1; *Swerian,* c. 1, Liebermann, *Gesetze,* 1:396.

10. E.g., *ASC,* s.a. 923 A (recte, 920), 920 A (recte, 917). Cf. Asser, *King Alfred,* chap. 91, trans. Keynes and Lapidge, pp. 101–102.

11. *ASC,* s.a. 874. The oath given by Asser, *Life of King Alfred,* chap. 46, ed. Stevenson, p. 35: "[Ceolwulf] iuravit, nullo modo se voluntati eorum contradicere velle, sed oboediens in omnibus esse," should be compared with the hold-oath. *Swerian,* c. 1, ed. Liebermann, *Gesetze,* 1:396.

12. BCS 303 (S 157). Cf. BCS 600 (S 368), where a thegn directed that an estate that he held by book-right should pass after his death to his son only "if he were willing to serve and obey the king."

13. *Rectitudines Singularum Personarum*, c. 1, ed. Liebermann, *Gesetze*, 1:444: "The right and privilege of the thegn is that he be worthy of his book-right." Cf. II *Edgar*, c. 2 = I *Cnut*, c. 11; I *Æthelred*, c. 1, § 14; II *Cnut*, c. 77, § 1.

14. *ASC*, s.a. 855, ed. Plummer, *Saxon Chronicles*, 1:66–67: "Gebocude Æthelwulf cyning teothan dæl his londes ofer eall his rice Gode to lofe and himselfum to ecere hælo." Cf. Asser, *King Alfred*, chap. 11, trans. Keynes and Lapidge, pp. 69–70, 232–234 (comments). On the "Decimation," see Stevenson, *Asser's Life of King Alfred*, pp. 186–191; Finberg, *Charters of Wessex*, pp. 187–213.

15. A number of cartularies contain what purport to be texts of Æthelwulf's "Decimation" of 855 (the documents are dated A. D. 854). See BCS 468 (S 304), 469 (S 308), 470 (S 305), 471 (S 302), 472 (S 303), 474 (S 307). These cannot be accepted as genuine in their present form, but Finberg has collated the various manuscripts to produce what he believes is the original text of the donation. *Charters of Wessex*, pp. 210–213.

Quapropter ego . . . Æthelwulf . . . pro meae remedio animae et regni prosperitate et populi ab omnipotenti Deo mihi collati salute consilium salubre cum episcopis, comitibus, et cunctis optimatibus meis perfeci, ut decimam partem terrarum per regnum meum non solum sanctis ecclesiis darem, verum etiam et ministris nostris in eodem constitutis in perpetuam libertatem habere concessimus.

Finberg, p. 210. But cf. comments of Keynes and Lapidge, *Alfred the Great*, p. 233.

16. *EHD* I:525–526; Campbell, *Charters*, no. 23, pp. 26–27; authenticated on p. xxiv.

17. BCS 467 (S 316).

18. According to Asser (chaps. 12–13), the king faced a rebellion by his eldest son, Æthelbald, upon his return, and was only saved by the loyalty of the majority of the nobility. To prevent civil war, Æthelwulf agreed to share the kingdom.

19. E.g., BCS 426 (S 287), 431 (S 288), 438 (S 292), 439 (S 291), 442 (S 293), 449 (S 296), and 467 (S 316).

20. *Æthelweard*, ed. Campbell, p. 42; Asser, *King Alfred*, chap. 52. Cf. *ASC*, s.a. 878. R. H. C. Davis, "Alfred the Great: Propaganda and Truth," *History* 56 (1971): 172–173, suggests, however, that the Chronicle may have exaggerated Alfred's difficulties in order to make his eventual victory more impressive.

21. See chap. 1.

22. The Danes avoided pitched battles, preferring to raid and then take refuge in their strongholds. See, e.g., *ASC*, s.a. 878, 894 (recte, 893), 895 (recte, 894), 896 (recte, 895).

23. Asser, *King Alfred*, chaps. 52–53, trans. Keynes and Lapidge, pp. 82–

83. See also *ASC*, s.a. 878. Æthelweard even suggests that some had submitted to the Danes even before the invasion: "Ast multos equitando per aduerterent ceruices, quoad haud habuere incolae dominatu insopituri, citius eorum cuncti mentes uertunt." *Æthelweard*, ed. Campbell, p. 42. Wulfhere, who had probably been King Æthelred I's ealdorman in Wiltshire (BCS 508 = S 336; BCS 886 = S 341), may have been among those who collaborated with the Danes, since we know that he forfeited his land for having broken his oath to "his lord King Alfred." See BCS 595 (S 362).

24. *Annales Bertiniani*, ed. Felix Grat, Jeanne Vielliard, and Suzanne Clémencet (Paris, 1964), pp. 74 (s.a. 857), 105, 113 (s.a. 864). Cf. also the evidence of cooperation between ninth-century Irish kings and the Norse of Dublin. Alfred Smyth, *Scandinavian Kings in the British Isles, 850–880* (Oxford, 1977), pp. 129–153. Ferdinand Lot suggests that Hincmar branded Pepin an apostate to discredit him. *Recueil des travaux historiques de Ferdinand Lot* (Geneva, 1970), 2:789–799, n. 1.

25. Asser, *King Alfred*, chaps. 53 and 55, trans. Keynes and Lapidge, pp. 83, 84. Cf. *Æthelweard*, ed. Campbell, p. 42.

26. Davis, "Alfred the Great," pp. 177–180.

27. Whitelock, *ASC*, p. 54; Plummer, *Saxon Chronicles*, 1:84. Edward the Elder preserved his father's arrangements. See, *ASC*, s.a. 920 (recte, 917).

28. *ASC*, s.a. 871, 896 (recte, 895), 901 (recte, 900). See J. H. Clapham, "The Horsing of the Danes," *EHR* 25 (1910): 287–293.

29. Plummer, *Saxon Chronicles*, 2:109, notes the remarkable similarity between Alfred's fyrd system and Amazon military practice as described in the Old English translation of Orosius sponsored by the king: "Hie [the Amazons' two queens, Marsepia and Lampida] heora here on tu todældon, other æt ham beon [?sceolde] heora lond to healdanne, other ut faran to winanne" ("They divided their army into two parts, one of which remained at home to guard their land, the other of which went out on campaign to wage war"). Cf. *ASC*, s.a. 894 (recte, 893), ed. Plummer, *Saxon Chronicles*, 1:84 (note especially the similar phraseology). If, as Plummer believed, the idea for Alfred's reform came from his reading of Orosius, then the purpose behind leaving one half of the fighting force becomes clear. Cf. Bately, *OE Orosius*, p. 220.

30. Carroll Gillmor, "Fortified Bridges," p. 5. Cf. Lot, "La grande invasion normande de 856–862," in *Recueil*, 2:714–715.

31. *ASC*, s.a. 905 B,C,D (recte, 903); Mercian Register, s.a. 902; Harmer, *Documents*, pp. 37–38 = BCS 1064 (S 1211); BCS 1065 (S 1212). Goda possessed bookland at Osterland in Kent and attested a grant by the Archbishop of Canterbury, ca. 905. BCS 638 (S 1288).

32. Harmer, *Documents*, pp. 37–38.

33. *ASC*, 894 C,D (recte, 893).

34. *ASC*, 896 C,D (recte, 895), 919 (recte, 916). Cf. Hollister, *Military Institutions*, pp. 29–30; Powicke, *Military Obligations*, pp. 8–14.

35. *Ælfrics Grammatik und Glossar*, ed. J. Zupitza, Sammlung englischer Denkmäler, no. 1 (1880; reprint Berlin, 1966), p. 34, l. 14 ("Grammatik"). Cf. ibid., "Glossar," chap. 2, l. 75: *gemotman* "contionator" (i.e., speaker at a popular assembly). See Asser, *King Alfred*, chaps. 91, 106, trans. Keynes and

Lapidge, pp. 102, 109–110, for the judicial authority of ealdormen, reeves, and thegns. One should also note that Alfred rotated his household. His *bellatores* and *nobiles ministri* spent one month at court and two at home, looking after their own affairs. Ibid., chap. 100, p. 106; Stevenson, pp. 86–87, Cf. IV *Æthelstan*, c. 7; IV *Æthelstan*, c. 5, § 4.

36. II *Æthelstan*, caps. 16; 20, § 1–4; VI *Æthelstan*, caps. 4; 5; 8, §§ 2–4. (These laws all concern the administration of boroughs.)

37. *ASC*, s.a. 901 (recte, 900).

38. Powicke, *Military Obligations*, p. 13.

39. *Alfred & Guthrum*, caps. 4, 5. Cf. II *Æthelred*, c. 6, § 2.

40. Dorothy Bethurum, ed., *The Homilies of Wulfstan* (1957; reprint Oxford, 1971), pp. 255–275; trans. *EHD* I:929–934. Note especially the archbishops's concern about slaves fleeing their masters only to return as viking raiders.

41. Cf. John, *Orbis Britanniae*, p. 139.

42. Wright and Wülcker, *Vocabularies*, 1: 193, 194, 304, 309, 429, 442; Napier, *OE Glosses*, § 1, ll. 387, 741, 893; § 2, l. 330.

43. Wright and Wülcker, *Vocabularies*, 1:450 (eleventh-century).

44. *ASC*, s.a. 1010; Whitelock, *ASC*, p. 190: "And many other good thegns [were killed at *Ringmere*] and a countless number of people." Cf. *ASC*, s.a. 896 (recte, 895), where only four king's thegns are said to have fallen in a rout of a London fyrd.

45. *ASC*, s.a. 894 (recte, 893).

46. DB, i. 189 (Cambridge).

47. *Dunsæte*, c. 7 establishes the value of a horse at 30 shillings, as compared to 30 p. (= 6 s.) for an ox. Cf. VI *Æthelstan*, c. 6, §§ 1–2 (one half pound for an average horse; 30 p. for an ox). II *Æthelstan*, c. 18 forbids selling horses overseas, a clear sign of their importance. Horses also appear in the bequests of nobles in the tenth and eleventh centuries, where they are often associated with swords and armor. See, e.g., Whitelock, *Wills*, no. 3, pp. 12, 14; no. 20, pp. 58–60. Magnates maintained their own stud farms. Finberg, *Agrarian History*, p. 498.

48. Cf. *ASC*, s.a. 1006, where Æthelred II called out the "whole nation" from Wessex and Mercia, which "cost the people of the country every sort of harm, so that they profited neither from the native army nor the foreign army." Again, there seems to be an implicit distinction here between those who fight—and ravage—and those who till the soil.

49. Campbell, *Anglo-Saxons*, pp. 150, 154. Cf. John, *Orbis Britanniae*, pp. 137–138.

50. *EHD* I:202.

51. On the history of this concept, see G. Duby, "The Origins of a System of Social Classifications," *The Chivalrous Society* (Berkeley, 1977), pp. 88–93. Nicholas Brooks assumes that Alfred was merely echoing "the ideas of the contemporary Carolingian monastic schools." Brooks, "Arms, Status, and Warfare in Late-Saxon England," in *Ethelred the Unready*, ed. David Hill, British Archaeological Reports, British Series, 59 (1978), p. 81. This argument, however, may be reversed, and the tripartite classification may have reached the

Continent through English writers. Certainly, Adalbéron's statement far more resembles Alfred's and those made by Ælfric and Wulfstan at the beginning of the eleventh century than the vague formulations that appear in Carolingian texts. Cf. Wallace-Hadrill, "War and Peace," pp. 172–174. See also D. Dubuisson, "L'Irlande et la théorie médiévale des 'trois ordres,'" *Revue de l'histoire des religions* 188 (1975): 35–61, esp. 58–63, for the possibility of Irish influence upon Alfred's system.

52. EHD I:919; *King Alfred's Old English Version of Boethius' De Consolatione Philosophiae,* ed. W. J. Sedgefield (1899; reprint Darmstadt, 1968), p. 40.

53. EHD I:928; *Die Hirtenbriefe Ælfrics in Altenglischer und Lateinischer Fassung,* ed. Bernhard Fehr, Bibliothek der Angelsächsischen Prosa, ed. C. Grein, 9 (1914; reprint Darmstadt, 1966), p. 225; Wulfstan, *Die "Institutes of Polity, Civil and Ecclesiastical,"* ed. Karl Jost (Bern, 1959), ch. 4, pp. 55–56. See discussion in chap. 7.

54. *Alfred,* c. 40, § 1.

55. Asser, *King Alfred,* chaps. 37–39. The English deployed *in response* to the vikings' decision to split their forces into two divisions of equal size.

56. ASC, s.a. 905 C,D (recte, 903).

57. John, *Land Tenure,* p. 115. Alfred's choice of Iley Oaks for his camp on the evening before the battle of Edington is interesting in this context, since we know it was the meeting-place of the Wiltshire Hundreds of Warminster and Heytesbury in the eleventh century. Asser, *King Alfred,* chap. 55; Keynes and Lapidge, *Alfred the Great,* p. 249, n. 105.

58. Asser, *King Alfred,* chap. 35, ed. Stevenson, p. 27.

59. Robertson, *Charters,* pp. 246–249, provides a convenient edition and translation, which should be used in conjunction with David Hill, "The Burghal Hidage: The Establishment of a Text," *Medieval Archaeology* 13 (1969): 84–92. The document is usually dated to the period 911–919 on the basis of internal evidence: Oxford and London only came into Edward's hands in 911 (ASC, s.a.); Buckingham was not built until 914 (ASC, s.a.; the reference to Buckingham may, however, be an interpolation, since the totals given exclude this burh); and Edward seized the rest of Mercia in 919 (ASC, s.a.). P. Wormald, "The Burhs," in Campbell, ed., *The Anglo-Saxons,* p. 152, proposes a date of composition prior to 886, the year that Alfred restored London to the Mercians. Wormald ignores, however, the inclusion of Portchester, which belonged to the bishop of Winchester until 904, when Edward the Elder obtained it by exchange. BCS 613 (S 372). He is on more secure ground in concluding that the Burghal Hidage "almost certainly reflects Alfredian policy." Ibid., p. 153. Cf. Stenton, *ASE,* p. 265.

60. Stenton, *ASE,* pp. 324–336. The "Mercian Register" stresses Æthelflæd's building of boroughs in Mercia. Among the boroughs she ordered built were *Scergeat,* Bridgnorth (912), Tamworth, Stafford (913), *Weardbyrig,* Runcorn (915). In addition, she and her husband were responsible for fortifying Worcester ("at the urging of Bishop Wærferth": Harmer, *Select Documents,* no. 13, pp. 22–23) and restoring the walls of Chester (ASC, s.a. 907; cf. ASC, s.a. 893). The two also played an important part in the refurbishment of Lon-

don's defenses, which they discussed at a conference held at Celchyth in 898 with Alfred and Archbishop Plegmund. See BCS 577 (S 1628), cited by Harmer, *Select Documents,* p. 106. For further discussion of Æthelflæd's role in the events of the early tenth century, see F. T. Wainwright, "Æthelflæd, Lady of the Mercians," in Peter Clemoes, ed., *The Anglo-Saxons* (London, 1959), pp. 53–69.

61. According to the "one man, one hide" rule of the Burghal Hidage. The hidages followed are those of Hill's restored figures."Burghal Hidage," p. 87.

62. For the Danes' use of fortifications, see Asser, *King Alfred,* chaps. 30, 35, and 36; *ASC,* s.a. 892. The Danes also used fortresses as administrative and military centers; much of the Danelaw was organized around the Five Boroughs of Leicester, Lincoln, Nottingham, Stamford, and Derby, an arrangement that predates Edward's and Æthelflæd's reconquest of these territories. For Charles the Bald's building program, see discussion below.

63. Biddle, "Towns," pp. 120–122.

64. Ibid.

65. Ibid., p. 137.

66. Asser, *King Alfred,* chap. 91, trans. Keynes and Lapidge, p. 101 (comments, pp. 24–25).

67. By comparison, in the beginning of the eleventh century Fulk Nerra spaced his strongholds on the route between Amboise and Angers at distances of between seventeen and thirty-three kilometers so that a cavalry force could ride between them and arrive in condition to do battle. Bernard Bachrach, "The Angevin Strategy of Castle Building in the Reign of Fulk Nerra, 987–1040," *American Historical Review* 88 (1983): 541–542 (see especially n. 27 on equine endurance). The fifth-century Roman military writer Vegetius believed that twenty Roman miles (thirty-two kilometers) was the maximum distance that a horse could be ridden in a day and still be battle-ready. Vegetius, *Epitoma rei militaris,* ed. C. Lang (1885; reprint Stuttgart, 1967), 1:28–29. Small mounted forces unencumbered by pack animals can, however, manage distances in excess of thirty-five miles under the proper conditions. Col. P. S. Bond, U.S.A. (ret.), ed., *Military Science and Tactics: Senior Division. Infantry* (Washington, D.C., 1938), p. 219. Donald Engels, *Alexander the Great and the Logistics of the Macedonian Army* (Berkeley, 1978), pp. 153–156. Alfred's armies, of course, would not have used mounts in battle except to pursue a fleeing enemy, and therefore a forced march would not have impaired their combat-readiness as much as it would have an army of medieval knights.

68. Robin Fleming, "Monastic Lands and England's Defence in the Viking Age," *EHR* 100 (1985): 247–265, argues that Alfred and his son incorporated strategically located monastic estates into the royal fisc in order to bolster the defense of the realm. The military importance of Alfred's royal *tuns* is reflected in their selection as the sites of battles during the viking wars. P. H. Sawyer, "The Royal *Tun* in Pre-Conquest England, in *Ideal and Reality in Frankish and Anglo-Saxon Society,* ed. P. Wormald with D. Bullough and R. Collins (Oxford, 1983), pp. 283–284.

69. Hinton, *Alfred's Kingdom: Wessex and the South 800–1500* (London, 1977), p. 34.

70. Ibid., p. 35; C. A. R. Ralegh Radford, "The Later Pre-Conquest Boroughs and their Defences," *Medieval Archaeology* 14 (1970): 94.

71. Hinton, *Alfred's Kingdom,* p. 40.

72. *EHD* I:540–541; BCS 579 (S 223).

73. E.g., *ASC,* s.a. 922 A (recte, 919): "In this year ... King Edward went with the army [*mid fierde*] to Thelwall and ordered the borough to be built, occupied, and manned [*het ge wyrcan tha burg, and ge settan, and ge mannian*], and while he stayed there he ordered another army, also from the people of Mercia, to occupy Manchester in Northumbria, and repair it and man it [*hie ge betan and ge mannian*]." *EHD* I:217; Plummer, *Saxon Chronicles,* p. 104. The conjunction of garrison duty and maintenance of the defenses tallies nicely with the wording of the Burghal Hidage.

74. Cf. Keynes and Lapidge, *Alfred the Great,* pp. 42–43.

75. *ASC,* s.a. 917 A (recte, 914).

76. *ASC,* s.a. 894 C,D (recte, 893).

77. *ASC,* s.a. 896 C,D (recte, 895), 921 A (recte, 918), 923 A (recte, 920).

78. *Capitularia regum Francorum,* 2, ed. A Boretius and V. Krause, *MGH, Legum Sectio II* (Hannover, 1883), no. 273, c. 27, p. 321.

79. Fernand Vercauteren, "Comment s'est-on défendu au IXe siècle dans l'empire franc contre les invasions normandes?" (1936), in idem, *Etudes d'histoire médiévale. Recueil d'articles du Professeur Vercauteren publiés par le Crédit Communal de Belgique* (Brussels, 1978), pp. 39–54, esp. 45–50; Kurt-Ulrich Jäschke, *Burgenbau und Landesverteidigung um 900, Überlegungen zu Beispielen aus Deutschland, Frankreich und England* (Sigmaringen, 1975), pp. 69–80; Carroll Gillmor, "Fortified Bridges," pp. 12–13.

80. J. M. Hassal and David Hill, "Pont de l'Arche: Frankish Influence on the West Saxon Burh?" *Archaeological Journal* 127 (1970): 188–195; Jäschke, *Burgenbau,* pp. 111–112. Keynes and Lapidge, *Alfred the Great,* p. 288, n. 23, note the parallels but conclude: "We may suppose that Alfred was intelligent enough to think of it himself." Nothing in the annal for 895, however, suggests that Alfred's decision to build a double-burh on the Lea was due to sudden inspiration, and the vikings' quick reaction to the construction of the forts shows that the tactic was not unfamiliar to them.

81. *ASC,* s.a. 896 C,D (recte, 895).

82. E.g., *ASC,* s.a. 894 C,D (recte, 893), on the siege of Exeter. On the defenses of the late ninth- and early tenth-century burhs, see Radford, "Pre-Conquest Boroughs"; Biddle, "Towns," pp. 127–129, 134–135.

83. *ASC,* s.a. 920 A (recte, 917), on the relief of Towcester and Maldon.

84. *ASC,* s.a. 892. Cf. the Norse occupation of the half-built fortified bridge at Pont de l'Arche in 865. *Annales Bertiniani,* s.a. 865. Cf. also Asser's remarks about forts "begun late in the day" so that "enemy forces burst in by land and sea." *King Alfred,* chap. 91, trans. Keynes and Lapidge, p. 102.

85. For a full discussion of "defense-in-depth," see Edward Luttwak, *The Grand Strategy of the Roman Empire* (Baltimore, 1976), pp. 131–135. Cf. John H. Beeler, "Castles and Strategy in Norman and Early Angevin England," *Speculum* 31 (1956): 581–601; Bachrach, "Angevin Strategy," pp. 556–557. Between 924 and 933 Henry the Fowler dotted eastern Saxony with fortified

towns that were to be used in tandem with a mobile field force. There is some reason to believe that Henry was inspired by the success of the English burghal system. Jäschke, *Burgenbau*, pp. 18–33, 115–121.

86. See, e.g., *Annales Bertiniani*, s.a. 865; *ASC*, s.a. 867 and 871.

87. Robertson, *Charters*, pp. 495–496; Hill, "Burghal Hidage," p. 91.

88. Hill, "Burghal Hidage," pp. 91–92; Wormald, "Burhs," in Campbell, *Anglo-Saxons*, p. 153. Exeter's allotment of hides, however, falls short. Radford, "Pre-Conquest Boroughs," pp. 101–102.

89. Hill, "Burghal Hidage," p. 90: "That is all 27,000 hides and seventy which belong to it; and 30 burhs belong to the West Saxons. And to Worcester 1200 hides. To Warwick 2400 hides."

90. Hill, "Burghal Hidage," p. 92; Stenton, *ASE*, p. 337; Biddle, "Towns," p. 126.

91. Local landowners may have been charged with finding as well as financially maintaining the boroughs' defenders, no small imposition in light of the numbers involved. The king, however, appears to have enjoyed lordship over these garrison troops. E.g., VI *Æthelstan*, c. 8, § 9. Cf. *Annales Bertiniani*, s.a. 869, which describes how Charles the Bald used *haistaldi*, poor free peasants, as royal military colonists in his newly built fortifications. (I owe this reference to Dr. Carroll Gillmor.) Cf. also K. J. Leyser, "Henry I and the Beginnings of the Saxon Empire," *EHR* 83 (1968): 1–32, reprint in idem, *Medieval Germany and its Neighbours, 900–1250* (London, 1982), pp. 11–42, on Henry the Fowler's employment of *agrarii milites* to garrison his Saxon strongholds. Vestiges of the Burghal Hidage's recruitment system can be seen in DB, i. 262b, which describes how Cheshire landowners in 1066 were required to supply on the sheriff's summons one man for each hide they owned to do wall-work and bridge repair. No mention is made in the Domesday custumal of garrison service. Oxford had a different arrangement in 1066, obliging those who dwelled in "mural houses" to do host service and wall-work [*excepta expeditione et muri reparatione*] in lieu of all other royal customs." DB, i. 154.

92. BCS 178 (S 92). See chap. two above.

93. Asser, *King Alfred*, chap. 91, ed. Stevenson, p. 77; *EHD* I:298 (I have given Whitelock's translation because of its fidelity to the wording of the original Latin).

94. Ibid., p. 79.

95. Cf. BCS 438 (S 292), Æthelwulf, king of the West Saxons, to his princeps Eanwulf, A.D. 842: "Arcium municionibus quod omni populo communis est." Phrases such as "communis labor" and "communium utilitatum necessitatibus" appear in tenth-century charters. For these and similar formulas, see Stevenson, "*Trinoda Necessitas*," pp. 689, n. 2; 689, n. 3; and 691, n. 16. Keynes and Lapidge, *Alfred the Great*, p. 271, n. 227, also read this passage to refer to the "common burdens."

96. Asser, *King Alfred*, chap. 91, ed. Stevenson, pp. 78–79; *EHD* I:299.

97. Ibid., "The other things for the common profit of the whole kingdom" seems to refer to Alfred's "frequent expeditions and battles against the pagans," which Asser mentions earlier in the same chapter.

98. Asser, *King Alfred*, chap. 106. Cf. Alcuin's letter to the nobility of Kent (A.D. 797), in which he addresses them as "viri fortissimi in bello et iustissimi in iudiciis," and presents them as being arbiters of justice. *Monumenta Alcuiniana*, Epistola, no. 86, pp. 369–372. Harmer, *Select Documents*, no. 18, pp. 30–33, 60–63 (comments) = BCS 591 (S 1445) provides a good illustration of the roles played by the local aristocracy and the king in the lawsuits of Alfred's reign. The king's dependence upon the nobility to maintain order and carry out the royal will comes out clearly in the law codes of the tenth century. Cf. II *Æthelstan*, c. 3; IV *Æthelstan*, c. 7; V *Æthelstan*, c. 1, § 4; VI *Æthelstan*, c. 11; III *Edgar*, c. 3; IV *Edgar*, c. 1, § 8. The ability of local magnates to thwart the royal will forms the subject of a series of laws in Æthelstan's codes. See III *Æthelstan*, c. 6; IV *Æthelstan*, c. 3; VI *Æthelstan*, c. 8, §§ 2–3.

99. Asser, *King Alfred*, chap. 91; EHD I:298. R. H. C. Davis, "Alfred the Great," pp. 177–178, 181–182.

100. Ibid. The difficulty of enforcing royal judgments in the tenth century is well documented. One late tenth-century charter (Robertson, *Charters*, no. 63, pp. 128–131 [S 877]) relates "the crimes by which Wulfbold ruined himself with his lord [*his hlaford*]," a title which is unintentionally ironic, since Wulfbold managed to escape retribution. Having robbed his stepmother and his kinsmen, he "made no amend [for his many crimes] up to the time of his death," ignoring with impunity the commands and judgments of the king. On four separate occasions his wergild was assigned to the king without any result. Cf. Harmer, *Select Documents*, no. 23, pp. 37–38, 66–68. See also II *Edward*, Preamble, 1 § 3; 2; II *Æthelstan*, c. 25, § 2; IV *Æthelstan*, c. 7.

101. Asser, *King Alfred*, chap. 91.

102. Although the Chronicle passes over the subject in discreet silence, Alfred clearly made large payments to the Danes. See BCS 533 (S 1278), a charter of 872, which refers to the "immense tribute paid the pagans" by the West Saxons. See also Alfred P. Smyth, *Scandinavian Kings*, p. 242.

103. Asser, *Life of King Alfred*, chap. 91. This seems to refer to ASC, s.a. 892: "They [the *micel here*] rowed their ships up the river as far as the Weald, four miles from the mouth of the estuary, and there they stormed a fortress [*fæstenne*]. Inside the fortification there were a few peasants, and it was only half made [*inne on tham fæ[ste]nne sæton feawa cyrlisce men on, & wæs sam worht*]." EHD I:201; Plummer, *Saxon Chronicles*, p. 84. Stevenson has dated the *Life* to 893. *Life of King Alfred*, p. lxxiv. This annal suggests that cierlisc men were included in the garrisons of the burhs. The term "sæton," used to describe the ceorls' activity in the half-finished fort, recalls the *gesettan* of the Burghal Hidage, which, as Robertson points out, means "garrison." *Charters*, p. 496. Cf. Chadwick, *Origin*, p. 160, and John, *Orbis Britanniae*, pp. 137–138, who contend that these ceorls were there to build the fortress, not to defend it.

104. Asser's rhetorical question, "Quid loquar de frequentibus contra paganos expeditionibus" (ch. 91, ed. Stevenson, p. 76), recalls the *expeditio contra paganos* of late eighth- and early ninth-century Mercian and Kentish charters. See, e.g., BCS 348 (S 177), 370 (S 186), and 487 (S 206).

105. BCS 848 (S 134). See discussion in chap. two.

FOUR: THE GROWTH OF ROYAL
LORDSHIP IN TENTH-CENTURY
ENGLAND

1. II *Æthelstan,* c. 13.

2. Chadwick, *Institutions,* pp. 219–227.

3. Stenton, *ASE,* p. 337. Hart adduces evidence for the shiring of the north and east Midlands during the reign of Edward the Elder. *The Hidation of Northamptonshire* (Leicester, 1970), pp. 12–14. Cyril Hart, *The Hidation of Cambridgeshire* (Leicester, 1974), pp. 30–31. Cf. C. S. Taylor, "The Origin of the Mercian Shires," in *Gloucestershire Studies,* ed. H. P. R. Finberg (Leicester, 1957), pp. 17–51. The Chronicle, s.a. 920 A (recte, 917), implies that Edward subdued Danish territorial districts attached to strongholds such as Northampton and Huntington, which were later to be shire towns.

4. E.g., Hertford (built by Edward in 912), Buckingham (914), Bedford (915), Huntingdon (restored and repaired in 917), and Nottingham (918).

5. II *Æthelstan,* c. 14. On the character and implications of the tenth-century currency reforms, see Campbell, "Observations," pp. 39–41, and authorities cited there.

6. I *Edward,* c. 1, § 1; II *Æthelstan,* c. 13, § 1; IV *Æthelstan,* c. 2. Edward and Æthelstan attempted to regulate commerce within the kingdom. On the changing nature of commerce in this period and its relation to Anglo-Saxon governance, see P. H. Sawyer, "Kings and Merchants," in *Early Medieval Kingship,* ed. P. H. Sawyer and Ian Wood (Leeds, 1977), pp. 139–158; Hodges, "State Formation," pp. 440–444, 446–449.

7. II *Æthelstan,* c. 20, §§ 1–4.

8. Cyril Hart, "Athelstan 'Half King' and his Family," *Anglo-Saxon England* 2 (1973): 115–144; Ann Williams, "*Princeps Merciorum Gentis:* The Family, Career and Connections of Ælfhere, Ealdorman of Mercia, 956–983," *Anglo-Saxon England* 10 (1982): 143–172; Katharin Mack, "Kings and Thegns in the Unification of Anglo-Saxon England," paper presented at the 20th International Congress on Medieval Studies, Kalamazoo, Michigan, 11 May 1985.

9. *ASC,* s.a. 922 A (recte, 919), 921 A (recte, 918).

10. *ASC,* s.a. 901 C,D,E (recte, 900). Cf. *ASC,* s.a. 900 A. The late tenth-century chronicler Ealdorman Æthelweard, who traced his descent from Æthelred I, suppressed all mention of the revolt. Keynes and Lapidge note that Alfred was not overly generous to his nephew in his will, which may have been still another source of the ætheling's disaffection. Keynes and Lapidge, *Alfred the Great,* p. 172.

11. Beer, *Führen und Folgen,* s.v. "bugan."

12. *ASC,* s.a. 917 A (recte 914), ed. Plummer, *Saxon Chronicles,* 1:100; trans. *EHD* I:213.

13. *ASC,* s.a. 920 A (recte, 917), ed. Plummer, *Saxon Chronicles,* 1:102; trans. *EHD* I:215–216.

14. Because the Danes commended themselves to Edward as their lord, they were not bound to follow his successors on the West Saxon throne. Hence Æthelstan, Edmund, and Eadred were each forced to secure the submission

of the Danes. See *ASC*, s.a. 926 D (recte, 927), 937, 941 D (recte, 940), 946 A, 947 D. (On the use of *here* to denote Danish landowners, see IV *Edgar*, c. 15, and discussion in Sawyer, *Vikings*, p. 123. Cf. the *Anonymous Life of St. Oswald*, in *EHD* I:913–914.)

15. *ASC*, s.a. 823 (recte, 825), ed. Plummer, *Saxon Chronicles*, 1:60: "East Engla cyning, and seo theod gesohte Ecgbryht cyning him . . . to munboran."

16. Asser, *Life of King Alfred*, chap. 80, ed. Stevenson, pp. 66–67; trans. Keynes and Lapidge, *Alfred the Great*, p. 96.

17. Stenton, *ASE*, pp. 259–260; Wainright, "Æthelflæd." Some Mercian nobles of royal blood may have preferred the overlordship of the vikings to that of the West Saxons, as we find Mercian æthelings fighting on the side of the Danes at the Battle of the Holme in 902.

18. Keynes and Lapidge, *Alfred the Great*, p. 38; Stenton, *ASE*, p. 259. But cf. Patrick Wormald, "Bretwaldas and the Origins of the *Gens Anglorum*," in *Ideal and Reality*, ed. P. Wormald, pp. 99–129, which argues that a sense of "Englishness" predated Alfred and may have aided his political efforts.

19. BCS 595 (S 362). Cf. BCS 225 (S 153), a contemporary text of a grant by King Cynewulf, dated 778: "Bican comiti meo ac ministro"; BCS 289 (S 153), contemporary text of a Mercian charter of 798: King Coenwulf to "Oswulf duci et ministro meo." See Chadwick, *Institutions*, pp. 322–325.

20. II *Edward*, c. 1, § 1: "and þæt lufian þæt he lufode, and þæt ascunian þæt he ascunode, ægther ge on sæ ge on lande." Cf. the hold-oath known as *Swerian*, c. 1 (text in n. 29).

21. II *Edward*, c. 5. Cf. IV *Æthelstan*, c. 3, § 2; VI *Æthelstan*, c. 10.

22. III *Edmund*, c. 1, ed. Robertson, *Laws*, pp. 12–13.

23. Liebermann, *Gesetze*, 2 (pt. 2), s.v. *Königstreue*, 7a, and *Mannschaftseid*, 2. Cf. the use of the *hwa*, "anyone," in II *Edward*, caps. 5 and 8; II *Æthelstan*, c. 20.

24. Attenborough, *Laws*, pp. 166–167: "Every reeve should exact a pledge from his own shire, that they would all observe the decrees for the public security."

25. See, e.g., the use of the term "meliores" in the *Liber Eliensis*, bk. II, chaps. 11, 11a, 25, ed. E. O. Blake, Camden, 3d Series, 92 (London, 1962).

26. Robertson, *Charters*, no. 78, p. 153 = KCD 755 (S 501). Cf. ibid., no. 83, pp. 162–165.

27. DB, ii. 130b: "De illis qui habent .xxx. acras iacet soca et saca in hundredo." Cited by Harmer, *Writs*, p. 476.

28. II *Cnut*, c. 71, §§ 1–2, distinguishes between the heriots of king's thegns and the thegns of other lords. Edmund's oath did not require the act of homage, "bowing," required by *Swerian*, c. 1 to complete the act of commendation.

29. Cf. *Swerian*, c. 1, ed. Liebermann, *Gesetze*, 1:396: "On thone Drihten, the thes halgdom is fore halig, ic wille beon N. hold and getriwe and eal lufian þæt he lugath and eal ascunian þæt he ascunath . . . and næfre willes ne gewealdes, words ne weorces owiht don þæs him lathre bith, with tham the he me halde, swa ic earnian wille, and eall þæt læste, þæt uncer formæl

wases, tha ic to him gebeah and his willan geceas. [In the presence of the
Lord, before whom this holy thing is holy, I am willing to be faithful and
true to N., and I will love what he loves, and discountenance what he discountenances ... and I will never do anything willfully or by my own accord,
either by word or by deed, which is hateful to him, provided that he hold me
as I deserve, and that he carry out on my behalf all those things that were
part of our agreement when I did choose his will and bowed to him.]"

30. Cf. *Capitularia Regum Francorum* 1, ed. A. Boretius, *MGH, Legum
Sectio II* (Hannover, 1883), appendix to no. 34 (Capitularia missorum spe-
cialia, 802), pp. 101–102: "Sacramentale qualiter repromitto ego, quod ab
isto die inantea fidelis sum domino Karolo piisimo imperatori, filio Piipini regis
et Berthanae regina, pura mente absque fraude et malo ingenio de mea parte
ad suam partem et ad honorem regni sui, *sicut per drictum debet esse homo
domino suo.*" Cited by James Campbell, "Observations on English Government from the Tenth to the Twelfth Century," *TRHS,* 5th Series, 25 (1975):
46–47. Cf. also *Annales regni Francorum,* ed. F. Kurze, *MGH SS* (Hannover,
1895), s.a. 757 (the oath of Tassilo III). F. L. Ganshof, *The Carolingians and
the Frankish Monarchy,* trans. Janet Sondheim (Ithaca, N.Y., 1971), pp. 112–
117.

31. Ibid. Cf. Charles the Bald's subject oath of 854: "Ab ista die et in
antea fidelis ero secundum meum savirum, sicut francus homo per rectum esse
debet suo regi." *MGH, Capitularia,* 2:278. The oaths that the Carolingians
demanded from their subjects and vassals increasingly emphasized the term
"rex" during the course of the ninth century. C. E. Odegaard, "The Concept
of Royal Power in Carolingian Oaths of Fidelity," *Speculum* 20 (1945): 279–
289, esp. 282–284.

32. Edmund seems to have experimented with a direct attempt to tie the
granting of bookland to commendation. BCS 814 (S 508): "Eatenus ut vita
comite tam fidus mente quam subditus operibus mihi placabile obsequium
praebeat. Et post meum obitum cuicunque meorum amicorum voluero eadem
fidelitate immobilis obediensque fiat. Sicque omnes posteriores praefatam terram possidentes in hoc decreto fideliter persistant sicuti decet ministro." Cited
by J. E. A. Jolliffe, *The Constitutional History of Medieval England* (London,
1937), p. 90, n. 3. Jolliffe's analysis of this charter is colored by his desire to
deny "feudalism" in pre-Conquest England and fails to draw the connection
between the charter's conditions of tenure and the Colyton oath.

33. E.g., Robertson, *Charters,* no. 63, cited above at chap. 3, n. 100.

34. *Alfred,* c. 1, §§ 1–8. Cf. II *Æthelstan,* c. 26, which deprives a perjurer
of the right to give oaths, and stipulates that he shall not be buried in consecrated ground unless his bishop testifies that he has made amends as his
confessor prescribed. Cf. also *Edward and Guthrum,* c. 11, where perjurers
are placed in the same category as witches and sorcerers.

35. *ASC,* s.a. 876. Asser, *Life of King Alfred,* chap. 49, describes the pagans as swearing upon Christian relics. Keynes and Lapidge, *Alfred the Great,*
pp. 245–246, n. 90, suggest that the received text of Asser's *Life* may be
corrupt or that Asser may have mistaken a pagan ring for a Christian relic.
A third possibility is that Asser was embarrassed by his hero's willingness to

engage in a pagan ceremony and deliberately suppressed the reference to Thor's ring.

36. Asser, *Life of King Alfred,* chap. 49, trans. Keynes and Lapidge, *Alfred the Great,* p. 83.

37. *ASC,* s.a. 942.

38. The extension of royal lordship over all free landholders was only one aspect of the developing conception of kingship in Anglo-Saxon England. The Church also acted to strengthen kingship, and under its influence the Anglo-Saxon monarchy increasingly assumed a theocratic character, as Alfred's preface to his translation of the *Cura Pastoralis* and the inauguration ritual of Edgar in 973 amply demonstrate. On this, see Wallace-Hadrill, *Germanic Kingship,* pp. 72–151; Loyn, "Church and State in England in the Tenth and Eleventh Centuries," in *Tenth-Century Studies,* ed. David Parsons (London, 1975), pp. 94–102; Janet Nelson, "Inauguration Rituals," in *Early Medieval Kingship,* pp. 66–70. In addition, the royal style took on a definite imperial tinge beginning with Eadred (946–955). See, e.g., Robertson, *Charters,* no. 30, pp. 56–57: "Angulseaxna Eadred cyning and casere totius Britanniae." The ideology of Anglo-Saxon kingship, however, lies outside the scope of the present work. Further discussion can be found in John, *Orbis Britanniae,* pp. 1–63.

39. See discussion in chap. 1.

40. *Ine,* c. 39.

41. *Alfred,* c. 37, §§ 1–2.

42. II *Edward,* c. 7; II *Æthelstan,* c. 22. The term "oferhyrnes" first appears in I *Edward,* caps. 1, § 1; 2, § 1. It is quite possible that it was an innovation of Edward the Elder.

43. III *Æthelstan,* c. 4, § 1; IV *Æthelstan,* caps. 4–5; V *Æthelstan,* c. 1, § 1.

44. II *Æthelstan,* c. 2, §§ 1–2.

45. See also the description of Edward the Martyr's death at the hands of his stepmother's thegns in the *Vita Oswaldi auctore anonymo,* in *Historians of the Church of York and its Archbishops,* ed. J. Raine, Rolls Series, 71 (London, 1879), 1:448–449; trans. *EHD* I:914–915. See KCD 692 (S 886), 699 (S 1301), 700 (S 893), 704 (S 939), 719 (S 926), 1289 (S 883), 1294 (S 877), 1295 (S 901), 1304 (S 927); A. S. Napier and W. H. Stevenson, eds., *The Crawford Collection of Early Charters and Documents* (Oxford, 1895), no. 8 (S 892). Cf. *ASC,* s.a. 993, 1002, 1006, 1015.

46. VI *Æthelstan,* caps. 3; 4; 8, § 1; I *Edgar,* c. 2; III *Edgar,* caps. 5–7; II *Cnut,* c. 20.

47. III *Æthelstan,* c. 7; III *Edmund,* c. 7; II *Cnut,* c. 31.

48. Harmer, *Writs,* no. 28 (Cnut, A.D. 1020), p. 183: "ofer swa gela thegena swa ic heom to lætan hæbbe." The same formula occurs in no. 38, a writ of Edward the Confessor, dated to 1042 X 1050.

49. *ASC,* s.a. 1052 D (recte, 1051), trans. *EHD* II:119–120: "All the thegns of Harold [Godwine's son] were transferred to the king's allegiance." Cf. *ASC,* s.a. 1048 E (recte, 1051), trans. *EHD* II:122: "Then the king asked for all the thegns the earls had had, and they were handed over to him."

Significantly, the exiled earls Godwine, Harold, and Swein recruited foreign mercenaries rather than relying on their English thegns. Similarly, Ælfgar, earl of Mercia, recovered his earldom with the aid of Irish and Welsh warriors. *ASC,* s.a. 1055 C,D; 1058 D.

50. E.g., DB, ii. 310b (Fordley, Suffolk). Eadric of Laxfield had been deprived of both his land and his men when he was outlawed. Upon his reconciliation with the king he received back his land, and Edward the Confessor issued a writ in his favor that permitted his former men to return to him: "Dedit etiam breuem et sigillum ut quicumque de suis liberis commendatis hominibus ad eum uellent redire suo concessu redirent." Harmer, *Writs,* Appendix IV, no. 17, p. 545.

51. *EHD* I:793–794. See discussion in chap. 1 at n. 17.

52. *ASC,* s.a. 1052 C. Godwine and his sons relied mainly, however, on Flemish and Irish mercenaries in the initial stages of their invasion. The "E" version of the Chronicle, although on the whole sympathetic to Godwine, relates that the exiled earls ravaged the southeast, coercing the local landowners to provide material support for their cause.

53. The structure of the fyrd will be discussed in chapter 8. Note also that "armies" are described as rendering legal decisions in the anonymous *Life of St. Oswald, EHD* I:840–841, and in *ASC,* s.a. 1049 C, where the king "and all the army [*here*]," declared Swein Godwineson a *nithing* and outlaw.

54. See discussion at n. 10 above.

55. II *Æthelstan,* c. 20, §§ 1–4; III *Æthelstan,* c. 6; IV *Æthelstan,* c. 3; VI *Æthelstan,* caps. 4; 5; 8, §§ 2–3. The last text is especially interesting: "And in addition, we shall send to the reeves in both directions, requesting from them the help of as many men as seems desirable . . . that the wrongdoers may be the more afraid of us because of our numbers. And we shall all ride out against them, and avenge the wrong done to us. And we shall ride forth and slay the thief and those who support him and fight on his behalf." Attenborough, *Laws,* pp. 163, 165. The police duties of the public assemblies meant that suitors were expected to come armed. Thus the hundred court of the northern Danelaw was known in the second half of the tenth century as a *wæpentac,* denoting the suitors' symbolic brandishing of their weapons to signal their assent. IV *Edgar,* c. 6. Stenton, *ASE,* pp. 504–505.

56. Harmer, *Writs,* no. 61, p. 249 (S 1109), a questionable writ purporting to be a grant of privileges by Edward the Confessor to Ramsey Abbey, contains an interesting and perhaps genuine legal formula to describe the status of the men over whom the abbot was to have sake and soke: *ferdwurthi, motwurthi,* and *faldwurthi,* "fyrd-worthy, moot-worthy, and fold-worthy." As the term "fold-worthy" implies, only property holders of a certain standing in the locality would be entitled and obliged to attend the hundred and shire courts. See Harmer, *Writs,* pp. 475–476, on property requirements for paying suit in these courts. Cf. David C. Douglas, ed., *Feudal Documents from the Abbey of Bury St. Edmunds,* British Academy Records in Social and Economic History, 8 (London, 1932), no. 16. The suitors in the various pleas recorded in the *Liber Eliensis* are described on occasion as "all the better sort" in the shire or the hundred [*omnes meliores*]. See, e.g., *Liber Eliensis,* bk. II, chaps.

11(a) and 25, ed. E. O. Blake, pp. 90, 99. The implications for fyrd service in middle and late Saxon England are obvious and important.

57. The Anglo-Saxon original of the *Libellus quorundam insignium operum beati Æthelwoldi episcopi* (bk. II, chaps. 1–49 of the *Liber Eliensis*) appears to have been composed at the end of the tenth century. E. O. Blake, "Introduction," *Liber Eliensis*, ed. Blake, pp. li–liii.

58. *Liber Eliensis*, bk. II, chap. 25, ed. Blake, p. 98.

59. Ibid., p. 9.

60. According to the account given in the *Liber Eliensis*, an Englishman named Wulfnoth held Bluntisham by charter. In fact, the vast majority of Ely's early donors who gave lands in Huntingdonshire and Cambridgeshire bore Anglo-Saxon names. Cyril Hart, *The Early Charters of Eastern England* (Leicester, 1966), pp. 215–230. The notion that Edward the Elder pursued a deliberate policy of colonization of the Danelaw is supported by two charters from Æthelstan's reign, BCS 658 (S 397) and BCS 659 (S 396; trans. *EHD* I:546–547), which tell of estates in Derbyshire and Bedfordshire. According to these charters, the two thegns who held the lands in Æthelstan's reign had purchased them "from the pagans, by order of King Edward" before Edward's successful assault on the territories belonging to Derby and Bedford. It is reasonable to assume that the English ruler wished to settle supporters in the areas of Danish settlement as beachheads for the planned military activity.

61. *Liber Eliensis*, bk. II, chap. 25, ed. Blake, p. 99: "Proprior erat ille, ut terram haberet, qui cyrographum habebat quam qui non habebat."

62. The royal tribute exacted from Cambridgeshire tenures in the third quarter of the tenth century appears to have been quite heavy. Ælfric, the son of Earl Hereric, for example, had to sell his two hides at Downham to the Abbey of Ely in order to pay the tribute. *Liber Eliensis*, bk. II, chap. 11, ed. Blake, p. 88: "Aluricus gravi tributo opprimebatur. Qui, cum pecuniam a se exactam non haberet, venit ad Ætheluuoldum episcopum et ad Brihtnotum abbatem."

63. Hart, *Hidation of Northamptonshire*, pp. 13, 15, 45–46.

64. BCS 599 (S 1285); Harmer, *Select Documents*, no. 17.

65. *ASC*, s.a. 921 A (recte, 918).

66. See the charters abstracted in Hart, *Charters of Eastern England*. The earliest surviving book from the Danelaw is dated 926. BCS 658 (S 397): Derbyshire. The holder of this book had possessed the land since at least 911.

67. Napier and Stevenson, eds., *Crawford Charters*, no. 5, pp. 10–11 = BCS 1347 (S 646). In the eleventh century the Danelaw had its own customary regulations on the neglect of the "common burdens." II *Cnut*, c. 65.

68. V *Æthelred*, c. 26, § 1; VI *Æthelred*, c. 32, § 3. Cf. II *Æthelstan*, c. 13, where fortress-work is an annual imposition.

69. Leslie Alcock, *"By South Cadbury is that Camelot..."* Excavations of Cadbury Castle 1966–1970 (London, 1972), pp. 194–201; Radford, "Pre-Conquest Boroughs," pp. 96–97.

70. Biddle, "Towns," pp. 140–141.

71. Radford, "Pre-Conquest Boroughs," pp. 86–91, 102. The stone walls

of non-Roman Alfredian boroughs are later additions, usually dated to the period 1000 X 1066.

72. Guy Beresford, "Goltho Manor, Lincolnshire: The Buildings and their Surrounding Defences," *Anglo-Norman Studies* 4 (1982):27–30. See also K. B. Davison, "The Origins of the Castle in England,"*Archeological Journal* 114 (1967):202–211.

73. On these changes, evidenced by the great late tenth-century fortresses excavated at Aggersborg, Fyrkat, Nonnebakken, and Trelleborg, see Hunter Blair, *Introduction,* pp. 93–98; Sawyer, *Vikings,* pp. 131–137. The best discussion of Danish fortresses in English is Klavs Randsborg, *The Viking Age in Denmark: The Formation of a State* (New York, 1980), pp. 96–103. Randsborg associates the construction of these fortresses with Harold Bluetooth's consolidation of power and creation of a secondary state in Denmark. Once thought to be mere barracks, Trelleborg and the other fortresses now appear to have been closer to the Edwardian burhs in function, controlling border provinces and regulating commercial traffic.

74. *ASC,* s.a. 1006. Cf. *ASC,* s.a. 994 E, trans. *EHD* I:235: "Olaf and Swein came to London . . . with 94 ships, and they proceeded to attack the city very stoutly . . . but there they suffered more harm and injury than they ever thought any citizens [*ænig burhwaru*] would do to them." Plummer, *Saxon Chronicles,* 1:129. The implied pacific character of the London *burhwaru* is unmistakable.

75. The navy that Alfred founded (*ASC,* s.a. 896) was developed and used extensively by his successors throughout the tenth century. Edward the Elder, for example, outfitted a fleet of about 100 ships in 910 (*ASC,* s.a.); Æthelstan sent a naval expedition to France in support of his nephew Louis d'Outremer's claims to Lotharingia (*Flodoard's Annals,* s.a. 939, *EHD* I:345); and Edgar chose a naval display to signal his imperial pretensions (ASC, s.a. 972 D [recte, 973]; Florence of Worcester, *Chronicon ex Chronicis,* s.a. 973, ed. B. Thorpe [London, 1848], 1:143–144). Cf. also *ASC,* s.a. 992, where we read that Æthelred II assembled a large fleet in London, comprising "all the ships that were any use," in order "to entrap the Danish army anywhere at sea." This naval expedition seems to have been organized territorially, since the Chronicler informs us that the Danes defeated the contingent from East Anglia and London.

76. G. N. Garmonsway, *The Anglo-Saxon Chronicle,* rev. ed. (London, 1960), p. 138.

77. Cf. *EHD* I:241, n. 3: "a warship from 310 hides." Plummer, *Saxon Chronicles,* 1:138 n. 4: C: "of thrim hundhrum and of tynum ænne scegth"; E: "[of] thrim hund hidum and of .x. hidon ænne scegth." On this see Plummer, *Saxon Chronicles,* 2:185. Cf. Florence of Worcester, *Chronicon,* ed. Thorpe, 1:160: "de ccc.x. cassatis unam trierem." Although the textual tradition of the Chronicle supports the existence of naval districts of 310 hides, the diplomatic evidence argues strongly for 300-hide ship-sokes. We know, for example, that the bishop of Worcester in the late tenth and the eleventh century enjoyed jurisdiction over the triple hundred of Oswaldslow, which constituted a *scypfylleth* or *scypsocne.* BCS 1135 (S 731); DB, i. 172. Similarly,

Bishop Æthelric of Sherborne complained in an early eleventh-century letter that he had suffered the loss of 33 hides from the 300 hides that other bishops had from their diocese for the ship-scot. (Apparently, the see of Sherborne was supplying the money for the construction and maintenance of a warship rather than the ship itself.) Harmer, *Writs*, no. 63, pp. 266–269 (S 1383), and comments at pp. 266–269, 482–486. Hollister, *Military Institutions*, p. 114. In light of this, I would tend to agree with Garmonsway's reading of the text.

78. Harmer, *Writs*, no. 63. On the authenticity of the *Altitonantis* charter, BCS 1135 (S 731), see Eric John, "War and Society in the Tenth Century: The Maldon Campaign," *TRHS*, 5th Series, 27 (1977): 192–193 (and references). Cf. R. R. Darlington, "Introduction," *The Cartulary of Worcester Priory* (Oxford, 1975), pp. xiii–xviii. The Domesday jurors of Worcestershire believed that the bishop's immunity (and presumably his ship-soke) dated back to "ancient times." DB, i. 172b. The will of Archbishop Ælfric, issued in either 1003 or 1004, grants one ship each to Kent and Wiltshire, the two shires in which his diocese of Canterbury and Ramsbury lay. Since Wiltshire is land-locked, this bequest strongly suggests that the prelate was helping these shires to fulfill their naval obligations, and if this were the case, then some sort of ship-soke system may well have been in place before 1008. Whitelock, *Wills*, no. 18, pp. 52–53, and comment at p. 163 (cf. p. 137). For further discussion of the ship-sokes, see John, *Land Tenure*, pp. 115–123, Hollister, *Military Institutions*, pp. 108–115.

79. V *Æthelred*, caps. 26, § 1; 27; VI *Æthelred*, caps. 32, § 3; 33; 34. Hollister, *Military Obligations*, pp. 104–108, emphasizes the relationship between fyrd service and naval obligation.

80. II *Cnut*, c. 79; Robertson, *Laws*, pp. 12–13: "And he who, with the cognisance of the shire, has performed the services demanded from a land-owner on expeditions either by sea or by land [*gewerod hæbbe on scyfyrde & on landfyrde*] shall hold [his land] unmolested by litigation during his life, and at his death shall have the right of disposing of it or giving it to whomsoever he prefers."

81. Simon Keynes, "The Declining Reputation of Æthelred the Unready," in Hill, ed., *Ethelred the Unready*, pp. 229–232.

82. See, e.g., EHD I:580, which tells of the treason of an Essex thegn, Æthelric of Bocking. Cf. ASC, s.a. 992, 993, 1003, 1013, 1016. But cf. Keynes, "Declining Reputation"; idem, *The Diplomas of King Æthelred "the Unready" 978–1016* (Cambridge, 1980), pp. 206–207.

83. The manner in which the English aristocracy invited Æthelred to return to the throne after the death of Swein is telling: "They said that no lord was dearer to them than their natural lord, *if he would govern them more justly than he did before.*" ASC, s.a. 1014, in EHD I:246–247. The monastic reform crisis of the 970s had created bitterness and division among the English aristocracy, especially among the thegns of East Anglia and western Mercia who had lost property to the restored monasteries, and this may help account for some of Æthelred's problems. John, "War and Society," pp. 176–183. Nor should one forget that Æthelred had come to the throne under a cloud.

Æthelred, who was but a child in 978, was probably innocent of the murder of his brother King Edward, but his failure to bring the culprits to justice must have seemed suspicious, especially to those who had supported Edward in life and now venerated him as a martyr.

84. Robertson, *Laws,* pp. 90–91.

85. E.g., Whitelock, *Wills,* nos. 4 (S 1491), 9 (S 1485), 10 (S 1498), 12 (S 1505), 17 (S 1536); Dorothy Whitelock, Neil Ker, and Lord Rennell, *The Will of Æthelgifu,* The Roxburghe Club (Oxford, 1968), l. 60 (S 1497); Harmer, *Select Documents,* no. 20 (S 1504); Robertson, *Charters,* nos. 38 (S 817), 45 (S 806), 69 (S 1456).

86. See references to *cynehlaford* and variants in Antonette DiPaolo Healey and Richard L. Venezky, *A Microfiche Concordance to Old English* (Toronto, 1980), C 16, pp. 179–183.

87. "Sermon of the Wolf," in Wulfstan, *Homilies,* ed. Bethurum, pp. 270, 275.

88. *EHD* I:838.

89. *Alfred,* c. 4. Cf. II *Æthelstan,* c. 4; III *Edgar,* c. 7, § 3.

90. V *Æthelred,* c. 30; VI *Æthelred,* c. 37; on deserting an army led by the king, V *Æthelred,* c. 28.

FIVE: FYRD SERVICE AND HIDAGE

1. E.g., Stenton, *English Feudalism,* pp. 117–120.

2. E.g., John, *Land Tenure,* pp. 140–161; idem, *Orbis Britanniae,* pp. 128–153; idem, in *The Anglo-Saxons,* ed. Campbell, pp. 168–169, 236–237. Cf. Hollister, *Military Institutions,* pp. 59–84, on the "select fyrd."

3. Douglas, *William the Conqueror,* pp. 346–356; Stenton, *ASE,* pp. 656–657; Sally Harvey, "Domesday and its Predecessors," *EHR* 86 (1971): 770–773; H. R. Loyn, "A General Introduction to Domesday Book," in *The 1986 Domesday Book Facsimile: Academic Edition* (London, 1986), pp. 5, 32.

4. *ASC,* s.a. 1085 E; *EHD* II:167.

5. Ibid., p. 168.

6. Ibid.; DB, ii. 450 (Colophon to Little Domesday). See V. H. Galbraith, *The Making of Domesday Book* (Oxford, 1961), pp. 180–188, 205; R. Welldon Finn, *An Introduction to Domesday Book* (London, 1961), pp. 92–94.

7. Galbraith, *Making of Domesday Book,* p. 160; idem, *Domesday Book: Its Place in Administrative History* (Oxford, 1974), p. 35. J. O. Prestwich has emphasized the importance of stipendiary troops for the Anglo-Norman kings in two important articles: "War and Finance in the Anglo-Norman State," *TRHS,* 5th Series, 4 (1954): 19–43; and "The Military Household of the Norman Kings," *EHR* 96 (1981): 1–35.

8. E.g., DB, i. 64b (Malmesbury, Wilts.); 154 (Oxford, Oxon.); 238 (Warwick, Warwicks.); 56b (Beds.); 79 (Hereford, Herefords.); 252 (Shrewsbury, Salops.).

9. DB, i. 56b.

10. See J. H. Round, *Feudal England,* pp. 36–69; Maitland, *Domesday*

Book and Beyond, pp. 357–490; John McGovern, "The Hide and Related Land-Tenure Concepts in Anglo-Saxon England, A.D. 700–1100," *Traditio* 28 (1972): 101–118; Charles-Edwards, "Kinship, Status and the Origins of the Hide"; Finberg, *Agrarian History*, pp. 412–416. Additional information can be found in the individual county studies in the "Domesday Geography" series edited by H. C. Darby et al., and in the introductions to the Domesday translations in the volumes of the Victoria County History.

11. *Domesday Book and Beyond*, p. 357.

12. Ibid., pp. 475–490.

13. E.g., R. W. Eyton, *A Key to Domesday: The Dorset Survey* (London, 1878), p. 15; J. Tait, "Large Hides and Small Hides," *EHR* 17 (1902): 280–282; R. R. Darlington, "Introduction to the Wiltshire Domesday," *VCH of Wiltshire* (London, 1955), 2:182–183.

14. Plummer, *Baedae Opera*, 2:40–41; Charles-Edwards, "Kinship, Status and the Origins of the Hide," pp. 5–7.

15. *H.E.*, I. 25; II. 9; III. 4, 24, 25; IV. 3, 13, 16, 19; V. 19.

16. E.g., Stenton, *ASE*, p. 279; Charles-Edwards, "Kinship, Status and the Origins of the Hide," p. 3: "In origin, the hide was the territorial expression of a particular form of kindred allied to a particular status system."

17. John, *Orbis Britanniae*, p. 103, an apparent repudiation of the position taken in *Land Tenure*, p. 3.

18. *Vita Wilfridi*, chaps. 8, 41, ed. Colgrave, pp. 16, 82. *Mansa* and *manens* were two terms commonly used to render "hide" in the early charters. H. P. R. Finberg concluded, based in part on C. S. Taylor's study of Gloucestershire hidage, that the hide was actually a "relic of the imperial system that survived because it was too efficient to be surrendered, no matter who held the reins of power." Finberg, "Some Early Gloucestershire Estates," in idem, ed., *Gloucestershire Studies* (Leicester, 1957), pp. 15–16. F. Seebohm made a similar suggestion in his *The English Village Community*, 4th ed. (London, 1890), pp. 289–290, 326. *Tributarius* was the Latin equivalent of *gafolgelda*.

19. BCS 265 (S 132), a tenth-century manuscript. Cf. BCS 60 (S 70), 85 (S 53), 145 (S 44), 236 (S 116).

20. S 256 (Sawyer, *List*, p. 136). Cf. BCS 61 (S 236), 213 (S 110). Note also the formula used in BCS 42 (S 10): "continet antiquo jure XLIIII manentes."

21. See Charles-Edwards, "Kinship, Status and the Origins of the Hide," p. 9.

22. Finberg, *Agrarian History*, pp. 413–415. David Herlihy's work on the Frankish *mansus* is also relevant to the nature of the eighth-century hide. Herlihy, "Carolingian *Mansus*," pp. 77–89.

23. Hart, "The Tribal Hidage," pp. 156–157. Cf. Davies and Vierck, "The Contexts of the Tribal Hidage," pp. 229, 236.

24. *H.E.*, I. 9, ed. Colgrave and Mynors, p. 176.

25. Plummer, *Baedae Opera*, 2:40–41.

26. *H.E.*, I. 25; III. 4.

27. *H.E.*, IV. 16.

28. Between the time that Bede wrote the *Historia* and the composition of the Tribal Hidage, Mercia had expanded from 12,000 (*H.E.,* III. 24) to 30,000 hides. Hart, "Tribal Hidage," pp. 138, 146–147.

29. Hart, *Northamptonshire,* pp. 13, 14, 39, 45–46.

30. Although one would hesitate to call this a late ninth- or early tenth-century innovation, there is no positive evidence that hidage was used to determine the extent of service before this time. See n. 68.

31. The hidages of twenty-seven of the thirty West Saxon burghal districts in the Burghal Hidage are divisible by ten; the majority, by one hundred. Cf. the figures for the County Hidage printed by Maitland, *Domesday Book,* p. 456.

32. *Liber Eliensis,* bk. II, chap. 11, ed. Blake, p. 88.

33. Regression analyses of hides on value for Buckinghamshire show clearly that the shire's hidage in 1066 was based on the economic capacity of its manors rather than its villages (see tables A1 and A1b). John McDonald and G. D. Snooks, who have pioneered the application of modern statistical methods to Domesday data, have gone further and argued that, contrary to received opinion, tax assessment was "built up from the manorial level" rather than cast down from above. McDonald and Snooks, "How Artificial Were the Tax Assessments of Domesday England? The Case of Essex," *Economic History Review* 38 (1985): 371. That this was *originally* the case is not at all clear. Nor do their findings account for the variation in the relationship between value and hidage in neighboring shires.

34. Henry Loyn, *Governance,* pp. 119–122. Loyn has astutely observed that the £134,000 recorded in the Chronicle as having been paid to the Danes between 991 and 1012 and the £82,500 exacted in 1018 as tribute by King Cnut "indicate not only the weight of fluid wealth available in England, but also the capacity to tap it." Ibid., p. 121.

35. Loyn, *Anglo-Saxon England,* pp. 309–310. On the County Hidage and the problems associated with its dating and interpretation, see Maitland, *Domesday Book,* pp. 455–459; Cyril Hart, *Northamptonshire,* pp. 15–16; P. H. Sawyer, *From Roman Britain to Norman England,* pp. 228–229. Cf. David Hill, *An Atlas of Anglo-Saxon England* (Toronto, 1981), pp. 96–97.

36. Round, "Danegeld and the Finance of Domesday," in *Domesday Studies,* ed. P. E. Dove (London, 1888), 1:119–120; idem, *Feudal England,* pp. 44–45; Hart, *Cambridgeshire.* Round's and Hart's grouping of nearby villages into five-hide units or multiples thereof comes dangerously close to begging the question. On the other hand, there are numerous examples in Cambridgeshire of five- and ten-hide villages comprising several manors that were not rated on a decimal basis. McDonald's and Snooks's alternate explanation, that there was a fixed relationship between the size of villages and the resource endowments of the manors they serviced, is neither supported by contemporary evidence nor inherently persuasive. "Tax Assessments," p. 361.

37. Round, *Feudal England,* pp. 36–69.

38. The Domesday survey of Middlesex provides not only the total geldable hides for each estate but also gives individual hidage assessments for the lord's demesne and the holdings of his tenants. Often the sum of the partic-

ulars does not equal the given total. Both Maitland and Vinogradoff believed that the hides assigned to the demesne and the land of the tenants represent "agrarian hides" measuring, roughly, the arable, while the geld-hides are "fiscal hides," units of taxation. Maitland, *Domesday Book,* p. 478; Vinogradoff, *English Society,* pp. 167–176. Vinogradoff concluded from his study of the different types of hides throughout the Domesday survey that "fiscal hides" were based "on real and local agrarian shares." Ibid., pp. 177–207. The term "hide" is used as a measurement of arable in *Liber Eliensis,* bk. II, chap. 11a, ed. Blake, pp. 89–91, 106. Cf. also DB, i. 149b: "[In Oakley, Bucks.] hae .v. hidae & .iii. virgae sunt .viii. hidae."

39. Round, *Feudal England,* p. 48.

40. Ibid., p. 63.

41. Some of the Domesday *valets, reddits,* and *valuits* may have been estimates rather than exact accounts of value. Nevertheless, it seems likely that the values given in the survey were closely related to the actual income derived from each property, through either rent or direct exploitation. John McDonald and G. D. Snooks recently demonstrated statistically that the valets correlate closely with manorial resources. "The Determinants of Manorial Income in Domesday England: Evidence from Essex," *Journal of Economic History* 45 (1985): 541–546. See also Sally Harvey, "Recent Domesday Studies," *EHR* 95 (1980): 129; Reginald Lennard, *Rural England: 1086–1135* (Oxford, 1959), pp. 113–141; R. Welldon Finn, *The Norman Conquest and its Effects on the Economy: 1066–1086* (London, 1971), pp. 6–18; and H. C. Darby, *Domesday England* (Cambridge, 1977), pp. 208–231.

42. Like so much else in Domesday, "ploughland" defies easy definition. Recently two scholars, Cyril Hart and Sally Harvey, studied this question in some depth, coming to diametrically opposed conclusions, the former seeing "ploughlands" as a vestige of Danish rule retained for the assessment of the "common burdens," hidage being used merely for the geld, and the latter regarding them as part of a post-Conquest process of reassessing the realm's resources. See Hart, *Northamptonshire,* pp. 24–28; idem, *Cambridgeshire,* pp. 38–54. Cf. Harvey, "Domesday Book and Anglo-Norman Governance," *TRHS,* 5th Series, 25 (1975): 186–189; idem, "Taxation and the Ploughland in Domesday Book," in Peter Sawyer, ed., *Domesday Book: A Reassessment* (London and Baltimore, 1985), pp. 86–103. Elaborate theories, however, are unnecessary for the "ploughland" of the Bedford-Middlesex circuit. In these counties the "ploughland" may well have meant what its formula, "terra est N carucis," says, that the local jurors deemed a particular holding to have enough arable for N ploughs. In other words, "ploughlands" here may simply represent an estimate of an estate's arable land. See Darby, *Domesday England,* pp. 99–101, 116–120.

43. See, e.g., H. C. Darby and R. Welldon Finn, eds., *Domesday Geography of South-West England* (Cambridge, 1967), pp. 15, 58, 105, 147.

44. Maitland, *Domesday Book,* pp. 464–465.

45. Ibid., pp. 469–471. Cf. McDonald's and Snooks's overly enthusiastic and anachronistic criticism of Maitland for failing to maintain the "equitable element" in hidation against Round. "Tax Assessments," pp. 357–360.

46. For the Domesday circuits, see C. Stephenson, *Medieval Institutions*, ed. Bruce Lyon (New York, 1954), pp. 184–205. I have concentrated on the south Midlands circuit in general because of the attention paid to and information given in these county surveys about lordship.

47. In an earlier essay, "Bookland and Fyrd Service in Late Saxon England," *Anglo-Norman Studies* 7 (1985):15–25, I presented the relationship between hidation and value as linear. But as G. D. Snooks pointed out to me in a private communication, the Domesday data violate one of the critical assumptions of the OLS technique by being heteroskadastic. In other words, as manorial value increases, the precise relationship between it and hidage changes. Therefore, all coefficient estimates obtained through a linear regression will be inefficient and tests for significance invalid. The actual functional form of the regression lines is curvilinear in most cases ($y = \alpha x^\beta$); it can, however, be made linear through a logarithmic transformation of the data for hidage and value ($\ln y = \ln \alpha + \beta \ln x$). This is, mathematically, the best explanatory model for the data in the majority of shires tested, and I have therefore used it as the basis for my regression analyses. But as we shall presently see, the curvilinear form may be misleading. It is probable that the original relationship between geld assessment and value was, in fact, linear and remained so for the majority of estates, especially those valued at less than £15. The statistical package that I used was *Minitab*, Minitab Project, Statistics Dept., Pennsylvania State University (1981).

48. Maitland attributed Leicestershire's ridiculously low total value to William's campaigning in the region, the assumption being that *valuit* does not represent the T.R.E. values in this shire but those of a later period. *Domesday Book*, pp. 464–472. Cf. the similar discrepancy between Yorkshire's assessment (10,609 carucates) and total value T.R.W. (£1,084).

49. At least one shire, Northamptonshire, underwent a radical reduction in its hidage between 1065 and 1086, due possibly to the damage done to the shire by Earl Morcar and his supporters in 1065 (*ASC*, s.a.). The County Hidage, which may reflect early eleventh-century conditions, gives Northamptonshire 3200 hides; a geld roll dating to the first decade of William's rule gives 2663½; and Domesday Book gives 1280 hides at the time of the Inquest. See Hart, *The Northamptonshire*, pp. 16–21; Loyn, *Governance*, p. 120. Domesday Book reveals that many estates throughout England were reassessed during William's reign.

50. To give but one example, King Edward held an estate in Blewbury, Berkshire, worth £50 and assessed at only 3 hides. DB, i. 56b. A local landowner named Anschill held five hides at nearby Aston Tirrold, which were valued at £3. DB, i. 60. See also Vinogradoff, *English Society*, pp. 176–186; R. S. Hoyt, *The Royal Demesne in English Constitutional History: 1066–1272* (Cornell, 1950), pp. 19–25; R. Welldon Finn, *An Introduction to Domesday Book*, pp. 253–255; J. A. Green, "The Last Century of Danegeld," *EHR* 96 (1981): 245–252.

51. W. A. Morris, *The English Medieval Sheriff to 1300* (Manchester, 1927), pp. 28–30.

52. Leofwine's £31 worth of land in Herts. was assessed at thirty-nine

hides and two virgates, one virgate more than Earl Harold's holdings in that shire, despite the fact that the earl's lands brought in £118 a year. Cf. also Ælfstan of Boscumbe, whose £45 in Herts. gelded as 11½ hides.

53. Stenton, *English Feudalism,* p. 118. There is no solid evidence for a "small" Berkshire hide, as Stenton himself admitted. Ibid., p. 118, n. 1.

54. DB, i. 64b, 100. Hollister, *Military Institutions,* pp. 49–52.

55. Ibid., p. 48. See also Maitland, *Domesday Book,* pp. 156–157, and Vinogradoff, *English Society,* pp. 31–34.

56. *Military Institutions,* pp. 49–53; Round, *Feudal England,* pp. 69–90. Cf. J. C. Holt, "The Carta of Richard de la Haye, 1166: A Note on 'Continuity' in Anglo-Norman Feudalism," *EHR* 84 (1969): 289–297. Holt suggests that a five-carucate rule formed the basis of fyrd assessment in pre-Conquest Lincolnshire. Lincolnshire Domesday itself implies that the local recruitment rule may have been less demanding than either Hollister or Holt has argued. Thus only one brother was to serve from the combined holdings of the sons of the thegn Godwine, and these lands apparently totaled more than twelve carucates. DB, i. 340b, 341b, 359b, 375b, 376. Cf. DB, i. 354 (Covenham, Lincs.).

57. See chap. 4 at n. 77.

58. *ASC,* s.a. 896; *EHD* I:205.

59. Whitelock, *Wills,* no. 18, p. 52.

60. P. G. Foote and D. M. Wilson, *The Viking Achievement* (London, 1970), p. 243.

61. Harmer, *Writs,* pp. 266–267.

62. M. K. Lawson, "The Collection of Danegeld and Heregeld in the Reigns of Æthelred II and Cnut," *EHR* 99 (1984): 737–738.

63. Ibid., p. 738. Florence of Worcester, *Chronicon,* ed. Thorpe, 1:195.

64. Robertson, *Charters,* no. 72, pp. 144–145, 389–392. See discussion in chap. 8, at n. 78.

65. Foote and Wilson, *The Viking Achievement,* pp. 235–236. This figure is consistent with the crew size of the viking ships engaged by Alfred in 896, or so it would seem from the casualty figures given in that annal. But cf. the "Eriksdrapa of Thord Kolbeinson," c. 9, which speaks of King Swein of Denmark's invasion of England with many ships of various sizes. *EHD* I:334.

66. DB, i. 1 (Dover), 3 (Sandwich).

67. *Gethynctho,* c. 2; *Northleoda laga,* c. 9; *EHD* I:468–469. The texts were edited in Liebermann, *Gesetze,* 1:456–462. For Archbishop Wulfstan's possible authorship, see Dorothy Bethurum, "Six Anonymous Old English Codes," *J. of English and German Philology* 49 (1950): 449–463.

68. BCS 201 [endorsement] (S 106); *EHD* I:501. John, *Land Tenure,* p. 80, interprets this text to support the five-hide rule by having Pilheard join the five soldiers owed, making the obligation six men from thirty hides. (John does not attempt to reconcile this with the charter's use of *tantum.*) Cf. Brooks, "Military Obligations," p. 70, n. 2. My own view is closer to that expressed by John Gillingham, "The Introduction of Knight Service into England," in *Anglo-Norman Studies* 4(1982):62, whose doubts about the universality of the five-hide unit parallel my own.

69. II *Æthelstan,* c. 16, ed. Attenborough, *Laws,* pp. 136–137.

70. *Rectitudines,* caps. 4, § 4; 21, ed. Liebermann, *Gesetze,* 1:447–448, 452; *EHD* II:876, 878.

71. E.g., II *Cnut,* caps. 12; 14; 15; 71, §§ 2–3. Cf. *Leges Henrici Primi,* c. 6, §§ 1–3a, ed. L. J. Downer (Oxford, 1972), pp. 96–98. The English monarchy's willingness to accommodate—and profit from—Welsh customs is evinced by the Domesday Book customs of Archenfield (DB, i. 179): "But if a Welshman has killed a Welshman, the relatives of the slain man gather and despoil the killer and his relatives and burn their houses until the body of the dead man is buried the next day about midday. The King has the third part of this plunder, but they have all the rest free."

72. For fyrdwite, see DB, i. 56b (Beds.), 154b (Oxon.), 172 (Worcs.), 179 (Hereford and Archenfield, Herefords.), 238 (Warwick, Warwicks.), 252 (Shrewsbury, Salop.). References to heriots in Domesday Book may be found in chap. seven, n. 17 and 45. For regional differences in heriot payments see also II *Cnut,* c. 71a, §§ 1–4.

73. DB, i. 1, 3. See also Maitland, *Domesday,* p. 209.

74. DB, i. 179, 181. Cf. DB, i. 64b, 100.

75. DB, i. 262b.

76. The conjunction of "five hides" and "to cynges utware" in *Gethynctho,* c. 3 and *Northleoda laga,* c. 9 implies that each hide owed a certain amount of service. On the term "utwaru," see Liebermann, *Gesetze,* 2, (pt. 2), p. 232, s.v. *utware.* Cf. F. M. Stenton, "Utwara," *Preparatory,* p. 7; "The Thriving of the Anglo-Saxon *Ceorl,*" ibid., p. 389, n. 1.

77. BCS 1136 (S 1368). On this letter, see Maitland, *Domesday,* pp. 304–318; John, *Land Tenure,* pp. 87–88, 142–147. Cf. Stenton, *English Feudalism,* pp. 123–131. Note also the use of "rata expeditione" to describe fyrd service in a number of late Anglo-Saxon royal charters. See, e.g., KCD 1277 (S 829), 1279 (S 843), 1292 (S 887).

78. In a number of these leases, the bishop gives the property free of all burdens, except for the common burdens and church-scot. See, e.g., BCS 1091 (S 1298), 1134 (S 726), 1201 (S 751), 1203 (S 1313), 1233 (S 1326), KCD 660 (S 1353), 668 (S 1357), 676 (S 1362), 677 (S 1364).

79. E.g., Robertson, *Charters,* no. 111, pp. 208–209: "And at the king's summons [*cyinges banne*] the holder shall discharge the obligations on these one-and-a-half hides at the rate of one." Cf. ibid., no. 112: "And he shall discharge the obligations upon them [the lands granted the thegn by Bishop Ealdred] at the rate of 2 hides."

80. DB, i. 209: "Bedford T.R.E. pro dimidio hundredo se defendebat et modo facit in expeditione et in navibus. Terra de hac villa nunquam fuit hidata nec modo est." Cf. DB, i. 366b (Wilsford, Lincs.), 368 (Somerby, Lincs.). In a number of entries, hidage is associated with *servitium regis.* See, e.g., DB, i. 75 (Dorchester, Dorset), 163 (Tewkesbury, Gloucs.), 173 (Bredon, Worcs.); DB, ii. 290 (*Gepeswiz* Hundred, Suffolk). Cf. Robertson, *Charters,* no. 81, p. 156 (Earle, *Land-Charters,* p. 235); no. 111 (KCD 804); no. 112 (KCD 923); KCD 797 (S 1058, of questionable authenticity); Harmer, *Writs,* no. 107. *Servitium regis* is clearly expressed in *Hemingi Chartularium Ecclesiae Wigorniensis,* ed. Thomas Hearne (Oxford, 1723), 1:81.

81. This formula appears frequently in the southern and south midland Domesday circuits (Stephenson's first and third circuits). It occasionally occurs also in the other circuits. See, e.g., DB, i. 75 (Dorchester, Dorset), 203b (Pertenhall, Hunts.).

82. Maitland, *Domesday Book,* p. 55; Vinogradoff, *English Society,* pp. 186–187. The connection between the term "defensio" and geld liability is confirmed by the Northamptonshire Geld Roll's use of the term *gewered* ("defended"). Robertson, *Charters,* Appendix I, no. 3, pp. 230–236. But note that Bedford "nunquam fuit hidata nec modo est," despite serving for a half hundred in the fyrd.

83. DB, i. 336b. Cf. Hollister, *Military Institutions,* pp. 49–50. In Lincolnshire the term "hundred" referred to a district consisting of twelve carucates. See Vinogradoff, *English Society,* pp. 102–103, 280–281; Douglas, *Social Structure,* pp. 29, 58.

84. II *Cnut,* c. 79, ed. Robertson, *Laws,* pp. 214–215. Note that military service was performed with the cognizance of the shire, which again indicates the military as well as the judicial functions of this assembly.

85. Harmer, *Writs,* pp. 450, 459–460.

86. On expeditio and carucates, see DB, i. 366b (Wilsford, Lincs.) and 368 (Somerby, Lincs.). In Kent the formula was "T.R.E. se defendit pro N solins." See E. M. J. Campbell, "Kent," (*Domesday Geography of South-East England,* ed. H. C. Darby and E. M. J. Campbell (Cambridge, 1962), p. 504.

87. DB, i. 209.

88. E.g., Lewes (DB, i. 26), Dorchester, Bridport, Wareham, and Shaftesbury (all DB, i. 75), Malmesbury (DB, i. 64b), Exeter (DB, i. 88), Oxford (DB, i. 154), Warwick (DB, i. 238); Colchester (DB, ii. 107b). Cf. *Exeter Book,* f. 88, in *Domesday Book, seu Liber Censualis Willelmi Primi Regis Angliae,* vol. 3 (*Addimenta*), ed. Sir Henry Ellis (London, 1816).

89. Robertson, *Charters,* no. 48, p. 100.

90. DB, i. 368 (Somerby). Cf. DB, i. 366b (Wilsford). DB, ii. 48 (Maldon, Essex). Cf. DB, i. 230 (Leicester, Leics.). Cf. also E. King, "The Peterborough 'Descriptio Militum' (Henry I)," *EHR* 84 (1969): 92, for a similar interpretation of the meaning of the post-Conquest phrase "serviunt cum militibus," and Thomas K. Keefe, *Feudal Assessments and the Political Community under Henry II and his Sons* (Berkeley and Los Angeles, 1983), pp. 35–37, for the use of *auxilium exercitum* to denote scutage in twelfth-century Normandy.

91. *Hemming's Cartulary,* ed. Hearne, 1:80; Henry Adams et al., *Essays in Anglo-Saxon Law* (1876; reprint S. Hackensack, New Jersey, 1972), Select Cases, no. 33. See also Robertson, *Charters,* Appendix I, no. 4, p. 236, on the dues pertaining to Taunton. Cf. DB, i. 162 (Taunton, Somerset).

SIX: BOOK-RIGHT AND MILITARY OBLIGATIONS

1. See chap. 1.

2. Robertson, *Laws,* pp. 214–215.

3. Penalties for desertion of the fyrd are given in V *Æthelred,* c. 28; VI *Æthelred,* c. 35; II *Cnut,* c. 77; Robertson, *Laws,* pp. 86–87, 102–103, 214–

215. Here and in II *Cnut,* c. 78, which concerns "men who fall on campaign before their lords," there is a presumption that those who fought in the fyrd were usually landowners. For an example of forfeiture for breaking the king's peace while on campaign, see, KCD 1304 (S 927).

4. II *Cnut,* c. 77, § 1. Cf. II *Cnut,* c. 13; Robertson, *Laws,* pp. 180–181.

5. Liebermann, *Gesetze,* 1:444–453; *EHD* I:875–879. On the composition of the *Rectitudines,* see Dorothy Bethurum, "Wulfstan," in *Continuations and Beginnings,* ed. E. G. Stanley (London, 1966), pp. 210–246. Cf. Finberg, *Agrarian History,* pp. 512–515, 519.

6. The phrase *wyrthe beon* often appears in Anglo-Saxon writs with the meaning of "to be entitled to" or "to possess lawfully" some privilege, estate, or office. See, e.g., Harmer, *Writs,* nos. 8, 12, 16, 28, 44, 51, 69, 80. Cf. Harmer's comments at pp. 63–64, 433, 475–476. See also I *Æthelred,* c. 1, §§ 7, 14; "The London Charter of William the Conqueror," chap. 2, ed. Robertson, *Laws,* pp. 230–231. The implication seems to be that one who is deserving of an honor is entitled to it.

7. Liebermann, *Gesetze,* 1:444, emends *frithscip* to *fyrdscip* on the supposition that this obligation was somehow connected with the ship-sokes. While the term *frithscip* may indeed be unique to this document, *unfrithscip* and *unfrithflota* are both found in the Chronicle, denoting an enemy or pirate ship or fleet. *ASC,* s.a. 1000, 1046 E (recte, 1049). Cf. *ASC,* s.a. 1009: *unfrithhere.* If the text of the *Rectitudines* is correct as it stands, then the *frithscip* would have been a "peace-keeping ship," conceivably associated with the duty of *sæward,* i.e., a vessel that patrolled the coast on watch for pirates or invaders.

8. *EHD* II:875; Liebermann, *Gesetze,* 1:444.

9. Ibid.; Liebermann, *Gesetze,* 1:445.

10. The actual labor upon the king's deer hedges was probably performed by cottars. *Rectitudines,* c. 3, § 4, ed. Liebermann, *Gesetze,* 1:446.

11. The "geneat's right" is similar to the dues owed the king both by his thegns in southern Lancashire T.R.E. (DB, i. 269b: "inter Ripam et Mersham") and by his sokemen in East Anglia and Cambridgeshire. The latter has been noted by Barrow, *Scots,* pp. 13–15. Cf. Davis, *Kalendar,* pp. xxxi–xxxv.

12. Cf. Frank Barlow, *Edward the Confessor* (Berkeley, 1970), pp. 147–148. Circuit 1 of Domesday Book, comprising the shires of Kent, Sussex, Surrey, Hampshire, and Berkshire, seems to use the phrase "N tenuit de rege" to express hereditary tenure. Even so exalted a lord as Earl Harold is said to have held Pyrford, Surrey, "from King Edward." DB, i. 32. This is, of course, a Norman interpretation of Anglo-Saxon tenurial practice, not unlike the use of the terms *relevatio* and *relevamentum* to describe the Old English heriot in Domesday Book (e.g., DB, i. 56), and cannot be used as contemporary evidence. See also DB, i. 151b (Drayton, Bucks.). One might also note how the relationship between a king's thegn and the king paralleled that between a landowner (*landagende*) and the lord of the estate (*landrica*) within which his lands lay in eleventh-century Northumbria. "Laws of the Northumbrian Priests," caps. 48–49, ed. Liebermann, *Gesetze,* 1:380–385; *EHD* I:471–476.

The landagende, whose status was lower than a king's thegn's but higher than a ceorl's (caps. 51–53), may well have been the Northumbrian equivalent of the West Saxon geneat.

13. DB, i. 269b.

14. Domesday Book records that the Bishop of Worcester's tenant at Huddington, T.R.E., held "as a rustic doing service." DB, i. 173b. Similarly, the entry for Kempsey refers to *rusticum opus*. Cf. DB, i. 67b (Durnford, Wilts.), where a tenant of the Church of Wilton served his landlord "as a thegn."

15. DB, i. 262b (county customs).

16. For territorial lords standing surety for their tenants, see III *Æthelstan*, c. 7, § 2. Cf. III *Edmund*, c. 7. For their right to fines incurred within their lands, see I *Æthelred*, c. 3, § 1; III *Æthelred*, c. 3, §§ 2–3; "Law of the Northumbrian Priests," caps. 49 (cf. 48); 54, § 1; 59. Cf. VI *Æthelstan* (the *Iudicia Civitatis Lundoniae*), c. 1, § 1. The landhlaford is equated explicitly with the holder of bookland in this last law, the clear implication being that the possession of a book conferred regalian rights. Cf. the glosses in the tenth-century supplement to "Ælfric's Vocabulary": *fundos, bocland vel landrice*. Wright and Wülcker, *Vocabularies*, 1:247. *Landrica*, "land-ruler," was used as a synonym for landhlaford in Æthelred's and Cnut's codes.

17. Robertson, *Laws*, pp. 54–55.

18. Ibid.

19. Robertson, *Laws*, pp. 68–69. The first and third codes of Æthelred II have points in common and may have been issued together. Patrick Wormald, "Æthelred the Lawmaker," in *Ethelred the Unready*, ed. Hill, pp. 63–64.

20. E.g., II *Cnut*, caps. 13; 13, § 1; 77; 77, § 1, in which we find bookholders commended to men other than the king. Many of the lesser bookholders in Domesday Book were commended T.R.E. to men of local importance, often to more powerful landholders within the same hundred. E.g., Burgræd, father of Edwin, dominated the lordship pattern within Stodden and Willey Hundreds, Bedfordshire, as did Ælmer of Bennington in Broadwater Hundred, Middlesex. Even well-endowed landowners occasionally "bowed" to lords other than the king T.R.E. Thus Aki, who held sixteen hides in Hertfordshire, was both a king's thegn and a "man" of Earl Harold. DB, i. 138, 142.

21. II *Cnut*, c. 77. Cf. Robertson, *Charters*, pp. 62, 66, 88, 168, 178.

22. E.g., II *Cnut*, c. 13, § 1; Robertson, *Laws*, pp. 180–181: "And if he [an outlaw] has bookland, it shall be forfeited into the hands of the king without regard to the question of whose man he is." Cf. II *Cnut*, c. 77, § 1; Robertson, *Laws*, pp. 214–215: "And the man who through cowardice, deserts his lord or his comrades on an expedition, either by land or by sea, shall lose all that he possesses and his own life, and the lord shall take back the property and the land which he had given him. § 1. And if he has bookland it shall pass into the king's hands." The principle that bookland was forfeited to the king and that loanland returned to the lord who had title to it was established by the beginning of the tenth century, as the Fonthill suit attests. See Harmer, *Select Documents*, no. 18, pp. 30–32.

23. Cf. Maitland, *Domesday Book*, p. 159.

24. DB, i. 172: "Quando rex in hostem pergit si quis edictu eius uocatus remanserit, si ita liber homo est ut habeam socam suam et sacam et cum terra possit ire quo uoluerit, de omni terra sua est in misericordia regis. Cuiuscunque uero alterius domini liber homo, se de hoste remanserit, et dominus eius pro eo alium hominem duxerit, .xl. solidos domino sui qui uocatus fuit emendabit. Quod si ex toto nullus pro eo abierit, ipse quidem domino suo .xl. solidos dabit; dominus autem eius totidem solidos regi emendabit." Note especially that the lord is expected to *lead* his men to the fyrd.

25. It is noteworthy that the customs concerning the Worcestershire fyrd directly follow a description of the royal profits of justice.

26. Round, *Feudal England,* pp. 20–30; Carl Stephenson, "Commendation and Related Problems in Domesday," *EHR* 59 (1944), reprint idem, *Medieval Institutions,* ed. Bryce Lyon (Ithaca, N.Y., 1954), pp. 159–165.

27. Harmer, *Writs,* pp. 475–476.

28. Robertson, *Laws,* p. 180: "These are the dues to which the king is entitled from all men in Wessex, namely [the payments for] violation of his *mund,* and for attacks upon people's homes, for assault and for neglecting military service, unless he desires to show special honour to anyone [by granting him these dues]." Cf. *The (So-Called) Laws of William I,* c. 2, §§ 3–4; Robertson, *Laws,* pp. 252–255. The Domesday customs of Nottinghamshire, DB, i. 280b, stress the king's authority over those thegns who held their land with sake and soke. Cf. DB, i. (Dover, Kent). On the meaning of sake and soke, see Maitland, *Domesday Book,* pp. 80–107, 282–283; N. D. Hurnard, "The Anglo-Norman Franchises," *EHR* 64 (1949): 289–327, 433–460; Helen Cam, "The Evolution of the Medieval English Franchise," *Speculum* 32 (1957): 427–442; reprint, idem, *Lawfinders and Law Makers in Medieval England* (London, 1962), pp. 22–43. Only Cam's interpretation takes into account the growing power of the Anglo-Saxon kings during the tenth and eleventh centuries.

29. See N. R. Ker, "Hemming's Cartulary," in *Studies in Medieval History Presented to Frederick Maurice Powicke* (1948; reprint Oxford, 1969), pp. 49–75.

30. DB, i. 172b–174. Cf. BCS 1136 (S 1368).

31. E.g., *Hemming's Cartulary,* ed. Hearne, 1:264; Benjamin Thorpe, *Diplomatarium Anglicum Aevi Saxonici* (London, 1865), pp. 450–451, which describes the lease of Crowle to Sigmund, a Danish miles: "Prior istius monasterii ei terram concessit possidendam vitae suae spatio, ea tamen conventione, ut pro ea ipse ad expeditionem terra marique (quae tunc crebro agebatur) monasterio serviret." Cf. DB, i. 174 (Crowle, Worcs.): "Sigmund held it. It was of the lordship [*de dominio*] and he rendered for it to the Bishop all service and geld [the latter written in suprascript], and he could not betake himself anywhere with this land."

32. Cf. the *Altitonantis* charter, BCS 1135 (S 731), which would date this immunity to Edgar's reign.

33. Hemming's version of the Domesday Worcester liberties contains a number of other small differences. *Hemming's Cartulary,* ed. Hearne, 1:287.

34. DB, i. 172b.

35. *Hemming's Cartulary,* ed. Hearne, 1:81: "Edricus, qui fuit, tempore regis Edwardi, stermannus navis episcopi et ductor exercitus eiusdem episcopi ad servitium regis." Cf. DB, i. 173b (Hindlip and Offerton): "Edricus stirman [in suprascript] tenuit et deserviebat cum aliis servitiis ad regem et episcopum pertinientibus." Cf. *Hemming's Cartulary,* ed. Hearne, 1:77: "Et [episcopus] deracionavit socam et sacam de Hamtona ad suum hundred de Oswaldes law, quod ibi debent placitare et geldum ad expeditionem . . . persolvere," cited by Maitland, *Domesday Book,* p. 308. See also John, *Land Tenure,* pp. 115–126; idem, *Orbis Britanniae,* pp. 149–151. Stenton's interpretation, given in *English Feudalism,* p. 128, is based upon the notion that fyrd service was an obligation of peasants, and does not take into account Hemming's description of the Crowle lease.

36. DB, i. 172 (the county customs); 172b (lands of Worcester); 174b (lands of Westminster); 175–175b (lands of Pershore); 175b–176 (lands of Evesham). See also Harmer, *Writs,* nos. 73–106, pp. 286–372 (referring to the Church of Westminster); nos. 115–116, pp. 407–411 (referring to the Church of Worcester).

37. DB, i. 172 (the county customs); 174b–175 (Pershore, Worcs.). Cf. Harmer, *Writs,* nos. 99–100, pp. 363–365.

38. The county customs state that the king usually reserved the forfeitures arising from breach of the peace (*frithbryce*), obstruction of justice (*foresteall*), forcible entry into a home (*heimfare,* elsewhere termed *hamsocn*), and rape (for which there was no monetary compensation, the only amends being *de corpore justicia*). The Church of Worcester was unique in possessing these forfeitures in its lands. See Harmer, *Writs,* p. 319. One should note the absence of fyrdwite from this list.

39. DB, i. 175b (*terra Sanctae Mariae de Persore,* Worcs.).

40. *Hemming's Cartulary,* ed. Hearne, 1:263, cited by Round, *VCH, Worcestershire,* 1 (London, 1901): 267.

41. DB, i. 172. Cf. Harmer, *Writs,* no. 100, pp. 364–365: "And I command and enjoin that all the thegns of the lands be henceforth subject to the minster, to the abbot and to the monks, and pay to Christ and St. Peter and the brethren all the rights [or dues] and the recognition [of lordship] which belong to me, for I will not permit that anyone have any authority there [Deerhurst and Pershore] except the abbot and the brethren." Cf. Harmer, *Writs,* no. 85, pp. 351–352.

42. Harmer, *Writs,* pp. 14, 52–54. Cf. DB, i. 262 (Chester), on the lord's receipt of a summons from the royal reeve ordering him to supply men for the repair of the city's walls.

43. There is a good deal of evidence for commoners bearing arms and attending the fyrd in eleventh-century England. See, e.g., *Northleoda laga,* c. 10; *EHD* I:469: "Even if a *ceorl* prospers, so that he possesses a helmet and a coat of mail and a gold-plated sword, if he has not the land, he is a *ceorl* all the same." Note also the implication of *ASC,* s.a. 1052 C: "Earl Harold came from Ireland . . . and the inhabitants, both from Somerset and from Devonshire, gathered to oppose him, and he put them to flight and slew there more than thirty good thegns *besides other men*" [emphasis added]. Plummer,

Saxon Chronicles, 1:179. Cf. DB, i. 50; ii. 275b, 409b, and 449, for notices of liberi homines who fell in the Battle of Hastings. See discussion in chap. 7 at, n. 94.

44. II *Cnut,* c. 65. Cf. VI *Æthelred,* c. 35, which associates the desertion of a fyrd personally led by the king with the forfeiture of property, and V *Æthelred,* c. 28, § 1, which states that he who deserts a fyrd led by someone other than the king must compensate the king with a payment of 120 shillings (= the *fyrdwite* of II Cnut, c. 65). It is possible that the punishment for neglect of fyrd service was increased between the reigns of Cnut and Edward the Confessor.

45. *Leges Henrici Primi,* c. 13, § 1, ed. Downer, p. 116: "Hec mittunt hominem in misercordia regis . . . contemptus breuim suorum et quicquid ad propriam eius personam uel mandatorum suorum contumeliatur inuriam."

46. *Rectitudines,* c. 1.

47. Cf. III *Edgar,* c. 3 and II *Cnut,* c. 15, § 1, both of which stipulate that a thegn who possesses jurisdictional rights is to forfeit his rank and privileges if found guilty of malfeasance. Robertson, *Laws,* pp. 24–25, 180–181. Cf. also VI *Æthelred,* c. 5, § 3, which states that a cleric is to be entitled (*wyrthe*) to the rights of a thegn (*thegenrihtes*), and 5, § 4, which adds: "And he who will not do what befits his order shall impair his status before God and man."

48. Cf. *Ine,* c. 51.

49. Stephenson, "Commendation," pp. 159–165.

50. Cf. Maitland, *Domesday Book,* p. 159.

51. DB, i. 56b: "Si rex mittebat alicubi exercitum de quinque hidis tantum unus miles ibat, et ad eius uictum uel stipendium de unaquaque hida dabantur et .iiii. solidi ad duos menses. Hos uero denarios regi non mittebantur, sed militibus dabantur. Si quis in expeditionem summonitus non ibat, totam terram suam erga regem forisfaciebat. Quod si quis remanendi habens alium pro se mittere promitteret, et tamen qui mittendus erat remaneret, pro l. solidis quietus erat dominus eius." *EHD* II:929.

52. Stenton, *English Feudalism,* p. 119, n. 1; idem, *ASE,* p. 583.

53. Hollister, *Military Institutions,* p. 73.

54. Ibid., p. 96.

55. DB, i. 56b. The term "dominicus" in Domesday Book most often appears in the context of landholding, to distinguish the "home-farm" of a lord from the *terra villanorum.* E.g., the phrase *dominicum manerium regis* in Bedfordshire Domesday: DB, i. 209 (Leighton), 209 (Luton), 209b (Houghton). Occasionally, however, it is applied to individuals; e.g., DB, ii. 203 (Rockland, Norfolk, where one Edwin is said to have been a "tenus dominicus regis"). The most telling instance occurs in the borough customs of Norwich and Thetford. Here we find that certain burgesses were so much King Edward's own men (*erant ita dominici regis*) that "they could not recede from him or do homage to another without his permission." DB, ii. 116, 119. As both Round and Stephenson pointed out, the Domesday formula "potuit recedere . . . sine licentia domini sui" refers to the right of free disposal of land. Round, *Feudal England,* pp. 20–30; Stephenson, "Commendation," pp. 159–

165. The *tainus uel miles dominicus,* then, may have been personally commended to the king and holding *de rege.*

56. Hollister, *Military Institutions,* pp. 73, 79–80, cites holdings "in parage" and thegnland tenures as proof. In the first case, however, one is dealing with a single estate held by co-heirs, at least in regard to utware, rather than with separate holdings, and in the second the arrangements made for military service were not with the Crown but with an ecclesiastical landlord.

57. F. L. Ganshof, *Frankish Institutions under Charlemagne* (New York, 1968), pp. 59–62 (and notes).

58. DB, i. 354; C. W. Foster and T. Longley, ed. and trans., *The Lincolnshire Domesday and the Lindsey Survey,* Publications of the Lincoln Record Society, 19 (1924; reproduced 1976), p. 103.

59. DB, i. 375b; Foster and Longley, pp. 212–215.

60. On parage, see Maitland, *Domesday Book,* pp. 145–146; Vinogradoff, *English Society,* pp. 245–290, 405. The phrase "in paragio" connotes a free tenure as well as one held by co-heirs in Domesday Book. The explanation for this dual meaning may lie in the intimate association between hereditary possession and book-right. Thus if sons had the right to divide their father's landed estates among themselves, then by definition the property must have been bookland.

61. Maitland, *Domesday Book,* p. 145. Maitland is undoubtedly correct that one of the parceners would have assumed the role of "first among equals" and that he would have been charged with representing the holding in respect of the king's demands. This seems to be the meaning of a passage in Buckinghamshire Domesday (i. 145b): [In Lavendon, Bunsty Hundred], "eight thegns held this manor; one of them, Alli, the man of King Edward [*homo regis E.*], was the senior of the others [*senior aliorum fuit*]. All could sell their own land." Cf. DB, i. 291 (Winkburn, Lythe Wapentake). The use of *senior* rather than *dominus* suggests that the superiority derived not from personal commendation but from the tenure that they possessed jointly, with the *senior* (the oldest son?) enjoying some undefined right over the lands of his fellow parceners.

62. The names are too common to determine the extent of their holdings in Lincolnshire. A Chetel and a Turuer are found together only in Covenham.

63. DB, i. 340b–341, 342, 359b, 360 (lands held by a man named Godwine who may have been Siwate's father; DB, i. 376; Foster and Longley, eds., *Lincolnshire Domesday,* pp. 218–219). The identification, however, is far from certain.

64. DB, i. 376.

65. Stenton, *English Feudalism,* pp. 118–122; idem, *ASE,* p. 583.

66. Hollister, *Military Institutions,* p. 64.

67. Maitland, *Domesday Book,* p. 115; Vinogradoff, *English Society,* pp. 130–134, 320–322; Frank M. Stenton, *Types of Manorial Structure in the Northern Danelaw,* Oxford Studies in Social and Legal History, 2 (1910), pp. 28–45. Kristensen, "Danelaw," pp. 45–49, 74–85, provides a provocative treatment of the problem of *soca.*

68. Kristensen, "Danelaw," pp. 42–49; Barrow, *Scots,* pp. 7–68. See discussion in chap. 1 at n. 47.

69. Stenton, *ASE,* pp. 518–519. Cf. Jolliffe, *Jutes,* pp. 39–68; Jones, "Multiple Estates," pp. 15–40; Davis, *Kalendar,* pp. xlvi–xlvii.

70. DB, i. 280b, 298b, 337.

71. See Stephenson, "Commendation," pp. 179–180; Kristensen, "Danelaw," pp. 74–85.

72. Ibid.

SEVEN: THE ANGLO-SAXON MILITES

1. Wulfstan, *Polity,* ed. Jost, pp. 55–56; trans. Michael Swanton, *Anglo-Saxon Prose* (London, 1975), p. 127: "Every lawful throne which stands perfectly upright stands on three pillars: one is *oratores,* and the second is *laboratores* and the third is *bellatores.* 'Oratores' are prayer-men who must serve God and earnestly intercede both day and night for the entire nation. 'Laboratores' are workmen, who must supply that by which the entire nation shall live. 'Bellatores' are soldiers, who must defend the land by fighting with weapons."

2. *Romans,* 13:4. The Vulgate does not contain the word *miles.*

3. *Cniht* originally meant "boy." The word was most commonly used to describe a household retainer. See n. 56 below.

4. *EHD* I:928; Ælfric, *Heptateuch,* ed. Crawford, pp. 71–72.

5. *Die Hirtenbriefe Ælfrics,* ed. Fehr, Latin Letter, 2a (to Archbishop Wulfstan, A.D. 1003–1005), p. 225: "De bellico apparatu suspicor non latere almitatem tuam tres ordines fore in ecclesia dei: Laboratores, bellatores, oratores." In this letter Ælfric used the tripartite scheme to argue against those clerics who wielded the secular as well as the spiritual sword.

6. Wulfstan, *Polity,* ed. Jost, pp. 55–56.

7. Ælfric, "De populo Israhel," in J. C. Pope, ed., *Homilies of Ælfric: A Supplementary Collection,* Early English Text Society, 260 (London, 1978), 2: 641, l.10.

8. Robert Weber, ed., *Biblia sacra iuxta vulgatam versionem* (Stuttgart, 1975), 1:93.

9. More accurately, Ælfric has restored the military flavor, since the Hebrew text uses the term *geber,* "men of military age" or "mighty men," rather than *ish,* "men." Cf. the use of *geber,* Exod. 10:11, 12:37; Num. 24:3, 15; 1 Sam. 16:18; 2 Sam. 23:1; and 1 Chron. 26:12.

10. Ælfric rendered the correlative pair *seu laicus seu miles* as *swa ceorl swa kempa.*

11. Swanton, *Prose,* pp. 113–114; G. N. Garmonsway, ed., *Ælfric's Colloquy,* 2d ed. (London, 1947), pp. 112–113.

12. Cf. "Sermon of the Wolf," ed. Bethurum, *Homilies,* p. 271.

13. Stenton, *ASE,* p. 475. Finberg adds, "to most of us he will seem well over the verge." *Agrarian History,* p. 514.

14. *Rectitudines,* c. 2; *EHD* II:875. Cf. Finberg, *Agrarian History,* pp. 514–515.

15. See discussion at n. 94 below and chap. 8, n. 102.

16. DB, i. 56b.

17. DB, i. 56: "Tainus uel miles regis dominicus moriens pro releuamento dimittebat regi omnia arma sua et equum, cum sella, alium sine sella." The customs go on to say that the dying man also had to offer the king his hounds and his hawk, if he had such animals. Cf. DB, i. 1 (Dover, Kent) and 280 b (Nottingham). Cf. DB, i. 1 (Kent), 280b (Nottinghamshire), for pre-Conquest "relief." The terms "heriete," "herigete," and "harieta" also appear in the survey. See e.g., DB, i. 189 (Cambridgeshire), 336b (Stamford); DB, ii. 119 (Thetford, Norfolk). "Relief" and "heriot" are used interchangeably in *Leges Henry Primi*, c. 14. Cf. II *Cnut*, c. 71, §§ 1–5.

18. King, "Peterborough 'Descriptio Militum,' " pp. 97, 100.

19. Douglas, *Feudal Documents*, pp. 11–14, 16, 55.

20. Douglas, *William the Conqueror*, p. 95.

21. For the Domesday references to the lands that these men held in chief, see Henry Ellis, *A General Introduction to Domesday Book*, vol. 1 (London, 1833), "Index to the Tenants *in Capite*," s.v. Eudo Dapifer and Bigot, Rogerus. Cf. ibid., vol. 2, "Index of Under-tenants of Land." Milites of this sort are sometimes termed "nobles" in the ducal charters of Normandy before the Conquest. See M. Fauroux, ed., *Recueil des Actes des Ducs de Normandie de 911 à 1066*, Société des antiquaires de Normandie, 36 (Caen, 1961), no. 43: [Richard II, Duke of Normandy, attests a grant] "cum suis episcopis atque militibus, scilicet Nigello, Osberno dapifero, atque aliis nobilibus"; no. 147: "a quodam milite et claro genere, Richardo [de Riviers] nomine."

22. Sally Harvey, "The Knight and the Knight's Fee," *Past and Present* 49 (1970), reprint in R. H. Hilton, ed., *Peasants, Knights and Heretics* (Cambridge, 1976), pp. 145–148. An unnamed Domesday miles may, however, have held more than one subtenancy. Harvey's failure to consider this possibility injures, but does not destroy, her thesis.

23. DB, i. 128b, 132. Cf. DB, i. 197 (Weston Colville), 198b (Wratworth), 198b (Caldecote), all in Cambridgeshire.

24. DB, i. 210 (Yelden, Beds.): "In dominio sunt .iii. carucae, & uillani habent .xi. carucas. Ibi [sunt] .xuii. uillani & unus miles & .xii. bordarii & .i. seruus." Cf. DB, i. 73 (Yatesbury, Wilts.), 133b (Hadham, Herts.), 140 (Thorley, Herts.). But cf. DB, i. 130 (Stanwell, Mddlx.), where we find bordars "dwelling under" (*manentes sub*) milites.

25. Fauroux, *Recueil*, no. 199, p. 387: [Duke William grants a manor at Flottemanville-Hague] "cum omnibus appenditiis suis que ad eum pertinebat, id est, ecclesiam et .xx. acras, et terram suam dominica [*sic*] ad tres carrucas . . . .v. liberos milites, et moldendinum." The qualification of the milites as "free" men is especially interesting. Cf. ibid., no. 208, p. 397: [Duke William grants at Arnieres-sur-Iton] "totum quod in dominio habebam, excepto feodo militum et nemore et aqua." Cf. also ibid., nos. 80, 85, 94, 140, 147, and 197.

26. This phrase is used to describe the abbey's Domesday tenants in the second part of the "Liber feoffamentorum abbatis Baldewini." Douglas, ed., *Feudal Documents*, pp. 165–166.

27. DB, ii. 372. Cf. the comments of Douglas, *Feudal Documents*, p. cvi, and of Harvey, "Knight's Fee," p. 143.

28. DB, i. 128 (Westminster, Mddlx.).

29. Vinogradoff, *English Society*, pp. 77–78; Harvey, "Knight's Fee," pp. 154–155.

30. Eadmer, *Vita Sancti Anselmi*, ed. R. W. Southern, Nelson's Medieval Texts (London, 1962), pp. 94–96, cited by Marjorie Chibnall, "Mercenaries and the *Familia Regis* under Henry I," *History* 62 (1977): 15. Both Southern and Chibnall note that the anonymous *De Similitudinibus*, cap. 80, and Alexander's *Dicta Anselmi*, cap. 10, preserve independent versions of this allegory, which must have been a favorite of Anselm's. Southern, ibid., p. 95, n. 1; Chibnall, "Mercenaries," p. 15, n. 2.

31. *The Ecclesiastical History of Orderic Vitalis*, ed. and trans. Marjorie Chibnall, vol. 6 (Oxford, 1978): 26–28. Cf. Harvey, "Knight's Fee," p. 159; Chibnall, "Mercenaries," p. 22; idem, "Feudal Society in Orderic Vitalis," *Anglo-Norman Studies* I (1979):46.

32. Chibnall, "Mercenaries," pp. 15–23; idem, "Feudal Society," pp. 43–44. Cf. the vivid portrayal of one military household in the *Vita Herluini*, in J. Armitage Robinson, *Gilbert Crispin* (Cambridge, 1911), pp. 87–90. Cf. also William of Malmesbury on Wulfstan II's armed retinue. *De Gestis Pontificum*, ed. Hamilton, p. 281; *Vita Wulfstani*, ed. R. R. Darlington, Camden 3d Series, 40 (1928): 46, 55.

33. William of Poitiers, *Gesta Guilelmi ducis Normannorum et regis Anglorum*, ed. R. Foreville (Paris, 1952), p. 151. Household milites figure prominently in the ducal charters of pre-Conquest Normandy. See, e.g., Fauroux, *Recueil*, no. 44.

34. See Prestwich, "Military Household"; Chibnall, "Mercenaries." Cf. Stenton, *English Feudalism*, pp. 136–142; Bryce Lyon, *From Fief to Indenture* (Cambridge, Mass., 1957), pp. 99–100.

35. Sally Harvey follows William of Poitiers in choosing this adjective for the feudal vassals. The archdeacon describes how the Conqueror addressed his military forces in order of rank, speaking first to his magnates, then to the *milites mediae nobilitatis*, and last to the *milites gregarii* (whom Harvey would identify with the professional men-at-arms). *Gesta Guilelmi*, p. 232. Cf. Harvey, "Knight's Fee," pp. 141, 158.

36. Harvey, "Knight's Fee," pp. 135–160, esp. pp. 136–141. Emily Tabuteau advances a similar argument about the milites of eleventh-century Normandy. "Transfers of Property in Eleventh-Century Norman Law" (Ph.D. diss., Harvard University, 1975), p. 362, n. 249.

37. Harvey, "Knight's Fee," pp. 136–141. A sheriff or royal steward could prove a valuable ally for a monastic house. For the tenancy of one sheriff, Haimo of Kent, see David C. Douglas, ed., *Domesday Monachorum of Christ Church, Canterbury* (London, 1944), fol. 7r.

38. Emily Tabuteau, "Definitions of Feudal Military Obligations in Eleventh-Century Normandy," in *On the Laws and Customs of England: Essays in Honor of Samuel E. Thorne*, ed. Morris S. Arnold et al. (Chapel Hill, N.C., 1981), p. 59, concludes that "it seems unlikely that precisely defined obliga-

tions were imported in developed form from Normandy to England in 1066. Instead, it is probable that at the time of the Conquest, Norman practices were many and various, and often not precisely defined, and that after 1066 these practices were gradually regularized both in Normandy and in England, perhaps more rapidly in the latter country."

39. Douglas, *Feudal Documents*, p. 4; Harvey, "Knight's Fee," p. 142. Cf. the formula used in the Peterborough "Descriptio Militum": "tenet de abbatia . . . et inde servit se .n. militum." King, "Peterborough 'Descriptio Militum,' " pp. 97–101.

40. DB, i. 130.

41. See, e.g., William of Poitiers, *Gesta Guilelmi*, chap. 37, ed. Foreville, p. 88, for miles as feudal vassal: "Hic [Herbert II Bacon] . . . Normanniae ducem Guilelmum, sub quo tutus foret, supplex adiit, manibus ei sese dedit, cuncta sua ab eo, ut miles a domino, recepit, cunctorum singulariter eum statuens heredem, si non gigneret alium" ["Herbert II Bacon . . . sought William, Duke of the Normans, under whom he would be safe, as a suppliant, did homage to him, and received from him all his possessions, as a *miles* from his lord, constituting him his only heir of all his goods, if he should sire no other"]. Cf. ibid., pp. 48 (chap. 22), 66 (chap. 29), 106 (chap. 43). William of Poitiers emphasizes the military sense of miles in ibid., pp. 76 (chap. 33), 108 (chap. 44), 110 (chap. 45), 232 (chap. 88), as does William of Jumièges, *Gesta Normannorum ducum*, ed. Jean Marx (Rouen, 1914), pp. 41, 77, 80, 82, 84, passim. The idea of service, however, is far from absent in the latter's work. Note especially his use of the verb *militare*, ibid., p. 51: "Hactenus militavimus duci, ulterius serviemus invictissimo regi." Orderic Vitalis's use of miles is varied, denoting at different times feudal retainer, mounted warrior, and noble. Consult the indices to Marjorie Chibnall, ed. and trans., *The Ecclesiastical History of Orderic Vitalis*, s.v. "knighthood" and "knights." For further discussion of the meaning of the term "miles" in the early medieval period, see K. J. Hollyman, *Le développement du vocabulaire féodal en France* (Geneva, 1957), pp. 126–134; Joachim Bumke, *Studien zum Ritterbegriff im 12 und 13 Jahrhundert* (Heidelberg, 1964), pp. 46–59, 74–76, 112–113; Georges Duby, "The Origins of Knighthood," in *The Chivalrous Society*, pp. 158–170.

42. *Beowulf*, ll. 20–25, 794–797, 2490–2507, 2631–2655, 2865–2883; *The Battle of Maldon*, ll. 185–190. Cf. ASC, s.a. 755 (recte, 757).

43. Liebermann, *Gesetze*, vol. 2, pt. 2, s.v. *Heergewate;* Whitelock, *Wills*, p. 100; Brooks, "Arms," pp. 81–93.

44. This will be the subject of a future article.

45. Brooks, "Arms," in *Ethelred the Unready*, ed. Hill, pp. 87–89. Although heriot payments appear in most of the extant late Anglo-Saxon wills, we find cash payment in lieu of weapons in only two bequests: that of Ælfric Modercope, an East Anglian thegn (Whitelock, *Wills*, no. 28), and that of a woman, Æthelgifu. In the second will the phrase "my lord's due payment" is used in place of the term "heriot." D. Whitelock, Neil Ker, and Lord Rennell, eds., *The Will of Æthelgifu*, p. 20. But as with so much else concerning Anglo-Saxon institutions, the subject of heriots is complicated by temporal and re-

gional diversity. II *Cnut,* c. 71, §§ 2, 3, and 5 stipulate that lesser thegns and those king's thegns who dwelled within the Danelaw could commute their heriots for money payments, and this is confirmed by DB, i. 269 (between the Ribble and Mersey, Lancs.), 280b (Notts.), 298b (Yorks.), and 376b (disputes, Lincs.). But cf. Whitelock, *Wills,* no. 34, pp. 88, 202–203. DB, i. 56b (Beds.) and 179 (Herefords.) describe king's thegns and the *burhwaras* of the Welsh march as rendering their heriots in arms.

46. *Cempa* could also connote a military retainer. See, e.g., *OE Orosius,* ed. Bately, p. 77, l. 32, where *cempan* renders *stipatoribus regis satellitibusque.* Cf. *Ælfric's Lives of Saints,* ed. W. W. Skeat, Early English Text Society, Original Series, 76 (1881; reprint 1963), 1:190. The term was also occasionally used as a title, much like minister and thegn. E.g., Harmer, *Select Documents,* no. 17, p. 30, in which Eadulf cempa is the second secular retainer of Bishop Denewulf to sign. His attestation precedes those of the king's ministri.

47. E.g., *H.E.,* IV. 13, 22. Cf. Bede, *Historia Abbatum,* chap. 1, ed. Plummer, *Baedae Opera,* 1:365–366; *Epistola ad Ecgberhtum,* in ibid., 1:415.

48. E.g., BCS 600 (S 368), 702 (S 407), 757 (S 469), 774 (S 483), 782 (S 492), 870 (S 531), 958 (S 609), 992 (S 642), 998 (S 647), 1053 (S 685), 1257 (S 777); KCD 736 (S 977), 1305 (S 918), 1308 (S 931).

49. E.g., Æthelweard, recipient of two grants from Bishop Oswald of Worcester: "meo fideli" (BCS 1232 [S 1318]); "meo minister" (BCS 1206 [S 1312]; KCD 667 [S 1356]); "meo militi" (KCD 646 [S 1346]). Cf. Æthelstan, Bishop Oswald's "fidelis miles" (KCD 631 [S 1343]). Cf. KCD 613 (S 1331).

50. *Encomium Emmae Reginae,* ed. Alistair Campbell, Camden 3d Series, 72 (London, 1949): 43.

51. *Vita Ædwardi Regis,* ed. Frank Barlow (London, 1962), p. 50.

52. *ASC,* s.a. 1065 C (*huskarlas*); 1065 D (*hiredmenn*). The *Vita Ædwardi Regis,* pp. 35–36, numbers men of noble birth among Tostig's milites, including a relation of the king, Gospatrick, who saved his lord from a robber band during his pilgrimage to Rome.

53. Byrhtferth of Ramsey is now generally accepted as the author. *EHD* I:911–912.

54. Ælfric, *Heptateuch,* p. 72.

55. *Ibid.* Cf. Robertson, *Charters,* no. 119, pp. 220, 472.

56. E.g., Whitelock, *Wills,* p. 235, s.v., *cniht,* for references to *cnihtas* in bequests; Robertson, *Charters,* no. 74, pp. 148–149: "Ælfgeat and Ælfweard, his [Edmund the Ætheling's] *cnihtas* and all the other men of his *household* [*hiredmenn*]." See also Wright and Wülcker, *Vocabularies,* 1:77: "cliens vel clientulus, cniht." This gloss is immediately preceded by "dominus vel herus, hlaford" and followed by "servus, theowa." See Stenton's discussion of *cniht* in *English Feudalism,* pp. 132–136. *Cniht* could also simply mean "boy." For the various meanings of this word, see Healey and Venezky, *Old English Concordance,* microfiche C6, pp. 86–103.

57. *Monumenta Alcuiniana,* ed. Wattenbach and Dummler, Epist. no. 174, p. 623. One must point out, however, that miles was not equated with the word cniht alone, and in fact was more often glossed by cempa, the word for

warrior. See, e.g., Healey and Venezky, *Old English Concordance,* microfiche C2, pp. 259–260, 273.

58. *Vita Oswaldi Archiepiscopi Eboracensis auctore anonymo,* ed. J. Raine, pp. 448–450; trans. *EHD* I:914–915.

59. Ibid., p. 449.

60. Ibid., p. 428: "miles egregius, nomine Æthelwinus" (Æthelwine "Dei Amicus," son of Ealdorman Æthelstan "Half-King"); p. 444: "belliger miles Alfwoldus" (Ælfwold, brother of Æthelwine); p. 445: "intrepidus miles Alfwoldus" (the same Ælfwold). The term "miles," like the term "thegn," which it often translated, gained prestige in the tenth and eleventh centuries as the Anglo-Saxon nobility became more and more identified with service to the king.

61. E.g., William of Jumièges, *Gesta,* ed. Marx, pp. 92, 130. But cf. ibid., p. 105, an interpolated passage attributed to Saint-Etienne de Caen, for a tale about a miles so impoverished that he lacked the wherewithal to make an oblation on a saint's day.

62. *Vita Oswaldi,* p. 445.

63. *The Bayeux Tapestry,* ed. David M. Wilson (New York, 1985). (I have followed Wilson's plate numbers throughout.) Recent scholarship on the Tapestry is summarized by Nicholas Brooks and H. E. Walker, "The Authority and Interpretation of the Bayeux Tapestry," *Anglo-Norman Studies* 1 (1979):1–34. See also Frank M. Stenton, gen. ed., *The Bayeux Tapestry,* 2d ed. (London, 1965).

64. Francis Wormald, "Style and Design," in Stenton, ed., *Bayeux Tapestry,* pp. 25–36; M. Forster, "Zur Geschichte des Reliquienskultus in Altengland," *Sitzungsberichte der Bayerischen Akademie der Wissenschaften* (Phil.-hist. Abt.), 8 (1943): 16–19; R. Lepelley, "Contribution a l'étude des inscriptions de la Tapisserie de Bayeux," *Annales de Normandie* 14 (1964): 313–341.

65. Brooks, "Arms," pp. 94–96; Brooks and Walker, "Bayeux Tapestry," pp. 19–20.

66. *Bayeux Tapestry,* plate 28; Brooks and Walker, "Bayeux Tapestry," pp. 10–11.

67. *Bayeux Tapestry,* plates 30, 31. Cf. *Vita Ædwardi,* ed. Barlow, p. 79; Florence of Worcester, *Chronicon,* 1:224.

68. *Bayeux Tapestry,* plates 22, 44, 51–53, 57–61.

69. Cf. *The Battle of Maldon,* ll. 5–8, where a cniht of Earl Byrhtnoth shows himself prepared for battle by letting loose his hawk. Cf. also the mounted retinue described in the *Miracula Sancti Swithuni* and Ælfric's homily on Swithun, quoted by Stenton, *English Feudalism,* p. 129, n. 2. The tenth-century *Miracula* remarks that it was the custom among the Anglo-Saxons (*ut mos est Anglis Saxonis*) for noblemen to travel accompanied by "large mounted entourages." Cf. also *Vita Oswaldi,* ed. Raine, 1:449.

70. Defined in the customs of Lincoln as one endowed with sake and soke. DB, i. 336. For further discussion, see Stenton, "Introduction," *The Lincolnshire Domesday,* ed. C. W. Foster and T. Longley, pp. xxix–xxx.

71. DB, i. 189.

72. Although the Cambridgeshire lawman's heriot does not precisely correspond to any of the categories in Cnut's law, the size of the money payment would associate it with that of a king's thegn (caps. 71, §1, 71, §4). Cf. also the heriots described in the wills, where we also find payments of horses, helmets, swords, shields, and coats of mail. E.g., Whitelock, *Wills*, nos. 19, 28, 31, 34.

73. Brown, *Normans*, pp. 94–98. Cf. R. Glover, "English Warfare in 1066," *EHR* 67 (1952): 1–18. The early eleventh–century illustrator of the Canterbury Hexateuch depicted Abram's men pursuing Lot's captors on horseback but engaging them on foot, which seems to support Brown's position. British Library, MS. Cotton Claudius B. IV, 25r.

74. J. H. Clapham, "The Horsing of the Danes." In addition to the literary evidence cited by Clapham, one should pay special attention to the gloss of *equitatus* in the early eleventh-century supplement to Ælfric's *Vocabulary*, Wright & Wülcker, *Vocabularies*, 1:229: *equitatus, ferdwerod* [fyrd-troop]. The early eighth-century *Vita Wilfridi* implies that the early Northumbrian fyrds rode to battle and fought on foot. *Life of Wilfrid*, chap. 19, ed. Colgrave, pp. 40–42. Cf. Chadwick, *Origin*, p. 159, n. 1.

75. DB, i. 56b; *EHD* II:929.

76. This assumes that "uel" is used here conjunctively. It is possible, however, that it is disjunctive. If so, the Berkshire *miles* might have been a retainer of lesser rank than a king's thegn, a *geneat*, for instance. Even if "uel" is conjunctive, as seems probable, the *taini uel milites* may well have included men of this rank.

77. John, *Orbis Britanniae*, p. 144, n. 3.

78. Loyn, *Anglo-Saxon England*, pp. 211, 215–217.

79. Although *thegn* appears to have originally meant "young man," its primary meaning in the early sources is "servant." Like the Latin word *puer,* the Welsh *gwas,* and even the Anglo-Saxon *cniht*, *thegn* came to denote a military retainer. See Green, *Carolingian Lord*, pp. 98–106. Cf. A. G. Little, "Gesiths and Thegns," *EHR* 4 (1889): 724–729. Even in its aristocratic form, thegn implied subordination to some greater man.

80. By the early eleventh-century the term "thegn" by itself could connote nobility. Thus we read in *Dunsæte, c.* 5 that the law was to apply to all men, "whether thegn-born or ceorl-born." Cf. Robertson, *Charters*, no. 77, p. 152. But whenever we find thegn used in this technical sense, we can be sure that the modifier *cynges* is understood. This comes out most clearly in the charters and writs of the early eleventh century. Thus while the standard formula of address in the writs is "N cyngc gret . . . ealle *mine* thegenas on Nshire freond-lice" [emphasis supplied], the phrase "ealle tha thegnas on Nscire" is used in a number of eleventh-century diplomas. Robertson, *Charters*, nos. 78 (p. 152), 87 (p. 172), 94 (p. 180), 106 (p. 202), 107 (p. 202). See also the legal citations gathered by Liebermann, *Gesetze*, 1, pt. 1, s.v. *thegn*, pp. 218–219.

81. Liebermann, ed. *Gesetze*, 1:456–461; trans. *EHD* I:468–470.

82. Note the Latin translation in the *Instituta Cnuti* III, c. 60, § 1: "de suo proprio allodio." Liebermann, ed., *Gesetze*, 1:457. Cf. Robertson, *Charters*, p. 414.

83. *EHD* I:468; Liebermann, *Gesetze,* 1:456.

84. Bethurum, "Six Anonymous Old English Codes," pp. 449–463.

85. Liebermann, *Gesetze,* 1:456; *EHD* I:468.

86. Little, "Gesiths," p. 722, n. 7. See Bosworth and Toller, s.v. *thegnian* and *thegnung.* Cf. Wulfstan's *Sermo Lupi ad Anglos,* ed. Bethurum, *Homilies,* p. 262; trans. *EHD* I:929–930: "Among heathen peoples one dare not in any way ill-use the servants [*thenan*] of false gods as one now does the servants [*theowum*] of God. . . ."

87. The organization of Domesday Book places the English *Taini Regis* on the same footing as those who held by sergeanty (*Servientes Regis*), listing both after the tenants-in-chief with the *Servientes Regis* given pride of place. In some instances, the two lists are combined under the rubric *Servientes Regis.* See Vinogradoff, *English Society,* pp. 66–68.

88. DB, i. 73b–74.

89. DB, i. 56: "ad eius uictum uel stipendium de unaquaque hida dabantur et .iiii. solidi ad duos menses. Hos uero denarios regi non mittebantur, sed militibus dabantur."

90. See discussion in chapter 5.

91. This is the impression received from the *Inquisitio Comitatus Cantabrigiensis* and the *Inquisitio Eliensis,* which, unlike Domesday Book, provide information on the holdings of individual sokemen. As with most generalizations, there are exceptions. One fortunate sokeman, Æthelberht, the steward [*dapifer*] and man of the abbot of Ely, held ten hides of thegnland from Ely in Cambridgeshire. DB, i. 201 (Impington, Milton, and Utbech). Cf. *IE:* 113–114.

92. Harvey, "Knight's Fee," pp. 150–151.

93. Hollister, *The Military Organization of Norman England* (Oxford, 1965), pp. 157–160, 211–213; Harvey, "Knight's Fee," p. 150.

94. See Freeman, *Norman Conquest,* 3:426–428, 742–744 (Note HH).

95. DB, i. 50 (Tytherley, Hampshire).

96. DB, ii. 409 (Ward Green, Suffolk), 275b (Shelfanger, Norfolk), 449 (Cavendish, Suffolk).

97. Freeman, *Norman Conquest,* 3:427.

98. Eric Wolf, *Peasants* (Englewood Cliffs, N.J., 1966), pp. 3–4.

99. DB, i. 50; ii. 409.

100. DB, i. 138.

101. Davis, *Kalendar,* xxxiv–xlvii; Kristensen, "Danelaw," pp. 43–45 (and references).

102. An early twelfth-century survey from Burton Abbey (1114–1118) may shed some light on the military duty of such individuals. Orm, a *censarius* of the Abbey, held eight bovates of "warland" in the manor of Branston, Staffordshire, with seven men holding under him. In addition to his rent, Orm was obliged to attend pleas at the shire court and the wapentake, lend his plough to the abbot twice a year, reap with all his men three times in August, do boon-works, go to the hunts when ordered, and go on military expeditions [*in exercitus*]. "The Burton Abbey Twelfth-Century Surveys," ed. C. G. O. Bridgeman, *William Salt Archaeological Society* (London, 1916), p. 216 and

comments at p. 269; *EHD* II:886. Since Burton Abbey did not owe knight-service in the Anglo-Norman period, the phrase *in exercitus* may refer to the post-Conquest fyrd. Hollister, *Military Organization,* pp. 243–244. Orm's military service, like his obligation to pay suit in court and to lend the abbot his plough, is represented as a condition of his tenure. For further discussion of the military service of tenants, see chapter 8.

103. DB, i. 154; DB, i. 238; DB, i. 64b.

104. Cf. DB, i. 26 (Lewes, Sussex): "Si rex ad mare custodiendum sine se mittere suos uoluisset de omnibus hominibus cujuscunque terrae fuissent colligebant .xx. solidos et hos habebent qui in nauibus arma custodiebant."

105. *ASC,* s.a. 1094.

106. Again, this should only be regarded as a general rule that admitted of exceptions. The bishop of Worcester, for example, apparently did not lead the troops raised from his estates T.R.E. but, as mentioned above, had a tenant named Eadric who served as the "steersman" of his ship and the captain of his fyrd contingent (*ductor exercitus ejusdem episcopi ad servitium regis*). *Hemming's Cartulary,* ed. Hearne, 1:81. A similar situation must have pertained for the lands of the bishopric of Hereford before 1056, for Bishop Æthelstan was old and blind from 1043 until his death in that year. Florence of Worcester, *Chronicon,* 1:214. He was replaced by the warrior-bishop Leofgar, who was killed in battle against Gruffydd eleven weeks after his consecration. *ASC,* s.a. 1056.

107. See discussion in chapter 6.

EIGHT: LORDS AND RETAINERS IN THE
KING'S HOST

1. *The Battle of Maldon,* ed. D. G. Scragg (Manchester, 1981); trans. R. K. Gordon, *Anglo-Saxon Poetry* (1926; rev. and reprint London, 1970), pp. 329–334. We also have Florence of Worcester's description of the battle of Sherstone (1016) (*Chronicon,* 1:174–175) and the various narratives of the battles of 1066, including the near-contemporary accounts of the Chronicle, William of Jumièges, William of Poitiers, and the Bayeux Tapestry. The poem on the battle of Maldon is, however, unique in providing us with a glimpse into the workings of the fyrd and the relationships between its members.

2. John, "War and Society," p. 188.

3. J. C. McKinnell, "On the Date of *The Battle of Maldon,*" *Medium Aevum* 44 (1975): 121–136. George Clark, "*The Battle of Maldon:* A Heroic Poem," *Speculum* 43 (1968): 52–71; N. F. Blake, "The Genesis of *The Battle of Maldon,*" *Anglo-Saxon England* 7 (1978):119–129. But cf. Scragg, ed., *The Battle of Maldon,* pp. 13 (and n. 48), 26–28, who argues cogently for a near-contemporary dating.

4. Blake, "*Maldon,*" p. 129.

5. Hooper, "Anglo-Saxon Warfare," p. 90.

6. Chadwick, *Origin,* p. 159; John, *Orbis Britanniae,* p. 138.

7. *Maldon,* ll. 211–224, trans. Gordon, *Anglo-Saxon Poetry,* pp. 332–333.

8. *Maldon*, ll. 187–201, trans. Gordon, *Anglo-Saxon Poetry*, p. 332.

9. *Maldon*, l. 154. Cf. l. 203 ("Æthelredes eorl") and ll. 52–53. The lordship bond between earl and king is also stressed in an eleventh-century Northumbrian tract known as "De obsessione Dunhelmi." This piece relates how Cnut attempted to seduce Uhtred, earl of Northumbria, away from King Æthelred with promises of honors and power. The author has Uhtred respond by declaring: "No reward could persuade me to do what I ought not to do. As long as King Æthelred lives I shall support him faithfully. He is my lord and father-in-law, by whose gift I have sufficient honor and riches. I will never be traitor to him." "De obsessione Dunhelmi" in Symeon of Durham, *Symeonis Monachi Opera Omnia*, ed. Thomas Arnold, Rolls Series (London, 1882), p. 218; trans. Cyril Hart, *The Early Charters of Northern England and the North Midlands* (Leicester, 1975), p. 148.

10. Scragg, ed., *Maldon*, "Glossary of Proper Names," s.v. Æthelric, Byrhtwold, Sibryht, and Wulfstan, son of Ceola. Cf. N. F. Blake, *"Maldon,"* pp. 127–128. Blake's rejection of the historicity of the poem in toto is unwarranted by the evidence.

11. *Maldon*, l. 24 (*heorthwerod*, "hearth-troop"); l. 204 (*heorthgeneatas*, "hearth-companions"); l. 261 (*hiredmen*, "household men").

12. *Maldon*, ll. 262–264.

13. On Byrhtnoth's connections, see Scragg, *Maldon*, pp. 14–20.

14. See discussion in chap. 5 at n. 84.

15. Robertson, *Laws*, p. 214: "77. Be tham the flith fram his laforde. And the man the fleo fram his hlaforde oththe fram his geferan for his yrhthe, sy hit on scypfyrde, sy hit on landfyrde, tholie he ealles thæs the he age and his agenes feores, and fo se hlaford to tham æhton and his the he him ær sealde. § 1. And gyf he bocland hæbbe, ga thæt tham cingce to handa.

78. Be tham the toforan his laforde fealleth. And se man the on fyrdunge ætforan his hlaforde fealle, sy hit innon lande, sy his ut of lande, beon tha heregeata forgyfene, and fon tha yrfenuman to land and to æhte and scyften hit swithe rihte." Cf. *Lex Baiuvariorum*, II:7, ed. Rivers, *Laws of the Alemans and Bavarians*, p. 126.

16. Cf. II *Cnut*, c. 13, § 1.

17. See, e.g., Whitelock, *Wills*, no. 34, pp. 88, 90: "the land let for services [*earninglond*] which my man Alfwold holds; and he is to occupy it during his lifetime." Cf. ibid., nos. 2 (p. 8), 17 (p. 48), 21 (pp. 58, 60), 29 (p. 76), 31 (pp. 82, 84).

18. Maitland, *Domesday Book*, pp. 73, 154–155. Cf. Stephenson, "Commendation," pp. 289ff.

19. E.g., DB, i. 193 (Croyden; ICC fol. 102b), 193 (Shingay; ICC fol. 102b), 193 (Abinton Pigotts, ICC fol. 102), 193b (Melbourn; ICC fol. 105b); passim. "De," "sub," and "homo" are used interchangeably in the surveys of Norfolk and Suffolk in Little Domesday. Barbara Dodwell, "East Anglian Commendation," *EHR* 63 (1948): 291–295, esp. 294, n. 1.

20. Robertson, *Charters*, no. 101 (KCD 804 [S 1409]), pp. 208–209.

21. Harmer, *Writs*, no. 21.

22. David C. Douglas, *Feudal Documents from the Abbey of Bury St.*

Edmunds, British Academy Records in Social and Economic History, 8 (London, 1932), pp. cxi–cxii; Harmer, *Writs,* pp. 149–150. Cf. Harmer, *Select Documents,* no. 19, pp. 30–32; *Liber Eliensis,* bk. II, chap. 32, ed. Blake, pp. 106–107; "King Eadgar's Charter of Confirmation to Thorney Abbey (973)," ed. Cyril Hart, *Charters of Eastern England,* p. 178: "Leofstan quidam miles ob patrocinium sui muninis episcopo mansam ac dimidiam in Ticcanmersce gratuite dedit."

23. "Nam quidam dives, Turkillus nomine, sub Haroldi comitis testimonio et consultu, de se cum sua terra quae Kingestun dicitur, ecclesiae Abbendonensi sic agere erat, quatinus praedictae villae dominatio sub hujus ecclesiae perpetuo jure penderet." *Chronicon Monasterii de Abingdon,* ed. Joseph Stevenson, Rolls Series (1858; reprint Wiesbaden, 1964), 1:484.

24. *IE,* fol. 141. Cited by Edward Miller, *The Abbey and Bishopric of Ely* (1951; reprint Cambridge, 1969), p. 52. Note also other references given by Miller.

25. DB, i. 180b.

26. Æthelric Bigga appears also in KCD 773 (S 1471) (with his son Esbearn), KCD 789 (S 1473), and KCD 1327 (S 981). He was dead by 1066, for his son Esbearn is found holding in his place in Domesday Book T.R.E. See DB, i. 1, 2, 10b, 12, 13. An "Aluredus Biga" appears in DB, i. 9, 9b.

27. Wright and Wülcker, *Vocabularies,* 1:115 (Ælfric): *commodum, læn; precarium, landeslæn.*

28. KCD 1338 (S 1502). Bodsham (Green) was thegnland of St. Augustine's, Canterbury, in 1086. DB, i. 12b. According to Domesday Book it had been held T.R.E. "by a certain *villanus.*"

29. DB, i. 162b.

30. Evidence for this assertion can be found, paradoxically, in the leases issued by Bishop Oswald of Worcester in the second half of the tenth century. As Eric John has observed in *Land Tenure,* pp. 129–139, the drafter of these loans thought of them as a form of bookland, albeit bookland of limited duration. See the references collected by John to Oswald's use of the terms "bocath" and "bec" in these leases. Ibid., p. 130, n. 1.

31. W. J. Corbett, "The Development of the Duchy of Normandy and the Norman Conquest," *The Cambridge Medieval History,* ed. J. R. Tanner, C. W. Previte-Orton, and Z. N. Brooke (1926; reprint Cambridge, 1957), 5:509. Frank M. Stenton, "English Families and the Norman Conquest," *TRHS,* 4th Series, 26 (1944): 1–12.

32. Complaints about the usurpation of Church lands by Norman lords during the Conqueror's reign abound in the various medieval cartularies. Undoubtedly, the Normans, eager to claim their antecessors' lands even when the property was a dependent tenure held from a monastery, posed a very real threat to the religious houses. Perhaps we ought to attribute the Normans' lack of restraint in robbing the monasteries to their attitude toward the English saints. William I's appointee to the abbey of Abingdon, Athelelm, scandalized the native monks by ridiculing St. Æthelwold and St. Edward as "English rustics." *Abingdon,* ed. Stevenson, 2:238.

33. See, e.g., Maitland, *Domesday Book*, pp. 303–318; Stenton, *English Feudalism*, pp. 124–130; John, *Land Tenure*, pp. 80–167.

34. Sawyer, *List*, nos. 1297–1374 (excluding no. 1368, Oswald's famous memorandum). Only S 1341 (KCD 625) is dubious, and even this is thought by Finberg to have an authentic basis. Finberg, *Charters of the West Midlands*, no. 313.

35. This includes Eadric, the bishop's *compater*, who is called Oswald's *thegn* in the charter's English addendum. Robertson, *Charters*, no. 43 (BCS 1182 [S 1310]). Cf. the addenda to BCS 1088 (S 1300), 1181 (S 1311), 1207 (S 1316), 1208 (S 1314), all of which are addressed to Oswald's ministri.

36. This includes Oswulf, the bishop's kinsman, also termed his *cniht*. Robertson, *Charters*, no. 46 (BCS 1233 [S 1326]).

37. BCS 1091 (S 1298) is a grant in favor of Ælfwold, a king's minister. Cf. BCS 1229 (S 772); BCS 1234 (S 773).

38. The meaning of a "three-life" læn is made explicit in KCD 645 (S 1348). As Maitland observed, at the end of such a lease the tenure could be renewed for another three lives. *Domesday Book*, p. 310; John, *Land Tenure*, p. 137; Stenton, *ASE*, p. 485. Such tenures were known as the thegnlands of the Church. On thegnland, see Vinogradoff, *English Society*, pp. 370–372; Miller, *Ely*, pp. 50–53; R. Welldon Finn, *An Introduction to Domesday Book*, pp. 28–29, 138–140 (for thegnland in Domesday Book).

39. Stenton, *English Feudalism*, p. 126.

40. John, *Land Tenure*, p. 131.

41. Maitland, *Domesday Book*, pp. 305–306, abstracted from BCS 1136 (S 1368).

42. Although Stenton discussed the similarities between Oswald's tenants and the geneats of the *Rectitudines*, he failed to notice their similarity to the thegns of that document. *English Feudalism*, p. 125; idem, *ASE*, p. 486.

43. BCS 1136 (S 1368): "fidos mihi subditos telluribus quae meae traditae sunt potestati per spatium temporis trium hominum, id est duorum post se heredum, condarem."

44. Robertson, *Charters*, no. 67, p. 138: "minum holdan and getriowan thegn . . . for his eadmodre hersumnesse" [to my faithful and true thegn . . . for his humble obedience]; BCS 1242 (S 1323): "ministro meo . . . ob ejus fidele obsequium"; BCS 1299 (S 1335): "meo uni fideli . . . ob ejus fidele obsequium."

45. Robertson, *Charters*, no. 111, p. 208 (KCD 804 [S 1409]).

46. Ibid. Cf. KCD 773 (S 1473).

47. Stenton, *English Feudalism*, pp. 127–130.

48. Robertson, *Charters*, no. 111. Cf. Hollings, "Survival," p. 467; John, *Land Tenure*, p. 147.

49. As the term "archiductor" would suggest. See *ASC*, s.a. 1049 D and 1054 C for Ealdred, Bishop of Worcester (1046–1062), leading fyrds. By the reign of Edward the Confessor, however, the see of Worcester's military contingent was led by a tenant of the bishop, Eadric, who acted as his *ductor exercitus*. *Hemming's Cartulary*, ed. Hearne, 1:81.

50. DB, i. 172b.

51. DB, i. 172b; *Hemming's Cartulary*, ed. Hearne, 1:287–288. The Domesday *cartula* is translated along with the additions from Hemming in *VCH of Worcester*, 1:288.

52. DB, i. 173b. Cf. the reference to *rusticum opus* in the entry for Kempsey. DB, i. 173. "Rustic work" would have included the actual construction of bridges and the tending of deer-hedges. See DB, i. 269b (Lancashire, between Ribble and Mersey), where certain "thegns of the king" were required to build hunting lodges and tend hedges for their royal lord "just as if they were villagers" (*Faciebat per consuetudinem domos regis et qua ibi pertinebat sicut uillani*). Cf. the reference in the Wiltshire Domesday survey to the tenant of the Church of Wilton who served his landlord "as a thegn" (*seruiebat sicut tainus*). DB, i. 67b (Durnford, Wilts.), cited by Hollister, *Military Institutions*, pp. 79–80.

53. DB, i. 173 (Bushley, Worcs.). On him and his father, a prominent landholder in Gloucestershire, see Freeman, *Norman Conquest*, 4: 109–110, 517–519. References to Beorhtric's holdings in Domesday Book can be found in Olof von Feilitzen, "The Pre-Conquest Personal Names of Domesday Book," *Nomina Germanica*, 3 (1937): 197. He appears also to have been a prominent councillor of King Edward, witnessing many of his charters. See T. J. Oleson, *The Witenagemot in the Reign of Edward the Confessor* (London, 1955), p. 122.

54. DB, i. 172b (Kempsey, Worcs.). *Hemming's Cartulary*, ed. Hearne, 1:266.

55. DB, i. 173 (Bushley, Worcs.).

56. DB, i. 173 (Fladbury, Worcs.). Cf. the dues enumerated in Hemming's account of the 1077 plea between Worcester and Evesham. *Hemming's Cartulary*, ed. Hearne, 1:80; Adams, Lodge, et al., *Essays in Anglo-Saxon Law*, "Select Cases," no. 33, pp. 377–378. Cf. *Hemming's Cartulary*, ed. Hearne, 1:77 (on Hampton).

57. DB, i. 173 (Bushley, Worcs.).

58. DB, i. 173. Cf. Maitland, *Domesday Book*, p. 310. A practice akin to the later "wardship and marriage" may have been customary in the see of Worcester, for we find Bishop Oswald stipulating in a lease to "his kinsman" Gardulf that after him his widow would be permitted to hold of the bishop, providing that, if she were to remarry, she should marry a subject of the bishopric. KCD 637 (S 1345).

59. *Hemming's Cartulary*, ed. Hearne, 1:81: "Edricus, qui fuit, tempore regis Edwardi, stermannus navis episcopi, et ductor exercitus ad servitium regis." Cf. DB, i. 173b.

60. DB, i. 173b.

61. DB, i. 172b.

62. DB, i. 208. *Abingdon*, ed. Stevenson, 1:484.

63. *Liber Eliensis*, chap. 97, ed. Blake, p. 167. The story may be legendary, but Guthmund's holdings were not.

64. The early–thirteenth-century Abingdon Chronicle relates that the thegns who had held of the abbey T.R.E. had fallen in great numbers at

Hastings; they were replaced after the Conquest by Abbot Æthelhelm's milites. *Abingdon,* ed. Stevenson, 2:3. Similarly, Bury St. Edmunds's tenants played an active role at Hastings, and the abbey suffered for their participation in the battle, losing the thegnlands held by those men who "stood in battle against [William] and there were slain." Douglas, *Feudal Documents,* p. 47; trans. *EHD* II:464.

65. DB, i. 174.

66. *Hemming's Cartulary,* ed. Hearne, 1:264; Benjamin Thorpe, ed., *Diplomatarium Anglicum Aevi Saxonici* (London, 1865), pp. 450–451: "ut pro ea ipse ad expeditionem terra marique (quae tunc crebro agetur) monasterio serviret."

67. E.g., DB, i. 173 (Bushley, Worcs.). This is reminiscent of the distinction drawn in the Worcestershire customs between those who held their lands with soke and sake and those who did not.

68. See chapter 6.

69. Robertson, *Charters,* no. 111, p. 208.

70. DB, i. 87b.

71. Exeter Domesday, in Vol. III of the Record Commissioner's edition of Domesday Book (London, 1816), f. 162. Cited by Vinogradoff, *English Society,* p. 118, n. 3. The Exchequer and Exeter Domesday accounts of Taunton are translated in the *VCH* of Somerset, 1:422–444.

72. Robertson, *Charters,* Appendix I, no. 4, pp. 236–239. See Robertson's comments at pp. 485–490.

73. Ibid., p. 485.

74. Exeter DB, f. 162; DB, i. 87b: "et omnes illi [the preceding ten mentioned manors] debent ire in expeditionem cum hominibus episcopi."

75. Robertson, *Charters,* p. 238, translates this as "the bishop's tenant." She admits (p. 487) that she is somewhat puzzled by the use of this phrase in connection with Dunna, since the lands he held, Oake and Tolland, did not lie within the bounds of the manor of Taunton according to Domesday Book. Consequently, Robertson suggests that *biscopes mann* should be interpreted to mean "the man responsible to the bishop for the payment of the dues" or taken as an indication "of a closer connection between the estates concerned and the manor of Taunton in the time of King Edward than existed in 1066." Is it not more plausible to accept the charter on its face, and translate *biscopes mann* simply as "the bishop's man"? In this construction, the tenants of Taunton were connected to the bishop of Winchester both tenurially and through the acceptance of his lordship.

76. Ibid., p. 487.

77. Ibid.

78. Ibid., no. 72, p. 144. Cf. Robertson's notes on the text, pp. 389–392.

79. It is likely that the assessments on these lands had changed between the date at which this memorandum was drawn up and 1066. Furthermore, a number of the estates named, such as "Tollandune" and "Coddenham," cannot be satisfactorily identified. The 350 hides must therefore be viewed as a very rough figure.

80. DB, i. 127 (Stepney) and 128 (Islington).

81. DB, ii. 11 (St. Osyth) and 13 (Tillingham).

82. A number of these estates appear in Domesday Book as demesne or home farms of St. Paul's. But it is possible that they had been used as thegnland in the early eleventh century.

83. See chap. 7, n. 29.

84. *Hiredmen* appear in a number of Æthelred's and Cnut's laws. See I *Æthelred*, c. 1, § 10; VII *Æthelred* (Latin version), c. 1, § 3; VII *Æthelred* (Anglo-Saxon version), c. 5; II *Cnut*, caps. 31, 31a. II *Cnut*, c. 20 implies that all men were either householders (*sy he heorthfæst*) or the followers of such individuals (*se he folgere*). A number of late Anglo-Saxon glosses associate *clientelae* with service in a household. E.g., Wright and Wülcker, *Vocabularies*, 1:383; Napier, OE Glosses, §1, no. 2809. *Hlaford* is also glossed by *paterfamilias*. Wright and Wülcker, *Vocabularies*, 1:310; Napier, *OE Glosses*, §1, no. 3386. One should also note the eighty fully armed warriors given, along with a warship, to King Harthacnut by Earl Godwine in an attempt to win his favor. Florence of Worcester, *Chronicon*, ed. Thorpe, 1:195.

85. See chap. 7, nn. 2 , 3.

86. Whitelock, *Wills*, p. 127; Stenton, *English Feudalism*, pp. 134–135.

87. Stenton, *English Feudalism*, pp. 133–134.

88. E.g., *ASC*, s.a. 1083, 1086 (recte, 1087), 1087 (recte, 1088), 1124.

89. Stenton, *English Feudalism*, pp. 129–132, esp. p. 129, n. 1.

90. Ælfric provides an interesting portrait of one such robber band. See Ælfric, *Heptateuch*, ed. Crawford, pp. 62–68. Cf. *Vita Ædwardi*, ed. Barlow, p. 51.

91. *ASC*, s.a. 755 (recte, 757); *Vita Oswaldi*, ed. Raine, p. 449.

92. E.g., *Alfred*, c. 40, §1; II *Edmund*, c. 6; IV *Æthelred*, caps. 4, 4, §1; II *Cnut*, caps. 12, 15, 62, 64. Cf. Harmer, *Writs*, pp. 79–80 (note esp. the Domesday citation, DB i. 154b).

93. Robertson, *Charters*, no. 63, pp. 128–131.

94. See chap. 7, n. 52.

95. Florence of Worcester, 1:223, has "milites"; "C," "huscarlas"; and "D" and "E," "hiredmen." Plummer, *Saxon Chronicles*, 1:190–191. Cf. *Vita Ædwardi*, ed. Barlow, p. 50: *curia*.

96. *EHD* II:132; Plummer, *Saxon Chronicles*, 1:185.

97. Ibid.

98. L. M. Larson, *The King's Household in England Before the Norman Conquest* (Madison, Wis., 1904), p. 164, nn. 2, 3.

99. Thus Tostig's housecarls are found living in his residence at York. The term "housecarl" itself means a household man.

100. *Maldon*, ll. 204, 261.

101. *Maldon*, ll. 288–294, trans. R. K. Gordon, *Anglo-Saxon Poetry*, p. 334.

102. *Maldon*, ll. 255–259: "unorne ceorl." John's attempt to ennoble Dunhere goes beyond the evidence. *Orbis Britanniae*, p. 138. Nor is Hollister's explanation—that the ceorl was a warrior representative serving for a collection of peasant holdings—convincing, since Dunhere is described by the poet as Byrhtnoth's personal retainer. Hollister, *Military Institutions*, p. 63.

103. J.C.H.R. Steenstrup, *Normannerne* (Copenhagen, 1882), 4:146–154, cited in Larson, *Household*, pp. 153–171; Stenton, *English Feudalism*, pp. 120–122; Hollister, *Military Institutions*, pp. 12–15.

104. Steenstrup, *Normannerne*, 4:147; Larson, p. 153.

105. Stenton, *ASE*, pp. 382, 384, 401.

106. Gwyn Jones, *A History of the Vikings*, rev. ed. (Oxford, 1984), pp. 127–128.

107. Ibid., p. 127, n. 1.

108. Cited by Jones, ibid. See also pp. 9–10.

109. Sven Aggeson, *Lex castrensis sive curie*, in *Scriptores Minores Historiae Danicae medii aevi, ex Codicibus Denvo Recensuit*, ed. Martin C. Gertz, (Copenhagen, 1917), 1:65.

110. Saxo Grammaticus, *Danorum regum heroumque historia*. Books x–xvi, ed. and trans. (with commentary) Eric Christiansen, British Archaeological Reports, International Series, 84 (1980), 1:155; Nicholas Hooper, "The Housecarls in England in the Eleventh Century," *Anglo-Norman Studies* 7 (1985):161–176. I am grateful to Mr. Hooper for allowing me to read a copy of his stimulating and provocative article prior to publication.

111. Saxo, *Historia*, ed. Christiansen, 1:44.

112. *Northleoda laga*, c. 10. *EHD* I:469.

113. Sven, *Lex castrensis*, c. 5, ed. Gertz, *Scriptores*, 1:74–75. Cf. *ASC*, s.a. 1012. See Larson, Household, pp. 159–161.

114. Saxo, *Historia*, ed. Christiansen, 1:28; 201, n. 135.

115. Thorpe, *Diplomatarium*, p. 611; *EHD* I:604.

116. VI *Æthelstan* (Iudicia civitatis Lundoniae), c. 8, § 2; *EHD* I:425. Note also c. 7, which deals with blood feuds.

117. Robertson, *Laws*, p. 214. The clause implies that men fought either under their lords or beside their *geferan*, "associates." The term *geferan, ferscipe*, also denoted guilds. See Thorpe, *Diplomatarium*, p. 610. *Geferan* and *ferscipe* could mean a guild or some other fellowship. Cf. I *Cnut*, c. 5a, § 3, where *geferscipe* denotes a monastery.

118. Larson, *Household*, p. 153.

119. Foote and Wilson, *The Viking Achievement*, p. 100.

120. Gwyn Jones, *The Vikings*, p. 267.

121. Randsborg, *The Viking Age*, pp. 31, 37–44.

122. Larson, *Household*, pp. 157–158, 170–171.

123. Freeman, *Norman Conquest*, 1:445; Powicke, *Military Obligation*, pp. 4–5.

124. DB, i. 75.

125. Sven, *Lex castrensis*, c. 6., ed. Gertz, *Scriptores*, 1:74–75.

126. Asser, *Life of King Alfred*, caps. 100, 101, ed. Stevenson, pp. 86–87; Keynes and Lapidge, *Alfred the Great*, pp. 106–107.

127. Keynes and Lapidge, *Alfred the Great*, p. 177; Harmer, *Select Documents*, no. 11, p. 18.

128. See *EHD* I:339–340. Note that the scald Thorarin Loftunga claimed to have received fifty marks as a reward for his encomium to Cnut.

129. Florence of Worcester, *Chronicon*, ed. Thorpe, 1:204, where *solidarii*

seems to mean household troops. William of Malmesbury comments in a well-known passage that Harold's army at Hastings was composed largely of *stipendiarii et mercenarii milites*, and that few "provincial" troops (*ex provincialibus*) were present. *De gestis regum Anglorum,* ed. William Stubbs, Rolls Series (1887; reprint Wiesbaden, 1965), 1:182. This may be, however, merely a logical inference based on the "E" version of the Chronicle, which says that Harold did not wait for all of his troops to assemble before advancing. See also Florence of Worcester, *Chronicon,* ed. Thorpe, 1:127. Hooper suggests that William's remark was a tendentious attempt to underline Harold's lack of popular support. "Housecarls," p. 171. William of Malmesbury, however, never suggests that Duke William was popular among his new subjects. *De gestis,* 2:312–313.

130. Quoted in Foote and Wilson, *The Viking Achievement,* p. 104.

131. *Beowulf,* ll. 2490–2496, trans. Donaldson, p. 44.

132. The differences, if indeed there were any, between these three groups are obscure. Some have suggested that the housecarls were the king's land-based stipendiary warriors, the *lithsmen,* his sailors, and the *butsecarlas,* the garrison troops of the coastal boroughs. The term "sciplithendan" was also used in a more general sense to mean a sailor; it need not have carried martial connotations. See, e.g., "The Nativity of Mary the Virgin," l. 14, ed. B. Assmann, *Angelsächsische Homilien und Heiligenleben* (1889; reprint Darmstadt, 1964), p. 117: "*Sciplidendum monnum* know directions by the sea-stars." The evidence, however, is too fragile to support anything more than the most tentative hypothesis. *Lithsmen* are mentioned in the Chronicle, s.a. 1036 E, 1046 E (recte, 1048), 1047 E (recte, 1050), 1052 C, 1055 C, and 1066. *Butsecarlas* appears in the entries s.a. 1052 C and 1066, and in DB, i. 64b (Malmesbury). Cf. DB, i. 26 (Lewes)1: "men who guard the arms in the ships". Further discussion of the royal mercenaries of late Anglo-Saxon England is to be found in Vinogradoff, *English Society,* pp. 20–21; Hollister, *Military Institutions,* pp. 16–19. Hooper, "Housecarls," pp. 170–171, has drawn a useful distinction between retainers and mercenaries.

133. *ASC,* s.a. 1049 C, 1050 C. See Stenton, *ASE,* pp. 430–431.

134. Liebermann, ed., *Gesetze,* 1:396: "The he me healde, swa lc earnian wille."

135. Larson, *Household,* p. 164, n. 3, has collected the references to housecarls in Domesday Book. Cf. Harmer, *Writs,* no. 1, p. 120: "King Edward to his housecarl Urk."

136. DB, i. 56 (Wallingford). See Stenton, *ASE,* p. 582.

137. Stenton, *ASE,* p. 597. But cf. Hooper, "Housecarls," pp. 17–18.

138. Hollister, *Military Institutions,* p. 12; Stenton, *ASE,* pp. 582–583.

139. Florence of Worcester, *Chronicon,* ed. Thorpe, 1:195–196.

140. *ASC,* s.a. 1054 C, D. William Kapelle, *The Norman Conquest of the North: The Region and its Transformation 1000–1135* (Chapel Hill, N.C., 1979), pp. 46–47.

141. For housecarls as tax collectors, see *ASC,* s.a. 1041 C; Florence of Worcester, *Chronicon,* ed. Thorpe, 1:195. For witnesses to charters, see Robertson, *Charters,* no. 115, p. 214.

142. See, e.g., Harmer, *Writs,* no. 1, p. 120, a grant of privileges to King Edward's *huskarl* Urk. Cf. KCD 1318 (S 969), a diploma attested by Urk, minister of King Cnut, and KCD 772 (S 1004), addressed by the Confessor to *meo fideli ministro* Urk. See Harmer, *Writs,* p. 576.

143. DB, i. 146–147 (Shenley, Bucks.) Cf. Ulf, DB, i. 129 (Hanworth and Hillingdon, Mddlx.).

144. Larson, *Household,* p. 154. Sven described Cnut's company of housecarls as his *Thinglith. Lex castrensis,* c. 3, ed. Gertz, *Scriptores,* 1:67.

145. *ASC,* s.a. 1053 D, 1063 D, 1055; Florence of Worcester, *Chronicon,* ed. Thorpe, 1:212–214.

146. DB, i. 179. Twenty-seven burgesses who were Harold's men are mentioned immediately after the customs, with the comment that "they had the same customs as the other burgesses." It seems likely that we should consider these twenty-seven to be a group apart from the 103, who were most probably the king's men. Harold, who was the earl of the shire in 1065, is the only lord mentioned by name.

147. Ibid.

148. DB, i. 64b.

149. DB, i. 154.

150. DB, i. 100. For the size of Domesday boroughs T.R.E., see Carl Stephenson, *Borough and Town: A Study of Urban Origins in England* (Cambridge, Mass., 1933), p. 221; Darby, *Domesday England,* pp. 295–298, 302–309.

151. DB, i. 252.

152. Cf. DB, i. 172 (Worcestershire customs).

153. Cf. DB, i. 269b. Note also the resemblance to the "Geneat's law" in the *Rectitudines.*

154. DB, i. 179.

155. Ibid. Cf. DB, i. 262b (Chester): 10s. "relief" or king took property. Cf. also DB, i. 56b (Berkshire), for heriot of a "tainus uel miles regis dominicus," also the deceased's horse and arms.

156. Stenton, *ASE,* p. 573.

157. DB, i. 181 (in Archenfield). See Florence of Worcester, *Chronicon,* ed. Thorpe, 1:212–214.

158. DB, i. 179 (in Archenfield).

159. DB, i. 181 (in Archenfield): "In Arcenfelde habet Rex .C. homines, .IIII. minus, qui habent .LXXIII. carucas cum suis hominibus. . . . Nec dant geldum aut aliam consuetudinem, nisi quod pergunt in exercitu regis si jussum eis fuerit. Si liber homo ibi moritur, rex habet caballum ejus cum armis. De uillano cum moritur, habet rex .I. bouem."

160. See discussion in chap. 7, at n. 43.

161. *ASC,* s.a. 1055 C, 1063 D.

162. V *Æthelred,* c. 28; VI *Æthelred,* c. 35.

163. Hollister, *Military Institutions,* is the classic exposition.

164. *ASC,* s.a. 1015, 1016.

165. *ASC,* s.a. 1016: "for the fifth time he [Edmund] collected all the English nation [*ealla Engela theode*]." Plummer, *Saxon Chronicles,* 1:151.

166. *ASC*, s.a. 1016; *EHD* I:248; Plummer, *Saxon Chronicles*, 1:147.

167. DB, i. 179 (Hereford).

168. Richardson and Sayles, *The Governance of Medieval England*, pp. 51–52, make the same point. Bernard Bachrach, who accepts the existence of the "great fyrd," recently calculated that there were between 240,000 and 375,000 "free men between the ages of 15 and 54 upon whom Harold could call to help defend their homes against the Norman invaders." "Some Observations on the Military Administration of the Norman Conquest," *Anglo-Norman Studies* 8(1986):24–25. This calculation itself argues against the existence of any such levy.

169. *ASC*, s.a. 1006: "tha let se cyng abannan ut ealne theodscipe of Westseaxum and of Myrcean." Plummer, *Saxon Chronicles*, 1:136. *EHD* I:240.

170. Ibid. A similar distinction between fyrdmen and peasants is drawn by the anonymous author of the *Encomium Emmae Reginae*, chap. 7, ed. Campbell, pp. 22–23. Here we are told that Cnut ordered London to be besieged "because the chief men and part of the army had fled into it, and also a very great number of common people" (*quia in ea confugerant optimates et pars exercitus et maximum, ut est populosissima, uulgus*).

171. Cf. *ASC*, s.a 1003, 1006, 1015.

172. *ASC*, s.a. 1016; Florence of Worcester, *Chronicon*, ed. Thorpe, 1:147. The breakup of this fyrd probably had less to do with constitutional niceties than with political intrigue. Æthelred's absence must have seemed suspicious to the *heafodmen* of the fyrd, especially in light of the ætheling's recent quarrel with his father.

173. Hollister, *Military Institutions*, p. 30.

174. Ibid., p. 28.

175. DB, i. 100.

176. *ASC*, s.a. 1001; Florence of Worcester, *Chronicon*, ed. Thorpe, 1:154–155.

177. Douglas, *William the Conqueror*, p. 213.

178. *Bayeux Tapestry*, plates 66–67 and 73.

179. See chap. 7, n. 96.

A NOTE ON THE STRUCTURE AND
ORGANIZATION OF LATE ANGLO-SAXON
ARMIES

1. Hollister, *Military Institutions*, pp. 91–102; John, *Land Tenure*, pp. 115–116; *Orbis Britanniae*, pp. 142–146; Powicke, *Military Obligation*, pp. 6–16. See also Hodgkin, *Anglo-Saxons*, 2:590–598. Powicke's attempt to distinguish between the personnel of the royal/provincial fyrds and the county militias, pp. 14–15, is unconvincing. His contention that royal and provincial fyrds rode while county militias marched on foot fails to take into account *Maldon*, ll. 1–3. (Byrhtnoth's fyrd is even cited by Powicke as an example of a county levy.)

2. *ASC*, s.a. 1056 C, D.

3. For Siward's campaigns see Kapelle, *Conquest of the North*, pp. 42–46.

4. *ASC*, s.a. 1004. For Ulfkell's career see Stenton, *ASE*, pp. 380–383; Hart, *Early Charters of Northern England*, p. 363.

5. *ASC*, s.a. 1013.

6. *ASC*, s.a. 1016.

7. Uhtred's loyalty to Æthelred is emphasized in the post-Conquest Northumbrian tract "De obsessione Dunelmi," in *Symeonis Opera*, ed. Thomas Arnold, 1:215–220. The relevant portions are translated by Cyril Hart, *Early Charters of Northern England*, p. 148.

8. E.g., *ASC*, s.a. 992, 993 (three king's thegns), 1018, 1049, 1051, 1052, 1054, 1055, 1056, 1063, 1066.

9. *Wyrdwriteras*, ed. J. C. Pope, *Homilies of Ælfric: A Supplementary Collection*, Early English Text Society, 260 (London, 1968), 2:728–732, cited in Keynes, *Diplomas*, pp. 206–207.

10. *ASC*, s.a. 1041; Florence of Worcester, *Chronicon*, ed. Thorpe, 1:195–196.

11. Keynes, *Diplomas*, pp. 206–207.

12. The division of the fleet into royal ships (*cynges scipu*) and levy ships (*landes manna scipu*): *ASC*, s.a. 1046 E (recte, 1049). Cinque Ports: DB, i. 3 (Dover, Sandwich), 4b (Romney), on which see Hollister, *Military Institutions*, pp. 117–119. *ASC*, s.a. 1052 E suggests that all the ships in the royal fleet belonged to the Crown, and that both the commanders and oarsmen of ship-fyrds were rotated.

13. Hollister, *Military Institutions*, pp. 91–95, esp. 92, n. 1. Cf. Powicke, *Military Obligation*, pp. 11–12; Barlow, *Edward the Confessor*, p. 171.

14. Æthelweard, *Chronicle*, s.a. 800, cited by John, *Land Tenure*, p. 116. Hollister, *Military Institutions*, p. 95, n. 4, voices his suspicion that the hundred was a military unit, but leaves the question open. See also Hollister, *Military Organization*, pp. 36–40, for discussion and criticism of John's hypothesis.

15. E.g., *Ælfrics Grammatik und Glossar*, ed. Zupitza, "Grammar," p. 34, l. 14; "Glossary," c. 2, l. 110.

16. DB, i. 208 (Declaration of jurors of Huntingdonshire): "Testantur homines de comitatu quod Rex Edwardus dedit Suineshefet Siuuardo comiti soccam et sacam et sic habuit Haroldus comes, praeter quod geldabant in hundredo et in hostem cum eis ibant."

17. On the integration of the boroughs into the hundred system for the payment of geld and rendering of royal service, see Stephenson, *Borough and Town*, pp. 104–107, esp. p. 107.

18. Dannenbauer, "Hundertschaft, Centena, und Huntari"; John, *Orbis Britanniae*, p. 143. See also discussion in chap. 1.

19. DB, i. 206. Kimbolton and its members gelded for twenty hides, three virgates.

20. Cam, "The 'Private Hundred' in England before the Norman Conquest," in idem, *Law-Finders*, pp. 59–70. Cam's list is not comprehensive, and should be used only as a starting point.

21. DB, i. 163–163b (Tewkesbury, Gloucs.). It is interesting to observe that Beorhtric held one hide in Oswaldslow from the bishop of Worcester. DB, i. 173b.

22. DB, i. 163: "et erant quiete ab omni seruitio regali et geldo praeter seruitium ipsius domini cujus erat manerium." At the end of the inquisition of this manor and its appendages, the commissioners noted that all ninety-five hides were "exempt and free from geld and all royal service."

23. DB, i. 172 (Worcester customs). See discussion in chapter 6.

24. Kristensen, "Danelaw," pp. 45–85. Cf. Kapelle, *Conquest of the North,* pp. 79–85, for Northumbrian shires.

25. J. F. Verbruggen, *The Art of Warfare in Western Europe during the Middle Ages from the Eighth Century to 1340,* trans. S. Willard and S. C. M. Southern (Amsterdam, 1977), pp. 72–76.

Works Cited

PRIMARY SOURCES

Chronicles, Narratives, and Literary Sources

Abingdon. *Chronicon Monasterii de Abingdon.* Ed. Joseph Stevenson. 2 vols. Rolls Series, 2. London: Longman, Brown, Green, Longmans, & Roberts, 1858; reprint ed., Wiesbaden: Kraus Reprint, 1964.

Ælfric. *Ælfric's Colloquy.* Ed. G. N. Garmonsway. 2d ed. London: Methuen, 1947.

————. *Ælfrics Grammatik und Glossar.* Ed. J. Zupitza. Sammlung englischer Denkmäler I. Berlin: Weidmann, 1880; reprint ed., Berlin: Weidmann, 1966.

————. *Die Hirtenbriefe Ælfrics in Altenglischer und Lateinischer Fassung.* Ed. Bernhard Fehr. Bibliothek der Angelsachsischen Prosa, 9. Ed. C. Grein. Hamburg: H. Grand, 1914; reprint ed., Darmstadt: Wissenschaftliche Buchgesellschaft, 1966.

————. *Ælfric's Lives of Saints.* Ed. W. W. Skeat. Early English Text Society, Original Series, 76. London: Trübner, 1881; reprint ed., London: Oxford University Press, 1963.

————. *The Old English Version of the Heptateuch, Ælfric's Treatise on the Old and the New Testament and his Preface to Genesis.* Ed. S. J. Crawford. The Early English Text Society, 160. London: Oxford University Press, 1922; reprint ed., London: Oxford University Press, 1969.

————. *Homilies of Ælfric: A Supplementary Collection,* vol. 2. Early English Text Society, 260. London: Oxford University Press, 1978.

Æthelweard. *The Chronicle of Æthelweard.* Ed. Alistair Campbell. London: Thomas Nelson & Sons, 1962.

Alcuin. *Monumenta Alcuiniana.* Ed. W. Wattenbach and E. Dummler. *Bibliotheca Rerum Germanicarum,* vol. 6. Ed. P. Jaffe. Berlin: Weidmann, 1873; reprint ed., Darmstadt: Wissenschaftliche Buchgesellschaft, 1964.

Alfred. *King Alfred's Old English Version of Boethius' De Consolatione Philosophiae.* Ed. W. J. Sedgefield. Oxford: Clarendon Press, 1899; reprint ed., Darmstadt: Wissenschaftliche Buchgesellschaft, 1968.

————. *King Alfred's Old English Version of Saint Augustine's Soliloquies.* Ed. H. L. Hargrove. New York: H. Holt, 1902.

Andreas and the Fates of the Apostles. Ed. K. R. Brooks. Oxford: Clarendon Press, 1961.

Angelsächsische Homilien und Heiligenleben. Ed. B. Assmann. Kassel: G. H. Wigand, 1889; reprint ed., Darmstadt: Wissenschaftliche Buchgesellschaft, 1964.

Anglo-Saxon Chronicle. *Two of the Saxon Chronicles Parallel.* Ed. Charles Plummer. 2 vols. Oxford: Clarendon Press, 1892–1899; reprint ed., Oxford: Clarendon Press, 1952.

————. *The Anglo-Saxon Chronicle.* Trans. G. N. Garmonsway. Rev. ed. London: J. M. Dent & Sons, 1960.

————. *The Anglo-Saxon Chronicle: A Revised Translation.* Ed. and trans. Dorothy Whitelock, David C. Douglas, and S. I. Tucker. London: Eyre & Spottiswoode, 1965. Reprinted in *English Historical Documents* I (ca. 500–1042) and *English Historical Documents* II (1042–1154).

Anglo-Saxon Poetry. Trans. R. K. Gordon. London: J. M. Dent & Sons, 1926. Rev. ed. London: J. M. Dent & Sons, 1970.

Annales Bertiniani. Ed. Felix Giat, Jeanne Viellard, and Suzanne Clémencet. Paris: C. Klincksieck, 1964.

Annales Regni Francorum. Ed. F. Kurze. *MGH SS.* Hannover: Hahn, 1895.

Asser. *Asser's Life of King Alfred.* Ed. W. H. Stevenson. Oxford: Clarendon Press, 1904.

————. *Alfred The Great: Asser's "Life of King Alfred" and Other Contemporary Sources.* Trans. Simon Keynes and Michael Lapidge. Harmondsworth, Mddlx.: Penguin, 1983.

The Battle of Maldon. Ed. D. G. Scragg. Manchester: University of Manchester, 1981.

The Bayeux Tapestry: A Comprehensive Survey Ed. Frank M. Stenton. 2d ed. London: Phaidon Press, 1965.

The Bayeux Tapestry: The Complete Tapestry in Color with Introduction, Description and Commentary by David M. Wilson. Ed. David M. Wilson. New York: Alfred A. Knopf, 1985.

Bede. *Venerabilis Baedae Opera Historica.* Ed. Charles Plummer. 2 vols. Oxford: Clarendon Press, 1896.

————. *Bede's Ecclesiastical History of the English People.* Ed. and trans. B. Colgrave and R. A. B. Mynor. Oxford Medieval Texts, 1969; reprint ed., Oxford: Clarendon Press, 1972.

————. *The Old English Version of Bede's Ecclesiastical History.* Ed. Thomas Miller. Early English Text Society. 4 vols. Oxford: Clarendon Press, 1890–1898.

Beowulf. Ed. F. Klaeber. 3d ed. Lexington, Mass.: D. C. Heath, 1950.

————. *Beowulf and the Finnsberg Fragment.* Trans. John R. Clarke Hall. Rev. ed. C. L. Wrenn. London: Allen & Unwin, 1950.

————. *Beowulf: A New Prose Translation.* Trans. E. Talbot Donaldson. New York: W. W. Norton, 1966.

Boniface. *S. Bonifatii et Lulli Epistolae.* Ed. Michael Tangl. *MGH, Epistolae,* III. 2d ed. Berlin: Weidmann, 1955.

Eadmer. *The Life of St. Anselm of Canterbury.* Ed. R. W. Southern. Nelson's Medieval Texts. London, New York, and Edinburgh: Oxford University Press, 1962.

Encomium Emmae Reginae. Ed. Alistair Campbell. Camden 3d Series, 72. London: Royal Historical Society, 1949.

The Exeter Book. Ed. G. P. Krapp and E. V. K. Dobbin. New York: Columbia University Press, 1936.

Felix. *Felix's Life of St. Guthlac.* Ed. B. Colgrave. Cambridge: Cambridge University Press, 1956.

Florence of Worcester. *Chronicon ex Chronicis.* Ed. B. Thorpe. 2 vols. London: English Historical Society, 1848–1849.

Genesis A. In *The Junius Manuscript.* Ed. G. P. Krapp. New York: Columbia University Press, 1931.

Gildas. *De Excidio Britanniae: Gildas' The Ruin of Britain and Other Works.* Ed. and trans. Michael Winterbottom. London: Phillimore, 1978.

Gnomic Poetry in Anglo-Saxon. Ed. Blanche C. Williams. New York: Columbia University Press, 1914.

The Goddodin: The Oldest Scottish Poem. Trans. K. H. Jackson. Edinburgh: Edinburgh University Press, 1969.

Gregory of Tours. *Historia Francorum.* Ed. W. Arndt and Bruno Krusch, *MGH, Scriptores Rerum Merovingicarum,* I. Hannover: Hahn, 1885; reprint ed., Hannover: Hahn, 1961.

Hemming. *Hemingi Chartularium Ecclesiae Wigoriensis.* Ed. Thomas Hearne. 2 vols. Oxford, 1723.

Liber Eliensis. Ed. E. O. Blake. Camden 3d Series, 92. London: Royal Historical Society, 1962.

Nennius. *British History and the Welsh Annals.* Ed. and trans. John Morris. London: Phillimore, 1980.

Orderic Vitalis. *Historia Ecclesiastica.* Ed. Marjorie Chibnall. Oxford Medieval Society. 6 vols. Oxford: Clarendon Press, 1969–1981.

Orosius. *Old English Orosius.* Ed. Janet Bately. Early English Text Society. Supplemental Series, 6. London: Oxford University Press, 1980.

Saxo Grammaticus. *Danorum Regum Heroumque Historia,* vol. 1. Books x–xvi, ed. and trans. (with commentary) Eric Christiansen. British Archaeological Reports, International Series, 84. Oxford, 1980.

Sven Aggeson. *Lex Castrensis sive Curie.* Ed. Martin Gertz. *Scriptores Minores Historiae Medii Aevi, ex Codicibus Denvo recensuit,* vol. 1. Copenhagen: G. E. C. Gad, 1917. Pp. 64–93.

Symeon of Durham. *Symeonis Monachi Opera Omnia.* Ed. Thomas Arnold. Rolls Series, 75. 2 vols. London: Longman, 1882, 1885; reprint ed., Wiesbaden: Kraus Reprint, 1965.

Vegetius. *Epitoma Rei Militaris.* Ed. Karl Lang. Leipzig: Tuebner, 1885; reprint ed., Stuttgart: Tuebner, 1967.

Vita Aedwardi Regis. Life of King Edward. Ed. Frank Barlow. London: Thomas Nelson & Sons, 1962.

Vita Oswaldi, Archiepiscopi Eboracensis, Auctore Anonymo. Ed. James Raine. *Historians of the Church of York and its Archbishops,* vol. 1. Rolls Series. London: Longman, 1879; reprint ed., Wiesbaden: Kraus Reprint, 1965. Pp. 399–475.

Vita Sancti Cuthberti Auctore Anonymo and *Vita Sancti Cuthberti Auctore Beda.* Ed. B. Colgrave. *Two Lives of St. Cuthbert.* Cambridge: Cambridge University Press, 1940.

Vita Herluini. Ed. J. Armitage Robinson, in idem, *Gilbert Crispin, Abbot of Westminster.* Cambridge: Cambridge University Press, 1911.

Vita Wilfridi. Ed. B. Colgrave. *The Life of Bishop Wilfrid by Eddius Stephanus.*

Cambridge: Cambridge University Press, 1927; reprint ed., Cambridge: Cambridge University Press, 1985.

Vita Wulfstani. Ed. R. R. Darlington. Camden 3d Series, 40. London: Royal Historical Society, 1928.

The Wanderer. Ed. G. P. Krapp and E. V. K. Dobbin. *The Exeter Book.* New York: Columbia University Press, 1936.

Widsith. Ed. Kemp Malone. London: Methuen, 1935.

William of Jumièges. *Gesta Normannorum Ducum.* Ed. Jean Marx. Société de l'histoire de Normandie. Rouen: A. Lestringant, 1914.

William of Malmesbury. *De Gestis Pontificum Anglorum.* Ed. N. E. S. A. Hamilton. Rolls Series, 72. London: Longman, 1870; reprint ed., Wiesbaden: Kraus Reprint, 1964.

_____. *Gesta Regum Anglorum.* Ed. William Stubbs. Rolls Series, 90. 2 vols. London: Longman, 1887, 1889; reprint ed., Wiesbaden: Kraus Reprint, 1965.

_____. *Vita Wulfstani.* Ed. R. R. Darlington. Camden 3d Series, 40. London: Royal Historical Society, 1928.

William of Poitiers. *Gesta Guilelmi Ducis Normannorum et Regis Anglorum.* Ed. R. Foreville. Paris: Les Belles Lettres, 1952.

Wulfstan. *The Homilies of Wulfstan.* Ed. Dorothy Bethurum. Oxford: Clarendon Press, 1957.

_____. *Die "Institutes of Polity, Civil and Ecclesiastical."* Ed. Karl Jost. Bern: Francke, 1959.

_____. *The Institutes of Polity.* Trans. Michael Swanton. *Anglo-Saxon Prose.* London: J. M. Dent & Sons, 1975.

_____. *Sermo Lupi ad Anglos.* Ed. Dorothy Whitelock. 3d ed. Exeter: University of Exeter Press, 1977.

York. *Historians of the Church of York and its Archbishops.* Ed. James Raine. Rolls Series. 3 vols. London: Longman, 1879, 1886, 1894; reprint ed., Wiesbaden: Kraus Reprint, 1965.

Charters, Laws, and Collections of Documents

Attenborough, F. L., ed. and trans. *The Laws of the Earliest English Kings.* Cambridge: Cambridge University Press, 1922; reprint ed., New York: AMS Press, 1963.

Birch, Walter de Gray, ed. *Cartularium Saxonicum.* 3 vols. London: Whiting, 1885–1893; reprint ed., New York: Johnson Reprint, 1964.

_____. *Index Saxonicus.* London: Phillmore, 1899; reprint ed., New York: Johnson Reprint, 1964.

Boretius, A., ed. *Capitularia Regum Francorum,* vol. 1. *MGH, Leges,* 2. Hannover: Hahn, 1883.

Boretius, Alfred, and Victor Krause, eds. *Capitularia Regum Francorum,* vol. 2. *MGH, Leges,* 2. Hannover: Hahn, 1897.

Bridgeman, C. G. O., ed. *The Burton Abbey Twelfth-Century Surveys.* William Salt Archaeological Society. Collections for a History of Staffordshire. London: Harrison & Sons, 1916.

Campbell, Alistair, ed. *The Charters of Rochester*. London: Oxford University Press, 1973.

Downer, L. J., ed. and trans. *Leges Henrici Primi*. Oxford: Clarendon Press, 1972.

Douglas, David C., ed. *Feudal Documents from the Abbey of Bury St. Edmunds*. British Academy Records in Social and Economic History, 8. London: Oxford University Press, 1932.

Earle, John, ed. *A Hand-Book to the Land-Charters and Other Saxonic Documents*. Oxford: Clarendon Press, 1888.

Eckhardt, K. A., ed. *Lex Salica*. Weimar: H. Böhlaus, 1953.

English Historical Documents, vol. I (ca. 500–1042). Ed. and trans. Dorothy Whitelock. David C. Douglas, general ed. 2d ed. London: Eyre Methuen, 1979.

English Historical Documents, vol. II (ca. 1042–1189). Ed. and trans. David C. Douglas and G. W. Greenaway. David C. Douglas, general ed. 2d ed. London: Eyre Methuen, 1981.

Fauroux, M., ed. *Recueil des Actes des Ducs de Normandie de 911 à 1066*. Memoires de la Société des antiquaires de Normandie, 36. Caen: Société d'impressions Caron, 1961.

Finberg, H. P. R., ed. *The Early Charters of Wessex*. Leicester: Leicester University Press, 1964.

————. *The Early Charters of the West Midlands*. Leicester: Leicester University Press, 1961.

Galbraith, V. H., ed. "An Episcopal Land-Grant of 1085." *English Historical Review* 44 (1929): 353–372.

Haddan, Arthur W., and William Stubbs, eds. *Councils and Ecclesiastical Documents Relating to Great Britain and Ireland*, vol. 3. Oxford: Clarendon Press, 1871; reprint ed., Oxford: Clarendon Press, 1964.

Harmer, F. E., ed. and trans. *Select English Historical Documents of the Ninth and Tenth Centuries*. Cambridge: Cambridge University Press, 1914.

————, ed. and trans. *Anglo-Saxon Writs*. Manchester: Manchester University Press, 1952.

Hart, Cyril, ed. "The Early Charters of Thorney Abbey." *The Early Charters of Eastern England*. Leicester: Leicester University Press, 1966.

————. "The Tribal Hidage." *Transactions of the Royal Historical Society*, 5th Series, 21 (1971): 133–158.

Healey, Antonette DiPaolo, and Richard L. Venezky, compilers. *A Microfiche Concordance to Old English*. Toronto: University of Toronto Press, 1980.

Kemble, John M., ed. *Codex Diplomaticus Aevi Saxonici*. 6 vols. London: English Historical Society, 1839–1848.

King, Edmund, ed. "The Peterborough 'Descriptio Militum' (Henry I)." *English Historical Review* 84 (1969), text ed. at pp. 97–101.

Liebermann, Felix., ed. *Die Gesetze der Angelsachsen*. 3 vols. (vol. 1: texts). Halle: S. M. Niemeyer, 1903–1916.

Lindsay, W., ed. *The Corpus, Epinal, Erfurt and Leyden Glossaries*. London and New York: Oxford University Press, 1921.

Mommsen, Theodor, et al., eds. *Codex Theodosianus*. Berlin: Weidmann, 1905.

Mühlbacher, Engelbert, ed. *Diplomata Karolinorum. MGH.* Hannover: Hahn, 1906.

Napier, A. S., ed. *Old English Glosses.* Anecdota Oxoniensis, Mediaeval and Modern Series, 11. Oxford: Clarendon Press, 1900; reprint ed., Hildesheim: G. Olms, 1969.

Napier, A. S., and W. H. Stevenson, eds. *The Crawford Collection of Early Charters and Documents.* Oxford: Clarendon Press, 1895.

Rivers, Theodore John, ed. and trans. *Laws of the Alemans and Bavarians.* Philadelphia: University of Pennsylvania Press, 1977.

Robertson, A. J., ed. and trans. *Anglo-Saxon Charters.* 2d ed. Cambridge: Cambridge University Press, 1956.

————. *The Laws of the Kings of England from Edmund to Henry I.* Cambridge: Cambridge University Press, 1925; reprint ed., New York: AMS Press, 1974.

Scott, S. P., trans. *The Visigothic Code.* Boston: The Boston Book Co., 1910.

"Select Cases in Anglo-Saxon Law." *Essays in Anglo-Saxon Law.* Boston: Little, Brown, 1876; reprint ed., S. Hackensack, N.J.: Rothman, 1972. Pp. 309–383.

Thorpe, Benjamin, ed. and trans. *Diplomatarium Anglicum Aevi Saxonici.* London: Macmillan & Co., 1865.

Whitelock, Dorothy, ed. and trans. *Anglo-Saxon Wills.* Cambridge: Cambridge University Press, 1930.

Whitelock, Dorothy, Neil Ker, and Lord Rennell. *The Will of Æthelgifu.* Oxford: Oxford University Press for the Roxburghe Club, 1968.

Wright, T., and R. P. Wülcker, eds. *Anglo-Saxon and Old English Vocabularies,* vol. 1. London: Trübner, 1884.

Zeumer, K., ed. *Lex Visigothorum. MGH, Leges,* 1. Hannover: Hahn, 1902.

Domesday Book and Its Satellites

Domesday Book

Domesday Book, seu Liber Censualis Willelmi Primi Regis Angliae. Ed. Abraham Farley. 2 vols. Record Commission. London, 1783. Indices. London: G. Eyre & A. Strahan, 1811.

Domesday Book, or the Great Survey of England of William the Conqueror, A.D. *1086.* Zincograph Facsimiles. Southampton: Ordnance Survey Office, 1861–1863.

Domesday Book: A Survey of the Counties of England. General ed. and trans. John Morris. 34 vols. Chichester: Phillimore, 1975–present.

The Lincolnshire Domesday and the Lindsey Survey. Ed. and trans. C. W. Foster and T. Longley. Publications of the Lincoln Record Society, 19. Horncastle: W. K. Morton & Sons, 1924; reprint ed., 1976.

Domesday Book. Translated with commentaries in the *Victoria County Histories* (usually in the first volume for each county). Published in 1900 and succeeding years.

Satellites

Domesday Book, seu Liber Censualis Willelmi Primi Regis Angliae, vol. 3: Addimenta (Liber Exoniensis and Inquisitio Eliensis). Ed. Sir Henry Ellis. Record Commission. London: G. Eyre & A. Strahan, 1816.

Inquisitio Comitatus Cantabrigiensis; subjicitur Inquisitio Eliensis. Ed. N. E. S. A. Hamilton. London: John Murray, 1876.

―――. Trans. Jocelyn Otway-Ruthven. Victoria County History of Cambridgeshire, vol. 1. London: Oxford University Press, 1938. Pp. 400–427.

The Domesday Monachorum of Christ Church, Canterbury. Ed. David C. Douglas. London: Royal Historical Society, 1944.

SECONDARY AUTHORITIES

Abels, Richard P. "The Devolution of Bookland Tenure in Ninth-Century Kent: A Note on BCS 538." Archaeologia Cantiana 99 (1983): 219–300.

―――. "Bookland and Fyrd Service in Late Saxon England." Proceedings of the Battle Conference on Anglo-Norman Studies, vol. 7. Ed. R. Allen Brown. Woodbridge, Suffolk: Boydell Press, 1985. Pp. 1–25. (Hereafter cited as Anglo-Norman Studies with volume number and year of publication.)

Adams, Henry, Henry Cabot Lodge, et al. Essays in Anglo-Saxon Law. Boston: Little, Brown, 1876; reprint ed., S. Hackensack, N.J.: Rothman Reprints, 1972.

Alcock, Leslie. Arthur's Britain: History and Archaeology, A.D. 367–634. Harmondsworth, Mddlx.: Penguin, 1973.

―――. "By South Cadbury is that Camelot . . ." The Excavations of Cadbury Castle 1966–1970. London: Thames and Hudson, 1972.

Armitage Robinson, J. Gilbert Crispin, Abbot of Westminster. Cambridge: Cambridge University Press, 1911.

Aston, T. H. "The Origins of the Manor in England." Transactions of the Royal Historical Society, 5th Series, 8 (1956): 59–83.

Bachrach, Bernard S. Merovingian Military Organization, 481–751. Minneapolis: University of Minnesota Press, 1972.

―――. "The Angevin Strategy of Castle Building in the Reign of Fulk Nerra, 987–1040." American Historical Review 88 (1983): 541–560.

―――. "The Military Administration of the Norman Conquest." Anglo-Norman Studies 8 (1986): 1–25.

Ballard, A. The Domesday Inquest. London: Methuen, 1906.

Barlow, Frank. William I and the Norman Conquest. London: English Universities Press, 1966.

―――. Edward the Confessor. Berkeley and Los Angeles: University of California Press, 1970.

Barrow, G. W. S. The Kingdom of the Scots. New York: St. Martin's Press, 1973.

Beeler, John. "Castles and Strategy in Norman and Early Angevin England." Speculum 31 (1956): 581–601.

Beer, H. Führen und Folgen, Herrschen und Beherrschtwerden im Sprachgut der Angelsachsen. Breslau: Priebatsch, 1939.

Beresford, Guy. "Goltho Manor, Lincolnshire: The Buildings and their Surrounding Defenses." *Anglo-Norman Studies* 4 (1982): 13–36.

Berger, Adolf. *Encyclopedic Dictionary of Roman Law.* Philadelphia: American Philosophical Society, 1953.

Bethurum, Dorothy. "Six Anonymous Old English Codes." *Journal of English and Germanic Philology* 49 (1950): 449–463.

————. "Wulfstan." *Continuations and Beginnings.* Ed. E. G. Stanley. London: Thomas Nelson & Sons, 1966. Pp. 210–246.

Biddle, M. "Towns." *The Archaeology of Anglo-Saxon England.* Ed. D. M. Wilson. London: Methuen, 1976. Pp. 99–150.

Blake, N. F. "The Genesis of *The Battle of Maldon.*" *Anglo-Saxon England* 7 (1978): 119–129.

Blunt, C. E. "The Coinage of Offa." *Anglo-Saxon Coins.* Ed. R. H. Dolley. London: Methuen, 1961. Pp. 39–62.

Bond, P.S., Col., U.S.A. (ret.), ed. *Military Science and Tactics, A Text.* Officers' Training Corps (Senior Division: Infantry), Washington, D.C., 1938.

Bosl, Karl. *Frühformen der Gesellschaft im mittelalterlichen Europa.* Munich: R. Oldenbourg, 1964.

————. "Adel und Freiheit, Gefolgschaft und Herrschaft." *Gebhardts Handbuch der deutschen Geschichte.* Ed. H. Grundmann, 9th ed. Stuttgart: Union Verlag, 1970.

Bosworth, Joseph, and T. N. Toller. *An Anglo-Saxon Dictionary.* Oxford: Clarendon Press, 1898; reprint ed., Oxford: Clarendon Press, 1972.

Boyer, Marjorie. *Medieval French Bridges.* Cambridge, Mass.: Mediaeval Academy of America, 1976.

Brooks, Nicholas P. "Anglo-Saxon Charters: The Work of the Last Twenty Years." *Anglo-Saxon England* 3 (1974): 211–231.

————. "The Development of Military Obligations in Eighth- and Ninth-Century England." *England before the Conquest.* Ed. Peter Clemoes and Kathleen Hughes. Cambridge: Cambridge University Press, 1971. Pp. 69–84.

————. "Arms, Status and Warfare in Late-Saxon England." *Ethelred the Unready.* Ed. David Hill. British Archaeological Reports, British Series, 59 (1978): 81–103.

————. "Ninth-century England: the Crucible of Defeat." *Transactions of the Royal Historical Society,* 5th Series, 29 (1979): 1–20.

————. *The Early History of the Church of Canterbury.* Leicester: Leicester University Press, 1984.

Brooks, Nicholas P., and H. E. Walker. "The Authority and Interpretation of the Bayeux Tapestry." *Anglo-Norman Studies* 1 (1979): 1–34.

Brown, R. Allen. *The Normans and the Norman Conquest.* New York: Crowell, 1968.

————. *The Origins of English Feudalism.* New York: Barnes and Noble, 1973.

Brunner, H., and C. von Schwerin. *Deutsche Rechtsgeschichte.* 2d ed. Leipzig: Duncker & Humbolt, 1928.

Brunner, Otto. *Land und Herrschaft*. Darmstadt: Wissenschaftliche Buchgesellschaft, 1975.

Bumke, Joachim. *Studien zur Ritterbegriff im 12 und 13 Jahrhundert*. Heidelberg: Winter, 1964.

Cam, Helen. "The Evolution of the Medieval English Franchise." *Speculum* 32 (1957): 427–442. Reprint in idem, *Law-Finders and Law-Makers in Medieval England*. London: Merlin Press, 1962. Pp. 22–43.

———. "*Manerium cum Hundredo:* The Hundred and the Hundredal Manor." *English Historical Review* 47 (1932): 353–376. Reprint in idem, *Liberties and Communities in Medieval England*. Cambridge: Cambridge University Press, 1944. Pp. 64–90.

Campbell, A. *Old English Grammar*. Oxford: Clarendon Press, 1959.

Campbell, E. M. J. "Kent." *Domesday Geography of South-East England*, ed. H. C. Darby and E. M. J. Campbell. Cambridge: Cambridge University Press, 1964.

Campbell, James. "Observations on English Government from the Tenth to the Twelfth Century." *Transactions of the Royal Historical Society,* 5th Series, 25 (1975): 39–54.

Campbell, James, Eric John, and Patrick Wormald. *The Anglo-Saxons*. Ithaca, N.Y.: Cornell University Press, 1982.

Chadwick, H. Munro. *Studies in Anglo-Saxon Institutions*. Cambridge: Cambridge University Press, 1905.

———. *The Origin of the English Nation*. Cambridge: Cambridge University Press, 1907.

Charles-Edwards, T. M. "Kinship, Status and the Origins of the Hide." *Past and Present* 56 (1972): 3–33.

———. "The Distinction between Land and Moveable Wealth in Anglo-Saxon England." *Medieval Settlement*. Ed. P. H. Sawyer. London: Edward Arnold, 1976. Pp. 180–187.

Chase, Colin, ed. *The Dating of Beowulf*. Toronto: University of Toronto Press, 1981.

Chew, Helena M. *The English Ecclesiastical Tenants-in-Chief and Knight Service*. London: Oxford University Press, 1932.

Chibnall, Marjorie. "Mercenaries and the *Familia Regis* under Henry I." *History* 62 (1977): 15–23.

———. "Feudal Society in Orderic Vitalis." *Anglo-Norman Studies* 1 (1979): 35–48.

Clapham, J. H. "The Horsing of the Danes." *English Historical Review* 25 (1910): 287–293.

Clark, George. "*The Battle of Maldon:* A Heroic Poem." *Speculum* 43 (1968): 52–71.

Clemoes, Peter, ed. *The Anglo-Saxons: Studies in some Aspects of their History and Culture presented to Bruce Dickens*. London: Bowes & Bowes, 1959.

Clemoes, Peter, and Kathleen Hughes, eds. *England before the Conquest*. Cambridge: Cambridge University Press, 1971.

Conrad, Hermann. *Der Gedanke der allgemeinen Wehrpflicht in der deutschen*

Wehrverfassung des Mittelalters. Wehrrechtliche Abhandlungen, 4. Berlin: F. Vahlen, 1937.

Corbett, W. J. "The Development of the Duchy of Normandy and the Norman Conquest." *The Cambridge Medieval History,* vol. 5. Ed. J. R. Tanner, C. W. Previte-Orton, and Z. N. Brooke. Cambridge: Cambridge University Press, 1926; reprint ed., Cambridge: Cambridge University Press, 1957. Pp. 481–520.

Dannenbauer, H. "Die Freien im karolingischen Heer." *Aus Verfassungs- und Landesgeschichte. Festschrift für Th. Mayer,* vol. 1. Lindau and Konstanz: Jan Thorbecke, 1954. Pp. 49–64.

————. "Hunderschaft, Centena, und Huntari." *Historisches Jahrbuch* 69 (1949): 155–219.

Darby, H. C., ed. *Domesday Geography of Eastern England.* 3d ed. Cambridge: Cambridge University Press, 1971.

————. *Domesday England.* Cambridge: Cambridge University Press, 1977.

Darby, H. C., and E. M. J. Campbell, eds. *Domesday Geography of South-East England.* Cambridge: Cambridge University Press, 1962.

Darby, H. C., and R. Welldon Finn, eds. *Domesday Geography of South-West England.* Cambridge: Cambridge University Press, 1967.

Darlington, R. R., ed. "Introduction." *The Cartulary of Worcester Cathedral Priory.* Oxford: Clarendon Press, 1975.

————. "Introduction to the Wiltshire Domesday." *Victoria County History of Wiltshire,* vol. 2. London: Oxford University Press, 1955.

Davies, Wendy. *Wales in the Early Middle Ages.* Leicester: Leicester University Press, 1982.

Davies, Wendy, and H. Vierck. "The Contexts of Tribal Hidage: Social Aggregates and Settlement Patterns." *Frühmittelalterliche Studien* 8 (1974): 224–293.

Davis, R. H. C. "East Anglia and the Danelaw." *Transactions of the Royal Historical Society,* 5th Series, 5 (1955): 23–39.

————. *The Kalendar of Abbot Samson.* Camden 3d Series, 84. London: Royal Historical Society, 1955.

————. "Alfred the Great: Propaganda and Truth." *History* 56 (1971): 169–182.

Davison, B. K. "The Origins of the Castle in England." *Archaeological Journal* 114 (1967): 202–211.

Deloche, M. *La trustis et l'antrustion royal.* Paris: l'Imprimerie nationale, 1873.

Dempsey, George. "Legal Terminology in Anglo-Saxon England: The *Trinoda Necessitas* Charter." *Speculum* 57 (1982): 843–849.

Dodwell, Barbara. "East Anglian Commendation." *English Historical Review* 63 (1948): 289–306.

Douglas, David C. *The Social Structure of Medieval East Anglia.* Oxford Studies in Social and Legal History, 9. Ed. Paul Vinogradoff. Oxford: Clarendon Press, 1927.

————. "The Norman Conquest and English Feudalism," *Economic History Review* 9 (1939): 128–143. Reprint in idem, *Time and the Hour.* London: Eyre Methuen, 1977. Pp. 161–175.

———. *The Norman Conquest and British Historians.* Glasgow: Jackson, 1946. Reprint in idem, *Time and the Hour.* London: Eyre Methuen, 1977.

———. *William the Conqueror.* Berkeley and Los Angeles: University of California Press, 1964.

Dubuisson, Daniel. "L'Irlande et la théorie médiévale des 'trois ordres.'" *Revue de l'Histoire des Religions* 188 (1975): 35–63.

Duby, Georges. "The Origins of Knighthood." In idem, *The Chivalrous Society.* Trans. C. Postan. Berkeley, Los Angeles, London: University of California Press, 1977.

———. "The Origins of a System of Social Classification." In idem, *The Chivalrous Society.* Trans. C. Postan. Berkeley, Los Angeles, London: University of California Press, 1977.

Dumville, David. "Kingship, Genealogies, and Regnal Lists." *Early Medieval Kingship.* Ed. P. H. Sawyer and Ian Wood. Leeds: The Editors, 1977. Pp. 72–104.

———. "The Ætheling: A study in Anglo-Saxon Constitutional History." *Anglo-Saxon England* 8 (1979): 1–35.

———. "Alfred, Ine, Kindred, and Lordship." Paper presented at the American Historical Association Centennial Meeting. Chicago, December, 1984.

Ellis, Henry. *A General Introduction to Domesday Book, Accompanied by Indexes.* 2 vols. London: Eyre & Spottiswoode, 1833.

Engels, Donald. *Alexander the Great and the Logistics of the Macedonian Army.* Berkeley, Los Angeles, London: University of California Press, 1978.

Ennen, E., and W. Janssen. *Deutsche Agrargeschichte.* Wiesbaden: Steiner, 1979.

Eyton, R. W. *A Key to Domesday: The Dorset Survey.* London: Taylor, 1878.

Fehr, H. "Das Waffenrecht der Bauern im Mittelalter." *Zeitschrift der Savigny-Stiftung für Rechtsgeschichte (germanistische Abteilung)* 35 (1914): 118–146.

Feilitzen, Olof von. *The Pre-Conquest Personal Names of Domesday Book.* Nomina Germanica, 3. Uppsala: Almqvist & Wiskells boktryckeri -a. -b., 1937.

Finberg, H. P. R. "Some Early Gloucestershire Estates." In idem, ed., *Gloucestershire Studies.* Leicester: Leicester University Press, 1957.

———. *The Early Charters of the West Midlands.* Leicester: Leicester University Press, 1961.

———. *The Early Charters of Wessex.* Leicester: Leicester University Press, 1964.

———. *Lucerna. Studies of Some Problems in the Early History of England.* London: Macmillan & Co., 1964.

———. "Anglo-Saxon England to 1042." In idem, ed., *The Agrarian History of England and Wales,* vol. 1, bk. 2. Cambridge: Cambridge University Press, 1972.

Finn, R. Welldon. *Introduction to Domesday Book.* London: Longman, 1963.

———. *The Norman Conquest and its Effects on the Economy 1066–1086.* London: Longman, 1971.

Fleming, Robin. "Monastic Land and England's Defence in the Viking Age." *English Historical Review* 100 (1985): 247–265.

Foote, P. G., and D. M. Wilson. *The Viking Achievement.* London: Sidgwick & Jackson, 1970.

Forster, M. "Zur Geschichte des Reliquienskultus in Alt-England." *Sitzungsberichte der Bayerischen Akademie der Wissenschaften.* Philologische-Historische Abteilung, 8 (1943).

Fowler, G. Herbert. *Bedfordshire in 1086: An Analysis of Domesday Book.* Quarto Memoirs of the Bedfordshire Historical Society, 1. Aspley Guise: The Society, 1922.

Fox, Cyril. *Offa's Dyke.* London: Oxford University Press, 1955.

Freeman, Edward. *The History of the Norman Conquest of England.* 6 vols. 2d ed. Oxford: Clarendon Press, 1867–1879; reprint ed., New York: AMS Reprints, 1977.

Galbraith, V. H. "An Episcopal Land-Grant of 1085." *English Historical Review* 44 (1929): 353–372.

———. *The Making of Domesday Book.* Oxford: Clarendon Press, 1961.

———. "Who Wrote Asser's *Life of Alfred?*" In idem, *Introduction to the Study of History.* London: C. A. Watts, 1964.

———. *Domesday Book: Its Place in Administrative History.* Oxford: Clarendon Press, 1974.

Ganshof, F. L. *Frankish Institutions Under Charlemagne.* New York: W. W. Norton, 1968.

———. *The Carolingians and the Frankish Monarchy.* Trans. Janet Sondheim. Ithaca, N.Y.: Cornell University Press, 1971.

Gillingham, John. "The Introduction of Knight Service Into England." *Anglo-Norman Studies* 4 (1982): 53–64.

Gillmor, Carroll. "The Mobilization of a Work Force on the Fortified Bridges of the Seine, 862–888." Paper presented at the Third Annual Meeting of the Haskins Society, Houston, Texas, 10 November 1984.

Glover, Richard. "English Warfare in 1066." *English Historical Review* 67 (1952): 1–18.

Goebel, Julius. *Felony and Misdemeanour.* New York: Oxford University Press, 1937.

Green, D. H. *The Carolingian Lord.* Cambridge: Cambridge University Press, 1965.

Green, J. A. "The Last Century of Danegeld." *English Historical Review* 96 (1981): 245–252.

Grierson, P. "Commerce in the Dark Ages: A Critique of the Evidence." *Transactions of the Royal Historical Society,* 5th Series, 9 (1959): 123–140.

Grimm, Jacob, and Wilhelm Grimm. *Deutsches Worterbuch.* Leipzig: S. Hirzel, 1852; reprint ed., Leipzig: S. Hirzel, 1951.

Guilhiermoz, P. *Essai sur l'origine de la noblesse en France au moyen age.* Paris: A. Picard et fils, 1902.

Harrison, Kenneth. *The Framework of Anglo-Saxon History.* Cambridge: Cambridge University Press, 1976.

Hart, Cyril. *The Early Charters of Eastern England*. Leicester: Leicester University Press, 1966.

——. "Æthelstan Half-King and His Family." *Anglo-Saxon England* 2 (1973): 115–144.

——. *The Hidation of Northamptonshire*. Leicester: Leicester University Press, 1970.

——. "The Tribal Hidage." *Transactions of the Royal Historical Society*, 5th Series, 21 (1971): 133–157.

——. *The Hidation of Cambridgeshire*. Leicester: Leicester University Press, 1974.

——. *The Early Charters of Northern England and the Midlands*. Leicester: Leicester University Press, 1975.

Harvey, Sally. "The Knight and the Knight's Fee." *Past and Present* 49 (1970): 3–43. Reprint in R. H. Hilton, ed., *Peasants, Knights, and Heretics*. Cambridge: Cambridge University Press, 1976. Pp. 133–173.

——. "Domesday Book and its Predecessors." *English Historical Review* 86 (1971): 753–773.

——. "Domesday Book and Anglo-Norman Governance." *Transactions of the Royal Historical Society*, 5th Series, 25 (1975): 175–193.

——. "Recent Domesday Studies." *English Historical Review* 95 (1980): 121–133.

——. "Taxation and the Ploughland in Domesday Book." In Peter Sawyer, ed., *Domesday Book: A Reassessment*. London and Baltimore: Edward Arnold, 1985. Pp. 86–103.

Hassal, J. M., and David Hill. "Pont de l'Arche: Frankish Influence on the West Saxon Burh?" *Archaeological Journal* 127 (1970): 188–195.

Hazeltine, H. D. "On Anglo-Saxon Documents" (1931). In A. J. Robertson, ed., *Anglo-Saxon Charters*. Cambridge: Cambridge University Press, 1956.

Herlihy, David. "The Carolingian Mansus." *Economic History Review* 18 (1960): 79–89.

Hill, David. "The Burghal Hidage: The Establishment of a Text." *Medieval Archaeology* 13 (1969): 84–92.

——, ed. *Ethelred the Unready*. British Archaeological Reports, British Series, 59 (1978).

——. *An Atlas of Anglo-Saxon England*. Toronto: University of Toronto Press, 1981.

Hinton, David. *Alfred's Kingdom: Wessex and the South 800–1500*. London: J. M. Dent & Sons, 1977.

Hodges, Richard. "State Formation and the Role of Trade in Middle Saxon England." *Antiquaries Journal* 58 (1978): 539–553.

——. *Dark Age Economics: The Origins of Towns and Trade A.D. 600–1000*. New York: St. Martin's Press, 1982.

Hodgkin, R. H. *History of the Anglo-Saxons*. 3d ed. 2 vols. Oxford: Clarendon Press, 1953.

Holdsworth, Philip. "Saxon Southampton: A New Review." *Medieval Archaeology* 20 (1976): 26–61.

Hollings, Marjory. "The Survival of the Five-Hide Unit in the Western Midlands." *English Historical Review* 63 (1948): 453–487.

Hollister, C. Warren. "The Norman Conquest and the Genesis of English Feudalism." *American Historical Review* 66 (1961): 641–664.

―――. *Anglo-Saxon Military Institutions.* Oxford: Clarendon Press, 1962.

―――. *The Military Organization of Norman England.* Oxford: Clarendon Press, 1965.

―――. "Military Obligation in Late-Saxon and Norman England." *Ordinamenti Militari in Occidente Nell'Alto Medioevo.* Settimane di studio del Centro italiano di studi sull'alto medioevo, 15 (1968): 168–186.

Hollyman, K. J. *Le developpement du vocabulaire feodal en France pendant le haut moyen age.* Geneva and Paris: Droz, 1957.

Holt, J. C. "The Carta of Richard de la Haye, 1166: A Note on 'Continuity' in Anglo-Norman Feudalism." *English Historical Review* 84 (1969): 289–297.

Hooper, Nicholas. "Anglo-Saxon Warfare on the Eve of the Conquest: A Brief Survey." *Anglo-Norman Studies* 1 (1979): 84–93.

―――. "The Housecarls in England in the Eleventh Century." *Anglo-Norman Studies* 7 (1985): 161–176.

Hope-Taylor, B. *Yeavering.* Department of the Environment Archaeological Reports, 7. London, 1977.

Hoyt, R. S. *The Royal Demesne in English Constitutional History, 1066–1272.* Ithaca, N.Y.: Cornell University Press, 1950.

Hunter Blair, Peter. *An Introduction to Anglo-Saxon England.* 2d ed. Cambridge: Cambridge University Press, 1977.

Hurnard, N. D. "The Anglo-Norman Franchises." *English Historical Review* 64 (1949): 289–327, 433–460.

Irsigler, Franz. *Untersuchungen zur Geschichte des frühfrankischen Adels.* Rheinisches Archiv, 70 (1969). Partially trans. in *The Medieval Nobility.* Ed. Timothy Reuter. Amsterdam: North-Holland, 1978. Pp. 105–136.

James, Edward. "Merovingian Cemetery Studies and Some Implications for Anglo-Saxon England." *Anglo-Saxon Cemeteries 1979.* The Fourth Anglo-Saxon Symposium at Oxford. Ed. Philip Rahtz, Tania Dickinson, and Lorna Watts. British Archaeological Reports, British Series, 82 (1980): 35–55.

Jäschke, Kurt-Ulrich. *Burgenbau und Landesverteidigung um 900.* Überlegungen zu Beispielen aus Deutschland, Frankreich und England. Sigmaringen: Jan Thorbecke, 1975.

Jobert, P. *La notion de donation, convergences: 630–750.* Publications de l'Université de Dijon. Paris: Les Belles Lettres, 1977.

John, Eric. *Land Tenure in Early England.* Leicester: Leicester University Press, 1960.

―――. *Orbis Britanniae.* Leicester: Leicester University Press, 1966.

―――. "The Social and Political Problems of the Early English Church." *Agricultural Historical Review* 18 (1970). Supplement: *Land, Church, and People: Essays Presented to Professor H. P. R. Finberg.* Ed. Joan Thirsk. Leicester: Leicester University Press, 1970. Pp. 39–63.

———. *"Beowulf* and the Margins of Literacy." *The Bulletin of the John Rylands University Library of Manchester* 56 (1974): 388–422.

———. Review of H. Vollrath-Reichelt, *Königsgedanke.* In *English Historical Review* 89 (1974): 611–614.

———. "War and Society in the Tenth Century: The Maldon Campaign." *Transactions of the Royal Historical Society,* 5th Series, 27 (1977): 173–195.

Joliffe, J. E. A. *Pre-Feudal England: The Jutes.* London: Oxford University Press, 1933; reprint ed., London: F. Cass, 1962.

———. "English Book-right." *English Historical Review* 50 (1935): 1–21.

———. *The Constitutional History of Medieval England.* London: A. & C. Black, 1937.

———. "Northumbrian Institutions." *English Historical Review* 41 (1956): 1–42.

Jones, G. R. J. "Early Territorial Organization in Northern England." *The Fourth Viking Conference* (1965): 67–84.

———. "Multiple Estates and Early Settlement." *Medieval Settlement.* Ed. P. H. Sawyer. London: Edward Arnold, 1976. Pp. 15–40.

Jones, Gwyn. *A History of the Vikings.* Rev. ed., London and New York: Oxford University Press, 1984.

Jones, Michael. "The Logistics of the Anglo-Saxon Invasions." *Naval History: The Sixth Symposium of the U.S. Naval Academy.* Ed. Daniel Masterson. Wilmington, Delaware: Scholarly Resources, 1987. Pp. 62–69.

Jones, P. F. *A Concordance to the Historia Ecclesiastica of Bede.* Cambridge, Mass.: Mediaeval Academy of America, 1929.

Kapelle, William. *The Norman Conquest of the North: The Region and its Transformation 1000–1135.* Chapel Hill, N.C.: University of North Carolina, 1979.

Keefe, Thomas K. *Feudal Assessments and the Political Community under Henry II and His Sons.* Berkeley, Los Angeles, London: University of California Press, 1983.

Ker, N. R. "Hemming's Cartulary." *Studies in Medieval History Presented to Frederick Maurice Powicke.* Oxford: Clarendon Press, 1948; reprint ed., Oxford: Clarendon Press, 1969. Pp. 49–75.

Keynes, Simon. "The Declining Reputation of King Æthelred the Unready." In *Ethelred the Unready:* Papers from the Millenary Conference. Ed. David Hill. British Archaeological Reports, British Series, 59 (1978). Pp. 227–253.

———. *The Diplomas of King Æthelred the Unready 978–1016.* Cambridge: Cambridge University Press, 1980.

King, Edmund. "The Peterborough 'Descriptio Militum' (Henry I)." *English Historical Review* 84 (1969): 82–101.

Kirby, D. P. "Bede's Native Sources for the *Historia Ecclesiastica.*" *The Bulletin of the John Rylands University Library of Manchester* 48 (1966): 341–371.

Kristensen, A. K. G. "Danelaw Institutions and Danish Society in the Viking Age." *Mediaeval Scandinavia* 8 (1975): 27–85.

Kuhn, H. "Die Grenzen der germanischen Gefolgschaft." *Zeitschrift der Sa-*

vigny-Stiftung für Rechtsgeschichte (germanistische Abteilung) 73 (1955): 1–83.

Larson, L. M. *The King's Household in England before the Norman Conquest.* Madison, Wis.: University of Wisconsin Press, 1904.

Lawson, M. K. "The Collection of Danegeld and Heregeld in the Reigns of Æthelred II and Cnut." *English Historical Review* 99 (1984): 721–738.

Lennard, Reginald. "The Hidation of 'Demesne' in Some Domesday Entries." Economic History Review, 2d Series, 7 (1954).

———. *Rural England, 1086–1135: A Study of Social and Agrarian Conditions.* Oxford: Clarendon Press, 1959.

Lepelley, R. "Contribution a l'étude des inscriptions de la Tapisserie de Bayeux." *Annales de Normandie* 14 (1964): 313–341.

Levison, Wilhelm. *England and the Continent in the Eighth Century.* Oxford: Clarendon Press, 1946.

Levy, Ernst. *West Roman Vulgar Law.* Memoirs of the American Philosophical Society, 29. Philadelphia: American Philosophical Society, 1951.

Leyser, K. J. "Henry I and the Beginning of the Saxon Empire." *English Historical Review* 83 (1982): 1–32. Reprint in idem, *Medieval Germany and its Neighbors, 900–1250.* London: Hambledon Press, 1982.

Little, A. G. "Gesiths and Thegns." *English Historical Review* 4 (1889): 723–729.

Lodge, H. Cabot. "Anglo-Saxon Land Law." *Essays in Anglo-Saxon Law.* Boston: Little, Brown, 1876; reprint ed., S. Hackensack, N.J.: Rothman Reprints, 1972. Pp. 55–119.

Lot, Ferdinand. *Recueil des Travaux Historiques de Ferdinand Lot.* Geneva: Droz, 1970.

Loyn, H. R. "Gesiths and Thegns in Anglo-Saxon England from the Seventh to the Tenth Century." *English Historical Review* 70 (1955): 529–549.

———. *Anglo-Saxon England and the Norman Conquest.* London: Longman, 1962.

———. "Towns in Late Anglo-Saxon England." *England before the Conquest.* Ed. Peter Clemoes and Kathleen Hughes. Cambridge: Cambridge University Press, 1971. Pp. 115–128.

———. "Kinship in Anglo-Saxon England." *Anglo-Saxon England* 3 (1974): 197–209.

———. "The Hundred in the Tenth and Early Eleventh Centuries." *British Government and Administration.* Ed. H. R. Loyn and H. Hearder. Cardiff: University of Wales Press, 1974. Pp. 1–15.

———. "Church and State in England in the Tenth and Eleventh Centuries." *Tenth-Century Studies.* Ed. David Parsons. London: Phillimore, 1975. Pp. 94–102.

———. "Domesday Book." *Anglo-Norman Studies* 1 (1979): 121–130.

———. *The Governance of Anglo-Saxon England, 500–1087.* Stanford, Calif.: Stanford University Press, 1984.

———. "A General Introduction to Domesday Book." *The 1986 Domesday Book Facsimile: Academic Edition.* London: Alecto, 1986.

Luttwak, Edward. *The Grand Strategy of the Roman Empire*. Baltimore: Johns Hopkins University Press, 1976.

Lyon, Bruce. *From Fief to Indenture*. Cambridge, Mass.: Harvard University Press, 1957.

Lyon, C. S. S. "Some Problems in Interpreting Anglo-Saxon Coinage." *Anglo-Saxon England 5* (1976): 173–224.

Mack, Katharin. " Kings and Thegns in the Unification of Anglo-Saxon England." Paper presented at the Twentieth International Congress on Medieval Studies, Western Michigan University, 11 May 1985.

Maitland, F. W. *Domesday Book and Beyond*. Cambridge: Cambridge University Press, 1897; reprint ed., New York: W. W. Norton, 1966.

Malinowski, Bonislaw. *Argonauts of the Western Pacific*. London: Routledge, 1922; reprint ed., London: Routledge and Kegan Paul, 1950.

Matthew, D. J. A. *The Norman Conquest*. London: Batsford, 1966.

Mauss, Marcel. *The Gift; Forms and Functions of Exchange in Archaic Societies*. 1925. Trans. I Cunnison. Glencoe, Ill.: Free Press, 1954.

Mayer, Theodor. "Die entstehung des 'modernen' Staates im Mittelalter und die Freien Bauern." *Zeitschrift der Savigny-Stiftung für Rechtsgeschichte (germanistische Abteilung)* 57 (1937): 210–288.

————. *Mittelalterliche Studien*. Darmstadt: Wissenschaftliche Buchgesellschaft, 1963.

McDonald, John, and G. D. Snooks. "The Determinants of Manorial Income in Domesday England: Evidence From Essex." *Journal of Economic History* 45 (1985): 541–556.

————. "How Artificial Were the Tax Assessments of Domesday England? The Case of Essex." *Economic History Review,* 2d Series, 38 (1985): 352–372.

————. *Domesday Economy: A New Approach to Anglo-Norman History*. Oxford: Clarendon Press, 1986.

McGovern, John P. "The Meaning of 'Gesette Land' in Anglo-Saxon Land Tenure." *Speculum* 46 (1971): 589–596.

————. "The Hide and Related Land-Tenure Concepts in Anglo-Saxon England, A.D. 700–1100." *Traditio* 28 (1972): 101–118.

McKinnell, J. C. "On the Date of the Battle of Maldon." *Medium Aevum* 44 (1975): 121–136.

Miller, Edward. *The Abbey and Bishopric of Ely*. Cambridge: Cambridge University Press, 1951; reprint ed., Cambridge University Press, 1969.

Mitteis, Heinrich. *Lehnrecht und Staatsgewalt*. Weimar: H. Böhlaus, 1933.

Morris, John. *The Age of Arthur; A History of the British Isles from 350 to 650*. New York: Scribner's, 1973.

————. "Appendix on Hidage." In idem, ed., *Domesday Book,* vol. 2: *Sussex*. London: Phillimore, 1976.

Morris, W. A. *The English Medieval Sheriff to 1300*. Manchester: Manchester University Press, 1927.

Nehlsen, Hermann. "Aktualität und Effektivität der ältesten germanischen Rechtsaufzeichnungen." *Recht und Schrift im Mittelalter*. Ed. Peter Classen.

Vörtrage und Forschungen, 23. Sigmaringen: Jan Thorbecke, 1977. Pp. 449–502.

Nelson, Janet. "Inauguration Rituals." *Early Medieval Kingship.* Ed. P. H. Sawyer and Ian Wood. Leeds: The Editors, 1977. Pp. 50–71.

———. "The Church's Military Service in the Ninth Century: A Contemporary View?" *Studies in Church History* 20(1983): 15–30.

Nesbitt, John. "The Rate of March in Crusading Armies in Europe." *Traditio* 19 (1963): 167–181.

Noble, Frank. *Offa's Dyke Reviewed.* Ed. Margaret Gelling. British Archaeological Reports, British Series, 114 (1983).

Odegaard, C. E. "The Concept of Royal Power in Carolingian Oaths of Fidelity." *Speculum* 20 (1945): 279–289.

Oleson, T. J. *The Witenagemot in the Reign of Edward the Confessor.* London: Oxford University Press, 1955.

Page, R. I. *Life in Anglo-Saxon England.* London: Batsford, 1970.

Parsons, David, ed. *Tenth-Century Studies: Essays in Commemoration of the Millennium of the Council of Winchester and "Regularis Concordia."* London: Phillimore, 1975.

Pearson, Michael Parker. "Economic and Ideological Change: Cyclical Growth in the Pre-State Societies of Jutland." *Ideology, Power and Prehistory.* Ed. Daniel Miller and Christopher Tilley. Cambridge: Cambridge University Press, 1984. Pp. 69–90.

Pollock, Frederick, and F. W. Maitland. *The History of English Law Before the Time of Edward I.* 2d ed. Cambridge: Cambridge University Press, 1898; reprint ed., Cambridge: Cambridge University Press, 1968.

Potts, W. T. W. "History and Blood Groups in the British Isles." *Medieval Settlement.* Ed. P. H. Sawyer. London: Edward Arnold, 1976. Pp. 236–253.

Powell, H. A. "Competitive Leadership in Trobriand Political Organization." *Journal of the Royal Anthropological Institute* 90 (1960): 118–145.

Powicke, Michael. *Military Obligation in Medieval England.* Oxford: Clarendon Press, 1962.

Prestwich, J. O. "The Military Household of the Norman Kings." *English Historical Review* 96 (1981): 1–35.

———. "War and Finance in the Anglo-Norman State." *Transactions of the Royal Historical Society,* 5th Series, 4 (1954): 19–44.

Radford, C. A. R. "The Later Pre-Conquest Boroughs and Their Defenses." *Medieval Archaeology* 14 (1970): 83–103.

Radley, J. "Excavations in the Defences of the City of York: An Early Medieval Stone Tower and Successive Earth Ramparts." *Yorkshire Archaeological Journal* 44 (1972): 38–64.

Ramsay, J. H. *The Foundations of England.* 2 vols. London: S. Sonnenschein, 1898.

Randsborg, Klavs. *The Viking Age in Denmark: The Formation of a State.* New York: St. Martin's Press, 1980.

Reuter, Timothy, ed. *The Medieval Nobility.* Europe in the Middle Ages: Selected Studies, 14. Amsterdam: North-Holland, 1978.

Richardson, H. G., and G. O. Sayles. *The Governance of Medieval England from the Conquest to Magna Carta.* Edinburgh: Edinburgh University Press, 1963.

———. *Law and Legislation in England, from Æthelberht to Magna Carta.* Edinburgh: Edinburgh University Press, 1964.

Roper, Michael. "Wilfrid's Landholdings in Northumbria." *Saint Wilfrid at Hexham.* Ed. D. P. Kirby. Newcastle-upon-Tyne: Oriel Press, 1974. Pp. 61–79.

Round, John Horace. *Feudal England.* London: S. Sonnenschein, 1895; reprint ed., New York: Allen & Unwin, 1964.

———. "The Domesday Hidation of Essex." *English Historical Review* 29 (1914): 61–79.

Runciman, W. G. "Accelerating Social Mobility: The Case of Anglo-Saxon England." *Past and Present* 104 (1984): 1–12.

Sahlins, Marshall. "On the Sociology of Primitive Exchange." *The Relevance of Models for Social Anthropology.* Ed. M. Banton. A.S.A. Monographs, 1. London, 1965. Reprint in *Stone Age Economics.* Chicago: Aldine-Atherton, 1972. Pp. 85–275 (relevant pp. 149–183).

Samouce, William. "General Byrhtnoth." *Journal of English and Germanic Philology* 62 (1963): 129–135.

Sawyer, P. H. *The Age of the Vikings.* 2d ed. London: Edward Arnold, 1971.

———. "Charters of the Reform Movement: The Worcester Archive." *Tenth-Century Studies.* Ed. David Parsons. London: Phillimore, 1975. Pp. 84–93.

———. "Kings and Merchants." *Early Medieval Kingship.* Ed. P. H. Sawyer and Ian Wood. Leeds: The Editors, 1977. Pp. 139–158.

———. *From Roman Britain to Norman England.* London: Methuen, 1978.

———. "The Royal Tun in Pre-Conquest England." *Ideal and Reality in Frankish and Anglo-Saxon Society; Studies Presented to J. M. Wallace-Hadrill.* Ed. P. Wormald, D. Bullough, and R. Collins. Oxford: Basil Blackwell, 1983.

Schrabram, H. "Bezeichungen für 'Bauer' im Altenenglischen." *Wort und Begriff "Bauer."* Ed. R. Wenksus, H. Jankuhn, and K. Grinda. Abhandlungen der Akademie der Wissenschaften in Göttingen, Philologisch-Historische Klasse, 3d Series, 89 (1975): 79–85.

Schlesinger, W. "Herrschaft und Gefolgschaft in der germanisch-deutschen Verfassungsgeschichte." *Historische Zeitschrift* 176 (1953): 225–275. Trans. and reprint in *Lordship and Community in Medieval Europe.* Ed. Frederic Cheyette. New York: Krieger, 1975. Pp. 64–99.

Schlesinger, W., and J. Werner. "Über den Adel in Frankenreich." *Siedlung, Sprache und Bevölkerungsstruktur im Frankenreich.* Ed. F. Petri. Darmstadt: Wissenschaftliche Buchgesellschaft, 1973. Pp. 175–185.

Schulze, H. "Rodungsfreiheit und Königsfreiheit." *Historische Zeitschrift* 219 (1974): 529–550.

Seebohm, Frederic. *The English Village Community.* 4th ed. London and New York: Longmans, Green, 1890.

Service, Elman. "Kinship Terminology and Evolution." *American Anthropologist* 62 (1960): 747–762.

Sisam, K. "Anglo-Saxon Royal Genealogies." *Proceedings of the British Academy* 39 (1953): 287–343.

Smyth, Alfred P. *Scandinavian Kings in the British Isles, 850–880.* Oxford and New York: Oxford University Press, 1977.

Staab, Franz. "A Reconsideration of the Ancestry of Modern Political Liberty: The Problem of the So Called 'King's Freemen.' " *Viator* 11 (1980): 57–69.

Stafford, P. A. "The Reign of Æthelred II: A Study of the Limitations on Royal Policy and Actions." *Ethelred the Unready.* Ed. David Hill. British Archaeological Reports, British Series, 59 (1978): 15–37.

Steenstrup, J.C.H.R. *Normannerne,* vol. 4: *Danelag.* Copenhagen: R. Klein, 1882.

Stenton, Frank M. *William the Conqueror.* New York and London: G. P. Putnam's Sons, 1908.

————. *Types of Manorial Structure in the Northern Danelaw.* Oxford Studies in Social and Legal History, 2. Oxford: Clarendon Press, 1910.

————. "The Supremacy of the Mercian Kings." *English Historical Review* 33 (1918): 433–452.

————. "English Families and the Norman Conquest." *Transactions of the Royal Historical Society,* 4th Series, 26 (1944): 1–12.

————. *The Latin Charters of the Anglo-Saxon Period.* Oxford: Clarendon Press, 1955.

————. *The First Century of English Feudalism, 1066–1166.* 2d ed. Oxford: Clarendon Press, 1961.

————, ed. *The Bayeux Tapestry.* 2d ed. London: Phaidon Press, 1965.

————. *Preparatory to Anglo-Saxon England, Being the Collected Papers of Frank Merry Stenton.* Ed. Doris M. Stenton. Oxford: Clarendon Press, 1970.

————. *Anglo-Saxon England.* 3d ed. Oxford: Clarendon Press, 1971.

Stephenson, Carl. *Medieval Institutions.* Ed. Bruce Lyons. Ithaca, N.Y.: Cornell University Press, 1954.

————. *Borough and Town: A Study of Urban Origins in England.* Cambridge, Mass: Mediaeval Academy of America, 1933.

Stevenson, W. H. "Trinoda Necessitas." *English Historical Review* 29 (1914): 689–702.

Swanton, M. J. *The Spearheads of the Anglo-Saxon Settlements.* London: Royal Archaeological Institute, 1973.

Tabuteau, Emily. "Transfers of Property in Eleventh-Century Norman Law." Ph.D. dissertation, Harvard University, 1975.

————. "Definitions of Feudal Military Obligations in Eleventh-Century Normandy." In *On the Laws and Customs of England: Essays in Honor of Samuel E. Thorne.* Ed. Morris S. Arnold et al. Chapel Hill, N.C.: University of North Carolina, 1981.

Tait, James. "Large Hides and Small Hides." *English Historical Review* 17 (1902): 280–282.

————. *The English Medieval Borough.* Manchester: Manchester University Press, 1936.

Taylor, Charles S. "The Origins of the Mercian Shires." *Gloucestershire Studies.*

Ed. H. P. R. Finberg. Leicester: Leicester University Press, 1957. Pp. 17–51.

Taylor, Christopher. *Village and Farmstead: A History of Rural Settlement in England*. London: George Phillip, 1983.

Toller, T. N. *An Anglo-Saxon Dictionary: Supplement*. Oxford: Clarendon Press, 1921; reprint ed., Oxford: Clarendon Press, 1972.

Turk, M. H. *The Legal Code of Ælfred the Great*. Halle: E. Karras, 1893; reprint ed., New York: AMS Press, 1973.

Vercauteren, Fernand. "Comment s'est-on défendu an IXe siècle dans l'empire franc contre les invasions normandes?" In *Etudes d'histoire medievale. Recueil d'articles du Professeur Vercauteren publiés par le Crédit Communal du Belgique*. Brussels, 1978. Pp. 39–54.

Vinogradoff, Paul. "Folkright." *English Historical Review* 8 (1898): 1–17.

———. *English Society in the Eleventh Century*. Oxford: Clarendon Press, 1908.

———. *The Growth of the Manor*. London: Allen & Unwin, 1911.

Vollrath-Reichelt, Hanna. *Königsgedanke und Königtum bei den Angelsachsen bis zur mitte des 9 Jahrhunderts*. Cologne: Böhlau Verlag, 1971.

Wainright, F. T. "Æthelflæd Lady of the Mercians." *The Anglo-Saxons*. Ed. Peter Clemoes. London: Bowes & Bowes, 1959. Pp. 53–69.

Waitz, G. *Deutsche Verfassungsgeschichte*, vol. 2, pt. 2. 3d ed. Berlin: Weidmann, 1882.

Wallace-Hadrill, J. M. *The Long-Haired Kings*. London: Methuen, 1962; reprint ed., Toronto: University of Toronto Press, 1982.

———. *Early Germanic Kingship in England and on the Continent*. Oxford: Clarendon Press, 1971.

———. "War and Peace in the Earlier Middle Ages." *Transactions of the Royal Historical Society*, 5th Series, 25 (1975): 157–174.

Whitelock, Dorothy. "Wulfstan and the Laws of Cnut." *English Historical Review* 63 (1948): 533–552.

———. *The Audience of Beowulf*. Oxford: Clarendon Press, 1951.

———. "Wulfstan's Authorship of Cnut's Laws." *English Historical Review* 69 (1954): 72–85.

———. "Forward." *Liber Eliensis*. Ed. E. O. Blake. Camden 3d Series, 72. London: Royal Historical Society, 1962. Pp. ix–xviii.

———. *The Genuine Asser*. The Stenton Lectures, University of Reading, 1968.

———. *The Beginnings of English Society*. Rev. ed. Baltimore, Md.: Penguin, 1977.

Williams, Ann. "Some Notes and Considerations on Problems Connected with the English Royal Succession." *Anglo-Norman Studies* 1 (1979): 144–167.

———. "*Princeps Merciorum Gentis:* The Family, Career and Connections of Ælfhere, Ealdorman of Mercia, 956–983." *Anglo-Saxon England* 10 (1982): 143–172.

Wilson, D. M. *The Anglo-Saxons*. 2d ed. Harmondsworth, Mddlx.: Penguin, 1971.

———. "Introduction." *The Archaeology of Anglo-Saxon England*. Ed. D. M. Wilson. London: Methuen, 1976.

Witney, K. P. *The Kingdom of Kent.* London: Phillimore, 1982.

Wolf, Eric R. *Peasants.* Englewood Cliffs, N.J.: Prentice-Hall, 1966.

Woolf, R. "The Ideal of Men Dying with their Lords in the 'Germania' and the 'Battle of Maldon.' " *Anglo-Saxon England 5* (1976): 69–81.

Wormald, Francis. "Style and Design." *The Bayeux Tapestry.* Ed. Frank M. Stenton. London: Phaidon Press, 1965. Pp. 25–36.

Wormald, Patrick. *"Lex Scripta* and *Verbum Regis:* Legislation and Germanic Kingship from Euric to Cnut." *Early Medieval Kingship.* Ed. P. H. Sawyer and Ian Wood. Leeds: The Editors, 1977. Pp. 105–138.

————. "Æthelred the Lawmaker." *Ethelred the Unready.* Ed. David Hill. British Archaeological Reports, British Series, 59 (1978). Pp. 47–80.

————. "Bede, *Beowulf* and the Conversion of the Anglo-Saxon Aristocracy." *Bede and Anglo-Saxon England: Papers in Honor of the 1300th Anniversary of the Birth of Bede.* Ed. R. T. Farrell. British Archaeological Reports, British Series, 46 (1978): 32–95.

————. "Bretwaldas and the Origins of the *Gens Anglorum.*" In *Ideal and Reality in Frankish and Anglo-Saxon Society; Studies Presented to J. M. Wallace-Hadrill.* Ed. Patrick Wormald, Donald Bullough, and Roger Collins. Oxford: Basil Blackwell, 1983. Pp. 99–129.

Index

Designer: U. C. Press Staff
Compositor: Auto-Graphics, Inc.
Text: 10/13 Sabon
Display: Sabon
Printer: McNaughton & Gunn, Inc.
Binder: John H. Dekker & Sons